LIBATION

An Afrikan Ritual of Heritage in the Circle of Life

Kimani S. K. Nehusi

University Press of America,® Inc.
Lanham · Boulder · New York · Toronto · Plymouth, UK

Copyright © 2016 by
University Press of America,® Inc.
4501 Forbes Boulevard
Suite 200
Lanham, Maryland 20706
UPA Acquisitions Department (301) 459-3366

Unit A, Whitacre Mews, 26-34 Stannary Street,
London SE11 4AB, United Kingdom

All rights reserved
Printed in the United States of America
British Library Cataloging in Publication Information Available

Library of Congress Control Number: 2015955031
ISBN: 978-0-7618-6710-4 (paperback : alk. paper)
eISBN: 978-0-7618-6711-1

∞™ The paper used in this publication meets the minimum
requirements of American National Standard for Information
Sciences—Permanence of Paper for Printed Library Materials,
ANSI Z39.48-1992

This book is dedicated to my Ancestors:
my parents, A. B. Drakes and Princess C. Drakes nee Alves
and to their parents also:
Maud Augusta Drakes nee Hollingsworth and Charles Drakes and Dorothy
Alves nee Tyrell and Jacob Alves as well as to all those others in the family
whose names we do not know
because of the terrible circumstances of the Maafa
but who became Ancestors before these who are named above

Endorsements of Libation:
An Afrikan Ritual of Heritage in the Circle of Life

"Libation as the offering of drink at a moment of power may seem a universal act, a sacred combination of gesture, word and thought still vibrant in societies around the world. Yet, the ritual may seem and feel obliterated in the dominant Euroamerican world of consumption that rationalises life as economy. We need to look outside the consumer horizon to recognise offering rituals still powerfully at work, in Africa and among Africans in Europe and the Americas. In this work Kimani Nehusi explores libation as an African essence, from contemporary worlds called popular culture, to monumental visual expressions of ancient Kemet. As links beyond time, stronger than a written genealogy, this living network finds here expression as a community of continuing and pervasive African rituals of libation. In its substance and in its method asserting radical unities, *Libation—an Afrikan Ritual of Heritage in the Circle of Life* delivers to any reader material new and old with new insight into ancient worlds and practices and their place in modern life. Essential reading that will require long contemplation."
—**Professor Stephen Quirke**, author of *Ancient Egyptian Religion*. Research Curator of the Petrie Museum of Egyptian Archaelolgy and Edwards Professor of Egyptian Archaeology and Philology, Institute of Archaeology, University College London (UCL), UK.

"Impressive knowledge of Ancient Egyptian historical antecedents, culture and language . . . a lucid and systematic explanation of the practice of libation . . . examines the meaning of the various elements and actions which comprise the complex of activities which make for libation, unveils the symbolic significance of the libation offerings, and propounds on the ethical and cosmological messages conveyed by the ritual. He establishes the pan-Afrikan spread of the custom both within the continent of Afrika and beyond, and the importance of maintaining libation as a sign of Afrikan historical and spiritual consciousness, of constantly renewed acknowledgement of and respect for our ancestors, and as a token of the unity of African peoples. This sign serves as a rejuvenation of commitment to concerted and self-interested action across space and through time . . . carefully illustrated and meticulously written."
—**Maureen Warner-Lewis**, author of *Yoruba Songs of Trinidad* and *Guinea's Other Suns*; Professor Emeritus of Linguistics, University of the West Indies, Mona, Jamaica

" . . . it shows an extremely refreshing and philosophically original approach. It is Afrocentric without being overbearingly so. I find it also serious in scholarship and well-written. It reads easily with no obscurity of either language or ideas. It takes the shroud off Egyptology. I think its break from Eurocentric leanings is one of its very fine points."

—**Kwesi Kwaa Prah**, Professor and Director, Center for the advanced study of African Society, Cape Town, South Africa.

"Professor Kimani Nehusi has written a powerful book on a most ancient and critical Afrikan ritual, libation. He masterfully demonstrates that libation must be understood within the Afrikan worldview and its emphasis on ontological unity and life eternal. Furthermore, his argument about the importance of cultural reclamation in the process of Afrikan renaissance is both timely and compelling."
—**Ama Mazama**, PhD, Department of African American Studies, Temple University.

"This is, undoubtedly, a masterly and monumental work on libation, an African ritual of heritage, that reflects the African world view from the earliest times until the present. In an admirably scholarly manner, the author tells the "lion's story" that amply explains the meaning and significance of the ritual of libation and restores African identity in a conscious manner that effectively counters the hazards of the Maafa. The African world owes an immeasurable debt of gratitude to Kimani Nehusi for this brilliant piece of work."
—**Kofi Asari Opoku**, PhD African University College of Communications, Accra, Ghana. Formerly Professor of Religious Studies, Lafayette College, Easton, PA. Author of *West African Traditional Religion*.

"Professor Nehusi's treatment of the ancient Afrikan tradition of Libations is an essential text for understanding the Afrikan worldview and way of being. Through this scholarly treatment, he has reconstructed a powerful and indispensable tool for our identity restoration."
—**Chike Akua**, author of *Education for Transformation: Releasing the Genius of African American Students*.

"The author measures the civilizational unity of African cultures and their own dynamics in the light of libation rituals which punctuate the highlights of African existence—initiations, weddings, funerals. An innovative approach, fully documented, that renews the intelligence of several millennia of African History—from the texts of ancient Egypt to the live rituals of the modern African worlds, including ones scattered abroad by the Soulless Trade."
—**Alain Anselin**, founder of the teaching of Ancient Egyptian at the University of Antilles-Guyane (1992-2012), and journals *Cahiers Caribbean Egyptology* and *i-Medjat*.

"Dr. Nehusi . . . shows how Libation is both a guide and Opener of the WAY, and how under varying circumstances Afrikans utilised whatsoever they had available to OPEN THE WAY . . . these rituals are affirmations of the

COSMIC UNITY, which at the same time celebrate DIVERSITY and INTERDEPENDENCE of component parts of the COSMIC WHOLE and UNITY . . . The book . . . is a further attempt by Afrikans globally to RECONSTRUCT the positive elements of our life and to give it credence in a societal situation that has historically attempted to negate the Afrikan contribution to planetary balance, equilibrium, education and high science. This book is a must read."
—*Oloye Orawale Oranfe of Ife, Otunba Atoodimu of Caribbean Region* (Worldwide Isese Agbaye Community). Oluto Alagba (Council of Traditional Afrikan Chiefs of Trinidad & Tobago) Chief Priest/ Administrator of Egbe Onisin Eledumare.

"Dr. Kimani Nehusi has produced a substantial work which does far more than to excavate, analyse and explain the ritual of Libation in African tradition from ancient to modern times. This work also demonstrates a continuous, distinctive and rationally organised African world in which libation functioned from ancient to contemporary Africa, including the Diaspora and despite the severe impositions of the *Maafa*: enslaveryment, colonialism and neo-colonialism that continues to plague Africans from attaining full freedom and liberation. This contribution provides an important roadmap to realise fully African post-coloniality by providing epistemic resources to make all Africans free, confident and full of pride, self-worth and self-reliance."
—**Mammo Muchie**, *Research Professor, Institute for Economic Research and Innovation, Tshwane University of Technology, Tshwane, South Africa*

"In his ground-breaking study about libation, Nehusi Kimani raises interesting questions about this far reaching Afrikan tradition. Nehusi's study not only looks at the functions libation has had for Afrikans in the past, but also what it can mean for people who has had the traumatic experience of enslavement, resulting in self denial. In this way Nehusi Kimani has contributed significantly to fill the gaps of education pertaining to our Afrikan heritage and its enlightening role for Afrikan people all over the globe."
—**Dr. Rose Mary Allen**, *University of the Netherlands Antilles*

Pour libation for your father and mother who rest in the valley of the dead. God will witness your action and accept it. Do not forget to do this even when you are away from home. For as you do for your parents, your children will do for you also.
—**The Book of Ani**

TABLE OF CONTENTS

List of Abbreviations	xiii
List of Illustrations	xiii
List of Photographs in the Photospread	xv
Note on Translation and Transliteration	xvii
Photographic Credits	xvii
Preface	xix
Acknowledgments	xxi
Introduction	xxiii
1. ḥr ḳbḥw: Concerning Libation	1
2. The Origins of Libation	41
3. The Origins and Evolution of the Offering Complex	69
4. On the Sacred Ancestors	97
5. Transmission across Space and Time	129
6. Ritual Significances	151
7. Some Conclusions	177
8. Some Questions and Answers	183
Bibliography	189
Index	201

LIST OF ABBREVIATIONS

BCE   Before the Current Era
CE   Current Era
CdE   *Chronique d'Égypte. Bulletin périodique de la Fondation égyptologique Reine Élisabeth*. Bruxelles.
IPEAFRO   *Instituto de Pesquisas e Estudios Afro-Brasileiros*.
JARCE   Journal of the American Research Center in Egypt
JCTAW   Journal of Culture and its Transmission in the African World
JEA   Journal of Egyptian Archaeology
ZÄS   *Zeitschrift für agyptische Sprache und Altertumskunde*. Leipzig and Berlin.

LIST OF ILLUSTRATIONS

1. The Divine Cosmic Order   7
2. Afrikan divinities in camouflage 131

*LIST OF PHOTOGRAPHS IN
THE PHOTOSPREAD*

1. Pouring libation onto the body of Asuru, the Corn Divinity

2. A woman making offerings in early Kemet (UC 14417)

3. Another illustration of a woman making offering in early Kemet (UC 14436)

4. Libation today in Afrikan communities abroad

5. An offering table from Kemet, the 12th Dynasty

6. Another offering table from 12th Dynasty Kemet

7. Pepi I making a two-handed offering of libation (BM 39.121)

8. Nsu Taharka offering libation to Hemen, the Falcoln Divinity

9. A Message from the Ancestors

10. Sylvia Thomas, informant of Colihaut, Dominica

11. Albert Severen, informant of Colihaut, Dominica

12. Vera Venture-Hinds of Queenstown Village, Essequibo Coast, Guyana

13. Water of Life in Kemet

NOTE ON TRANSLATION AND TRANSLITERATION

Many of the concepts used in this book were first written down in the: 𓌃𓂧𓊹 Mdw Nṯr, the *Medew Netjer* (Hieroglyphics). Their reproduction in the following pages generally follows a standard formula employed by scholars. First there is the rendition in the Medew Netjer: 𓌃𓂧𓊹. Then there is a rendition in the International Phonetic Alphabet: Mdw Nṯr, followed by the nearest equivalent, using the Roman script in italics: *Medew Netjer*, which is often followed by a translation into English: "the words of the divinity." It should be noted that since the Ancient Egyptians did not write the vowels, scholars are usually not very certain about the exact representation of each word, as many vowels are little more than informed guesses.

PHOTOGRAPHIC CREDITS

Petrie Museum, University of London, UK: UC 14417 and UC 14436
Brooklyn Museum, USA: BM 39.121
Denise Ellis: Ancestral Message
Kamau Drakes: Libation in the Diaspora today
Des Robinson: Hatshepsut pouring Libation, offering Tables from Kemet, Priest pouring Libation over Asar, Water of Life in Kemet.
Villeneuve George: Sylvia Thomas and Albert Severin
Vera Venture-Hinds: Vera Venture-Hinds

On the front cover: A kneeling Hatshepsut making a two handed Libation. Cario Museum. Photograph by Des Robinson.

PREFACE

The immediate impulse for this work lies partly in the urgent necessity to fulfil some of the most important needs of Afrikan people. These needs were identified in questions and demands that arose out of practical political activity pursued by many people, Afrikan as well as non-Afrikan, but mostly Afrikans. All are determined to change the fate and fortunes of Afrikan people across the world. The author is but one of these.

One characteristic of the broad movement for Afrikan liberation, at this historical juncture, is the increasing awareness of identity (history and culture) as a very significant factor in determining world-view and the ability to identify, defend, pursue and sustain genuine interests, including spiritual, cultural and economic liberation and development. There is a consequent conviction among many that the reclamation of Afrikan history, culture and identity, and their refurbishment where necessary, is a prerequisite to real liberation. Study of the Anti-Apartheid Movement offered further and convincing evidence of the danger of colonialists colonising the Afrikan struggle and emphasised the fact, as Walter Rodney observed, that liberation is something that only a people can do for themselves.

One result of these understandings has been the clarification, and redefinition where necessary, of the roles of both Afrikans and non-Afrikans in the struggle for genuine Afrikan liberation. Politically, this led to the insistence that Afrikans direct and lead their own struggle; all others are welcome once they recognise the Afrikan right to and duty of self-determination and accept their role as allies.

This position has led to an increasing emphasis on the reclamation, development and practice of Afrikan cultural institutions. It has also resulted in an increased emphasis upon Afrikan awareness of Afrikan history. Afrikan centered scholarship has been fed by these streams and has fed them in return.

Utilising these principles, especially from in the early 1990s, several progressive organisations led the way towards Afrikan redemption in London, though their activities often impacted elsewhere. Foremost among these were the Association for Pan African Studies and Initiatives (APAS), the Pan Afrikan Grassroots Educational Network (PAGEN), Afrika Liberation Support Campaign (ALISC), the Pan Afrikan Congress Movement (PACM), the All African People's Revolutionary Party (AAPRP), New Initiatives, the Alkebulan Revivalist Movement (ARM), the Auser Auset Society, the Afrikan United Action Front (AUAF) and other Afrikan centered organisations in the UK. These organisations maintained a climate in which enlightened attitudes towards Afrikanity were encouraged. APAS, in which Femi Biko was a major driving force, organised many opportunities for study, discussion and practice. So did the PACM. ALISC later followed. All of these organisations became increasingly concerned with the study and explanation of Afrikan history and Afrikan cultural institutions. Some tried to emphasise the daily living of Afrikan culture. It is in this context that a growing number of Afrikans in London and other parts of the UK began to investigate and practice Naming Ceremonies, the Libation ritual and Kwanzaa. Within the ALISC and the AUAF, Bro. Explo Kofi Nani was an early fountain of knowledge and example in the practice of libation. Finally, the work of the Association for the Study of Classical Afrikan Civilizations (ASCAC) was and continues to be a major influence upon the evolution of knowledge, understanding and practice among many conscious Afrikans in communities abroad as well as in Afrika itself.

The reclamation of Afrikan social history is a major objective of Afrikan liberation, so it is a major task of all Afrikans. Much of what passes for the history of Afrikans, irrespective of whether it is written by Afrikans or non-Afrikans, is written from the points of view of non-Afrikans and functions to balkanize, demean, deny and ultimately disable Afrikans. History teaches us that no group of people: family, clan, community or nation, has ever become successful when they are ignorant or confused about their identity. Self-knowledge is the one sure basis of recognising and pursuing one's own interests and of recognising, understanding and fulfilling one's own potential. It is not at all co-incidental that of all the peoples in the world, Afrikans are the most untutored and ill informed about their own history and culture and are also the most disabled and underdeveloped people. These two facts are related; the first is perhaps the most important contributory factor to the condition described by the second. There is a particular wisdom saying from the beloved continent which warns us that: "Until lions have their own historians, tales of hunting will always glorify the hunter," and that is true. Others say that the victors always write history, and that, too, is substantially true. But each of these is merely part of an even greater truth concealed therein. It is that those who make and write their own history will eventually be victorious, for the construction and recording of one's own history are the most fundamental proofs of victory.

    Kimani Nehusi
    London
    17 March, 2007

ACKNOWLEDGMENTS

Many individuals have also played important roles in bringing this offering to the public. Vee Marshall, then a student at the University of East London, was first to read a very early draft. She showed it to her elderly aunts, Irene Mallory and Elizabeth Hallett, who directed that it be completed and published. In the USA, certain members of my family were always willing to provide all kinds of support. My nephew Kamau provided some of the photographs. I had numerous fruitful discussions on matters in this book with my brothers, Rudy and Dr. Terrence Olufemi Drakes. My sister Yvonne, and brothers Deryck, Arnold and Lennox provided encouragement and practical support in many forms. So too did Keith Miller, Randolph Sampson and Courtney Jones. Help was also forthcoming in London and elsewhere. Des Robinson read the text, made suggestions for improvement and provided most of the photographs. Villeneuve George took the photographs of the informants from Dominica. William Daley, then Reference Librarian in the Medgar Evers College, CUNY, has become an ancestor. He helped to procure some of the images used in this work. James Mingo (jgmingo@earthlink.net) enhanced most of them. Eusi Kwayana, for many decades now a leading theorist and practitioner of Pan Afrikanism, Robin Walker, Nah Dove, Prof. Herbert Ekwe Ekwe of the African Renaissance Associates, Stephen Quirke, Curator of the Petrie Museum of Egyptian Archaeology and Professor of Egyptology, Institute of Archaeology, University College London, Joseph Clayton, Egyptologist at the University of London, Rita Christian of the Department of Caribbean Studies at London Metropolitan University, Prof. Stafford Griffith of the School of Education, University of the West Indies, Mona, Jamaica, Ananta Alva, formerly of the African Cultural Development Association in Guyana, Dr. Amon Saba Saakana of Karnak House, Shurwin Semple, Oswald Kendall, Tessa Fraser, Egbezor Uchendu and Earnest Ebele Obumselu interrogated the text, made many useful suggestions and so helped to ensure a better product. Rita Christian and Cecily Hermel-Atherley assisted with translations from French and German respectively. Ezra Blondel conducted interviews in Dominica. Colleagues in the CREATE research group at the University of East London provided a useful space for the discussion of some of the ideas reproduced here. Two of them, Dr. Patricia Walker and Dr. John Preston, kindly undertook most of my academic responsibilities while I was away for a semester researching and writing drafts of some of the following chapters. Jervine Young undertook most of the initial formatting. Finally, the editorial pencils of Albert Straker, Ezra Blondel and Audrey Burnham and the typesetting skills of Ashton Franklyn helped to ensure a significantly more easily readable text.

This work has therefore not been produced in a social vacuum. It is the result of a wide range of meaningful interactions in the constant search for greater human dignity. Foremost in these exchanges have been those with other practitioners in the field of Afrikan Liberation. But my interactions have also been with other scholars as well as with texts and other kinds of sources that are incorporated into this effort to reconstruct, describe and analyse a very important aspect of Afrikan culture.

These and many other providers of example, knowledge, space and inspiration, emphasise the spiritual and social nature of intellectual enterprise, and indeed of all production. In undertaking this work I therefore undertook a conversation with our community: with our ancestors, with those here and with those yet to come. I have also conversed with people of other communities. I shall always be grateful for the assistance they have each rendered to me, for such help was often critical in the fulfilment of the numerous tasks I gave myself in embarking upon this project. Bringing this resulting book into the public domain is perhaps the best way of thanking them all. I do so here without any reservation.

INTRODUCTION

1.1: A Plenitude of Sources, a Paucity of Scholarship

There is a multitude of references to libation in the existing literature on Afrika.[1] References occur both in many sources and in many kinds of sources. This significant ritual is also attested by many artefacts as well as by a large number of images of those artefacts, some of which are reproduced in this book. This large number of references confirms the presence of libation among Afrikan people throughout a time frame stretching from the earliest of times to the present. It also confirms the distribution of the ritual in a physical space that defines itself as the Afrikan continent as well as other places to which Afrikans have migrated, or were forced to migrate. The sacred ritual of libation therefore occupies a spiritual, cultural, socio-historical and geographical space that is the Afrikan world. From the time of its beginnings millennia ago, libation has existed wherever and whenever the Afrikan existed. It is still present everywhere Afrikans live today. We shall see, *en passant*, that libation is to be found even beyond this Afrikan world; that is, among non-Afrikan peoples and their cultures.

Yet, for all its persistence through time and space, this ancient and important ritual, which continues to live among Afrikan people, has received no extended treatment by the academic and intellectual community of Afrika and the world. This is a very surprising and potentially expensive gap in our knowledge, especially in an age of instant communication that has shrunk the world into much more of a global village, vastly increased the fact of interaction among peoples and institutions of differing histories and cultures, and so also imposed an even greater premium upon our understanding of ourselves and of each other.

The study of libation demands attention for another reason. This ritual must be understood and explained in partial fulfilment of the need for Afrikans everywhere to reclaim, reconstruct and fully repossess their own history and cultural heritage. Such processes of repossession will constitute a restoration of identity that is perhaps the most important prerequisite for Afrikans to fulfil, once again, their own vast potential and undertake their own development according to their genuine interests. This is the only legitimate way for Afrikans to contribute to the proper development of the emerging global community, in which Afrikans must have their own independent voices. Afrika must recover its own stories, reconstruct itself on its own terms and (re)create its own libraries on these bases.

The rebuilding of Afrikan identity will reverse the fundamental damage of the *Maafa* or Afrikan Holocaust. The United Nations has recognised the importance of identity in the education and socialization of all humanity. In *The Convention on the Rights of the Child*, adopted by its General Assembly on 20th

November, 1989, this world body emphasises, in the Preamble, and adumbrates at Articles 2, 4, 8, 17, 29 (c) and 30, that each signatory state is bound by these agreements to respect and promote the identity of each child, who must be educated to respect her/his own identity and that of others.[2] These principles are further repeated and emphasised in the documents of numerous other conventions and agreements.[3] The UN has also held the World Conference against Racism, Racial Discrimination, Xenophobia and Related Intolerance in Durban, South Africa, in 2001, where it adopted the Durban Declaration and Programme of Action, which seeks to institutionalise a global response to discrimination. Later on the UN also declared 2011 the Year for People of African Descent.

Clearly, there is an urgent need for comprehensive investigation of this important subject.

1.2: Ancient Sources

The oldest sources of information on the ritual of libation are those generated by ancient communities in ⌐𓅓𓏏𓊖 Kmt: Kemet (Ancient Egypt) in particular, and the Nile Valley in general. Perhaps the oldest known source is an incense burner found at Qustul,[4] though the more recent uncovering of a settlement and worshipping complex at Nabta Playa in the far south of Egypt[5] may attest an even earlier date. By virtue of their attestation of the ritual complex in which libation normally occurred, both the Nabta Playa temple complex and the Qustul burner may constitute indirect references to the practice of libation in organised political entities that existed before and beyond the state of Kemet. In these examples, the association of libation with the ritual complex that includes sacrifice and other offerings represent neither isolated instances nor a practice confined only to the distant Afrikan past. This very ritual complex is attested throughout the history of Afrika, though, like much else in culture, there has been a number of variations and changes.

Other references to libation occur in some of the earliest writings in the world, thus further illustrating the great antiquity of this ritual. The sacred literature of Kemet, a representative sample of which is contained in the writings now known as the *Pyramid Texts*[6] and its successor texts, the *Book of Vindication*, popularly known in the west as the *Coffin Texts*,[7] the *Book of Going Forth into Enlightenment*,[8] usually termed *The Egyptian Book of the Dead* in western scholarship, as well as several other texts, also provide some of the earliest recorded information on libation. Even more information on libation is contained in other documents as well as in artistic representations generated by the people of Kemet throughout the 3000 and more years that this state existed.

Libation vases, statues, temples, tombs and other artefacts, mostly but not only from Kemet, that either directly attest this ritual, or bear inscriptions that do so, or both, admit another category of extant sources. The daily temple Offering Ritual to consecrate images and the Ritual of Opening the Mouth are the subjects of some of these inscriptions. Both provide evidence of libation. Much scholarly enquiry is based upon this particular group of sources. Examples abound. From this category this project employs the works of Yellin,[9] Guarnori and Chappaz,[10] Schäfer,[11] Gardiner,[12] and Assmann.[13]

Almost all of the sources mentioned above, with the exception of the last five, are primary sources, which constitute the bases of numerous studies that mention the ritual and often provide some details. The five latter studies are secondary sources, a number of which are general investigations of ancient Egyptian society. From this category the study of J. Gardner Wilkinson,[14] first published well over a century and a half ago, is still in some respects very useful. But there is one source that appears to defy easy categorisation, partly because it embraces the boundaries of both primary and secondary sources. This is the work of the Greek scholar, Herodotus.[15] Though ancient today, it was written at a time when the state and society of Kemet were still extant, though nearing the end. Herodotus' work is unusual for being in part an eyewitness account of such a relatively early date; it was written in live *cultural situ* and provides much valuable information, particularly his "remarks on daily life, religion and the country itself . . . "[16] But it is necessary to be cautious about his conclusions on account of his methodology,[17] for while his personal observations have often been validated by history and archaeology, information about the political history of Kemet, supposedly passed on to him by informants, has been frequently disputed by some scholars.[18] Though highly advanced in his time, Herodotus' techniques are far from the leading edge of the investigative sciences of today. It is also necessary to be aware of a likely Eurocentric bias in Herodotus, for like most of the interpreters of Kemet, he was from Europe, even though it was ancient Europe. A necessary question that accompanies the use of Herodotus' work is therefore whether he could view Kemet on Kemet's own terms, or only through the distorting eye of Europe. His work is therefore employed here mainly for corroborative purposes.

1.3: Modern Sources

As may be expected, the largest number of sources that mention our subject is constituted by the works of modern scholarship. These include numerous studies that focus on Kemet and the Nile Valley, as well as studies of modern Afrika, especially the spiritual system, which is commonly referred to as Afrikan traditional religion. Two of the earliest and most known modern studies of the Afrikan spiritual system are contained in two books by John Mbiti. His somewhat enlightened approach recognises the strong similarities and continuities running through history and culture in Afrika, without denying divergence and discontinuity. Yet Mbiti's work, as Molefe Asante and Ama Mazama point out, is rooted in his adherence to Christianity, and for this reason is marked by contradiction and ambivalence in his conception of the traditional Afrikan spiritual system. Mbiti insists "on a plurality of religions in Africa," while the title of one of his books, "African Religions and Philosophy, suggests his own ambivalence about the nature of this unity," since in that title the term "Religions" is problematic in insisting on plurality while "African Philosophy" articulates unity and perhaps, even more fundamentally, singularity.[19]

Despite these severe shortcomings, Mbiti does represent some movement towards the consideration of the Afrikan continent as a single entity[20] in ways similar to how Kofi Opoku[21] as well as J. Omosade Awolalu and P. Adelumo Dopamu[22] approach their studies of "religion" in West Afrika. This aspect of the methodology of these works was anticipated by Harry Sawyerr, who concentrated his attention on the idea of the Creator among three groups of people in West Afrika. Sawyerr's work is significant because it recognises the similarities in the idea of the Creator among the Akan, Mende and Yoruba.[23]

Some works are specific to particular groups within the Afrikan nation. Here we must mention the works of Jomo Kenyatta on the Gikuyu in Kena,[24] John Anenechukwu Umeh on the Igbos in Nigeria[25] and E. Bolayi Idowu on the Yorubas, also in Nigeria.[26] J. Olumide Lucas is somewhat unusual in having both a work dedicated to the spiritual system of the Yoruba[27] and another that attempts to explain the links between spirituality in Kemet and West Afrika.[28] It is on account of his recognition of this linkage that Lucas is in advance of his contemporaries as well as many who wrote after him. Ancient Egypt and modern West Afrika are remote from each other in both space and time. In postulating links between Afrikans across these two different geographical areas of the continent, as well as across different historical epochs, Lucas was in fact confirming the accounts of some of the oldest sacred and secular narratives, the myths and legends, of the peoples of West Afrika. He was also anticipating the conclusions of a growing number of scholars whose works show that humanity did not grow out of the ground in West Afrika and is therefore not autochthonous to the region in that most fundamental sense, since they migrated there, from the Nile Valley[29] and more than likely also from other regions of the continent.

In raising questions about the origin of West Afrikans and their connection to ancient Egypt and the Nile Valley, Lucas positioned the scholarship on West Afrika for significant advance along a new trajectory. More recent scholarship may question some of his techniques and thus, perhaps, some of the specifics of his conclusions. However, in conceptualising West Afrikans as people with a deeper historical past than that allowed by "traditional" perspectives, Lucas moved the study of West Afrika forward by moving it closer to the study of the beginnings of the people of the region. This aspect of his methodology holds important implications for the study of all Afrika. "Traditional perspectives" do not look beyond the region. Such perspectives therefore balkanize the concept of Africa by disconnecting African people from the early parts of their social history. In questioning this particular idea of the origins of West Africans, Lucas therefore opened the way for all Africans to repossess their entire social history.

The text entitled *Traditional Religion in West Africa*, edited by E.A. Ade Adegbola,[30] particularly the many contributions of Modupẹ Oduyọye, shares with the work of Lucas the important principle of including Kemet as a vital part of Afrikan history. But in this entire work the inclusion of Kemet in the concept of Afrika does not always represent, as it should, a positive development in the study of Afrika. It is easy to underestimate the significant contribution of Oduyọye to the advancement of the scholarship of Afrika, a contribution that is also well represented in his other works.[31] However, Oduyọye, like most of the other contributors to this text, and like Mbiti above, is a Christian, which is their main distinguishing feature. Unfortunately, their Christianity also appears to be the source of much unscientific bias. Jewish sacred literature, in the form of the bible, is consistently regarded as a primary and unimpeachable source. The Hebrew language is similarly privileged. Such uncritical acceptance of any source is clearly illogical and in the work in question it often yields misleading results. It is an error to regard belief, never mind how strongly and sincerely held, as fact. It is also an error to accord Eurochristianity an anteriority it does not possess and an authority it does not deserve. One glance at the chronology of Afrika is enough to establish the fact that Kemet and the *Medew Netjer* (ancient Egyptian language, hieroglyphs) are infinitely older than the basic materials from which Adegbola's text is constructed: the bible, Christianity, the Hebrew language and the spiritual system of modern West Afrika. Further, the Nile Valley spiritual system is the common basis of, and/or shares a common ancestry with the spiritual system of modern West Afrika and with much of the doctrines of the bible and Christianity.[32] Consideration of this text establishes just how urgent it is for the scholarship of Afrika to understand and apply the chronology of Afrika and the centrality of the continent to its own early development, as well as to distinguish Christianity from European values and culture, and modernity from progress.

Modern sources of information on libation also include studies of Afrikan languages. Numbered among these must be the 𓌃𓏛𓊹: Mdw Nṯr: *Medew Netjer*, literally "the words of the Divinity," the language of Kemet (commonly called Hieroglyphs[33]), the first language in the world to be written and thus the earliest inventory of the conception and practice of libation—and of much more also. This group of sources also includes numerous dictionaries and grammars. Of particular importance to this study is the dictionary of Erman and Grapow[34] as well as that of Faulkner[35] and the grammars of Gardiner[36] and Allen.[37] Each of the last two contains an important word list. Linguistic analysis of the *Medew Netjer* helps to establish the origins, nature, practice and *raison d'être* of the ritual of libation in early times. Comparative study of the *Medew Netjer* and modern Afrikan languages establishes continuities between the ancient Nile Valley and modern Afrika and helps to clarify concepts which may be vague in the *Medew Netjer*. It is the same with other aspects of culture. Language and libation are not exceptional in this regard, though for obvious reasons they receive much attention in this study.

One of the most significant advances in modern scholarship of Afrika is the two volume work on the Afrikan spiritual system edited by Molefe K. Asante and Ama Mazama and entitled *Encyclopedia of African Religion*.[38] Composed of the work of many of the leading scholars from the Afrikan world and of the Afrikan world, it is distinguished by a methodology which looks at Afrika through the eyes of Afrika. Contributors are unanimous in including Kemet as an aspect of Afrika and in the demonstration of one continuous indigenous culture and spiritual system, with diverse expressions, in the social history of the people of the Afrikan world. The result is the first comprehensive work on this subject, a work about Afrikan thought and practice of Afrikan spirituality from the earliest times to the present. It is regrettable that these volumes did not arrive in the public domain early enough to receive full consideration in the construction of the present text.

Much like the *Encyclopedia of African Religion*, the present work does not restrict itself to the continent of Afrika, from ancient through to modern times. It pursues libation to most places Afrikans have gone or were taken; that is, to most of the Afrikan world. The study of Afrikan communities abroad, chiefly in the Americas and the Caribbean, became relevant and important for this reason. Here the project relied a great deal on the works of Zora Neale Hurtson,[39] Maya Deren,[40] Raul Canizares,[41] Abdias do Nascimento[42] and Marta Moreno Vega,[43] among others. It is unfortunate that the relevant details of the Afrikan presence in Papua-New Guinea, the Solomon Islands, other places in the Indian and Pacific oceans and on the Indian sub-continent, are not presented here. The presence of libation in these areas should constitute a line of future research on libation and other aspects of Afrikan humanity.

Almost all of the categories of sources mentioned so far fall into the realm of the academic and scholarly texts that result from some form of investigation of the living reality of Afrika, mostly through the human sciences, particularly but not only religion and anthropology. But the presence of libation in Afrikan life, like all other aspects of Afrikan culture, is also reflected in and therefore may be accessed through works of the creative imagination of Afrikans on the continent and abroad. This is a fact which helps to illustrate the relations, within the Afrikan world-view, among the reality represented in the narratives that are termed myths or legends, whether "sacred" or "secular," and the historically more recent fiction and other aspects of contemporary Afrikan popular culture.

A partial listing of the group of creative writers who wrote from a location on the continent, and whose work reflects the presence of libation in Afrikan communities, should include Chinua Achebe,[44] Ayi Kwei Armah,[45] Elechi Amadi,[46] Flora Nwapa,[47] Ben Okri[48] and Ben Hansen.[49] A similar presence of libation in Afrikan communities abroad is registered in the work of such writers as Jan Carew,[50] Edward Kamau Brathwaite,[51] Roy A. K. Heath,[52] Austin Clarke,[53] Brenda Flanagan[54] and, more recently, Lawrence Hill.[55] Libation is of course also present in the popular culture of Afrikans and so reflected in artistic works in contemporary popular genres. The kaiso from the Caribbean yields "Play One" by the Mighty Stalin[56] and the Mighty Sparrow's "Tribute to Melody."[57] Hip Hop from inner city USA gives us, among others, 2Pac Shakur's deep and wonderfully descriptive "Pour out a little liquor"[58] and the equally telling "Just a Moment" from Nas.[59] These references confirm that Stephen C.

Satell's inclusion of libation in his fictionalisation of gang life in Philadelphia, Pennsylvania, between 1968 and 1975[60] amounts to an authentic expression of the survival and continuation of this Afrikan ritual in severely challenged Afrikan communities across the USA.

Myth is more often encountered in the form of narrative represented in stories, drama, dances and other forms people employ to communicate ideas. Myths are therefore always relevant as a potent source of a people's thought: their history, their cosmogony, cosmology, theology, art, psychology, sociology, literature, poetry, song, dance, drama; of every means through which they seek to represent their ideas about themselves and their reality.

The presence of libation in the myth of Afrika therefore offers an important source of information on our subject, particularly its role and status in Afrikan society. It is certainly a comment upon the underdevelopment of scholarship on libation, and of the scholarship on Afrika in general, that before this work, myth has not been exploited as a source of understanding and explanation of this important ritual.

Contemporary records from the time of physical enslavement of Afrikans in the west sometimes attest the continuity of the ritual of libation among Afrikans during that time of terror. These sources therefore constitute another significant, though often underutilized source of information on the social history of the Afrikan people. The narratives of enslaved Afrikans, which are the foundation texts of a genre usually termed the "slave narrative," are an important part of this category. Other writings that emerged from this period, usually the observations of Europeans, make up another aspect of this category of sources, as does works of scholarship that often employ both of the foregoing groups, normally in conjunction with other kinds of sources. In this project the work of Esteban Montejo[61] represents the voice of the enslaved Afrikans. Other contemporary observers are represented by the work of John Stedman[62] and John Smith.[63] Modern scholarship on this period is present in the work of Clinton Hutton,[64] Jacob Carruthers,[65] Maureen Warner-Lewis[66] and a number of other sources which form a substantial basis of Chapter Six.

It should not at all be surprising that the sources for the study of libation reflect the changing condition of Afrikans and Afrika through the ages. Some sources are strictly period pieces: they mirror the prevailing values and attitudes of their time. Others attempt, sometimes successfully, to rise above the narrowness and resulting limitations that beclouded the judgement, restricted the vision and lessened the scholarship of some. Perhaps the most instructive story to be discerned from these sources begins with the recognition that the earliest sources on libation were produced by Afrikans from their own points of view. Then, conquest and domination began to reflect themselves in Arab and European influence and/or control over the processes of production, representation, interpretation, distribution, dissemination and internalization of information about libation. It was not only the land and the people of Afrika that were colonised; information about them, including images, was also colonised. The resulting works were not always distinguished by an attempt to be objective. Afrikans were no longer writing about themselves from their own perspectives.

There is much significance in the fact that the largest group of sources on libation, as on much else about Afrika at the present juncture, is generated from within this dominant trend of hegemonic narratives. These are predominantly the product of non-Afrikans who are usually bent on controlling Afrika and Afrikans and repositioning them in diminished and demeaning ways. So persistent has been this trend that even the earliest works on libation, those generated by Afrikans, have arrived in this era mediated by Europeans. Today television programming about ancient Egypt is usually dominated by Arab and European actors posing as ancient Egyptians and the programmes are fronted by Europeans and Arabs. Such narration is made and controlled by Arabs and Europeans. The Afrikan creators of this civilization are normally absent from their own story. The resulting misrepresentations have a substantial basis in the need of all colonizers to falsify the history of both themselves and those they colonize.[67] Thus it is that in the study of all Afrika, including Kemet, the challenges usually posed to scholarship by the compulsion to investigate and make judgements across historical eras and across cultures are often, though not always, aggravated by the limitations imposed by arrogance and prejudice.

But Afrikans have always resisted Arab and European domination. In the more recent historical era intellectual resistance has been marked by the Afrocentric or Afrikan centered movement: the insistence on the deployment of a rigorous methodology, which is usually multi-disciplinary and sometimes transdisciplinary, for the reclamation of the full history, heritage and identity of Afrika and a vision of self and the world that is anchored in Afrikan experiences and perspectives. Some Afrikans have decided to own themselves and their own social history once again. This is in full recognition and in practice of the principle that every people has the right and the responsibility of participating—in the very least, equally with other interested parties—in the writing of their own history. They also have the duty of doing so from their own perspectives. Afrikans shall once again be present as fully human in their own social history. They shall be present in the events and processes they initiated and sustained as conscious and knowing actors, not as mere objects. They shall be present as agents and not as passive bystanders in their own stories. The restoration of consciousness, knowledge and agency to Afrikans is substantially a process of self-repair and a prerequisite to an honest presentation of Afrikan social history, for Afrikans were very much present, as Afrikans, in the distinctive and intelligently organised world they themselves created long before the arrival of foreign intruders. The present study is largely a product of this movement, which is increasingly producing texts of robust quality. Some of the texts from this group relied upon the most here have been mentioned above. Others include the works of Théophile Obenga,[68] Maulana Karenga,[69] Jacob Carruthers,[70] Molefe Asante and Abu S. Abarry.[71]

The last group of sources consulted in this work is composed of living Afrikans who practice libation and/or recall its presence in bygone days. Some

Introduction xxxi

are elders; others are of middle age or early middle age. The result is a good mix of persons who practiced or still practice libation and related rites, and/or who recall the practice of these aspects of Afrikan tradition. This material from living Afrika was gathered mainly through interviews, conducted chiefly by this writer with persons who hail from his home village of Queenstown, on the Essequibo Coast of Guyana in South America[72] and by Ezra Blondel among residents of the town of Colihaut, Dominica.[73] Strictly speaking, the afore-mentioned works of Hurston, Canizares and Vega bear a strong similarity to this category of sources through being informed by participant observation and other forms of first hand experience. However, those works are also distinguished from the category of interviewees because they are also informed by sources additional to the direct personal experiences of the writers. In this work the information obtained through interviews from each of these living witnesses has not been treated as verified fact. It has been used mainly to corroborate information from other sources that are independent of each individual who was interviewed, these sources sometimes being other witnesses themselves.

1.4: Conceptual Isolation and Other Limitations

But for all the enormity in number, the dominant characteristics of the sources of information on libation are brevity and conceptual isolation to specific groups among the Afrikan people. There is no extended treatment of this most important subject, either across the many variations of the Afrikan people and their practice, or across the many historical eras in which they have lived. It is symptomatic of the existing scholarship on this subject that the Right Reverend Dr. Peter Kwasi Sarpong's very brief text, of fifty pages,[74] is distinguished in this regard. It is the only work so far that makes libation its exclusive concern. Despite sharing most of the characteristics of the existing sources on libation: brevity, concentration on one group of Afrikans (in this case the Asante model), restriction to the contemporary era, as well as its focus upon attempting to reconcile this aspect of Afrikan culture to the doctrine of the Catholic Church, Dr. Sarpong's work is informed by many scholarly approaches. He deploys substantial knowledge of the subject and an awareness of culture in other parts of Afrika. He emerges with a text that is neither isolationist nor ill informed. The present investigation found no other work that takes libation as its only subject matter and none that accords it the substantial treatment it deserves.

The restriction of references to libation to specific groups within Afrika ignores the tremendous underlying unity and continuity in Afrikan history and culture. This balkanization of information about Afrika pretends that there are no spiritual, genetic, cultural, social and historical relationships among Afrikans. It is as if the ritual of libation, as much else, exists independently in origin, structure and function in every one of the prodigious number of groups into which hegemonic scholarship likes to divide Afrika. But such a profusion of independent origins of a single ritual is very obviously impossible. The conclusion of multiple origins, stated or implied, is therefore illogical. Such an approach to the study of libation, and by extension to the study of Afrika, provides, at best, merely a partial understanding of the subject. That approach is defective in another way. It is deeply misleading and damaging to a full and proper understanding of Afrika, its history, its culture and its identity—both to Afrikans themselves and to the rest of the world.

Therefore while the profusion of references in the literature may at first sight suggest substantial engagement with libation, the nature of the vast majority of these references argues a virtually unexplored and certainly a not fully understood subject. Hence, while there is no shortage of references on this subject, there is no thorough investigation of libation, and there is a resulting and regrettable paucity of scholarship, knowledge and understanding of the ritual and its great significance.

1.5: Research Questions and Methodology

What, really, is libation? What are its origins? How does it fit into the Afrikan cosmogony and cosmology, into the Afrikan world view? What does it tell us about this world view, about Afrikan philosophy? This ritual was enacted in the Nile Valley in ancient times and is still alive all over the Afrikan world. How and why did it spread? Why does it appear to embrace the full dimensions of Afrikan existence? Has it evolved in its journey over place and time? Existing scholarship offers no full answer and often no answer at all, to any of these queries. In fact, at present, scholarship rarely if ever asks such imperative questions and goes in search of answers to any of them.

The state of our knowledge about libation has been underdeveloped for far too long. The present undertaking attempts to put an end to this deficient condition. It builds upon the previous engagements with libation. It consciously attempts to break out of the factual and conceptual limitations that characterise the currently available sources. It makes libation its major subject of enquiry. It begins as close as possible to the beginnings of the ritual. In bringing together the information contained in all of these sources, this work connects the practice of libation throughout the prodigious time/space correlation occupied by the Afrikan experience of life, connects Afrikans to their social history, and so to themselves across generations in different spaces and times. The methodology is at once both multi-disciplinary and inter-disciplinary, and may even approach transdisciplinarity. The methods and techniques of history, linguistics, cultural studies, literature and other human arts and sciences are deployed to pursue answers to the research questions concerning the origins, structure, purpose, meaning and significance of libation, developments and change within the ritual, and its distribution in the Afrikan world.

These, then, are the basic materials we shall deploy and the major approaches we shall employ in the following pages in our attempt to recover, reconstruct, analyse, evaluate and understand libation.

NOTES

1. Afrika. For an explanation of this spelling consult Kimani Nehusi, "From 𓂋𓏤𓈖 *Medew Netjer* to Ebonics" in Clinton Crawford (2001, ed.) *Ebonics and Language Education of African Ancestry Students* (Sankofa World Press, New York and London), p.104.
2. The text of this convention is widely available. A good example is http://wboesww.org, where it is available in full in sixteen languages.
3. Numerous examples include internet sources at http://eurochild.gla.ac.uk/; http://www.crin.org and http://www.unicef.org. See also UNICEF (2002). *A World Fit for Children*. (New York, USA) and UNICEF and UNESCO (2007). *A Human Rights Based Approach to Education for All*. (New York, USA and Paris, France).
4. Bruce Williams (1985). "The Lost Pharaohs of Nubia" in Ivan Van Sertima (ed.). *Nile Valley Civilizations* (Journal of African Civilizations, Ltd. New Brunswick, USA), pp. 29–43; James E. Brunson (1991). *Before the Unification: Predynastic Egypt. An African-centric View* (The Author, DeKalb, Illinois), pp. 107–111.
5. Richard H. Wilkinson (2000). *The Complete Temples of Ancient Egypt*. (Thames and Hudson, London), p.16; Jeff Hertaus. "Nabta Playa" http://www.mnsu.edu/emuseum/archaeology/sites/africa/nabtaplaya.html. [Accessed 6th April, 2007].
6. Raymond O. Faulkner (ed. and trans., 1969). *The Ancient Egyptian Pyramid Texts* (Oxford University Press; Aris and Phillips, Warminster).
7. R. O. Faulkner (ed. and trans.1994). *The Ancient Egyptian Coffin Texts* 3 Vols. (Aris and Phillips Ltd., Warminster).
8. Several translations are available. The principal ones are based on the work of R. O. Faulkner. Those consulted in this text are Faulkner (ed. and trans. 1985, 1996, 2005). *The Ancient Egyptian Book of the Dead* (British Museum Press, London; Barnes and Noble, New York); Faulkner (ed. and trans., 1994, 1998) *The Egyptian Book of the Dead: The Book of Going Forth by Day* (Chronicle Books, San Francisco). See also E. A. Wallis Budge (translation and transliteration, 1895, 1967). *The Egyptian Book of the Dead (The Papyrus of Ani)*. (Dover Publications Inc., New York) and T. G Allen (ed. and trans., 1974). *The Book of the Dead or Going Forth by Day: Ideas of the Ancient Egyptians Concerning the Hereafter as Expressed in their own Terms*. Studies in Ancient Oriental Civilization 37. (The University of Chicago Press).
9. Janice W. Yellin (1988). "Abaton-style milk libation at Meroe" in N. B. Millet and A. L. Kelley (eds.). *Meroitica*. Proceedings of the Third International Meroetic Conference, Toronto, 1977. (Akademie-Verlag, Berlin), pp. 151–155.
10. S. Guarnori and J. Chappaz (1983). "Deux tables d'offrandes et un basin à libations du Musée d'Art et d'Historie à Genève CdE. Vol. LVIII, Nos. 115–116, pp. 73–82.
11. Heinrich Schäfer (1898). *"Eine altägyptische Schreibersitte" ZÄS*. No. 36, pp. 147–148.
12. Alan H. Gardiner (1902–03). "Imhotep and the scribe's libation." *ZÄS*. No. 40, p.146.
13. Jan Assmann (Trans. D. Lorton, 2005). *Death and Salvation in Ancient Egypt*. (Cornell University Press, Ithaca and London).
14. J. Gardner Wilkinson (1853, 1994). *The Ancient Egyptians: Their Life and*

Customs. 2 Vols. (Senate, London).
15. Herodotus (trans. A. de Sélincourt, revised A. R. Burn, 1972). *The Histories.* (Penguin).
16. Jean Vercoutter (1992, trans. R. Sharman). *The Search for Ancient Egypt.* (Harry N. Abrama, Inc., New York), pp. 20–21, as quoted in Charles A. Grantham (2003). *The Battle for Kemet* (The Kemetic Institute, Chicago), p.41.
17. See, for example, A. R. Burn, "Introduction" in Ibid., pp.10, 25–27, 31, etc.
18. Grantham, *Ibid.,* pp. 41, 43, 49.
19. M. K. Asante and Ama Mazama, "Introduction" in M. K. Asante and A. Mazama (2009, eds.). *Encyclopedia of African Religion.* 2 Vols. (SAGE Publications, Inc., Los Angeles, London, etc.), p. xxii.
20. John Mbiti (1969, 1988). *African Religions and Philosophy* (Heinemann, London) and Mbiti (1975, 1986). *Introduction to African Religion* (Heinemann, London).
21. Kofi Asare Opoku (1978). *West African Traditional Religion* (FEP International Private Ltd., Accra).
22. J. Omosade Awolalu and P. Adelumo Dopamu (1979). *West African Traditional Religion* (Onibonoje Press and Book Industries (Nig.) Limited, Ibadan).
23. Harry Sawyerr (1970). *God. Ancestor or Creator? Aspects of traditional belief in Ghana, Nigeria and Sierra Leone.* (Longmans, London).
24. Jomo Kenyatta (1965). *Facing Mount Kenya: Tribal Life of the Gikuyu* (Vintage Books, New York).
25. John A. Umeh (1997, 1999). *After God is Dibia: Igbo Cosmology, Divination and Sacred Science in Nigeria.* Vols. I & II. (Karnak House, London).
26. E. Bolayi Idowu (1960, 1994). *Olódùmarè: God in Yoruba Belief* (A&B Publishers, New York).
27. J. O. Lucas (1948). *The Religion of the Yorubas* (CMS Bookshop, Lagos).
28. J. O. Lucas (1970). *Religions in West Africa and Ancient Egypt.* (Nigerian National Press, Apapa).
29. See, for example, Ayi Kwei Armah (2006). The Eloquence of the Scribes: A Memoir on the Sources and Resources of African Literature (Per Ankh, Popenguine, Senegal), pp. 171–198; Abouncry M Lam, (2004). "L'origine des Peul: les principales thèses confrontées aux traditions africaines et à l'égyptologie" Ankh: Revue D'Égyptologie et des Civilisations Africaines. Nos. 14/15 and 12/13, 2003 2004, pp. 90–108; Lam (2006a). "Égypte ancienne et Afrique noire: quelques nouveaux faits qui éclairent leurs relations" Ankh Nos. 14/15, 2005–2006, pp. 115–127; Lam (2006b). La Vallée du Nil: berceau de l'unité culturelle de l'Afrique noir (Khepera, Paris and Presses Universitaires de Dakar); Boubacar Diop Buuba (2006). "Les migrations Sereer: jalons de la saga arficaine et sénégalaise" Ankh Nos. 14/15, 2005–2006, pp. 137–147; C. A. Diop (1987). Precolonial Black Africa. Trans. H. Salemson. (Lawrence Hill and Co. Westport, Connecticut), pp. 212–234; Théophile Obenga (2004a). "Comparaisons morphologiques entre l'Égyptien ancient et le Dagara" Ankh Nos. 14/15, 2003–2004, pp. 48–63; Obenga (2004b). African Philosophy: The Pharaonic Period: 2780–330 BC. (Per Ankh, Senegal); Mouhamadou Nissire Sarr (2006). "Cours d'eau et croyances en Égypte pharaonique et en Afrique noire modern" Ankh Nos. 14/15, 2005–2006, pp. 128–136.
30. (1998). *Traditional Religion in West Africa.* (Sefer Books Limited, Ibadan). First published by Daystar Press, Ibadan, 1983.
31. See in particular M. Oduyoye (1996). *Words & Meaning in Yoruba Religion: Linguistic Connections in Yoruba, Ancient Egyptian & Semitic* (Karnak House,

London), *passim*. Note in particular his observation on pp. 74–75. See also M. Oduyọye (1988). "The Spirits that Rule the World: African Religions & Judiasm" in A.Saakana (ed.). *Afrikan Origins of the Major World Religions* (Karnak House, London), pp. 59–98.

32. The sources for this assertion are many and growing. See, for example, Lucas (1970). *Religions in West Africa and Ancient Egypt*; Jacob Carruthers, "Forward" in Maulana Karenga (1984). *Selections from the Husia: Sacred Wisdom of Ancient Egypt* (Kawadia Publications, Los Angeles), p. ix; Karenga, "Introduction," *Ibid.*, p. xiii; Théophile Obenga (2004b, trans. A. K. Armah, 2004). *African Philosophy: The Pharaonic Period: 2780–330 BC* (Popenguine, Senegal). See also most of the texts listed in notes 66–69 below.

33. From the Greek *hiero* = divinity and *glyph* = carved writing; a fairly accurate translation of the correct name.

34. Adolf Erman and Hermann Grapow (1926, 1963, 1982). *Wörterbuch der Aegyptischen Sprache*. 5 Vols. (Akademie Verlag, Berlin).

35. R. O. Faulkner (1962). *A Concise Dictionary of Middle Egyptian* (Griffith Institute, Oxford).

36. Alan H. Gardiner (1927, 1988). *Egyptian Grammar: Being an Introduction to the Study of Hieroglyphs*. 3rd Edition, revised. (Ashmoleum Museum, Griffith Institute, Oxford).

37. James P. Allen (2000). *Middle Egyptian: An Introduction to the Language and Culture of Hieroglyphs* (Cambridge University Press, London and New York).

38. See note 15 above.

39. Z. N. Hurston (1938, 1990). *Tell My Horse: Voodoo and Life in Haiti and Jamaica*. (Harper and Row, New York).

40. M. Deren (1953, 1970). *Divine Horsemen: The Living Gods of Haiti* (Mc Pherson and Co. Ltd., New York).

41. Raul Canizares (1993). *Walking With the Night: The Afro-Cuban World of Santeria* (Destiny Books, Rochester, Vermont).

42. Abdias do Nascimento (1995). *Orizás: Os Deuses Vivos da África* (IPEAFRO/Afrodiaspora, Rio de Janeiro).

43. Marta M. Vega (2000). The Altar of My Soul: The Living Traditions of Santeria (One World, The Ballantine Publishing Group, New York).

44. Chinua Achebe (1958, 1987) *Things Fall Apart* (Heinemann, London).

45. Ayi Kwei Armah (1974). *Fragments* (Heinemann, London), pp. 5–12, 13 637,223, 263; Armah (1979).*The Healers* (Heinemann, London), pp. 55–56, 161, 209–211.

46. Elechi Amadi (1975). *The Great Ponds* (Heinemann, London), pp.28, 64, 85, 86, etc.

47. Flora Nwapa (1966, 1978) *Efuru* (Heinemann Educational Publishers, London); Nwapa (1970). *Idu* (Heinemann Educational Books Ltd., London). See especially pp. 68, 85, 108–109, 121, 141, 146, 160, *passim*. See also Nwapa (1975, 1992). *Never Again* (Tana Press, Nigeria; Africa World Press, Inc., Trenton, NJ). There is growing critical appreciation of Nwapa's work. For examples see Marie Umeh (1998). *Emerging Perspectives on Flora Nwapa: Critical and Theoretical Essays* (Africa World Press, Inc., Trenton, NJ) and Femi Nzegwu (2001) *Love, Motherhood and the African Heritage: The Legacy of Flora Nwapa* (African Renaissance, Dakar, Senegal).

48. Ben Okri (1991). *The Famished Road* (Vintage, London), pp. 51, 57, 65, etc.

49. Ben Hansen (1999) *Takadini* (Lantern Books, Literamed Publications Ltd.,

Lagos), pp. 122.
50. Jan Carew (1958, 2009). *Black Midas* (Peepal Tree Press, Leeds), pp. 114, 133 and 247.
51. Edward Brathwaite (1967, 1973). *The Arrivants* (Oxford University Press), pp. 89–99.
52. Roy A. K. Heath (1978). *The Murderer* (Allison and Busby Ltd., London), p. 11
53. Austin Clarke (2003). *The Polished Hoe* (Ian Randle Publishers, Kingston, Jamaica), p. 337
54. Brenda Flanagan (2005). *You Alone Are Dancing* (University of Michigan Press, Ann Arbor), p.178.
55. Lawrence Hill (2007). *The Book of Negroes*. (HarperCollins Publishers Ltd., Toronto), p. 360. This work has been published in the USA in 2007 as *Someone Knows My Name* (W. W. Norton & Co.).
56. The Mighty Stalin (1979). "Play One." *To The Caribbean Man*. LP. (Wizards MCR-147, Makossa M2342), Side A, Track 1 as well as other relevant releases listed at www.calypsoarchives.co.uk. [Accessed on 16th March, 2007].
57. Mighty Sparrow (2000, re-issue). "Play One for Melo." *Down Memory Lane*. CD. Millennium Series, Track 6.
58. 2Pac. "Pour Out A Little Liquor." Lyrics and accompanying video available at youtube.com [Accessed 10th May, 2008].
59. Nas. "Just a Moment" from the album *Street's Disciple*. Lyrics available at anysonglyrics@hotmail.com. [Accessed 1st May, 2008].
60. Stephen C. Satell (2013). *No Gang War in '74: Past, Present and Future*. (Xlibris Corporation), p. 43.
61. Esteban Montejo (1968, 1993. Translated by Jocasta Innes). *The Autobiography of a Runaway Slave*. (The Macmillan Press Ltd., London)
62. Richard Price and Sally Price (eds. 1992) *Stedman's Surinam: Life in an Eighteenth Century Slave Society*. (The Johns Hopkins University Press, Baltimore and London).
63. John Smith. *Journal*, as quoted in Emilia Viotti da Costa (1994). *Crowns of Glory, Tears of Blood: The Demerara Slave Rebellion of 1823*. (Oxford University Press, Oxford and New York).
64. Clinton A. Hutton (2005). *The Logic and Historical Significance of the Haitian Revolution and the Cosmological Roots of Haitian Freedom* (Arawak Publications, Kingston, Jamaica.)
65. Jacob Carruthers (1985). *The Irritated Genie: An Essay on the Haitian Revolution* (The Kemetic Institute, Chicago.)
66. Maureen Warner-Lewis (2003). *Central Africa in the Caribbean: Transcending Time, Transforming Cultures* (University of the West Indies Press).
67. Kimani Nehusi (2011) "Introduction: The Strategic Intellectual Importance of Kemet" in Karen Exell (ed.) *Egypt in its African Context* (Archaeopress, Oxford), pp. 11–13.
68. Théophile Obenga (1995). "La parenté égyptienne: Considérations sociologiques" *Revue D'Égyptologie et des civilisations africaines* Nos.4/5, pp. 139–183; Obenga (1989). "African Philosophy of the Pharaonic Period (2780–330 B. C.)" in I. van Sertima (ed.). *Egypt Revisited* (Transaction Publishers, Trenton, New Jersey), pp.286–324; Obenga (Trans. Ahmed Sheik, 1992). *Ancient Egypt and Black Africa*. (Karnak House, London); Obenga (2004b, trans. A. K. Armah, 2004). *African Philosophy. The Pharaonic Period: 2780–330 BC* (Popenguine, Senegal).
69. Maulana Karenga (1991). "Towards a Sociology of Maatian Ethics: Literature

and Context" in Ivan van Sertima (ed.) *Egypt Revisited* (Transaction Publishers, Trenton, New Jersey); Karenga (1984, ed.). *Selections From the Husia: Sacred Wisdom of Ancient Egypt* (Kawaida Publications, Los Angeles); Karenga (1990). *The Book of Coming Forth by Day: The Ethics of the Declarations of Innocence* (University of Sankore Press, Los Angeles); Karenga (1999, ed.). *Odù Ifä: The Ethical Teachings* (University of Sankore Press, Los Angeles) and Karenga (2004). *Maat: The Moral Ideal in Ancient Egypt: A Study in Classical African Ethics.* (Routledge, New York and London).

70. Jacob Carruthers (1985). *The Irritated Genie: An Essay on the Haitian Revolution* (The Kemetic Institute, Chicago); Carruthers (1995). *Mdw Ntr: Divine Speech* (Karnak House, London).

71. Molefe K. Asante and Abu S. Abarry (1998, eds.). *African Intellectual Heritage: A Book of Sources* (Temple University Press, Philadelphia).

72. Interviews conducted by this writer in 2006 with Ms. Patsy Russell, 54 years; Ms. Ms. Vera Venture, 82; Ms. Lorine James, 44 years; Ms. Voi James, 68 years; Ms. Evelyn James, 40 years and Ms. Eunice Walcott, 72 years.

73. Interviews were conducted by Ms. Ezra Blondel in 2006 with residents of the town of Colihaut on the island of Dominica, in the Caribbean Sea, chiefly with Sion Adams, 100 years, Albert Severin, 87 years, Ratcliffe St. Louis, 91 years and Sylvia Thomas, 76 years.

74. Rt. Rev. Dr. Peter Kwasi Sarpong (1996). *Libation.* (Anansesem Publications, Accra).

Chapter One

ⲡ ⲁ 𓏤𓏤 ḥr ḳbḥw: CONCERNING LIBATION

2.1: A Ritual of Heritage in the Circle of Life

Libation is a Ritual of Heritage within the Afrikan Circle of Life. In the worldview of Afrika this Circle is described and represented by transformations through different stages and states in the human journey through existence: from dwelling in the Spirit World, coming into this sphere (the physical world), birth and naming, puberty, initiation and adulthood, marriage and procreation, eldership, transition into the Spirit World again, Ancestorship, and, sometimes, elevation into divinity. Each stage in this Circle is marked by appropriate Rituals of Heritage that indicate status transformation and also clarify and make smooth each process of transformation, thus rendering the entire journey easier. Such rites include Naming Ceremonies, Initiation Ceremonies, Marriage Ceremonies, Transition Ceremonies and Rites of Elevation to Divinity. Libation is an important part of each of these aspects of the Afrikan ritual universe, and so of Afrikan existence.

But libation recognises, indicates and acknowledges far more than humanity's transition and change through spaces and space, and times and time. In fact, as we shall shortly see, libation is founded upon two elementary and demonstrable truths about the cosmos. The first is that the universe is a single integrated whole composed of interdependent elements. The second is that to impair any of the relations that hold these elements together in a harmoniously functioning order is ultimately to threaten the existence of all the elements in the whole and therefore the entire cosmos itself. At the very basis of libation, therefore, is a fundamental idea of the Afrikan world-view, which is that there is a oneness, or unity, with consequent interconnection and interdependence, balance and harmony, within and among all beings and things in the cosmos.

The cosmology and cosmogony of Afrika, which articulates this worldview, also orders the universe and legislates for every conceivable relationship within it, human and non-human. The details of this world view are preserved in and communicated through the sacred and secular narratives of the Afrikan people, that is, the mythical and legendary narratives contained in stories, dances, drama and other forms of communication. These narratives therefore illustrate and explain this cosmic order, provide a value system and ethical precepts and supply other archetypes through which are transmitted models of good and acceptable behaviour, the basis of social institutions and therefore the boundaries of approved personal and social interaction and development, including the responsibilities of individuals to self, family, society, the environment and the universe.

Libation is consequently an important every-day ritual in which Afrikans regularly acknowledge and symbolically unite all beings and things in eternity. The motivation for doing libation is provided by the desire or compulsion to maintain the appropriate relationships or connections with those who are living, with the ancestors, with those who are yet to come, with the lesser divinities, with the Creator and with the physical environment that s/he made and in which we live.

The intention of libation is therefore always to promote what the people of Kemet termed ≳∘ʃ— (variation ʃ°) M3ᶜt: *Maat*. This concept means acting consistently to ensure the optimum existence of the fundamental principle of the cosmic order. It includes proper human and environmental relations, which are achieved through the affirmation and maintenance of the proper balance and relationships within each human individual and group, among all humanity, as well as between humanity and the different beings and things in eternity. Maintaining this order also means the reaffirmation of these relationships through conciliatory words and gestures if and when they are threatened, or acting to repair or restore them when they are impaired or severed. Libation may be viewed, somewhat anthropocentrically and therefore somewhat subjectively, as a way for humans to make contact with the spirit world in order to fulfil the human need for order and balance, (for *Maat*), both within ourselves individually and collectively and within our world as a whole.

2.1.1: The Offering Complex

In Afrikan culture there are a number of closely related ideas and practices, with libation at the centre, that have occurred together from time immemorial. Most of these ideas and practices are still enacted today, either unchanged or in slightly changed forms, both in Afrika and in its communities abroad. These related ideas and practices therefore constitute an Afrikan culture complex. We may call them the Offering Complex, since making offerings is the central idea that dictates all of these activities. Besides libation itself, this complex includes a collection of fundamental and related beliefs, values, attitudes and behaviours towards the Creator, the Ancestors, humans (including such notions as spirit, soul and other vital forces, the name and other aspects of the person), and towards the physical environment, particularly as represented in sacred places and special features therein. The complex also includes other rituals, such as sacrifice, censing (burning incense), first fruits or harvest, prayers, and specific articles of great importance to this ritual, such as incense, candles, water or other liquids such as alcohol, but especially clear spirits, and honey. It is scarcely possible to understand libation without some reference to these beings and things, ideas and practices, upon which libation is founded and with which this ritual is inextricably associated.

There is a great likelihood that this culture complex was extant before the Qustul incense burner or even the Nabta Playa ceremonial complex, which has been dated to 11,000 years ago (see Chapter Two), both of which predated the establishment of the unified state of ⌐𓈖𓂀 Kmt: Kemet. But there is much certainty that it can be accounted for from Kemet to the present, on the Afrikan continent and in Afrikan communities abroad, an attested history of well over 5000 years. Like much else in Afrikan culture, the offering complex is both transgenerational and transcontinental;[1] this complex is an aspect of that spirituality that permeates the time/space correlation of Afrikan existence. It is here that we find the tremendous feat of the generations in continuously passing on to succeeding generations, for more than 5000 years, that which was inherited, even through the savage times of the last 2000 years of disruption by Persians, Greeks and Arabs and 500 years of continuing Arab and European disruption. It is here, too, in Afrikan cultural transmission across times and spaces, that we find a potent source of Afrikan redemption and we find some of the best potential foundations for Afrikan unity.

It was always a dynamic process. Libation, like the wider behavioural complex of offerings of which it is a part, has been continuously subject to adaptation and change. Libation evolved in Afrika as part of a single integrated ritual. It has been erased or distorted by Arab and European attempts to assassinate Afrikan cultural and historical identity. Libation has been taken across the Atlantic and preserved almost intact in Afrikan communities of resistance outside of Afrika, even at the same time that it was severely truncated in other communities that resulted from that identical horror of forced migration. Libation is now being reclaimed with increasing confidence and practised with increasing vigour over the last decades of what Abdias do Nascimento appropriately terms *"nussa diáspora complusória:"* our compulsory diaspora.[2]

There has always been variation and change n the ritual of libation. This is very normal with culture as a generality. It has been so whether variation and change have resulted from the slow and often almost imperceptible processes usually afoot in all cultures. It has been so, too, when both variation and change, or just one of these, has been the more immediate and so easily perceptible creative adaptations of our culture. In many instances such changes in Afrikan culture were in response to specific discordant and challenging factors in new and differing circumstances that confronted Afrikans, often violently, in their progress through place and places, and time and times. Variation and change demonstrate to all humanity that each Afrikan individual and every Afrikan group is compelled, by the very fact of their own humanity, to live a specific representation of being Afrikan, which is in turn this particular group's way of being human. Each must respond to differences in time, place, opportunity and their own inclinations. Therefore, for a people like the Afrikans, variation and change are both natural and inevitable. This is so firstly because Afrikans are the first people on this planet, so no one else's history is longer than Afrikan history. Secondly, the Afrikan continent is the second largest land mass on the earth (only the combined land mass called Eurasia, Asia and Europe, which is really its peninsula, is greater). It is also known that Afrikans migrated to foreign lands to people the world and sometimes to change in response to long residence in a different environment and become other people. The Afrikan existence therefore occupies tremendous expanses of time and space. In addition there is hardly any people who have been confronted by the multitude of challenges Afrikans have faced, from those challenges that resulted in their founding of the first civilisations in the Nile Valley to those they continue to confront in the long and continuing season of oppression and destruction Afrikans call the *Maafa*, the Great Afrikan Holocaust. Afrikans have had to become adaptable, to change, while continuing to retain their distinctive cultural values and practices that make them Afrikan. This much is shown in the different ways of practising libation, which illustrate a common understanding that there are different ways of being Afrikan, and that no one way is necessarily either superior or inferior to the others, just as there are different ways of being human, without implying inequality.

2.2: The Cosmic Model

Implied in the various stages in the Circle of Life acknowledged by Afrikans, is a certain way of conceptualising the world as being divided into beings and things. James Allen is quite explicit on how the ⌂𓏤 ... or ⌂ ... , the rmṯ n kmt (Coptic remenkemi), "the people of Kemet," visualized the world:

> The ancient Egyptians divided their world into three classes of sentient beings: the gods (𓊹𓊹𓊹 Nṯrw), the akhs (𓐍𓏲 ȝḫjw), and the living (𓂝𓈖𓐍𓇋 ȝḥw). The gods were the original forces and elements of nature, whose wills and actions governed all life. The akhs were the spirits of those who had died and made the successful transition to life after death. They do not live in some heavenly paradise, but in this world, among the living.[3]

We may add here two other categories of beings and things that were recognised, known and named by the people of Kemet—other animals besides humans, and inanimate things; in short, the physical environment. In this understanding of the cosmos, every being and everything in the universe, including lesser divinities, is brought into being by the Creator, ≐ℓ *Atum*, (later variously *Ra*, *Amun*, *Atum-Ra*, *Amun-Ra*, *Ptah*, *Khnum* and the *Aten*), who is thus nb tm: the "Lord of Totality," and is at once both male and female.[4] Every being and thing was given a ⊔ K3: *ka*, a "life force," "vital force" or "energy" emanating from the Creator.[5]

This way of understanding and explaining the world arises directly from and is in fact a part of the creation stories of Kemet, perhaps the oldest known explanations of the universe. In this cosmology everything in the universe derived from the possibilities inherent in the ○○○≡ *Nun*,[6] or primordial waters, for the nun is the oldest substance in the cosmos and contains all the possibilities of existence, that is, all reality everywhere that ever was, is and will be, all possible examples of anything. In this definition of existence everything and its opposite as well as every possibility on the continuum between the two is included.

This very same model of the cosmos exists among the contemporary successors of the people of Kemet, both on the continent of the ancestors and in the numerous Afrikan communities abroad. Of course, there have been some developments and variations. None of this ought to surprise us. Asante and Abarry assert that "[t]he ancient African along the Nile River was in contact with the spiritual world of the ancestors in ways that are similar to the expressions of ancestral relations found in African societies throughout the continent."[7] This observation has been confirmed by Ali Mazuri.[8] To this we may add the many Afrikan communities abroad where this cosmic model, as well as other aspects of Afrikan culture, is lived daily. The reason for this tremendous continuity is not difficult to discern. We turn again to Asante and Abarry, who explain that as Afrikan culture and society developed and became more complex and distant, in both space and time, from its ancient sources in the Nile Valley, "new interpretations, revelations, and permutations occurred," but that "in all cases the ideas of [Afrikan spirituality] kept the societies close to the fundamental principles of harmony between humans, humans and the environment, and humans and the spirit world."[9]

The details vary among different groups of Afrikans, but all who retain Afrikan culture continue the ancient Egyptian concept of the world, which is clearly the model of John Mbiti's division of the contemporary Afrikan world into five categories:

> *God* as the ultimate explanation of the genius and sustenance of both [hu]man[s] and all things.
>
> *Spirits* being made up of superhuman beings and the spirits of [humans] who died a long time ago.
>
> *[Hu]man[s]* including human beings who are alive and those about to be born.
>
> *Animals and plants*, or the rest of biological life.

Phenomena and objects without biological life[10] [i.e. the rest of the physical environment].

Mbiti goes further, telling us that "in addition to the five categories, there seems to be a force, power or energy permeating the whole universe." God is the origin and "ultimate controller" of this force, but the spirits and certain humans also have access to it.[11] Sarpong's explanation of this arrangement is irresistible: "The divinities and the ancestors exercise executive powers only in as far as he permits them."[12] This "force, power or energy" that is in everything is the same as the *ka* of Kemet,[13] the *kra* of the Akans in Ghana and Ivory Coast and most Afrikans in Suriname, and also the same as the *asé* (pronounced ashay) of the *Orisas* (Orishas) that are propitiated by Afrikans (and sometimes by non-Afrikans) in Yorubaland. This very spiritual system, which features the Orishas, is called Orisha in Trinidad, where the same force is also propitiated, as it is among adherents to *Voodoo, Candomblé* and *Santería* in Haiti, Cuba, Jamaica, Brasil, the USA and other places and Kumina in Jamaica. It is also the same as the *ike* and *chi* of the Igbos,[14] and *ntu* of Afrikans in central and southern parts of the continent, the Bantu, from whom this concept has been translated as "vital force."[15] This life force, found in all nature, is also recognised by all the Afrikan people in East Afrika, where it is often termed *Jok* among the speakers of the Luo tongue.[16] Odudoye provides even further evidence of these connections, showing a linguistic link between this ka in the *Medew Netjer* and *chi* in Igbo, and noting that the likely influence is from the ancient Egyptians to the Igbos, not vice versa.[17]

Clinton Hutton shows us that "Ase ... is cosmologically the primordial cosmic material, the creative essence, the creative force..."[18] Robert F. Thompson informs us that asé is a "morally neutral," "spiritual command, the power-to-make-things-happen, God's own *enabling light* rendered accessible to men and women."[19] Raul Canizares tells us that the ontological meaning of asé "refers to a sense of order and balance in the universe. Ashé is the ultimate source of everything."[20] Order and balance are fundamental ideas in the concept of *Maat*, which we have referred to above as good order in the cosmos and which is further explained below. When Afrikans in Brazil greet each other in Portuguese with *"Muito axé para você"* [Much axé for you] or with *"Tremendo ashé pá ti"* [Tremendous axé for you] in Cuba, Puerto Rico and other places where the Spanish language predominates,[21] they are in fact wishing each other empowerment as well as good order and balance within both themselves as individuals and of communities of which they are members. They are also wishing them well in their individual and collective pursuits.

Further close similarities and continuities, in both form and function, may be noted with the ancient Nile Valley spiritual system, though it is not appropriate to burden this text with much of the details. For example, like *Atum*, then *Ra* and *Atum-Ra* of Kemet, who are the sole source of *ka*, Olodumare, also known as *Olorun*, the supreme divinity of the Yorubas, is the sole source of *asé*, which s/he parcels out to the *orisas*. Again like *Atum, Ra* and *Atum-Ra*,

Olodumare is both male and female, dwells in a place that is remote from human habitation, and is the Creator of the world.[22] Among the Igbos the Creator is *Chukwu* (Great Chi) or *Chineke* (*chi[nke]naeke* i.e. *chi* who creates] who also dwells far away from humanity[23] and is a gender neutral divinity. The archetype of the supreme divinity who dwells in a place remote from humans, usually as a direct result of some human weakness, may be encountered in the Myth of Libation, which is recounted in Chapter Two of this work. The lesser divinities in each of these three expressions of the Afrikan spiritual system are each a specific aspect of the Creator, either as a personification of a principle or a natural force or, less often, a deified ancestor. The same or very similar conceptualization of the world is extant among Afrikans everywhere and is either clearly stated or clearly implied in studies of the Afrikan world.[24] Ayi

THE CREATOR (GOD)	THE SPIRIT WORLD OR THE UNSEEN WORLD (SPIRITUAL RELATIONSHIPS)
LESSOR DIVINITIES (or GODS)	
ANCESTORS and other SPIRITS	
HUMANS	THE 'NATURAL' WORLD OR THE SEEN WORLD (SOCIAL AND ECOLOGICAL RELATIONSHIPS)
OTHER ANIMALS	
INANIMATE THINGS	

Illustration 1: The Divine Cosmic Order

Kwei Armah, a foremost spokesperson of the Afrikan story, says definitively that "This outlook is common to African society everywhere"[25] and that "No African society anywhere could find this outlook anything but familiar."[26] This order resides in the popular consciousness of many Afrikans, not the least in Afrikan communities abroad. One example will be enough to illustrate the point here.

When greeted with the standard enquiry about their welfare, some Afrikans would respond with a statement that says something to the effect "By Divine order I am quite all right, thank you." Here the person is signalling that all's relatively well with her/him personally as well as with all of their relationships in the cosmic order, which they acknowledge to be divine. This is so closely related to the greetings of Afrikans in Brazil, Cuba, Puerto Rico and other places where the Portuguese and Spanish languages predominate, that it may well be the response to those same greetings, which are mentioned on the previously. When we remember the common origin of Afrikans these similarities and continuities will make much sense.

These observations articulate the fundamentals of spirituality as the overwhelming presence and importance of spirit as the basis of the cosmos and everything within. This includes individual human beings, as well as the connections or relationships among beings and things. Spirituality also encompasses the compulsion to respect, and on occasion restore, but always to maintain these relationships in a harmonious working order.

In this divine cosmic order, which is illustrated in the diagram above, humans are ranked below the Creator, below other divinities, and below ancestors and other spirits. However, humans are ranked above other animals and above inanimate elements of the physical environment. Spirit animates everything, and when the material person or thing is no more, spirit alone continues, on a higher plane. Spirit is first and foremost; animate and inanimate life, in all its variations, amount to but differing manifestations of spirit. However, the poor vision, poor understanding and inordinate self-centeredness of some humans have led them to try to place themselves at the centre of the universe, above all else and therefore outside of the cosmic order. The consequences have often been disastrous. Today the modern scourge of environmental degradation and destruction threatens every living thing on the planet, including humans.

The being(s) and/or things in each category of things in the cosmos have a specific relationship to the others within that category, and each category also bears a particular relationship to the other categories. For example, humans worship the Supreme Being and lesser divinities, venerate the ancestors, and respect each other and the physical environment. These relationships are respectively spiritual, social and ecological relationships, for our relations to our gods or divinities, to our ancestors and to our unborn are spiritual relationships; those among us living are social relationships; those to our environment are ecological or environmental relationships. They are all based upon awareness of this order and the consequences of both acting to maintain it or not acting to maintain it.

It is necessary to stress that this awareness of spirituality, this oneness, connectedness and interdependence of everything in the cosmos, compelled Afrikans to live in respect for and in harmony with the physical environment. Humanity lives in this environment, a habitat that is absolutely necessary for sustaining life through the many indispensable resources it provides. It is therefore necessary for the environment to be recognised as a very precious resource bank which needs to be owned and managed intelligently in order to secure a decent and dignified living for all and for all times. This is what the ancestors understood and practised. It explains their attitude to the land, which can neither be allowed to be idle while people are land hungry, or be alienated from common ownership to become the property of any individual, which is often a certain step towards land hunger. In the Afrikan understanding of things, land is sacred. That is why groups of Afrikans have always had at least one divinity of the earth. The instances are legion, from ancient through to modern times. For example, in Kemet there was 𓐍𓂋𓏏𓊹 Gb: Geb [Old Kingdom 𓎼𓃀𓃀 Gbb] and 𓄿𓈎𓂋 ꜣkr: Akr: Aker. The latter was both an earth divinity and the earth itself.[27] As is shown in Figure 1 in the photospread, in this ancient Afrikan country there was also Asaru, a divinity of corn, which was an important staple. The presence of these divinities among the gods of Kemet reinforces the fact that the earth was held to be a sacred being.

The very same is true in modern Afrika, where numerous earth divinities are to be found. Among the Igbo in eastern Nigeria, there is *Ani*, which is also a personal name in Kemet, and its variants *Ama*, *Ala* and *Ale*. In Twi in Ghana, there is *Asaase Yaa*, (*Adaase Afua* in the Fante dialect), and *Aberewa:* Old Mother, a general name. *Ayi* and *Li* are the names of the earth goddess among the Ewe.[28] *Oto* is the earth divinity among the Edo. Other examples of current Afrikan earth divinities include *Isong* among the Ibibio and *Dugbo* among the Mende and Kono in Sierra Leone. These are all female earth divinities, whereas in Kemet both of the earth divinities, *Geb* and *Aker*, were male. However, there are also male earth divinities in Afrika today. *Amakiri* is a male earth divinity among the Ijaw, as is *Sopono* among the Yoruba, with the variation *Sapata* among the Fon, Ewe and Eguns.[29] There are many more earth divinities across Afrika. That is why, too, Afrikans always pour libation into Mother Earth, directly or symbolically. Further, Mother Earth is a living, active entity, possessed of some of the same qualities as beings in the other categories of existence. And, like each of these, the physical environment was also made and given by the Creator. This physical environment is also a manifestation of the Creator and is indeed an aspect of the Creator, inviolable and divine. Therefore it is natural to treat the physical environment as a living, breathing and sacred entity according to the tradition handed down by our ancestors. That is why Afrikans have always revered nature and treated Mother Earth as a sentient being. Relations to the earth are simultaneously ecological, spiritual and social relations. In the deepest tradition of Afrika notions of being and existence are anchored in the overriding necessity to preserve the environment. It is logical for development in Afrika to be consistent with this cultural principle and not merely concern itself with the introduction of aspects of European modernity.

This is the idea of Mother Earth that is embedded in Afrikan spirituality, which is deeper and bigger than mere religion. This is the basis of what is now termed environmentalism by some arrogant non-Afrikan latecomers to history, who, in their tremendous ignorance and pursuit of individualism and materialism, have disregarded the Afrikan principle of existing and working in harmony with nature, have tried to conquer nature, and have nearly destroyed the earth. These people now trumpet environmentalism as though it were a recent invention of theirs. Further, they try to impose it upon others without regard to the living traditions in these dominated societies. Afrikans have, from uncounted generations ago, articulated the principle of environmentalism in their daily lives. A good example is through their names, where families and clans are named for a representative ancestor, animal, plant or object. This principle, which is known as totemism in some literatures, is also the basis of prohibitions against killing or eating or interacting in certain other ways, usually specified, with one's representative animal or thing, referred to as taboos.

The earliest known representation of this system, in Afrika and in all humanity, is in the society of Kemet. There the term for the concept of taboo was 𓃀𓅱𓏏 bwt.[30] This system of representative animals or things and the prohibitions against certain kinds of interaction with them spread a comprehensive form of species protection and preservation, without guns and fences, from community to community throughout Afrika. What is known today as environmentalism is a cultural principle of Afrika that was lived daily in prohibitions against killing or eating the representative animal of one's family, clan or community, against cutting down trees needlessly or indeed against the wanton destruction of any life form. Additionally, there was also the compulsion to propitiate the relevant divinity whenever nature was to be interfered with in any way, for example, if a single tree were to be cut down, an animal taken in the hunt, or warfare undertaken.

There are many profound truths in this world-view and the understanding of reality that it instructs. These have been handed down from ancient times by our Afrikan forebears. In simple language that tells these fundamental truths, to maintain the proper relations means life: healthy, vigorous and redemptive identity for communities and people. To continue the present disconnections means a declining standard of life: continuously diminishing spiritual and material existence—and eventual but most certain cosmic death.

In this cosmic order there is ultimately no real death in the ordinary sense of the word, only decline and decay followed by periodic rejuvenation, often called re-birth. Nature had pointed the way, for nature was her first children's first teacher; Afrikans learnt first by direct observations of nature. (The accumulation of knowledge and distillation of wisdom—the results of the interaction of experience with intuition, insight and analysis—would necessarily come later.) The violent, threatening and at first even terrifying but ultimately refreshing and regenerative annual flood of the Nile, or the fire on the grassland; these and many other examples of nature's regenerative power were observed by Afrikans.

This continuing regeneration in nature has often been misunderstood as mere death and destruction by the uncomprehending, those who do not look beyond the immediate and the individual and so do not apprehend the big picture of unending (re)creation and so unending life. This is the significance of the new growth that is always occasioned by the river in flood or the new shoots which unfailingly follow the fire on the grassland. The individual, just like any particular day, or a specific fire or flood or season, is comparatively temporary and fleeting. S/he decays and is soon physically no more. But in a normal healthy environment the collective is permanent and enduring, for individuals are always being replaced, and in healthy circumstances their beliefs and rituals, knowledge, skills and insights are handed on to succeeding generations by those ultimate bringers and signifiers of continuity and progress we term socialisation and education. Therefore the community never dies, and so its work is never done. Hence the collective is always greater than the individual; this is a fundamental principle of Afrikan life. Therefore there can be no ultimate death other than cosmic death where an entire species is extinguished. For though an individual may physically decline and die, the species continues to replenish itself through millions of individual recreations at every level—from a single cell to an entire individual to communities composed of many individuals, to countries and civilizations that are in turn composed of numerous communities and countries.

Creation is an ever continuing process alive in all life in all time. It is not a finite event which took place at a particular moment in the past. Spirit is the basis of the universe; not matter, which really amounts to differing and rather specific expressions of spirit, each limited in its own regard by its own specificities and so its own possibilities. And spirit never dies. (We inherit this from the Almighty through our ancestors.) Spirit always returns, hence the principle of the indestructible and returning soul, as illustrated in such Afrikan personal names as ⌘: Nfrtyti = Nefertiti (Kemet, "The beautiful one is come again,") Babatunde (Yoruba, "Father has returned,") Iyabo (Yoruba, "Mother has come back") and so on. Certain physical aspects of the individual may decline and disintegrate, but spirit, the basic element of all matter, continues in reconstituted form.

In Kemet the maintenance of cosmic relations by each individual was examined at death. The soul of the deceased was required to make a series of forty two declarations affirming that while on earth its owner did not infringe any of these relations among the Creator, the lesser divinities, humans past, present and future, and the environment. These are known today as the Declarations of Innocence, which may be found in Chapter 125 of *The Book of Going Forth Into Enlightenment*, which is discussed in Chapter Two.[31] The Declarations are the intellectual basis of both the good moral life in Kemet and the Ten Commandments in Christianity.

It was, it is and it will always be necessary to maintain this divine cosmic order, or ⌘ (variation ⌘) M3ʿt: *Maat*, a concept first encountered and articulated in Kemet, where it was also rendered as the feather ⌘ and personified as the female divinity of the same name: ⌘, also rendered ⌘ and ⌘. Like many other ideas from one language and culture sphere, it is either very difficult or not possible to translate *Maat* into other languages and culture spheres with the greatest precision. This difficulty in especially increased because the concept is at once profound, pervasive and multifaceted. Interpretations therefore vary. This concept has been variously translated as truth, justice, righteousness, order, balance, harmony and reciprocity.[32] However, these terms merely describe some of the parameters of the idea, which is elastic and simultaneously inclusive of all of them.³³

The opposite of *Maat* is [hieroglyph] [variation [hieroglyph]] isft: *isfet*. Logically, this is the absence of *Maat*, the lack of truth, balance, justice, righteousness, harmony or reciprocity. Such a condition must mean wrongdoing, evil, disorder and chaos.

Maat has been described as the "key idea in the traditional African approach to life" which today "recurs in most African societies as the influence of right and righteousness, justice and harmony, balance, respect and human dignity."³⁴ We have seen above that notions of order and balance represent a deeper meaning of asé, which is therefore conceptually a continuation and restatement of *Maat*. The two—or maybe the two labels of the same thing—are also linked in practice, for libation is about maintaining *Maat* for the people of Kemet as it is about maintaining asé for the practitioners of the Way of the Orisas, of Voodoo, Kumina, Candomblé, Cumfa, Macumba, Mayal and Santería. In Afrikan thought and practice, Libation is an affirmation of and a path to the divine cosmic order.

The maintenance of this order, that is, all these relationships, has always been achieved by a periodic show of this respect—or by making appeasement and restoration when something has gone wrong. And things go wrong usually through some inappropriate action by humans. Respect and appeasement of the divine forces were both achieved through making offerings, by sacrifice and by pouring libation.³⁵

The notion of healing as restoration of this ancient cosmic order within each individual, family, clan and indeed within the entire nation therefore finds a very powerful resonance among Afrikans who are aware of and determined to bring about the redemption of the race, which they know to be achievable only through unity. This in turn can be rebuilt only upon the restoration and upkeep of the proper cosmic relations: of understanding their common origin and heritage, of up-keeping their own rituals, of telling their own story and ensuring that it is passed on to future generations, so that all engage in what Ayi Kwei Armah describes as "a long ritual involving members of a community of affection so extensive as to embrace living members in present time, members who [have] lived and died but whose memory it [is] the responsibility of the living to keep alive, and members yet to come, who would inherit the common memory and manage its flow into the future."³⁶ The ability and determination to reinstate and keep this covenant of the generations will be a decisive influence upon the future of Afrika and the world.

Respect for and understanding of this cosmic order confers order, meaning, purpose, value and motivation on the Afrikan way of life. The traditional Afrikan way of life is therefore marked by the urge to be humble and to be grateful and give thanks to those who are both greater than us humans as well as responsible for our presence in this dimension of time. There is security in a belief and a faith that both spring eternally from the knowledge of and respect for the universe; an integrated universe of beings and things, which holds an importance and significance over and above humans and above that of the individual: I am because we are, and because we are therefore I am.[37] The Native Americans remind us that we humans do not weave the web of life, but we are a part of it.[38] The most sacred and powerful parts of this universe are made up of the Supreme Being or Creator, known to Afrikans by different names in different places and at different times, of the other but lesser divinities and of the ancestors also. It is known and understood that these beings or forces exist, that they are greater than humans are, and that they can take action on our behalf once we conduct our lives in the proper way.

Offerings are therefore an important part of the Afrikan spiritual practices that together make up an important part of the Afrikan way of life. These include thoughts that are expressed in words in the form of prayers. They also include any number of the choicest articles available in a community. Offerings are presented by humans to the Supreme Being, to other divinities and to our ancestors in recognition of their divinity and/or superiority over us and as a way of renewing or restoring the ties to other aspects of the cosmic order. Such articles normally include the first fruits. These are the first and choicest portions taken in the hunt, or gathered in the harvest, or generally obtained in human production. Indeed anything that is considered good enough for the divine and for the ancestors may be presented, including food. Utterance 936 in the *Coffin Texts* gives a very good example of the list of articles put on an offering table in the time of Kemet. This Utterance also provides some idea of the order in which the entire offering ritual proceeded,[39] an order which may also be gleaned from the propitiatory text that forms Utterance 926.[40] Sacrifice, which is the offering up of the life of an animal, also falls into this category of offerings. Offerings are normally accompanied by libations and the burning of incense. In Kemet the latter two were normally offered simultaneously, or one immediately after the other.[41]

The use of each was both sacramental as well as pacificatory. They were offered to divinities to continue or restore balance and harmony in the universe or some aspect of it, and/or in return for the grant of certain virtues and powers to those who offered—or in whose name an offering was made. Incense and certain oils were employed in order to create a cleansing, calming and enabling atmosphere; one receptive to communication among the forces at work on such occasions, when such aids were considered indispensable. The origin, development and significance of the Offering Complex form the subject of Chapter Three.

2.3: Definition

Libation is a highly distinctive combination of thought, word and gesture which together constitute a ritual drama that has been sacred to Afrikans for as long as humanity has counted time, and perhaps even before then. It is a powerful moment of profound significance in which divinity and ancestors are invoked, the environment acknowledged, and all the generations within the entire time/space correlation represented by the experience of living are united before the invoked forces.

Libation therefore crosses many boundaries to unite forces from every domain of the cosmos in a fusion of space: the here/not here, and a fusion of time: the past/present/future.

At this most potent moment of this ritual process a drink offering is made and favours sought. In the current historical era the offering is made with the right hand—to the Supreme Being, to lesser divinities, to the ancestors, and/or to the environment or aspects thereof. This is done in order to receive the support of these forces for our general well-being and/or for a specific purpose or purposes that the libationer seeks. This spiritual help is sought and normally secured through propitiating these forces or making reparations in order to ensure the repair and restoration of ruptured relations among the beings and things in the universe, or to affirm this good order (*Maat, asé*) if it is threatened, to give thanks for an achievement, to call down cosmic damnation on an enemy, or for any combination of these. The specific purpose(s) for which the support may be solicited would be made clear in each libation statement.

We shall see that in practice the meaning of libation also incorporates purification as preparation for the ritual, so that libation may be properly regarded as purification of mind and body in order to better and properly solicit and receive blessings and other forms of strength and support from the Almighty, from lesser divinities and from our sacred ancestors upon whose shoulders we stand, as well as the actual ritual and its purposes in which such solicitations form a central part. An important idea in libation is therefore ritual purification, including restoration or repair, through running water. This is demonstrated below in Chapter Six.

The liquid with which libation is poured may be water, milk, honey, oil, wine, gin, palm wine, white rum, etc. It is normally poured into the ground, into sacred recesses such as natural chasms, over altars and/or sacrificial animals, or into sacred vessels like a calabash, or a cup, or a bowl. One historically recent adaptation to life in a cold climate, to where many Afrikans have migrated, is the pouring of the liquid into the soil of a potted plant inside of a building. The soil and the plant symbolize Mother Earth. The liquid is poured in a ceremonial act in which salutations, proclamations and petitions may also be made, either silently or aloud, though they are normally made aloud, especially at communal ceremonies.

Libation is an Afrikan Ritual of Heritage usually enacted at the very beginning of the day, at meal times and as part of most Afrikan ceremonies, though libations may also be poured at any point of a ceremony, even at the end. Critically, special libations are poured in times of need to satisfy the demands of particular circumstances.

In this ritual an individual, the libationer, that is, the one who pours, enters into contact with any or all of the higher powers of the world: The Supreme Being, the divinities, the ancestors and the environment. The libationer may also solicit the spiritual presence of humans who are alive but are not physically present at the particular enactment of the ritual and who are known to share the aims of the libationer and would support the petition.

The libationer enters into contact with the spirit world to promote his/her interests (if s/he is pouring and asking on her/his own behalf) and/or on behalf of those assembled, or on behalf of any individual(s) and/or group(s) named in the ritual. The named individual(s) and/or group(s) may include persons who are not physically present or even have direct knowledge of that particular enactment of the ritual. However, such individual(s) and/or group(s) may have the same or similar interests, wishes and spiritual connection and alignment. Therefore they may be directly represented and/or would have wished to be represented in the enactment of the ritual and may therefore be spiritually present. This connection between those who are physically there and those who are not physically there is also illustrated in the presence of inhabitants of the spirit world: The Supreme Being, other divinities, the ancestors and the unborn. These spiritual presences are central to the understanding and practice of libation.

Libation is therefore a recognised and proclaimed way of articulating, maintaining, safeguarding or repairing the relationship between humanity and the higher powers as well as among humans and between humanity and the physical environment. The process of invoking the spiritual presences is always an important part of libation.

During the ritual, at least one petition is addressed to the higher power(s) to whom the libation is poured, though there may be more than one petition, particularly if one considers the usual requests (i.e. petitions) for general guidance and protection.

The format of libation, as well as the *Medew Netjer* term 𓂋𓏏𓉔𓂋𓅱 pr(t)-ḥrw-(ḥtpw)-nṯr, which means "voice offerings" or "prayers of the spirits," which is discussed in the next two chapters, show that this ritual contains the most ancient, or one of the most ancient, forms of the libation statement or prayer. Libation is a dramatised appeal by human beings to the Most High Divinity, to the lesser divinities, to the ancestors and to the environment. This ritual demonstrates the Afrikan understanding of these spiritual forces. It shows the way in which living beings and things are connected to and relate to the spiritual world, indeed to the entire cosmos. Libation also indicates the cosmic order in which all these forces exist in relation to each other.

Without a doubt libation has influenced, in fact determined, the form as well as the functions of prayers in Christianity, Judaism and Islam. These are religions that arose long after the establishment of the classical Afrikan traditions and took many of their principles and practices, sometimes directly and sometimes indirectly, from those traditions, especially the ways in which they were expressed in Kemet.

The ritual of libation is one example. The multitude of references to libation in the Bible, both as "libation" and as its synonym "drink offering," in both their singular and plural forms, numbers at least 67, beginning at Genesis 35:14.[42]

These references occur over 2000 years after libation was first attested in Kemet, and show the form and significance of libation to be derived from the pre-existing Afrikan tradition, much of which passed into the Eurochristian tradition through Moses, who is now considered by many to have been an ancient Egyptian or man of Kemet who gave to the Jews their religion and culture, which is essentially that of the people of Kemet.[43]

The notion of purification through running water, which is the origin and basis of the Christian baptism, also has its archetype in the Libation Ritual and the related practice of purification by the ritual pouring of water, though it must be mentioned *en passant* here that Afrikan deep thought[44] finds absurd the doctrine that proposes humanity to be born in sin.[45]

Today in most enactments of this ritual there is only one libationer and a simple format is followed. This is usually enacted in homes by individuals on behalf of themselves or for small groups. Anyone, including children, may pour libation on such occasions. However, on special occasions there may be an elaborate and complex ritual and more than one libationer, usually a leading or chief libationer and an assistant or a number of assistants. On such occasions the libationer or chief libationer is usually a male: a priest, the head of the household, the head of a lineage, of a clan, or of a particular branch of the Afrikan nation. Traditionally this is so because of the way in which Afrikans arrange their affairs so that roles such as these are often placed in the male domain of responsibilities, not because of gender inequality. In fact, anyone may be deputed to pour libation on behalf of the group.

Women were priestesses, poured libation and generally made offerings in Kemet from very early times. Figures 2 and 3 in the photospread show women making offerings in early Kemet and help to illustrate a central role for women in the offering rituals of that country, though it must be made clear that such facts by themselves do not establish gender equality beyond any doubt. In some Afrikan communities abroad, for example in Suriname, the leading libationer may be either female or male, while on certain occasions a male and a female perform the leading role jointly.

Today there appears to be a growing number of Afrikan women who pour libation on community occasions. This is especially noticeable in the communities abroad, where increasing numbers are reAfrikanising themselves. A good illustration of this practice is shown in Figure 4 in the photospread, where priestess Okomfo Nana Akosua Baakan pours libation and conducts the entire naming ceremony of the author's niece, Nia Drakes. This increasing participation of women in this role within the ritual may also in some instances be part of a reaction to perceptions of male dominance in the way in which the ritual has often been practised, and indeed in life in general.

The libationer, the one who performs the ritual, enters into this undertaking in order to recognise and proclaim the existence and superiority of spiritual beings, to solicit and obtain their blessings for a particular individual or a particular group, to repair imbalance in a person, a family, a clan, a specific part of the Afrikan nation or in the entire nation or in the physical environment, or to nullify the perceived threat of such imbalance, to obtain blessings for a project that is to be started, or for one that has already been started or has been completed, to issue a curse upon ill wishers or evil doers, or for any combination of these foregoing reasons, and usually to obtain general blessings and all other benefits—psychological, spiritual or otherwise—that arise from the recognition, acknowledgement and benevolence of those powers that are greater than us mere humans.

To summarise, a particular libation may have one or any combination of the following purposes:

(i) Giving thanks to the Supreme Being, to the lesser divinities and to the ancestors for all life and for the things which sustain life, for example for any of the following: a meal, a successful hunt, a catch of fish, anything else reaped from mother nature and/or derived through the processes of human production.

(ii) Asking general blessings of the Divine Spirit, the lesser divinities and the ancestors.

(iii) Asking help and guidance of the Divine Spirit, the lesser divinities and the ancestors in work (that is, a particular project) to be undertaken.

(iv) Giving thanks to the higher powers for guidance, sustenance or help in some way in attaining some milestone (e.g. another Earth Day) or in completing a project.

(iv) Asking for evildoers to be damned.

(v) Asking the Supreme Being and/or other divinities or ancestors to intervene to restore the cosmic balance (*Maat*) if in any of the spiritual relationships that constitute it is ruptured or endangered or is likely to be threatened through some forthcoming action(s), for example cutting down trees or going to war.

In a libation any divinity or combination of divinities, any ancestor or combination of ancestors, or any of the spirits of the environment resident in natural phenomena such as a river, or any combination of divinities, ancestors and environmental spirits, may be invoked. In addition to any of these combinations, the spiritual strength of the absent living may also be invoked.

A libation may be poured with any drinkable liquid, including water, milk, wine, beer, or strong spirits, although alcohol has been the dominant choice for some generations now. More often than not clear spirits are chosen on important occasions: palm wine, gin or *schnapps* in Ghana, Nigeria and other parts of West Afrika, *clairin* in Haiti, white rum in Jamaica, Guyana, Trinidad, Suriname and other places. In Suriname the preferred white rum is Palm. In Ghana the community made white spirits used is *akpeteshie*, in Nigeria it is *ogogoro*, in Trinidad it is puncheon, less often *babash*, and in Dominica it is *Zai-id* or Mountain Dew.

The predominance of clear spirits as the most popular choice is almost certainly because of its physical resemblance to pure water, the significance of which is explained below. However, in arriving at a conclusion on this matter it is also necessary to consider a practice that evolved during the centuries of the European trade in enslaved Afrikans. Many Afrikan chiefs were in complicity with the European traders; some by force of circumstances, others through sheer greed or through some combination of the two. But they were junior functionaries to the Europeans in the largest crime against humanity. It became a common practice for chiefs to try "to make an extra profit on every sale [of their fellow Afrikans] by insisting that the Europeans [the buyers of humans] should give them a present of [alcohol] before they started business."[46] This is a likely explanation—or part of the explanation—of the custom of presenting chiefs with gin or schnapps, both clear alcohol and both used extensively in libation. Whether this practice initiated the predominant choice in West Afrika or merely influenced a pre-existing custom is at this point open to some degree of conjecture. It is however very clear that this ought to be a line of future investigation.

At this historical moment certain Afrikan divinities may have their individual preferences about drink and food. This is more than an echo from Kemet, where "certain oblations [were] suited to particular gods, others inadmissible to their temples, and some more peculiarly adapted to prescribed periods of the year."[47] Esteban Montejo, an ancestor who was enslaved by Europeans in Cuba, attests to the continuation of these attitudes and practices among Afrikans on that island during his lifetime, from the 1850s to the 1960s. Shango's favourite food there was *harina de amalá*, Ochún's was *Ochinchin*. "All the [Afrikan gods]" Esteban tells posterity, "had their special foods. Obatalá had a dish of kidney beans, and there were many others . . . "[48] Today, in Nigeria, Ogun's drink is palm wine. Among the loa (divinities) of Voodoo in Haiti, the liquid of libation "varies according to the god. It is sweet liquor if it is Damballa, rum for Ogun, Loco or Legba."[49] It is red wine or any home-made wine or puncheon or babash (Trinidad moonshine) for Shango in Trinidad. In Candomblé in Brazil, Oshun's favourite food is *Xinxin de galinha*, that of Shango is *maala* or *caruru*, Obatala's is white rice, *abará vatapá*, *acarajé*. The preference of Tano in Ghana is eggs, fowls and wine. Mashed yam, sometimes along with hard boiled eggs, is offered to the ancestral spirits at Odwira in Ghana.

In current West Afrikan practice there is a sharp distinction between some things that are done with the right hand and other things that are to be done only with the left hand. Libation is poured with the right hand because this is the hand reserved by historically more recent Afrikan tradition for such activity as offering, eating and drinking. A libation often accompanies offerings of food and other things considered good and worthy of the higher powers, but libation should not be confused with those other offerings or with entire ceremonies of which it may form a part. For example, from the earliest known times, libations are always poured as part of the rituals which mark the Afrikan cycle of life:

Naming Ceremonies, Initiation Ceremonies, Marriage Ceremonies and Transition Ceremonies (funerals). Libation is also poured at other occasions, such as to mark the settlement of a dispute, before chopping down trees (individually or parts of a forest), at the enstoolment of chiefs, at the many festivals in the Afrikan calendar, at the opening of Voodoo, Orisha, Candomblé and other Afrikan spiritual gatherings, and indeed in every ceremony and gathering in the Afrikan way of life. Even these do not exhaust the occasions for libation. The general purpose is to safeguard or make amends and seek forgiveness for infracting any of the relationships in the cosmic order, but the specific occasions and themes in libation may be many, as is illustrated by Abu Abarry's consideration of Ga libation oratory[50] or in the Igbo invocations,[51] or indeed in the libation practice of the many existing groups of Afrikans.

As can be expected, a Libation Statement will reflect the occasion or specific purpose(s) at hand. It will also tell whether it is a simple or a complex enactment of the ritual as well as the general circumstances and aim(s) of those who have organised the gathering.

If properly done, the person, the family, the clan, the community or the nation (i.e. those present and participating and/or those on whose behalf the libation is poured) may receive several benefits from a libation. They may benefit through being fortified by the renewal and/or restoration which this ritual offers. They may also receive benefit through the psychological security that comes from the knowledge of the spiritual connection and oneness with the Supreme One, with the lesser divinities, with the ancestors, among themselves singly and collectively, and with the physical environment. It is the preservation of these connections and the beneficial results of understanding and maintaining them that this ritual represents and promotes.

Libation, like any activity that is at once both sacred and communal, is useful and important because it helps to overcome fears, anxieties and frustrations. It promotes knowledge of and respect for elders and the ancestors, hope and healing, unity and harmony. It achieves all of this through the reinforcement of common bonds. Through the promotion of togetherness, it also lends itself towards the achievement of communal solidarity, which results from common participation in any such communal activity.

Libation also functions beneficially by helping those present to be psychologically prepared for a task at hand, especially through the self-confidence that grows from the knowledge that not only that all is well within the self and in our relationships with the powers in the cosmic order, but also by becoming focused upon what is to be done during a specific forthcoming undertaking. The latter is normally achieved by rehearsing, interrogating and if necessary, refining our plan of action in one's mind before actually embarking upon the undertaking(s) in question. In a similar way libation is also helpful because it empowers us to focus upon all the tasks and expected challenges in a particular venture or during a specific day—or indeed within any time period—that may be unfolding before us and which may be addressed in the Libation Statement. The strategic location of the morning libation at the very beginning of the day is especially helpful in the daily review process. In short, by promoting critical review of our plans and focus upon upcoming commitments, libation helps us to imagine the future, recognise forthcoming challenges in the way of its attainment and plan effectively towards the realization of our goals. In this way, libation may help boost self-confidence and create an enabling psychological climate for success in forthcoming action.

However, libation must not be a substitute for human labour or human struggle, as Christian and Muslim prayers are sometimes viewed. The idea that a god or saviour introduced by some Arabs or Europeans could and would save Afrikans, if they close their eyes to the reality of their own oppression by those two groups, pray hard and follow the rules devised by their oppressors, has been popular among some Afrikans who spend their lives in worship of the ancestors of those who oppress them and never organise their own liberation. No one should worship the gods of their oppressors, for that is the surest sign of their spiritual and mental enslavement, the deepest kind of oppression.

A particular libation may be part of an occasion specifically devoted to the Supreme Being, or to a particular divinity, or to an ancestor, or even to a living leader, but every part of Afrikan society is usually acknowledged in the statement accompanying the pouring, including families, clans and the entire collective.

We have seen that one moment for doing libation is generally at the beginning of the day. In addition, libation is also done at meal times, or at a special ceremony to honour the Supreme Being, or a particular divinity, or an ancestor. The beginning of a day is a particularly significant time at which to site a libation ritual. The birth of each day is another beginning, a time when everyone is part of a re-awakening world that shows humanity as an intimate aspect within the rhythm of nature. Plants, humans and other animals begin to stir after their overnight rest and recuperation, all informed by the rising of the sun which signals the start of another cycle of activity. This is a time when humans are more disposed to the possibilities of the new day. Here, invigorated by the previous night's rest, in the calm of the infant day that lies mostly unrevealed and unfulfilled before them, people are generally more reflective and enthusiastic about visualizing the immediate opportunities and challenges, about establishing and planning the accomplishment of their goals for the unfolding new segment of time that they musc inhabit profitably.

Libation may also be an important part of a ceremony arranged specifically to mark the commencement of an important piece of work (e.g. the building of a house,) at the completion of a significant piece of work (the building of a house, or its cleansing or dedication, if these are not done on the same occasion,) or in recognition of an important achievement (success at exams, an earthday, the attainment of a certain stage in spiritual growth, the end of a period of struggle, recovery from illness, and so on.) J. Gardner Wilkinson tells us that in Kemet, "[t]hanksgiving for the birth of a child, escape from danger, or other marks of divine favour, were offered by individuals through the medium of priests. The same was done in private; and secret as well as public vows were made in the hope of future favours."[52] The material quality of the offering was of course dependent upon the means of the offerer(s).[53] Today, as far removed from Kemet in place and time as Guyana is, Afrikans who remain true to this part of their traditions still hold a ceremony and feast of thanksgiving to mark such an important landmark in the life of a person or a community, such as a birthday, success in an examination, promotion on the job, and so on. Such a ceremony is called a "Come True" or simply a "Service" or a "Thanksgiving," which are terms for the same activity that is widespread in the Caribbean and the Americas, where the synonymous term *bembé* is employed in Santería.

The recognition and acknowledgement of our ancestors, the divinities and The Supreme One, as well as our connection with them, is always a very special occasion for Afrikans. It is not therefore necessary to have a special earthly occasion for one to pour libation. So individuals and groups may pour libation at any time they have the urge to do so. A particular libation may be addressed to any divinity or ancestor or cosmic force or to any combination of such forces to whom the person or group feels close or perceives the need to contact and propitiate.

2.4: The Divine Presence and Sacred Space

In order to show respect to the higher powers certain acts of submission are made in acknowledgement of divine superiority, especially by the person who does the offering, but these may also be made by anyone else present. These acts of submission include bowing, kneeling, baring the shoulders, removing the shoes, covering the head (in some parts baring the head,) touching the ground with one's hands, and prostrating oneself.

These are very ancient ways of showing supplication. To stand in the Divine Presence is to stand on holy ground. Afrikans have demonstrated submission to the Almighty on such occasions by removing their footwear and remaining barefooted, that is, in direct and solid contact with Mother Earth at that particular spot.

One of the earliest known examples of this practice is clearly shown on the Narmer Palette from early Kemet, which has been widely reproduced in the literature on Kemet. This palette has been dated to about 5000 years ago. Here ꜣ Narmr: Narmer, a name which literally means "Striking Catfish" but is more probably to be interpreted as "The Assertive Survivor,"[54] the ꜣ nsw: nesu or Pharaoh[55] who may have had a decisive role in the unification of Upper and Lower Kemet, is shown on each side of the palette. The Pharaoh is ritually barefooted in each instance.

The great importance and significance placed upon the Pharaoh being barefooted is emphasised by the presence of one of his functionaries. This is the person who occupied the post of Sandal Bearer and Footwasher. He is holding the Pharaoh's sandals and a small water vessel, which we must presume is filled. This official is placed immediately behind the *Nsw* Narmer—on each side of the palette. The location of this official, and his repetition on each side of the palette, attempt to ensure that the observer does not miss the point: the nsw is barefooted and this fact is of the greatest significance.

It seems clear that a symbolic and ritual context is indicated by these and other details on the palette. It is also apparent that the event being recalled, described and commemorated, took place in a sacred area. Therefore it is necessary to conclude that *Nsw* Narmer was barefooted because he was in a sacred space.[56]

Very deep significance should be attached to this conclusion. The nsw or Pharaoh was himself a divine being. He was also a temporal king, being in effect also owner of the country. For such an all-powerful functionary to remove his footwear publicly must indicate a conscious, deliberate and willing supplication to an authority he knew, recognised and wished to be recognised, to be superior even to himself. The inescapable conclusion is that the Pharaoh knew that he was in divine presence, on sacred ground and before the Supreme Being.

There is a great likelihood that Narmer was practising a tradition which had been inherited from previous generations. But it is certain that going barefooted when in sacred spaces became a custom in Kemet from the very earliest of times. The practice was handed down from generation to generation. So too was the ritual of smiting of the enemy. There are numerous scenes in the literature of Kemet in which a pharaoh is depicted symbolically smiting an enemy. Again the *nsw* is usually barefooted, indicating that he is knowingly performing a sacred act in a sacred space.

The conclusion that being barefooted indicated presence in a sacred space is further strengthened by the way in which the people of Kemet depicted the *Heb Sed*: the rejuvenation and jubilee observations of the *nsw*. In every depiction of this ritual, this most important figure runs, symbolically around the boundaries of the state, and is barefooted. This also appears to be true every time the nsw conducts an offering ritual, even though there are images of other offerers wearing sandals. Therefore going barefoot in ritual space appears to be a fundamental rule in Kemet. Other examples of this practice that may be seen in other self representations of the people of Kemet, including the so-called Scorpion Macehead, a very early example, which is now housed in the Ashmolean Museum in Oxford University, England.

Eighteen hundred years after Narmer, and nearly contemporaneous with Tutankhamon, Moses, himself a son of Kemet, would also follow this identical ancient Egyptian practice and remove his shoes in the presence of the Almighty. This is represented in the Bible at Exodus 3:5, where Moses is said to be directed by the Almighty to remove his shoes, with the explanation being that it was because he was standing on holy ground, doubtless because he was in the Divine Presence and the space was therefore sacred.

In more historically recent times, but at a point still somewhat remote from today, it was compulsory to remove both hats and shoes when addressing particular Mutapas, the leaders of Monomotapa. The Mutapa state that flourished from the fifteenth to the eighteenth centuries was located in an area that included what is now northern Zimbabwe. It is still compulsory to remove these items when entering the presence of spirit mediums[57] or in any holy spaces. Removal of head and foot wear on certain sacred occasions is maintained among many other Afrikan people, where this act has an identical significance. For example, among the Asante in Ghana, it is customary for a libationer to bare his chest as well as to take off his headwear and footwear before commencing ritual duty. These are acts of supplication to show reverence for the Creator, for the lesser divinities and for the ancestors. In Afrika, people take off their shoes to honour someone.[58]

Taking off of shoes before entry into households is also good hygiene, since it helps to prevent the spread of pollutants and other unwanted material. This action also shows respect for the ancestral spirits of the home, and therefore for the entire household. Taking off the shoes before entry into temples shows respect for the divinity served in each temple. These are practices that are current in most Afrikan communities, including those in the diaspora. These related ideas of Divine Presence and sacred space also inform the contemporary Afrikan worldview and practise of libation.

2.5: Formula

The form a libation takes may vary from the simple to the elaborate, depending upon the grandeur of the occasion, the specific purpose of the ritual, the spiritual and material circumstances of the organiser(s) and also the particular variation of the ritual that is practised in the locality. On very grand occasions the libation may be very elaborate, with all the stages being observed and the chief libationer being assisted by others. A libation poured for a simple every day meal may vary in some details from a libation poured on the occasion of a wedding feast, a Thanksgiving, or a dedication ceremony. The Afrikan people have the longest history on earth and have lived in many diverse environments, both on the ancestral continent and in communities abroad. Variations in the daily practice of their common cultural principles have therefore developed naturally. It is also true that in their historical experience there have been some variations that have developed out of the experience of the Maafa. Some of these that pertain to libation are discussed below, in Chapter Five. Libation may therefore also vary according to which particular group within the Afrikan nation is performing this ritual. But wherever libation is poured in the Afrikan world, whether it is in Lagos or London, in Bamako or Bridgetown, Georgia or Georgetown, it is the very same principles, discussed above, from the very same source in the bosom of Mamma Afrika that will be observed and celebrated.

There have been regular debates among people in the conscious Afrikan community about the most appropriate language(s) in which their rituals and ceremonies, including libation, must be conducted. Non-Afrikan languages have been widely rejected on the ground that they are invariably the languages of oppression. It is thought that such languages ought to be used only as a last resort. Afrikan languages are widely preferred because it is felt that the ancestors will recognise and understand them, as well as be more appreciative of the libationers, when their sacred presences are invoked in their own languages. These languages are part of their ancestors' own creations and part of their legacy to subsequent generations, which of course include the libationers, who, in fact, represent the living generations at each libation. Here no one must forget those languages created by the much beloved company of sacred ancestors in the depths of cultural genocide during that time of naked terror called enslavement, or the Maafa as a generality. These languages are Kwéyòl, Creole, Ebonics, Papiamentu, Srantongo, Pidgin English and others. These are Afrikan languages which are valid for libation and other sacred or secular purposes.

Employing Afrikan languages in Afrikan rituals and ceremonies is of the greatest importance for other reasons. Such a practice amounts to a demonstration of the fact that Afrikans value and respect their own languages and culture, and therefore they value and respect themselves and their own identity. This practice is also the only one that ensures that the great majority of Afrikan people are included and treated equally on these most important occasions, for these are the languages with which that majority is most familiar and so can function in with the greatest ease and effectiveness. The alternative practice of conducting Afrikan sacred rituals in languages that are unfamiliar to the majority of the Afrikan people serves to exclude that majority, and is therefore undemocratic, un-Afrikan and counter-productive as a device for cultural re-affirmation.

When a people speak their own languages at the most sacred and important of occasions, they include, celebrate and honour to the highest, their own selves, their families, their ancestors, their communities, their traditions; themselves. It is one of the best ways of honouring themselves collectively as a people. This is what Boukman Dutty did in the Haitian Revolution. (See Chapter Five.) Embracing their own languages is another way in which Afrikans must begin to return to themselves. Afrikans must maintain Afrikan languages as their only sacred languages. That is a good way of demonstrating love and respect for themselves—and commitment to their own cause of self liberation and sustained development in their own interests.

When the name of each divinity or ancestor is intoned in the libation ritual, the pourer pours out a little of the drink and invites the named divinity or ancestor to come and drink. There is no fixed number of times to pour, but it is normal to pour at least once for each spirit being invoked and once for each petition made.

It is of the greatest importance that everyone performing this ritual sticks to the inherited form and principles, for a ritual is, above all else, always doing sacred things in good order, in the right way. It is this preservation and continuation, through space and time, of the same ritual actions in the same order for the same purpose which, more than anything else, makes libation the recognizable and important sacred drama that it is and invests it with the power to unite all Afrikans in eternity and so attain a significance that transcends the ritual itself. From the earliest times much importance has been placed on repeating the formula precisely. Great pains are also taken to ensure exact repetition of any incantation (prayer invoking a spirit force) that may accompany a libation. Anyone who departs from a formula, but especially from the sacred principles, does so on pain of offending the Supreme Being, the lesser divinities and the sacred ancestors. The immediate result may be violating the mission and bringing shame and disrepute upon the celebrants and ultimately weakening their communities and the entire nation.

The following model of a Libation Statement is taken from Ewe customary tradition still alive in parts of Ghana, Benin, Togo and Nigeria. It was given to this writer by Brother Explo Nani-Kofi, who obtained it from Kofi Kogi MD, an elder who is much interested in these matters. The information here is corroborated by examples of libation from other sources employed in this work. It shows continuities with much of the practice in other Afrikan communities and indicates the essential elements of a Libation Statement.

The ritual drama of libation is therefore a process that is likely to be identified by all or by a combination of some of these stages:

1. Invocation of the Creator.

2. Invocation of lesser divinities.

3. Invocation of the ancestors.

4. Introduction of the self (i.e. the person pouring the libation,) including a statement of his or her genealogy.

5. Statement of the mission (i.e. of the specific purpose of the particular Libation.) This needs not be one purpose.

6. The petition or request for blessings, support and protection in pursuit of the stated purpose or purposes.

7. The pouring of the liquid.

8. Announcement of the return from the mission.

9. Welcome by the crowd.

10. Sipping from the common cup.

1) Invocation of the Creator or Supreme Spirit

The Supreme Spirit is invoked or called out — 𓏤𓐍𓏏 *nis*, for reasons outlined above. The Supreme One is known by many different names throughout Afrika, but all over the Afrikan world it is the identical creative force that is observed. The name of the Supreme One is intoned (called out with great respect) and some of the liquid poured.

Sometimes the Supreme Spirit or Creator is invoked along with Mother Earth (in Twi, *Asaase Yaa*, in Igbo, *Ani*, *Ala*, etc.) and the drink is poured to both of them.

2) Invocation of Lesser Divinities

There are a great number of lesser divinities throughout Afrika, with particular groups having their own divinities. Each represents some aspect(s) of the Creator. The names of those divinities considered relevant and helpful to the occasion are intoned in turn and some of the liquid is poured for each one of them.

3) Invocation of the Spirit of the Ancestors

This is achieved by intoning the names of the ancestors, beginning with the most distant ancestors and proceeding to those who have departed this dimension more recently.

Throughout the social history of Afrika the ancestors have been considered to be intermediaries between humans and the divinities, with power to help or hinder the human condition.[59] They are not dead, with a finite separation at the point of the demise of the physical aspect of the person, as in the European belief about things. They are living forces. Our ancestors exist both within our memory as well as independently of our memory, that is, whether or not we remember, memorialise and propitiate them. They can be contacted to play meaningful roles in our daily lives, but only if we treat them with due respect and reverence.

Birago Diop's important poem "Souffles"[60] tells this understanding of the status of our ancestors. It is a poem that has justifiably received widespread attention from observers of the human condition in Afrika,[61] most recently by Ayi Kwei Armah,[62] whose statement on the connection among those past, those present and those yet to come may be equally regarded as a good articulation of the important aspect of the Afrikan world-view which is at the very basis of Diop's poem: "This concern with connections is a constant motif in all autonomous African culture. It comes from an ethos that says death cannot be the end; that beyond death remains connection, between those here now, those who were here but are no longer here but elsewhere, and those who are not yet here but are elsewhere, destined to come some day."[63]

Calling out the names of the ancestors establishes that point of connection and a unity with the ancestors, with an entire culture and an entire history. In Afrika a name is a cultural seed and a sacred word of power. It tells who one is, and who one's people are. A name often tells even more about its owner. Intoning the names of the ancestors keeps the names and so the memories and spirits of the ancestors alive, an injunction sacred to Afrikans from at least the time of ⌁𓎡𓐝𓏏 Kemet, where the eldest son was normally the foremost person charged with this responsibility:

> I remember the names of my ancestors. I speak the names of those I love. I speak their names and they live again. May I be so well-loved and remembered. In truth, may the gods hear my name.[64]

It is very important to say clearly that all ancestors are being called, so that if the name of any ancestor is not mentioned it is not because that ancestor is excluded. Rather it is because time does not normally permit the mention of the name of every known ancestor. Besides this, it is impossible to proclaim the names of all the ancestors in the lineage of any given Afrikan since no one knows the names of all the ancestors stretching right back to those just after the very first African, the very first and common ancestor, who was the first human being. It is also true that no one knows the names of some ancestors who lived at a time nearer to the generations in the present time. The barbaric circumstances in which they were kidnapped, terrorised and raped away from the Motherland during the *Maafa*, with their names, personal histories and other aspects of identity assassinated, amputated or distorted, have wiped out this particular detail of the Afrikan heritage. But such inhumanity could not erase memory of those times, nor the collective duty and desire to propitiate those sacred ancestors.

Remembering and reciting the names of one's ancestors have always been part of Afrikan tradition, for this is an inescapable aspect of the narratives of remembrance, through which Afrikans keep permanently open the lines of communication among ancestors, the living and those who are not yet born. Memory is an imperative for keeping these human connections alive. In the context of the *Maafa*, where one objective of the oppressors is the assassination and/or distortion of Afrikan historical memory, narratives of remembrance have by their very nature become narratives of resistance and irrefutable testimony to the fundamental fact of survival. In these continuing circumstances of oppression the possession of Afrikan memory, the very act of remembrance, is in itself an act of resistance.

The people of Kemet regarded the ancestors as being present among the family, which was an extended family and included the unborn, the living and the dead. In the tombs, the names and likenesses of ancestors were often listed among the living family members, for in Kemet as in contemporary Afrika, to keep a name alive is to keep its owner alive. That is one reason why names are intoned at libations, and why names of the departed are given to the new born. These are acts of remembrance. They reinforce connection and so help to guarantee continuity.

In Kemet there were also family shrines in houses, with alters upon which were placed busts of ancestors to be propitiated.[65] The ancestors who lived exemplary lives on Mother Earth, could each therefore recite the Forty-two Declarations of Innocence, without any doubt or other blemish, on her or his day of judgement before Wsir (Osiris) and forty two other divinities in the Great Hall of Maati, can be recognised by the appearance of certain words after their names. These words formed a title or a sort of affirmation, for the deceased became mꜣꜥ ḫrw: *maa kherew*, literally "true of voice," but "vindicated,"[66] "pure and vindicated,"[67] "justified" or innocent or even triumphant, in terms which are more familiar to today's reader in the English language. These are the blessed dead, those who attained the ancient Egyptian heaven.

In the Great Hall of the Ancestors in the temple of Pharaoh Seti I there is a list of royal ancestors to which we shall refer again in Chapter Four. It covers hundreds of generations. In Kemet there is evidence that, at least on one monument, the High Priests of the divinity Ptah listed their descent and inheritance of the office from father to son for some three hundred generations.[68]

On the Afrikan continent today and in its communities abroad, many families and clans have kept this tradition, which is in many instances represented in the identical practice of family shrines and altars, though there are, as can be expected, many variations also.[69] Families know the names of their ancestors, starting from many generations ago and covering many hundreds of years. Persons in these families and clans often recite their genealogy clearly, for great emphasis is placed upon remembering genealogies precisely. Such memory is often in the custody of griots and other groups of professional or semi-professional praise singers. This is an additional source of great strength and direction to those who have such detailed knowledge of their own blood line. Mbiti tells us that "[t]he genealogy gives a sense of depth, historical belongingness, a feeling of deep rootedness and a sense of sacred obligation to extend the genealogical line."[70] It is through genealogy that all the generations are linked up upon the continuum of time and everyone in every generation is clearly sensitised about and completely and securely aligned to the sacred foundations of their people and so to her/his individual self and to the recognition, defence and promotion of her/his interests. In some parts of Afrika people trace their genealogies to a historically remote "first" human who, as Walter Rodney says to us, is often "a very vague figure on the borders between history and legend."[71] Among the large number of examples from throughout Afrika may be listed Eze Chima of the Igbo west of the Niger,[72] Tsoede, regarded as "ancestral hero and mythical founder of the Nupe Kingdom"[73] and of course, Shongo of the Yoruba, also in West Afrika and Kintu of the Baganda in East Afrika. In other instances the alignment may be to a more contemporary national hero or shero. In all cases this focus upon a common ancestor provides the group with "a sense of pride and satisfaction."[74] Much time and energy is given over to this aspect of the most important duty of remembering, for to remember the ancestors is to keep them alive, to refresh our connection with them and therefore our alignment and location in space and time, to ensure that we do not lose the meaning of ourselves or lose sight of our purpose in the universe and so lose direction. For the Afrikan people, it is to keep ourselves Afrikan centered.

In passing it is to be noted that this is only the most recent part of the genealogy which is normally recited, since no one knows all of the names of all of the Ancestors going as far back as the First Ancestor, the very first human being. But we do know the name of this First Ancestor, a woman who lived 4.7 million years ago. The name *Dinkinesh*, an appropriate Amharic name which means "You are a miracle," was conferred upon her by the Ethiopian community in whose land her remains were unearthed.[75] It is of the greatest importance to have knowledge of such details, as well as to understand the lesson that is to be derived from them. The most important lesson is that all Afrikans spring from a common ancestor and so have a common genealogy from which different groups of Afrikans branched off and further sub-divided at various points in time in the very long history of the Afrikan nation.

The known genealogies hardly, if ever, link current generations securely to ancestors who lived in the most distant past and are common to all and in some cases to many groups of Afrikans. Most Afrikans describe a genealogy that begins only at the foundation of their own sub-group or "tribe," and consciousness mostly extends only to a founding figure of such a sub-group of Afrika or to the birth of a nation state constructed by Europeans along European lines for the purpose of Europeans. Afrikans have been Afrikans for millennia, but Ga, Yoruba, Gikuyu, Zulu, etc. for far less time, and Kenyans, Ghanaians, Nigerians etc. for even less time, indeed merely for a few generations. The different sub-groups or "tribes" in Afrika are specific, more recent and varying expressions of an ancient and common heritage. They are historical, regional and local expressions of an ancient self. Each is no less valid than any other way of living those ancient values, which every Afrikan is challenged by necessity to do in specific and concrete ways in a specific historical era, and perhaps to a lesser extent nowadays, in a particular geography. Our very humanity compels everyone to exist in a rather specific time/space correlation. The clearer each person is about the identity through which everyone is also compelled to express our humanity, the more purposeful and successful will the living of each life become. When any Afrikan interprets his or her particular expression of being Afrikan, whether that is at the individual or group level, in ways that negate these common origins and common cultural values, that person or group therefore negates the most ancient and fundamental aspects of themselves. They violate a fundamental law of nature, which is to remember and be instructed by all of one's own history and culture. Such behaviour is often the product of disablement that results from erasure or distortion of history, culture and identity. The results are often visible as disunity and division, as well as the failure to recognise elders, brothers and sisters, in destructive rivalries and in other forms of backwardness and weakness.

The confusion between identity and nationality is another cause of this diminishing of consciousness of our ancestors and of historical consciousness in general. There were Afrikans and Afrikan communities, states and even empires long before the carving up of Afrika by Europeans at the Berlin conference in 1884. There were Afrikans and Afrikan communities before the consequent spate of Afrikan states that have been even more recently founded upon these divisions made and imposed by non-Afrikans. Yet many Afrikans define themselves exclusively by way of reference to these foreign constructs, many of which represent cultural balkanization and are economically and otherwise unviable. It is entirely logical that the restoration of these older, deeper and more meaningful links, which are more valid, must be part of the project of Afrikan redemption.

In the Afrikan communities in the Diaspora detailed knowledge of the ancestral lines does not normally stretch beyond the contact with western Europe and the horrors of enslavement, the trade in enslaved Afrikans and the plantation. In fact the state of genealogical knowledge in many families does not go beyond the plantation. This historical amnesia exists because of the nature of the living presence of the Maafa in the lives of the Afrikan people in this particular part of the Afrikan world. That is partly why, in a growing number of Afrikan communities outside Afrika, one part of the Libation Ritual is occupied by the Lamentation that it is not possible to intone the names of all of the ancestors. One part of the explanation is of course that time will never permit them to intone the name of each ancestor, going right up to the First Ancestor, even if they did possess that important knowledge. The other reason is that Afrikans do not know and can never know all the names anyway. This is because of the profoundly inhuman but human-made context, referred to above, in which some of their ancestors were terrorised, kidnapped, taken away from their Motherland and deposited in Arab and European controlled lands to be conditioned over many generations into forgetting their identity, into self-hate, confusion and disempowerment. One aspect of this destruction was the erasure of the precise genealogies of most Afrikan families in the Americas and the Caribbean. This also happened in Afrika itself in some instances. Numerous actions contributed to this cultural genocide. These include the erasure of Afrikan names and the imposition of Arab and European names, the imposition of Arabs and Europeans at the head of some Afrikan genealogies, the deliberate and regular break up of Afrikan families and the banning of reading and writing on pain of death, or only in Arabic or European languages with content that functioned largely to distort or destroy Afrikan identity.

These numerous barbarities have robbed many Afrikans of the names of many of their ancestors and of other precious memories. Still, Afrikans shall continue to recall the tremendous pain and suffering that company of ancestors endured, for theirs is an important part of the Afrikan story, as valid as any other. Afrikans revere this company of their ancestors for triumphing over that trial of their humanity and so preserving that of their successors. Their living descendents are the most telling evidence of their triumph. These are increasingly determined to remember. They swear never to forget. In remembering this particular company of their ancestors they recall their sacrifice for those who are alive today. And so they renew their determination to restore that what was destroyed by those who, in trying to dehumanise one section of humanity, succeeded only in clearly demonstrating their own inhumanity.

The condition of ignorance of genealogy, as of Afrikan history in general, is being transformed. There is a small number of attested instances of Afrikans born overseas reciting the names of known ancestors as part of devotion,[76] but a growing number of individuals and families are embarking upon the reclamation, reconstruction and documentation of their ancestral lineage. The most celebrated example of this growing repossession of ancestral self is undoubtedly Alex Haley's classic work, aptly entitled Roots.[77] But other works that concern themselves with Afrikan ancestors have also been placed in the public consciousness[78] and many individuals and families are working towards this most important objective,[79] which is also partly evident in the remarkably increasing number of family reunions in Afrikan communities outside of the Motherland. But Afrikans in the communities abroad know the outlines of their heritage and are increasingly making meaningful reconnections with their ancestry and with the classical traditions of Afrika, which are the most ancient traditions on earth. Furthermore, increasing numbers of Afrikans abroad are beginning to repossess these traditions and this heritage by accepting the challenge of living them every day, which is the best way possible of possessing them. In these ways the psychic disconnection from their ancestors is being repaired and increasing numbers of Afrikans are beginning to be Afrikans again, in full splendour and in deeply meaningful ways.

The invocations of the Supreme Spirit, the Spirits of lesser divinities and the Spirits of the Sacred Ancestors mark an extremely important moment in the libation ritual. The person pouring is considered to have crossed into sacred space in order to invite these Sacred Presences. The invocation transforms the area of the gathering into sacred space because of the Supreme Presence, other Divine Presences, the Ancestral Presence and those of other cosmic forces invoked.

4) *Introduction of the Person Pouring the Libation*

Here the person states his or her name, then gives his or her genealogy, calling out the names of his/her parents, fore-parents and other relatives. The libationer introduces her/himself to the forces addressed in order to be identified, which s/he cannot properly do merely by way of reference only to her/himself, but only through her/his lineage. In Afrikan life no one exists alone, without family and community.

This is an opportunity to recite a lineage and therefore a chance to familiarise or re-familiarise oneself with the lineage of the person performing this task, as well as to reinforce knowledge and the significance of lineage, of remembering.

5) *Statement of the Mission*

Here the person states clearly the purpose of the gathering. This purpose may vary from the personal to the communal, from celebrating success in some venture, to asking for success in an upcoming venture, or any combination of these or other purposes outlined above.

6) The Petition or Request for Blessings and Protection

Here the person asks the Supreme Being, the other Divine Ones and the ancestors for blessings, for support in the undertaking at hand and perhaps in any mission to be pursued by anyone in the gathering.

The pourer of the libation next asks the rivers, mountains or other natural phenomena to ward off enemies or bad omens so that those in the gathering are not distracted from their mission or prevented in any way from being successful in the undertaking. In arriving at a correct understanding of this request we must recall something that has already been mentioned in this chapter, which is that Afrikans recognise an invisible life force in all phenomena (*ka, kra, asé, chi, ntu, Jok*, etc.;) whether they are animate or inanimate, all beings and things are the expressions and the work of the Supreme One.

Together these natural phenomena make up the habitat or environment in which humanity lives. Afrikans have always regarded this environment as a sacred, living whole that must be respected, protected and used intelligently, for they recognised that to disregard and destroy the environment is to disregard and destroy humanity by undermining our chances of survival through irrevocably depleting the resources we depend upon for daily life and living.

This protection helps to create an appropriate context that is free from any distraction so that the emissary may be empowered to concentrate fully upon the task in hand.

7) The Pouring of the Libation

The standard practice is to pour the drink three times. This number has always been significant in Afrikan society. (See Chapter Six.)

The pourer then turns his/her back to the gathering and drinks from the libation cup to those ancestors who left in unusual circumstances or in ways not approved by the community, for example those who died by suicide. They are still remembered and included in the ritual. The formula for referring to this group is "to those who do not drink in the midst of others."

The pourer then spits three times.

Ritual spitting is another extremely ancient aspect of libation known from the practice of Kemet. This is also explained below in Chapter Six.

At any point in the ritual, the libationer may enter into a direct and audible interaction with the gathering. (A basic principle of Afrikan drama, ritual or otherwise, is the involvement of the audience in the narrative.) This is done in an orderly fashion that gives respect to all involved. The pourer may be reminded by members of the audience about particular divinities and/or ancestors who should be invoked. As the libationer pours, everyone present, including the libationer, is encouraged to intone the names of particular spirits, or ancestors, one at a time. The audience responds with a general "Asé!" for each name invoked. Expressions of approval and encouragement for the one pouring may also be given by the audience.

The format that emerges here is the call and response pattern that is so typical of Afrikan communications behaviour. This is how Afrikans today, especially in communities abroad, help to promote the Afrikan community spirit, to concretise in their daily behaviour the maxim by which they must live: *One for all and all for one.* In this way too they remember not only their divinities, but also both the personal ancestors of those present and the political and ideological ancestors and guides of all Afrikans, that is, those Afrikans who have distinguished themselves by their work in advancing the Afrikan cause.

There are many possibilities for innovation, and therefore of variation, within the Libation Ritual and Afrikan culture in general while remaining true to the foundational values of the Afrikan tradition. For example, instead of an Asé when the name of a sacred ancestor is intoned there may be a drum roll—or there may be both an Asé and a drum roll. The libationer may briefly narrate the history of the Afrikan people, highlighting those aspects and issues that are relevant to the assembly and the occasion and showing how these fit into the wider story. Afrikans in different generations and in different groups within the Afrikan nation, in different spaces and different times, may therefore express the principles of the Afrikan Classical Traditions in ways which are not always completely identical, but which nevertheless remain Afrikan; that is, remain true to the fundamental principles of those traditions.

8) *Announcement of the Return from the Mission*

The pourer next makes an announcement saying that he/she has returned from the mission (to whichsoever force s/he had departed.) This announcement marks the return of the libationer from the sacred space. It also simultaneously releases the Supreme One, the ancestors and other spirits and therefore returns the space from its existence as sacred space. It is normal space again. Those who are greater than humanity have departed, leaving their blessings but maintaining their watchful presence from afar. The Afrikan divinities will always be with the living Afrikans in spirit—but only if the living behave correctly by holding fast to Afrikan traditions and by deepening and extending them. Heads, torsos and feet may now be covered again, for the gathering is no longer in Divine Presence.

9) *Welcome by the Crowd*

The crowd now welcomes back the libationer, who was in effect their emissary to the Sacred Presences. This welcome is a simple statement of "Welcome" or "Welcome back." In addition, the libationer may be accorded applause, a drum roll and other appropriate expressions of welcome and appreciation of the mission just completed.

10) *Sipping from the Common Cup*

During the ritual, if the drink is not poured directly into the earth or into a plant, it would be poured into a receptacle, usually a calabash or something else of Afrikan cultural significance and value. If the liquid was poured into the earth or a plant, the remains would be poured into a receptacle. If necessary, this receptacle would be topped up to suit the number of persons in the gathering. It is then passed around the gathering. This liquid has become sacred because it has been presented to and has been accepted and blessed by the divine and sacred presences. Everyone takes a symbolic sip. This is sacramental. If a person does not wish to drink the liquid used, for example alcohol, then that individual may elect to pour a little onto Mother Earth, or onto the floor, as a symbolic act of participation. This symbolic drink is their way of participating in the ritual and it is as valid as swallowing the liquid.

Community or group participation is very central to Afrikan ceremonies and rituals. In fact it is fundamental to the Afrikan way of life. This may be participation in the distinctive call and response type of community interaction common to all Afrikans. Examples of this distinctive kind of interaction are expressed at worship, in ring games, in popular entertainment, in eating a common meal like the ritual eating of food from a sacrificed animal and in the ritual drink from the Communal Cup at the end of the libation. If the libation is part of a larger ritual of offering then the entire gathering may participate in a communal feast and/or receive gifts of food and other articles which were offered up. Those in need are given preference. This practice is effectively a redistribution of resources along humanist principles, which announces the Afrikan attitude to charity. This way of living the Afrikan version of humanity, which is still very prevalent throughout the Afrikan world, may be traced with great certainty to Kemet, where it was known as the "Reversion of the Offering."[80] A much earlier origin is entirely likely, but must be established through further research. The sharing of the kola nut is symbolic in a similar way, but it is used in a slightly different manner. Perhaps the most relevant example for this discussion is the audience response reported above. Let us remind ourselves here that communal rituals give to each participant a powerful sense of belonging to the group, thereby promoting group solidarity and unity. The more sacred and frequent the ritual, the greater is the depth of attachment to those with whom one shares this special occasion. This is a particularly inexhaustible and important source of unity and strength among Afrikans.

NOTES

1. As far as this writer knows, this terminology belongs to Asante and Abarry, who restricted its application to "religious" ideas. Consult Molefe K. Asante and Abu S. Abarry (eds., 1996). *African Intellectual Heritage: A Book of Sources* (Temple University Press, Philadelphia), p. 60.
2. Abdias do Nascimento (1995). *Orixás: Os Deuses Vivos da África* (Rio de Janeiro: IPEAFRO), p. 75. For the similar formulation, "forced Diaspora," see Marimba Ani (2000) "Introduction" in K. Kia Bunseki Fu-Kiau and A. M. Lukondo-Wamba (1988, 2000). *Kindezi: The Kôngo Art of Babysitting*. (Inprint Editions, Baltimore, Maryland).
3. James P. Allen (2000). *Middle Egyptian*, p. 31. For a view that differs slightly in listing the *nswt* or pharaoh as a separate category, see John Baines (1991), "Society, Morality and Religious Practice" in B. E. Shafer (ed., 1991). *Religion in Ancient Egypt: Gods, Myths and Personal Practice* (University of Cornell Press, Ithaca and London), p. 129.
4. James P. Allen (1988). *Genesis in Egypt: The Philosophy of Ancient Egyptian Creation Accounts* (Yale Egyptological Studies 2, New Haven, CT), pp. 9–10, 60–63.
5. Ibid., p. 14 and note 85 on p. 69. See also Allen, (2005), "Introduction." R. O. Faulkner (trans.). *Ancient Egyptian Book of the Dead*. (New York, Barnes and Noble), p.11; O. Goelet, Jr. (1994), "A Commentary . . . " in R. O. Faulkner (trans. 1972). *The Egyptian Book of the Dead: The Book of Going Forth by Day*, p.152.
6. Hunter Adams' definition of this term is instructive: "The concept of *Nun* (incessant oscillation or fluctuation) also embodies notions of darkness (*Kuk*), formlessness (*Huh*), inscrutability or hiddenness (*Amon*), and implicitly boundlessness and timelessness (*neheh* or *djet*). Nun attempts to describe the '*that which is not yet*', the pre-creation state where even conflict had no existence." See H. Adams, "Ma'at: Returning to Virtue—Returning to Self," (The Author), p. 18, note 11.
7. Asante and Abarry, Ibid., p. 12.
8. Ali A. Mazuri (1986). *The Africans: A Triple Heritage*. (BBC Publications, London), p. 50.
9. Ibid., p.59.
10. Mbiti. *African Religions and* Philosophy, p.16. Emphases in the original.
11. Mbiti, Ibid.
12. Sarpong. *Libation*, p.2.
13. See, for example, Faulkner. *The Pyramid Texts*, Note.2, p. 247; Allen, "Introduction" in Faulkner (trans.) *Ancient Egyptian Book of the Dead*, p. 11.
14. Chinua Achebe (1998), "'Chi' in Igbo Cosmology" in E. C. Eze (ed.). *African Philosophy: An Anthology* (Blackwell Publishing Ltd., Malden, MA), pp. 67–72, renders *chi* as " . . . god, guardian angel, personal spirit, soul, spirit double, etc." (p. 67). *Chi* may therefore be a category into which is collapsed such ancient Egyptian notions as *ba, ka, akh*, etc. More investigation of this possible relationship is needed. This is a certainly another line of research and consideration for (re)generating knowledge about Afrika.
15. See, for example, Placide Temples (1959, 1998), "Bantu Ontology" in E. C. Eze (ed.) *African Philosophy*, pp. 429–434.
16. Mazuri, *The Africans*, p. 50.

17. Modupe Odudoye. *Words & Meaning in Yoruba Religion,* p. 129.
18. Clinton Hutton (2007). "The Creative Ethos of the African Diaspora: Performance Aesthetics and the Fight for Freedom and Identity" *Caribbean Quarterly.* Vol. 53, Nos. 1 & 2. March-June, 2007, p. 128.
19. Robert F. Thompson (1983, 1984). *Flash of the Spirit: African and Afro-American Art and Philosophy* (Vintage Books, New York), p.5. Emphasis added. In the Yoruba language the word *asé,* a word also represented as *aché,* (*axé* in Brasil), means life force, divine energy flow, and power. Marta Moreno Vega (2000). *The Altar of My Soul: The Living Traditions of Santeria* (One World, The Ballantine Publishing Group, New York), p. 281 supplies this definition: Aché is "[t]he invisible, elusive life force of Olodumare that was distributed to the Orishas. Aché is the life force present in nature." From Candomblé, Abdias do Nascimento. *Orixás,* p. 149, supplies this definition: "Cosmic energy, vital force which gives life and movement to all beings. Used also as a salutation, similar to 'long life!' " For a fuller exposition consult Thompson, *Flash of The Spirit,* pp. 5–16. See also Henry L. Gates, Jr., "A Myth of Origins: Esu-Elegbara and the Signifying Monkey" in Asante and Abarry (eds.) *African Intellectual Heritage,* p. 163; Raul Canizares, *Walking with the Night,* pp. 4–7, *passim* and E. C. Eze (1998), "The Problem of Knowledge in 'Divination': The Example of Ifa" in *African Philosophy: An Anthology,* p.173.
20. Canizares, *Walking with the Night,* p.5. Canizares distinguishes ashé in Santeria from asé of the Yoruba, but if there is any difference between the two terms it exists only in the orthography and thus no distinction will be recognised in this work.
21. Félix A. Omidire (2008). "The Yoruba *ase* as a social capital among Afro diasporic peoples in Latin America" in Tunde Babawale and Akin Alao. *Global African Spirituality, Social Capital and Self-reliance in Africa* (Malthouse Press Limited, Lagos, Benin, Ibadan, etc.), p.287.
22. For the divinities of Kemet see Joyce Tyldesley (ed., 2004), "The Destruction of Mankind" and "Commentary on the Destruction of Mankind" *Tales from Ancient Egypt* (Rutherford Press Ltd., Bolton), pp. 11 and 13 respectively; For Olodumare see Canizares, Ibid., pp. 3, 5, 54, 57, *passim*.
23. Kalu Ogbaa (1992). *Gods, Oracles and Divination: Folkways in Chinua Achebe's Novels* (Africa World Press, Trenton, NJ), p. 10; Awolalu and Dopamu. *West African Traditional Religion,* pp. 56–64, 214–215.
24. See, for example, J. O. Lucas (1948). *The Religion of the Yorubas* (CMS Bookshop, Lagos), pp. 34 and 119 for clear statements. The categorization is implied in the entire work. Most of the works consulted in this book fall into the latter category. Note also Sarpong, *Libation,* pp. 1–5 and Awolalu and Dopamu, pp. 70–74; Ogonna Agu (1997). *The Book of Dawn and Invocations: The Search for Philosophic truth by an African Initiate* (Karnak House, London), pp. 12–13, and others.
25. Ayi Kwei Armah (2006). The Eloquence of the Scribes: A Memoir on the Sources and Resources of African Literature (Popenguine, Per Ankh), p. 195.
26. Armah (2006), "Who were the Ancient Egyptians?" *New African.* No. 450. (April, 2006),p.12.
27. See Faulkner, *Concise Dictionary,* p. 6. Variant determinatives include ⸱⸱, ⸱⸱⸱ and ⸱.
28. The obvious linguistic transformations from Ani (Mdw Ntr) to Ala, Ale, Ama (Igbo) and Ayi and Li (Ewe) should constitute part of another line of research in the social history of Afrika.
29. Lucas. *Religions in West Africa and Ancient Egypt,* pp. 100–112; Adelumo and Dopamu. *West African Traditional Religion,* pp. 85–115.

30. Erman and Grapow. *Wörterbuch* I, pp. 453-454; Gardiner. *Egyptian Grammar*, pp. 476, 564, 605; Faulkner. *Concise Dictionary*, p. 82.
31. See especially Note 14 and its corresponding text in Chapter Two.
32. Two of the best critical essays on *Ma'at* are Maulana Karenga (1991), "Towards a Sociology of Maatian Ethics: Literature and Context" in Ivan Van Sertima (ed.). *Egypt Revisited* (Transaction Publishers, New Brunswick), pp. 352–395 and Hunter Adans (1994), "Ma'at: Return to Virtue–Return to Self." (The Author). Adams' definition replaces righteousness with compassion. The best extended treatment of this concept is M. Karenga (2004). *Maat. The Moral Ideal in Ancient Egypt: A Study in Classical African Ethics* (Routledge, New York and London). See also J. Carruthers (1984). *Essays in Ancient Egyptian Studies* (University of Sankore Press, Los Angeles), pp. 54–56; Allen. *Genesis in Egypt*, pp. 25–27; Allen. *Middle Egyptian*, pp. 115–117; Richard H. Wilkinson (1998). *Reading Egyptian Art* (Thames and Hudson, London), pp. 36–37 and 102–103 and Obenga. *African Philosophy*, pp. 189–190, 191–193, 203 and 220–222 *passim*.
33. Karenga. *Maat. The Moral Ideal in Ancient Egypt*. The entire text is an elaboration of the meaning and interpretation of *Maat*. For definitions see pp. 6–11, 53, 55, 89, etc.
34. Asante and Abarry, p.59.
35. Among many other sources see Asante and Abarry, Ibid., p.61; Mbiti, *African Religions and Philosophy*, p. 9; Abu S. Abarry, "Recurrent Themes in Ga Libation (Mpai) Oratory" in Asante and Abarry (eds.) *African Intellectual Heritage*, pp. 92 93; Armah, "Who Were the Ancient Egyptians?", p. 14; *The Eloquence of the Scribes*, pp. 23–24.
36. Armah, *The Eloquence of the Scribes*, p. 195; Armah, "Who were the Ancient Egyptians,?" p. 12. For another statement of this concept of community consult Awolalu and Dopamu. *West African Traditional Religion*, p. 275.
37. Mbiti, *African Religions and Philosophy*, p.117.
38. Chief Seattle, Native American Leader (1786–1866). See Duane Bristow, "Chief Seattle's Thoughts".http://www.kyphilom.com/www/seattle.html. [Accessed on 23 rd April, 2007].
39. R. O. Faulkner (trans., ed.). *The Ancient Egyptian Coffin Texts*. Vol. III, pp.70–77.
40. Ibid., p. 66.
41. A. M. Blackman (1912), "The Significance of Incense and Libations in Funerary and Temple Ritual" *Zeitscrift Für Agyptische Sprache und Altertmuskunde (ZÄS)*. Leipzig, Berlin. Vol. 50. p. 69; J. Gardner Wilkinson (1853, 1994). *The Ancient Egyptians: Their Life and Customs* Vol. I (Senate, London), pp. 264–266; Papyrus No. 10188 (British Museum) as quoted in E. A. Wallis Budge (1934, 1988). *From Fetish to God in Ancient Egypt* (Dover Publications, Inc., New York), p. 527.
42. Rev. Joseph Osei-Bonsu. (n.d.), "Libation" as quoted in Rt. Rev. Dr. Peter Kwasi Sarpong (1996). *Libation* (Anansesem Publications, Accra), p.31.
43. Sigmund Freud (1964, 1985. Trans. A. Richards). "Moses and Monotheism" in *The Origins of Religion* (Penguin), pp. 239–386; Jan Assmann (1997). *Moses the Egyptian: The Memory of Egypt in Western Monotheism* (Cambridge University Press, Cambridge, Mass. and London).
44. For the formulation of "Deep Thought" in preference to "philosophy," consult Jacob Carruthers, *Mdw Nṯr Divine Speech*. Note p.14.
45. For example, see Marimba Ani's demolition and rejection of this view in M. Ani (1980, 1997). *Let The Circle Be Unbroken: The Implications of African Spirituality in the Diaspora* (Nkonimfo Publications, New York), pp.35–36. See also Maulana

Karenga (1990). "Introduction" in *The Book of Coming Forth by Day: The Ethics of the Declarations of Innocence* (University of Sankore Press, Los Angeles), pp. 26–27 and T. Obenga. *African Philosophy*, pp. 177–178.
46. Walter Rodney (1967). "West Africa and the Atlantic Slave Trade" Historical Association of Tanzania. Occasional Paper No. 2. (East African Publishing House, Dar-Es-Salaam), p. 16.
47. J. Gardner Wilkinson. *The Ancient Egyptians*, Vol. I, p. 263.
48. Montejo, *The Autobiography*, p. 101.
49. Zora Neale Hurston (1938, 1990). *Tell My Horse: Voodoo and Life in Haiti and Jamaica*. (Harper and Row, New York), pp. 175, 235.
50. Abu S. Abarry, "Recurrent Themes in Ga Libation (Mpai) Oratory" in M. K. Asante and A. S. Abarry. *African Intellectual Heritage*, pp. 92–95.
51. See "Igbo Invocations" in Ibid., pp. 96–97.
52. J. Gardner Wilkinson. *The Ancient Egyptians*. Vol. I, pp. 260–261.
53. Ibid., pp. 261–263.
54. Orly Goldwasser (1995). *From Icon to Metaphor: Studies in the Semiotics of Hieroglyphs*. Orbis Biblicus et Orientalis No. 142. (University of Fribourg Press and Vandenhoeck & Ruprecht, Göttingen), Chapter 1, Note 35, pp. 12–13.
55. From the Hebrew vocalization of the Ancient Egyptian term פֿרעה pr-ꜥ3 :*Per-aa*, literally, "Great House," a term of reverence employed in Kemet instead of the actual name of the *nesu*, in a similar way that terms such as "the Kremlin," "the White House" and "Downing Street" are used today as allusions respectively to the presidents of Russia and the USA and the Prime Minister of the UK. However, in the instance of Kemet, this formulation was instructed by the urge to be respectful to the *nsw*, which was indicated by the avoidance of any direct mention of his name. This very attitude of respect is alive in many Afrikan communities today, where it is good manners for the direct mention of the name of someone who is older than the speaker to be prefixed by "Mother," "Auntie," "Brother," "Cousin" or some such term of respect. In Guyana defaulters in this respect are guilty of calling the offended party "full mouth."
56. There are other interpretations of Narmer's barefootedness. One example is W.A. Fairservis, Jr. (1991), "A Revised View of the Narmr Palette" *JARCE* Vol. XXVIII, pp. 8 and 15. The absence of footwear is interpreted as "a sign of contempt for his enemies," but no reason is advanced for this conclusion.
57. David Lan (1985). *Guns and Rain: Guerrillas and Spirit Mediums in Zimbabwe* (James Currey, London and University of California Press, Berkeley and Los Angeles), p. 68.
58. Amadou Hampaté Bâ (1972. Translated by Susan B. Hunt). "Wisdom and the Linguistic Question in Black Africa." Chapter 2 of *Aspects of African Civilization (Person, Culture, Religion)*. Originally published as *Aspects de la civilization africaine: personne, culture, religion* (Présence africaine, Paris, 1972). www.ese.upenn.edu [Accessed 12 June, 2008].
59. Sources on Ancient Egypt include Lanny Bell (1996), "Ancestor Worship and Divine Kingship in the Ancent Nile Valley" in T. Celenko (ed.). *Egypt in Africa*, pp. 56–58; R.B. Parkinson (1991). *Voices from Ancient Egypt: An Anthology of Middle Kingdom Writings* (British Museum Press, London), pp. 142–145; Ian Shaw and Paul Nicholson (1995). *The British Museum Dictionary of Ancient Egypt* (The British Museum Press, London), pp. 160–161. Sources on contemporary Afrika include Mbiti. *African Religions and Philisophy, passim*; Chapurukha M. Kusimba (1996), "Ancestor Worship and divine kingship in Sub-Saharan Africa" in T. Celenko, Ibid.,

pp. 58–61; Opoku, *West African Traditional Religion*, pp. 35–53 and others. See also notes 18–41in Chapter 4.
60. Birago Diop (1960). "*Souffles*" in *Luerres et Lueurs* (Présence Africaine, Paris).
61. Some of the examples are Wole Soyinka. *Myth, Literature and the African World*, pp. 131–133, Ogbu U. Kalu (2000), "Ancestral Spirituality and Society in Africa" in J. K. Olupona (ed.). *African Spirituality: Forms, Meanings and Expressions* (The Crossroad Publishing Co., New York), p. 54 and Janheinz Jahn (1958, trans. by M. Grene 1961). *Muntu: An Outline of the New African Culture*. (Grove Press, Inc., New York), p. 108. The poem has also been set to music by Ysaye M. Barnwell and recorded for albums by the Afrikan American *acapella* women group, Sweet Honey in the Rock (1980) *Good News (Flying Fish) and* (1997) *Selections 1976–1988* (Flying Fish/ Rounder Records Corp., Cambridge, Mass.), Disc Two, track 17.
62. Armah, The Eloquence of the Scribes, p.198.
63. Armah, "Who were the Ancient Egyptians?" *New African*. April, 2006, p. 12. For similar observations See also Armah, *The Eloquence of the Scribes*, pp 22–24 and especially 196.
64. The Book of Ani, Chapter XXX in Normandi Ellis. (Translator, 1988). *Awakening Osiris*. (Phanes Press, Grand Rapids, Miossouri), p. 54.
65. Example, see R. David (2002). *Religion and Magic in Ancient Egypt*. (Penguin Books), pp. 74–75, 222, 272–273, 274–277; Gardiner. *Egyptian Grammar*, p. 170.
66. Karenga. *The Moral Ideal in Ancient Egypt*, pp. 63 and 137.
67. E.g. Faulkner, *Coffin Texts*, Vol. III, Spell 831, p.20.
68. O. Berlev (1997). "Bureaucrats" in S. Rocatti. *The Egyptians* (The University of Chicago Press, Chicago and London), p. 110.
69. E.g. John Mbiti (1975). *Introduction to African Religion* (Heinemann), pp. 123 124; Mbiti. *African Religions and Philosophy*, pp. 73–74, 83.
70. Mbiti, *African Religions and Philosophy*, p. 105.
71. Walter Rodney (1969, 1978, 1971,). *The Groundings With My Brothers*. (Bogle L'Ouverture Publications, London), p. 53. See also Rodney, "African History in the Service of the Black Liberation." Lecture presented at the Congress of Black Writers, Montreal, Canada, 12th October, 1968.
72. J. Okoro Ijoma (2010). *Igbo Origins and Migrations*. Nsukka History Series Vol.1. (Great AP Express Publishers Ltd., Nsukka, Nigeria), pp. 13–18.
73. J. Okoro Ijoma (2010). *The Igala and their Neighbours: Historical Glimpses* Nsukka History Series, Vol. 2 (Great AP Express Publishers Ltd., Nsukka, Nigeria), pp.19–22. The quote is on p. 20.
74. Mbiti, *African Religions and Philosophy*, p. 105.
75. Private communication with Dr. Amon Saaba Saakana. 29 June, 2006; Telephone conversation with Ms. Alganesh Messel. 30 June, 2006. See also Molefe Asante (2007). *The History of Africa: The Quest for Eternal Harmony* (New York and London: Routledge), p. 12 for Dinquesh, a different orthography. The European scientific community calls this First Ancestor by a European name, Lucy, a non Afrikan name.
76. Marta Moreno Vega (2000). *The Altar of My Soul: The Living Traditions of Santeria* (The Ballantine Publishing Group, New York), p.40.
77. Alex Haley (1976). Roots. (Doubleday, New York).
78. Examples include Paul Crooks (2002). *Ancestors* (BlackAmber Books Ltd., London) and D. H. Matthews (1998). *Honoring the Ancestors: An African Cultural Interpretation of Black Religion and Literature* (Oxford University Press).
79. Examples from Guyana include Wosley Semple (Compiler, 1989, 1990, etc.). *The*

Semple Family Tree (The Compiler, Howard University, Washington, D.C.). Other families known to be contributing to this healthy recent trend include the Scott Family, the Pilgrim Family, the Miller Family, the Drakes Family. [79]
80. Example, Faulkner, *Coffin Texts*, Vol. III, Spell 936, pp. 75 and 77.

Chapter Two

The Origins of Libation

3.1 𓆎𓅓𓏏𓊖 : *Kemet*

At this historical moment our surest knowledge of Afrikan culture stretches as far back as Kemet, 5000 years ago. Less is known about 𓎡𓄿𓋴: Kas, later rendered 𓎡𓄿𓋴: K3š: Kash (or Kush), or about 𓇾𓈀: Ta Seti, literally "Land of (those who carry the) Seti Bow" or Nubia and other Afrikan states that preceded Kemet and gave it the fundamentals of its culture and indeed much more. Even less is generally known about the long period of time that stretches from the very beginnings of Afrikans, and so of humanity, probably in the Nile/Great Lakes region of Afrika, to the era of these states that preceded Kemet.

There is a particular incense burner which offers a good indication of the anteriority of censing (the ritual burning of incense) higher up the Nile Valley before the time of Kemet. This burner was found in the Nile Valley at Qustul, in Lower Nubia, near to the current border between the Sudan and Egypt.[1] Its presence in that place at a time before Kemet shows that both censing and, by implication, the ritual behavioural complex to which censing belongs, a complex that includes libation, were practised by Afrikans before they built the state of Kemet.

At this moment scholarship is even less certain about the significance for our subject of the Nabta Playa ceremonial complex, which is mentioned in Chapter One. The importance of the site as a ritual centre dates from the early Holocene era, about 11,000 years ago. It was occupied up to about 4,800 years ago, with the majority of its stone structures dating from about 7,000 to about 6,500 years ago.[2] But there is not much certain knowledge about this complex.

It is therefore wholly necessary to be cautious in making conclusions about the Qustul incense burner, and especially about the Nabta Playa temple complex. Nevertheless, it may be of some significance that both sites are in the south of Egypt, near to the present border with the Sudan. Such a location fits in with the known general trajectory in the early spread of humanity, development and civilization in ancient times from south to north along the valley of the Nile River. Further, both a ritual centre and an incense burner suggest the presence of beliefs and behaviours that belong to an offering complex. It is not possible to make firm conclusions beyond this. The specificities of these rituals, and the terminologies through which they were articulated by their celebrants, are at present unknown.

However, the methodology of this work is to begin with Kemet while paying homage to all those Afrikan communities that were before Kemet and upon whose achievements Kemet stands; just as Afrikans today exist because of the work of all of their ancestors, including those who built Kush, Nubia and Kemet. This way of proceeding is instructed by an understanding of the absolute importance of beginning at the beginning, or as close to it as one can get, which is outlined above. This is true for any and every aspect of anyone's story.

It is almost certain that libation originated somewhere in the upper Nile Valley or beyond, somewhere in inner Afrika, and was taken down the valley, by both land and water, and eventually to other parts of the continent by migrating Afrikans as part of their inalienable cultural equipment, something almost inseparable from themselves. If the significance suggested of the Nabta Playa complex and attached to the Qustul incense burner is tenable, then the libation complex must have made this journey along the Nile uncounted generations ago. Scholarship is on firmer ground from the time of Kemet; there is a mass of detail about libation from very early on in the history of this country.

But cultural influence, certainly in the case of libation, did not travel only in one direction along the Nile, and not only overland from the heart of Afrika. There is evidence that particular styles of libation, visible in Kemet in later eras, impacted back upon the ritual in places further up the Nile Valley, towards the south, the source of both the river and this cultural practice. One example is Meroe.[3] Despite Eurocentric misrepresentations to the contrary, it is also certain that Kemet-style libation, as well as the very idea and practice of this ritual, were passed on to Alexandrian Egypt, Greece, Carthage and Italy.[4] This information thus confirms more general conclusions about the transmission of knowledge and culture made by Herodotus, George G. M. James, Cheikh Anta Diop, Théophile Obenga, Martin Bernal and others.[5] It also illuminates the historical context of the references to offerings, including libation, made by Homer.[6] Libation was also extant in ancient Mesopotamia. The fact of the practice of the ritual in these other places is depicted and so confirmed by the written references and graphic representations of the ritual in Greece, Rome,

Mesopotamia and other parts of the ancient world. In addition, libation is practised today in places such as India.

3.2: Legend, Myth and Divinity

The origins of the ritual of libation are so ancient that even to the people of the ancient Afrikan state of Kemet they were obscure, lost in the mists of time, and therefore accounted for in legend and myth. Yet, libation was so important to the people of Kemet that in their sacred narratives it was located in the realm of divinity, that is, in the spiritual aspect of existence.

One such account of things may have originated as an oral form before the invention of writing and the state of Kemet. This account was probably handed down by word of mouth through an untold number of generations. It is certain that this particular version of the beginning of libation was eventually committed to writing, first perhaps in the New Kingdom era (about 1550—1080 BCE,) as it is absent from the written literature of the preceding eras (the Old Kingdom, about 2650—2040 BCE and the Middle Kingdom, about 2040—1550 BCE.) So far as is known, this earliest written account of the origin of the ritual of libation was inscribed on the largest of the gilded wooden shrines that enclosed the coffin of Nsu Tutankhamon. This text was also written on the walls of four other royal tombs in the Valley of the Kings during the New Kingdom, with the tombs of Seti I and Ramses II housing the most complete accounts. Copies are also to be found in the tombs of Ramses III and Ramses IV.

In this account of the beginning of the ritual, the sun Divinity *Ra* retreated in anger from humans and from the earth because of humanity's irreverence in plotting against him and ridiculing him because he had grown so old that he drooled. *Ra* sent his daughter, *Hathor*, to avenge his hurt. She decided to wipe out humanity and proceeded so well that *Ra* changed his mind and wanted to stop the slaughter. But *Hathor's* blood lust could not be easily quenched. Eventually she was stopped by a trick. She was served copious quantities of red beer. She drank, believing it to be blood, and became so drunk that she forgot about killing. And so humanity was saved.[7]

Most interpretations of this myth, from within Egyptology circles, miss its obvious reference to libation. Leonard H. Lesko provides a good example. He speculates that "[i]t may have been an attempt to rationalize plague as a divine punishment that had miscarried . . . " and asserts that this myth "also provides an explanation for the origin of beer and for the drinking of beer, perhaps to excess, at the Festival of Hathor."[8] This assessment is doubly burdened, being both minimalist and negative. It is the Afrikan centered scholar, Ayi Kwei Armah, who provides the explanation. "This legend," he asserts, "explains the rise of a propitiatory custom found everywhere on the African continent: libation, the pouring of alcohol or other drinks as offerings to ancestors and divinities."[9] To be very precise, as we shall see, the drink offering is also made to other beings and to things, and the ritual is also practised in Afrikan communities outside of the Afrikan continent.

In Egyptology this myth is widely known as "The Destruction of Mankind" and "The Deliverance of Mankind." George Hart terms it "The Myth of cataclysm."[10] This term is perhaps more appropriate, especially if the notion of myth here is read as a *double entendre*. The first title is both erroneous and misleading, since humans were not destroyed by these events, but endangered then restored by them. This conclusion is sustained by Obenga, who asserts that "[t]he ultimate theme of this narrative . . . is salvation, not destruction."[11] Further, titles such as the first two risk being too anthropocentric, for humanity is quite certainly the author of the script and so ultimately, perhaps, the real arbiters of the action in which they (humans) are involved. However, it is not they, but divinities who are the central characters in the drama, which is a parable on the maintenance of the entire cosmos, not just an account of the survival of humanity. Most of the action takes place in the realm of the ancient Afrikan Gods, with *Ra, Hathor, Djhuti* and *Maat* being the principal actors. All the decisions determining the outcome of the story are taken here, for in the Afrikan world-view it is here, in the realm of the divine, i.e. of the spiritual, that ultimate power lies. Humanity is initially the active source of preliminary discord. But the human role is very quickly overshadowed by divine action and becomes purely passive; first as the recipient of *Ra's* anger, then *Hathor's* wrath and finally salvation arising from a drink offering made by other divinities to the enraged *Hathor*. This drink offering was made in order to appease the divine wrath and restore and help guarantee the correct relations within the cosmos.

The genesis of libation is therefore meant to be located in the realm of divinity. Cosmic relations are impaired and endangered, the consequences are potentially catastrophic, and the entire condition is triggered by human failure that is manifested by their ingratitude to Ra in plotting against him because he had become old and physically enfeebled. In disrespecting their Gods and disrespecting age, humanity had in fact transgressed two very important principles of the Afrikan code of social behaviour. These are respect for the Gods and respect for the aged. We have seen, in the preceding chapter, that these foundational principles are anchored in the Afrikan world-view that posits a oneness and therefore also an inter-relatedness and interdependency of all beings and things in the cosmos. The interrelatedness and interdependency of all in the cosmos are demonstrated in this Myth of Libation, as discordant actions by one group of beings (humanity), have very significant ramifications for the entire cosmos (divinity, humanity, the environment).

First to suffer are relations between *Ra* and humans: human ingratitude leads to *Ra's* anger and physical withdrawal from earth, then to *Hathor's* wanton slaughter of humanity, which in this myth is the most serious manifestation of actual impairment of the cosmic order. But there is the latent threat of worse to come, for *Hathor* does not heed the will of *Ra* and the other divinities by ending her destructive behaviour. Her disobedience and intransigence in turn thus both threaten the cosmic death of humanity and endanger relations among the divinities. Finally, the cosmic order is restored and secured by the intervention of *Djhuti* and *Maat*, who are, significantly, respectively the divinities of knowledge, and of order and balance. This intervention leads to the offering of alcoholic drink to *Hathor*, whose significance in this sacred narrative is her representation of destructiveness and the threat of the cosmic death of humanity, since the latter would have been obliterated if she had not been stopped. The restoration and security of the entire cosmic order, including the place of humanity in it, is therefore achieved both by the making of the drink offering and equally by the acceptance of the offering, which Hathor shows by drinking it, thus rendering effective both the alcohol and the myth. By this action *Hathor* also observes and so pays homage to the principle of reciprocity, which is an essential element of *Maat*.

Drink offering is very significant in this archetype of libation and so it is central in all enactments of this ritual. In this First Libation the beer is a drink offering by divinities to another divinity in order to restore and preserve good relations in the cosmic order. This drink offering is, literally as well as figuratively, an exchange for the blood of humanity and the restoration and preservation of the cosmic order. The role of liquid offering is central in the ritual of libation, the ultimate meaning of which is the necessity for the restoration and maintenance of the cosmic order. This story may be mined for many more meanings, particularly if some attention is given to the possibilities raised in the definition of myth provided in the opening chapter of this work. But all additional meanings are likely to be subsidiary to this fundamental explanation.

There is reward in considering the significance of liquid in this First Libation, and therefore in the restoration of cosmic balance as well as a recipe for the prevention of cosmic imbalance in the future. Water, a gift from the Creator, is transformed into alcohol by human creativity and labour. This product of human ingenuity and industry is then exchanged for the blood (read essence) of humanity. The objective is to satiate the blood lust of a divinity, a purpose achieved through trickery. Water is a basic component of both the beer and the blood for which it was exchanged to propitiate the angry divinity. This centrality of water in the mythical origins of libation is an accurate reflection of the importance of this substance in the social history of the people of Kemet, as among the Afrikan people as a generality, which is the subject of part of Chapter Six. This importance is reflected in the Spiritual System as well as in the language of the people of Kemet. Water is the ultimate cleanser in the Afrikan universe. Its role in the First Libation finds powerful linguistic parallels in its presence in the derivation, orthography and basic meanings of the terms for libation in the *Medew Netjer*, as well as in the descriptive term for libation, i.e. "pour water," which has been synonymous with libation in many Afrikan languages for more than 5,000 years. It is worthwhile noting here that "pour water" is but one of the descriptive terms for libation. Other terms refer to the pouring of a small portion of liquor. These include the Twi term *nsaguo*, which is discussed later in this chapter, and the descriptive ritual instruction delivered by 2Pac Shakur, "Pour out a little liquor," echoed by Nas as "pour out some liquor," which are discussed in Chapter Five.

The function of this mythical narrative of the First Libation is to provide the intellectual basis and the performance model for the ritual drama known as libation. This narrative gives an origin and an explanation of the ritual. It also supplies a reference to the great importance to be attached to the ritual by locating it mainly among the highest and most powerful category of beings in the Afrikan cosmology, the realm of divinity.

In human society time has a way of picking out the best qualities in individuals among us. As the processes of myth making unfold, such individuals may then be elevated to newer and higher levels until, if they are worth it—or, more to the point perhaps, if the circumstances of their community are thought to demand it—they attain the highest of all levels in the human estimation: that of the divine. Then, when all their frailties and faults; their vices and other imperfections are forgotten, and victories and virtues alone are remembered, invented, ascribed and celebrated, these human beings may thus cease to be human. In this way, individuals are transformed into symbols that dwell in the realm of the superhuman, the supernatural, the extraordinary, the mythic, the magical and the divine. Heroes are made legendary, the legendary may become mythical, and finally, if necessary for the developing myth, divine. Thus, in time, may men and women become gods and goddesses: Osiris, Isis, Shango, Jesus. The process begins with an outstanding human, the hero or heroine, and each step renders him or her less human, the process taking her/him further and further away from humanity. He (and most often nowadays it is indeed a male) is made increasingly bigger, less fallible and more powerful, while his companions, contemporaries and eventually all other humans are rendered more and more powerless, and less and less equal to the mythical figure created in the process.

We may also note a somewhat parallel development that focuses more upon group behaviour rather than on individual achievement. The best practice in daily living becomes social ideals and may then be made into divine laws and guidance. Sometimes best practices amount to the ones most favourable to the survival and continuation of a ruling elite that exercises dominant influence upon choices through its control of state institutions, particularly those media that propagate ideas and perspectives.

In both processes there is a tendency to lose those details that are considered unnecessary for illustrating the central tenets of the story. This has occasioned Wole Soyinka's insightful observation that "myth is always careless about detail,"[12] a truth that finds more than an echo in the words of Modupe Odudoye, who, in discussing folk theology or mythology, concluded that "Folk theology does not stop to consider [certain] details."[13] Fortunately, the very processes of reification and deification are also often marked by the development of parallel traditions, as people migrate, stories travel with them and are handed down, different versions evolve from a single source, and details lost in one version may be preserved in another, and *vice versa*. Thus multiple traditions may aid the processes of recovery of individuals from legend and history from myth, mysticism, magic and divinity. If we are careful enough, the process of recovery of lost details, through the assembly of multiple versions, can therefore help in both the reconstruction of our story, and the preservation of our humanity. The mythical narrative may thus in some cases suffer the good fortune of being ambushed by history.

3.3 Sacred Literature

The great importance of libation, to the people of Kemet, is indicated by the location of the origin of this ritual among the heroic, the legendary, the mythical, the magical and the divine. The tremendous importance of this ritual is also reflected and reinforced by its status within the sacred literature of the Classical Afrikan Tradition. This tradition was over 3000 years of development and evolution in ⌒𓈎𓅓𓏏 Kmt: Kemet (ancient Egypt) alone. It had undergone uncounted generations of fashioning even before Kemet, where libation is an ancient command from the practice of our sacred ancestors. The regular performance of this ritual drama is therefore made mandatory upon all Afrikans. Libation is so ancient and so important that there are libation utterances in the *Pyramid Texts*,[14] the oldest substantial writings in the world, and Utterance 598 in the *Book of Vindication* (the *Coffin Texts*) may well be a libation utterance.[15] In his 𓊪 𓇋𓏭𓐟𓂋𓏏 *Sebayt* or teachings, 𓇋𓏠𓈖𓀀: *Ani*, an ancient wise man from the New Kingdom era of Kemet, commands us thus:

> Pour libation for your father and mother who rest in the valley of the dead. God will witness your action and accept it. Do not forget to do this even when you are away from home. For as you do for your parents, your children will do for you also.[16]

3.4: Language: 𓂋𓏤𓊹𓏥 : The *Medew Netjer*

𓊖𓈎𓅓𓏏 Kmt: Kemet (Ancient Egypt) is the oldest Afrikan society about which we have much detailed knowledge. There are many words in the 𓂋𓏤𓊹𓏥 *Medew Netjer*, the language of Kemet, that are connected with the concepts, paraphernalia and activities germane to the complex of offerings mentioned above. Examples of such terms include the following:

𓊵𓏏𓊪 Htp: *Hotep*. Gardiner supplies "rest, go to rest, be at peace, pleased,"[17] while Faulkner yields "be pleased," "be happy," "be gracious," "pardon," "be at peace," "be peaceful," "become calm," "rest," "go to rest," "satisfy," "make content," "pacify."[18] Clearly, *Hotep* is a most important term, perhaps the key term for our understanding of libation, for it conveys the ultimate objective of libation and related rituals such as sacrifice, which was to please the divinities and ensure peace among humanity. Its presence in the origin, structure and meaning of the vocabulary of the offering complex demonstrates how this concept is foundational to and reverberates in the rituals and paraphernalia through which and by which devotion to the divinities was articulated.

𓊵𓏏𓊪 Sḥtp: propitiate, pacify.

𓊵𓏏 ḥtp: table of offering, altar.

𓊵𓏏𓏥 ḥtp(w), ḥtpt: "offerings;" "food offerings."

𓊵𓏏𓊹𓏥 ḥtpw nṯr, "offerings" to the spirits or 𓉐𓂋𓏏𓊹𓏥 pr(t)-ḫrw-(ḥtpw)-nṯr: literally, "sending forth/sending up of voice offerings (to the) divinity,"[19] i.e. "voice offerings (prayers) to the divinity," hence "divine offerings." This is the oldest recorded reference to what would become, over millennia of evolution, the Libation Statement and prayers.

𓏌𓏌𓏌𓎺𓏥 snw "food offerings."

𓊃𓈖𓏏𓂋 :sntr; [variation 𓊃𓈖𓏏𓂋 :snṯr] sen-netjer "incense," a writing and a meaning which may indicate and reinforce the predominant notion of the article as a sweet-smelling enabler of the divine presence.

𓐝𓂋𓎛𓏏 mrḥt = anointing oil.

𓊃𓂧𓏏 sdt = anointing oil. It seems that there were different kinds of anointing oil.

𓐝𓂧𓏏 mḏt = ointment.

𓏏𓂓𓅱 tk3w: tekaw = candles[20]

𓊃𓏏𓊃𓏏 st3t: censor.[21] A device used for burning incense.

𓎗𓂉 (abbreviation 𓎗; later writing 𓎗𓂉):wḏḥw = "table of offerings."[22]

𓉔𓈖𓎡𓏏 ḥnkt: henket = "beer."

𓇋𓂋𓊪 or 𓇋𓂋𓊪𓏊 irp = wine.

𓈗 mw = water, "sometimes specified as mw n r(n)py" or "mw rnp: fresh water,"[23] meaning purifying and rejuvenating water[24] or "cool" water as is discussed below.

𓎡𓂋 k3r = shrine.

𓇋𓂋𓏏𓏏 irtt (Old Kingdom); 𓇋𓂋𓏏𓏏 irtt (New Kingdom) = milk.

𓈎𓃀𓎛𓅱 (variations 𓈎𓃀 and 𓈎𓃀𓈗): ḳbḥw = "libation."

Every one of these terms listed above is connected to all the others. These are connections that together spell out libation and the wider offering complex and related ideas, articles and actions to which libation belongs. Yet, there are other terms that further emphasise the presence of this complex in the society of Kemet. Such terms include various kinds of 𓏏𓏐 t: bread, 𓐍𓊪𓈙 : ḫpš *Khpsh*, the leg of an ox, normally used in offerings; 𓃀𓂝𓏏 : wʿb.t: wab.t, ritually pure meat; 𓄿𓊪𓂧𓅱 :3pdw or *apdu* = birds, and indeed any kind of food, which were all often included in the 𓉐𓂋𓏏 prt-ḫrw or *peret khrew*: "invocation offerings" that were regularly presented to the divinities and to ancestors. In fact, offering formulae from Kemet included a standard declaration that contained the words "𓐍𓏏𓎟𓏏𓄤𓏏𓃀 ḫt nb(t) nfr(t) wʿb(t) ʿnḫt nṯr," literally: "all things good and pure (upon which) a divinity lives." Other items such as flowers, fruits, grain, fresh plants, linen garments and amulets were also regularly offered.

It is important to ground our understanding of libation and associated ideas and practices at least partly in these terms, for a group of humans do not invent terms in their language to represent concepts that do not already exist in their physical, social and intellectual universe; that is, in their living reality. The facts, namely that these terms exist in the Medew Netjer and are indigenous to it, therefore must mean that the ideas and practices they represent existed in the social reality of the speech community of the people of Kemet, who were the inventors and users of the Medew Netjer. The existence of a number of related categories of these terms in this language further emphasises the presence of an elaborate offering complex of which libation was a part. This complex was composed of related materials, ideas and practises surrounding offering of libations, food, prayers, sacrifice, and other things considered good and worthy, to the environment or features thereof, to the ancestors, to divinities and to the Supreme One. This also means that this entire behavioural complex existed in Afrikan culture from very early times, certainly from the time of the people of Kemet, and most probably before then, as is indicated by the Nabta Playa temple complex and the Qustul incense burner. These terms therefore argue that this set of ideas and practices was of the greatest importance to the Afrikan people from a very long time ago. They have remained so. This knowledge, with its related understandings, beliefs and practises, and the ritual of libation in which they find a specific expression, therefore comprise a most important part of Afrikan culture and so, of Afrikan identity.

The fundamental importance of libation to the Afrikans in Kemet is indicated in the Medew Netjer, the language of the people, or at the very least the way in which they represented that language in writing. The special ceremonial vessels used for ritual libations are represented in the five netjers, or signs, from W14 to W18 in Gardiner's Sign List. These are, respectively, 𓎿, 𓏊, 𓏋, 𓏌 and 𓏎. Each forms the determinative or sense sign that indicates the class of meaning of words that range, respectively from "water pot," "jar" and "praise;" "be cool" and its derivatives, "libate;" "libation" and its derivatives, to "racks for water pots." It is from this latter that is derived the word 𓏎⸗[variation 𓎱] ḫnt, meaning "in front of" and its derivatives,[25] clearly from the rebus principle in which it is the sound and not so much the picture of the thing that is deployed to make meaning.[26] The first of these signs, 𓎿 ḥst = water pot, features regularly as a determinative for "libation," "pure" and "purity." Termed amphoras[27] in the literature of Egyptology, these ritual vessels are ubiquitous in the representation of libation in Kemet.

Therefore in the language of Kemet we also find a number of terms that are based upon these sense signs. The morphological, etymological and semantic significances of these terms are important for our understanding of libation and are the basis of the discussion in the following paragraphs.

First, spellings of the words for "libate" and "libation" are known: ⌬ 𓎡𓃀𓏤 (variant determinative 𓏋): ḳbḥ = "libate;" ⌬ 𓎡𓃀𓏤𓈗: ḳbḥw = "libation."[28] R.O. Faulkner also offers: ⌬ 𓎡𓃀𓏋: ḳbḥw = "cold water;" the abstract noun ⌬ 𓎡𓃀𓏤𓏌𓈗 ḳbḥw "coolness," with ḳbḥw 𓏋𓈗 and 𓏋⸗ ḳbḥt, being uncertain renditions of "libation-vase."[29]

Linguistically these words appear to have originated in two different words that manifest themselves in many derivatives that concern us here. These two roots are 𓎿 or 𓎿𓈖: cool through water and 𓐍𓃀 ḳb: "to humble oneself (before a divinity)."[30] Each of these concepts is fundamental to our understanding of libation. 𓎿 or 𓎿𓈖 originated in 𓎿 ḥst (from the Old Kingdom ḥzt), a water pot,[31] plus 𓈖 the sign for water. The idea of cooling by pouring water is unmistakably conveyed here.

It appears that over time these two different words with different meanings became fused into the single and composite concept of libation. Fusion appears to be a fact in both the structural and semantic domains. Hence the orthography of each of these words is a composite of the two roots and both of these meanings appear to inform the concept of libation, which is articulated through 𓐍𓎿𓈖, 𓐍𓃀𓎿: ḳbb = "(be) cool, cold, cooling, calm, quiet, secure, be purified" and 𓐍𓎿: ḳbb = "purify, present libations." The resulting concept is related in the noun 𓐍𓎿: ḳb = "cold," the adjective 𓐍𓃀𓎿 ḳbb: "be cool" and the verb 𓐍𓎿𓈖 ḳb = "pour a libation."[32] Each of these words demonstrates a particular aspect of a general concept and is formed from two elements; the two determinatives, 𓎿 and 𓈖, and the root 𓐍𓃀. Yet these terms by themselves, singly or collectively, do not cover all the nuances and the full meaning of the concept.

The *Wörterbuch* contains an extensive listing of the cognates. This list includes to humble oneself before a divinity, cool, to be cool, the act of cooling oneself, and several meanings of cool which originate in the physical state produced by pouring cooling water over the body. Further, these meanings extend themselves in a continuum ranging from this latter physical state to include related mental, emotional and spiritual conditions. All of these conditions, and therefore the lexical items that represent them in the *Medew Netjer*, are semantically related because they are all induced by this act of water pouring and/or are similar to a state created by the act. The terms include "to freshen up," "comfortable," "relaxed," speech that is careful (and therefore unexcited and non-threatening), "to restore to health" or "rejuvenate," "satisfied" (from ritual sacrifice), "left in peace," "happy state."[33] Water as the agent of cooling is evident, in fact pre-eminent, both through the construction of almost all these words, with the sign 𓈖 predominant in the orthography and also because water, or a state brought about by water, is invariably clearly present or strongly implied in each meaning.

Yet, the central concept in almost all these meanings arises from the states of satisfaction and even pleasure that are born from the absence of impurity and discomfort, the pleasant conditions that are induced by the cooling property of water. It is this basic meaning that is extended to embrace the many shades of meaning that arise in all of these words. Thus, aspects of the person (for example the mouth and other organs,) places, and even actions, may be cool, may be in a cool state or may be done in a cool manner. The significance of water in bringing about these desirable conditions ought to be noted here. The further significance of water is discussed at some length below in Chapter Six.

This basic notion of "cool" in the Medew Ntejer, meaning "to be all right," is also instructive. The identical usage of this term is extant among the Igala in Nigeria. Here, the Ata or king is required by tradition to utter the following invocation at the Ocho festival, which deals with the land shrine and issues of communal land use: "May I live long, let the eyes that see me today see me another year, *let it be cool throughout my land.*"[34]

Further, it is precisely this meaning which is popularly articulated today in the very term "cool" among Afrikan American and Afrikan Caribbean people, especially the younger generations. This section of the Afrikan people also extend the metaphor by the deployment of the term "chill" as in "chill out," meaning to "cool down," to calm or to refresh oneself. The aim here is for one to generally exist in a peaceful state, even if not satisfied with the state of the general environment. This general environment is often oppressive and a direct contradiction to the calm it takes to negotiate life in such circumstances. In practice, dominant forces in that environment often function to undermine such calm. Use of the term "cool" with this meaning was popularised in the late 1940s by jazz greats Charlie Parker and John Coltrane.[35] Recall examples of these usages such as "cool dude," the pop group "Kool and the Gang," and the film "Cool Runnings," this latter based upon the experiences of a Jamaican bobsled team.

More research on this matter may be necessary to prove linkage or mere coincidence. However, by appearances alone it seems that at a very deep level Afrikans in the Americas and the Caribbean have continued and extended the use of the very ideas represented for the first time in writing millennia ago in this Ancient Egyptian term and that this usage is still extant in at least one ritual in West Afrika. If this is so, then Afrikans in the Americas and the Caribbean have re-invented or retrieved, repossessed and certainly preserved a specific expression of the notion of "cool" as any kind and all kinds of wellness—and a parallel usage may still be detected in at least one tradition in Nigeria. This is a meaning of 'cool' that was first articulated in the Nile Valley, as far as is known, millennia ago by the ancestors of both West Afrikans and Afrikans in that compulsory diaspora in the Caribbean and Americas.

The term ⌂ 𓈎𓃀𓏏 or 𓈎𓃀 ḳbḥ: the title of a priest and one of the titles of the pharaoh[36] may indicate the role of these functionaries in maintaining Maat and therefore the cosmos in a "cool" or peaceful, purified and satisfactory or even pleasant state.

Faulkner lists ⌂𓈎𓃀 ḳb = "pour a libation" as an intransitive verb. However, libation is always poured into something (Mother Earth or a receptacle such as a calabash, a potted plant or a bowl), into aspects of the environment, to ancestors and/or to divinities, who are therefore always, in this grammatical sense, its objects (in addition to the specific objective(s) of the libation when these may be different). Faulkner's view of ⌂ 𓈎𓃀 ḳb is an exact parallel to his view of the verb 𓋴𓏏 s3t [z3t] = "make libation," which he also lists as intransitive.[37]

The English language term "libation," the etymology of which may be traced to the Latin libare, meaning "to take a portion" or "to taste," appears consistent with this meaning from the Medew Netjer, which is an infinitely older language. We have seen that the concept and practice of libation is native to Afrika and have a far longer history there than anywhere else. It is also true that the concept and practice of libation passed from the Nile Valley to the Greeks and Romans during the late stage of the history of Kemet.

In Twi, the predominant Afrikan language in Ghana, the term for libation is Nsaguo, derived from *nsa* = "a drink" and *gu* = "to pour." In Gikuyu the term is *goitangera ngoma njohi*, which means, literally, "to pour out or to sprinkle beer for spirits" and refers to the sprinkling of a few drops of any drink onto the ground for the ancestors as well as the larger quantity of beer specially brewed and offered to the ancestors on communal occasions.[38] Once again we must note that all over Afrika and in Afrikan communities abroad, wherever Afrikans practice their culture, these actions invariably form parts of that practice. This is a clear illustration of the cultural unity of Afrika.

The Twi term nsaguo appears to have survived in parts of the Caribbean, certainly in Antigua, where among the older generations a drop of rum or indeed a drop of any alcohol is referred to as sagua. Here the etymology appears clear from the retention of the structure of the item. On the semantic level there appears to have been some shift, since the meaning is now a small portion of liquor that is usually referred to in the context of social drinking; the word has lost its restricted association with its initial context of libating. However, a clue to its origin lies in the fact that an Nsaguo is really also a small portion of rum or alcohol, but employed for libation and not for social drinking.

The terms *Mpaee*, *Mpaebo* and *Mpaeyie*, literally "praying" but also "the act of pouring together with a prayer [that is, request(s) to one or more divinities]" may also be used for this activity. *Mpaebo*, from *mpaee* = "prayer" [or request to a divinity or to divinities] and *bo* = "to show, to offer," means, when used for libatory prayer, "a libation in which blessings and other beneficial graces are requested for those on whose behalf the libation is poured."[39] *Apaeeyie* is derived from *apaee* = a curse, and *yi* = "to remove;" hence a libation in which the petition is for the undoing of curses or the forestalling of evils and accidents. *Mmusuoyie*, from *mmusu* = evil; *yie* = to remove, and *Nsanom* = "the taking of drink," are terms applied to libation as the removal of bad things in particular areas of Asanteland. Other specific terms are also applied to libations with specific purposes.[40] This development of specific terms, or specialization, for different kinds of libation indicates a high frequency level of practice, a high level of sophistication and a high level of importance attached to this activity in this particular speech community. These facts argue a fundamental importance of the ritual of libation among this group of Afrikans.

In Ancient Egyptian there is also 𓎟 w^{c}b: *wab* (adjective) = "pure;" 𓎟𓀀 (variation 𓎟𓀁): w^{c}b, *wab* (noun) = an ordinary priest,[41] literally, "the (ritually) pure one" as well as 𓎟𓏏 ⌠w^{c}bt = "priestess,"[42] and 𓎟 w^{c}b ḥmt = "priestess,"[43] literally "the (ritually) pure woman." These terms clearly refer to men and women who have undergone purification rites and are therefore ceremonially or ritually pure. Ritual purity was a fundamental condition of all priests. It is apparently upon this understanding that both Obenga and Allen translate the term ⌂≡⚶ somewhat literally as "*le prêtre-purificateur*,"[44] i.e. "the purifying priest" or "cleaner."[45] The latter term risks being too restrictive, even though it does not undermine the fact that the idea of purity is central to the construction of the concept of priest in Kemet, a notion that is also sustained and reinforced in △ ∥⋔ or ḳbḥ ⋔≡, the title of a priest and a term that we have met before. The ⌂≡⚶: wʿb and ⌂₀∥ wʿbt were the basis and most numerous of the ≤₀*⚶ (variant writing ⚶∣,) wnwt: the priesthood of Kemet.

The generic term for priest in the Medew Netjer is ¶₁⚶ (variation ¶₁) ḥm-nṯr, *hem-netjer*, literally "servant of the divinity."[46] The idea of the priesthood, its organisation and the roles within it evolved and changed over the very long period—well over 3000 years—occupied by the history of the state of Kemet. In the Old and Middle Kingdoms the leading roles of the priests were undertaken by state officials as part of their civic duties. Lesser functions were usually performed by a corps of local persons on tours of duty. It was this group that became identified with the roles that came to be designated by the title ⌂≡⚶: wʿb, *wab*. In the New Kingdom the priesthood may have evolved into a permanent profession with a more clearly defined hierarchy in each temple. The foremost or high priest was the ¶₁℘□ (or ¶₁) ḥm-nṯr tpj the "first servant of the divinity," which was just below the rank of the ¶⚶ (or ○¶) it-nṯr: "father of the divinity," described by Gardiner as the "name of a class of elder priests."[47] The First Servant was followed in the hierarchy by the Second, Third and Fourth servants of the particular divinity. Next were several specialist priests, such as the ⌂▥∥: ḥry-ḥbt, "the master of the ritual book" or lector priest and the ⋔or ⍟, the ḥm-k3: *hem-ka* or "soul priest," with the entire structure resting upon the ⌂≡⚶.

The existence of the terms ⌂₀∥ wʿbt = "priestess," and ⚶⚶ wʿb ḥmt = "priestess," literally "(ritually) pure woman," shows clearly that women were a part of this profession and that ritual purity was a prerequisite for the participation of women in this office as it was for men. This was so from the inception. ⌂₀⚶st: Ast or Auset (Greek Isis, Isata in Ethiopia in modern Afrika) is the divinity who was the chief functionary in libations to the departed in Kemet. One of her attributes was ḳbḥt: *kebhet*, literally "the female libationer."[48] As these facts indicate, women were always a very important part of the profession, a clear contradiction of Herodotus, who states that "[n]o woman holds priestly office, either in the service of goddess or god; only men are priests in both cases."[49] On this matter Herodotus is quite clearly privileging men and simultaneously relegating women. This is an imposition of his own Eurocentric view of humanity, across cultural boundaries, upon the people of Kemet. In the society of Kemet, as in all Afrika when there are no foreign influences, women were generally at least relatively equal to men.

The roles of women within the priesthood, like those of men, naturally evolved and changed over the long period occupied by the history of Kemet. Much of this is attested from other sources. For example, from the Middle Kingdom onwards, women assumed powerful positions within the priesthood. Perhaps the most powerful of these posts was God's Wife of Amun, the titular of a high priestess, part of whose duties included pouring libations before the images of divinities.[50] Ahmose Nefertari, one of the founders of the New Kingdom, was in fact the initiator and first occupant of this office.[51] Such facts permit Obenga to arrive at this valid conclusion:

> *Dans l'Égypte ancienne, le clergé comptait en son sein un personnel feminine exerçant tout naturellement des charges sacerdotales, dès l'Ancien Empire: femmes prêtresses de déesses et de dieux, filles de prêtres ayant reçu en heritage la fonction de leur père, femmes musiciennes ou chanteuses dans les temples.*[52] [In ancient Egypt, the clergy welcomed feminine personnel to perform sacerdotal functions: women priests to Gods and Goddesses, priests' daughters having received the heritage of their fathers' duties, women musicians and singers in the temples.]

The tradition of at least female participation, if it was not gender equality in the priesthood, appears to have been more or less maintained, though not without challenge from patriarchal ideas and practices, throughout Afrika and its communities abroad. For example, it was a mambo or Voodoo priestess who was director of the entire ceremony, which contained a number of rituals, organised in the forest known as the Bois Caïman on the night of 21st August, 1791 to launch the military stage of the Haitian Revolution.[53] Powerful women were among the foremost Voodoo leaders in New Orleans before 1900. Sanité Dédé, Marie Saloppé and Marie Laveau may be mentioned in this regard.[54] A woman in a position of spiritual leadership in Afrika abroad was not uncommon then. It is not uncommon now. Today women are still priestesses all over the Afrikan world.

w‘b = "serve as a priest," with the noun w‘bwt = "priestly service."[55] The duty of this official, who was required to be physically and morally pure, was to ensure the purity of offerings. In the Medew Netjer, the term used to describe this priest therefore indicated both the state of ritual purity expected of this official and the main function s/he performed.

ibḥ = "a priest who poured libations or the like."[56]

[variation]: ibḥw = libationer.[57] The *Wörterbuch* has the identical transliteration, meaning and variation, but has a slightly different orthography for the verb: . Here the meaning is ibḥw = 'Wasser sprengen . . . auch als Priestertitel.'[58] ["To sprinkle water . . . also a priest's title."] The notion of pouring water in libation is the semantic root of these terms.

(abbreviation) ‘bw: *abu* = "purification," with ibw-r = "breakfast."[59] The latter is derived from two words: = "purification" and = "mouth," hence literally "the purification of the mouth." In the last term both structure and meaning are clearly derived from the timing of this meal in terms of its proximity to this particular act of purification, which, consequently, must have been regarded as a most important rite. It still is among Afrikans today. One of the first tasks of a new day is the purification of the mouth with water and kola nut or alligator pepper. The importance of purifying the mouth is examined in this chapter below.

A number of factors therefore together provide further proof of an elaborate practice of libation, with distinct aspects of the ritual, special gear, specialised or at least differentiated functions and specialised functionaries. First is the presence of this variety of terms for libation in the language of Kemet. Another is the fact that these terms are closely related in origin, structure and meaning. A third factor is the existence of a term for a priest who specialised in pouring libations and related matters. These facts help to show the deep importance and elaborate development of libation in Kemet and thus in Afrikan society from very early times. We have seen that it is the same among the speakers of Twi. It is much the same in other Afrikan languages and communities.

The significance of the origins of the Medew Netjer term "libation" in other terms with meanings like "cool," "clean" and "pure" should not be allowed to escape the reader. This morphological and semantic relationship and proximity of the idea of libation to the ideas of coolness (i.e. pleasantness), cleanliness and ritual purity reflect the spiritual practice of Kemet, represents an extension in the meaning of the word itself and in reality indicates other levels of meaning and significance of the ritual. These are the most powerful and potent levels of meaning and significance of the ritual and it is of the greatest importance to understand them.

3.5: Social History

The linguistic evidence for libation in Kemet obtained from content analysis of the language of Kemet is corroborated by evidence from the social history of the people of Kemet. Janssen and Janssen show that the custom of pouring water (i.e. libating) for a deceased was widespread in Kemet throughout its very long history,[60] a custom that is attested in the integrated offering ritual which is examined in the next chapter. Libating with water was also done for Imhotep and, more than likely, for the very few other outstanding private individuals who were elevated to divinity after their transition to the spirit world.[61] The sage Neferti gives independent corroboration of this latter custom when he writes that "The learned man will pour out water [i.e. make a Libation] for me, when he sees what I have spoken come to pass."[62] Other authorities agree with this meaning of the passage from the Medew Netjer. For example, John A. Wilson offers the same translation. Lichtheim offers "And he who is wise will libate for me,"[63] while a more recent source, R. B. Parkinson, renders it: "The sage will pour an offering of water for me."[64]

More historically recent testimony than Neferti, in fact from the Late Period of Kemet, towards the end of Pharoanic Civilisation, provides a strikingly similar formulation. Papyri from Akhmim or the surrounding area dated to the 1st century of the Current Era (CE) demonstrate this usage. For example, Column II of P. Berlin 8351 yields "receive .. a .. libation" (line 1), "receive water," "receive a libation," (3) "pour out a libation (4,5,)" "pour out wate" (12,) "given a libation" (17) and "water will be poured out" (19.) All of these terms are used interchangeably to refer to libation.[65] Further, the term *mw n mw*, "libation of water,"[66] makes it clear that in this ritual context "water" is synonymous with "libation."

There is more evidence. The papyrus numbered 10188 in the British Museum contains these lines: "Cool water and incense shall be offered by them as to the honourable kings of the South and North who are in the Other World."[67] The notion of libation as an offering of "cool" water, perhaps extended here to mean blessed, sanctified or pure, is inescapable. In each instance of this usage the meaning is unmistakable.

Yet, it is important to differentiate between the two customs involving libation. It seems that libation to a revered ancestor, for example to Imhotep, is distinguished by the fact that while the normal libation to the deceased was poured at the graveside at specific times and by the family of the deceased or by someone paid to do so by the family, libation to Imhotep was done by all scribes, that is, by an entire occupational group as a professional practice in tribute to him. This tribute was not confined to his burial place, which in his case was itself the focus of votive offerings by people from far and wide; libation to Imhotep was conducted wherever and whenever a scribe was about to write something.

Utterance 23 of the *Pyramid Texts* is perhaps the oldest known libation spell on this planet. The instruction "Pour water," which comes at the end, makes it plain that this is a Libation Ritual and that that particular libation was poured with water.[68] It may be of some significance that in the languages of both Kemet and contemporary Afrika there are specific words for libation, yet there is also the formulation "pour water" that is often employed to render this meaning. We can conclude from the discussion above that in this ritual context the notion of "water pouring" as well as the formulation "pour water," which is the same as "pour libation," were popular lexical currency in Kemet. It does appear probable that this very form of words was taken to different parts of the continent by Afrikans migrating out of the Nile Valley. Alternatively, this formula may have even been extant in a linguistic environment that was common to both Kemet and other parts of Afrika and was taken into Kemet from much earlier times. The explanation may even lie in a combination of these two possibilities. In any event, we are certain that this expression has been retained in the different Afrikan languages where today it reflects the lexical archetype and sustains the exact meaning of ancestors who dwelt in the Nile Valley thousands of years ago.

References to libation with water are distributed throughout the Pyramid Texts. Some of the formulae have been preserved. Here is an example:

[hieroglyphic text]⁶⁹

Libations for you Ausur! Libations for you, Oh Wenis, which have come forth before your son, which have come forth before Heru! I have come. I have brought to you the Heru-eye that your heart may be cool possessing it. . . . I offer you the moisture that has issued from you, that your heart may not be still possessing it.⁷⁰

The people of Kemet consciously pointed towards the south as their place of origin and so a place of great significance. Their language tells the same story.⁷¹ The South, the headwaters of the Nile in the Great Lakes region of Afrika, where humanity was born, is a sacred place. In Kemet water drawn from the River Nile, especially from the region of the First Cataract, was highly prized for the pouring of libation, since tradition had it that the water drawn from this area was guaranteed to be pure because it was near to the symbolic source of the river.⁷² Such a conclusion appears to be verified in the name the people of Kemet gave to this region of their country. It is [hieroglyph] ḳbḥw: *Kebhu*,⁷³ which must mean, literally, "pure land" or "pure region" because of the meaning of the root [hieroglyph] ḳbḥ combined with the determinative or sense sign [hieroglyph], which imposes the very general classification "hilly, desert or foreign land." Any doubt about this meaning ought to be erased by the variant writings of this term, which are given in the *Wörterbuch*: [hieroglyphs].⁷⁴ These writings supply a precise orthography and an exact meaning. This term is also consistent with the name the people of Kemet gave to the extreme south of their country, (of which this region was a part): [hieroglyph](variation[hieroglyph]) Wpt-ṱ = "Earth's beginning,"⁷⁵ (literally, "the beginning of all land," "the place where the water comes out of the land.") This was obviously a sacred place to the citizens of Kemet, who knew that that was the direction of their origin. In fact they referred to Afrika south of their country by names such as *Ta-Kenset*, literally "placenta-land," *Khenti* = "land of beginnings" and *Ta-Iakhu* = "the land of the spirits," that is, "where the souls of ancestors dwell."⁷⁶ This belief that the southern region of their country was a sacred and perhaps even a pristine place also finds expression in the term "Herr ([hieroglyph])des Kataraktengebiets"⁷⁷ one of the titles they gave to Khnum, who we must note was a Creator Divinity. The knowledge of inner Afrika "as the chief source of the spiritual—"The Land of the Gods" or "The Land of the Spirits" has persisted even after the Arab invasion and domination of Kemet.⁷⁸

The offerings made to the ancestors and to the divinities must be pure. The Chief Libationer must also be pure, both physically (hygienically) and spiritually. In terms of both physical and spiritual cleanliness, the priests of Kemet washed ritually, five times daily, with water from a special pool constructed for this purpose near to each temple. It was believed that the pool contained primordial water.⁷⁹ Priests also regularly shaved off all body hair, were circumcised, and abstained from eating certain foods, though this varied according to which divinity was served, the rank of the priest in question and the area in which the temple was located. For example, it is known that although priests could be married and have sexual relations when they resided with their wives, once it was their turn for service, they were required to reside within the temple and to abstain from any physical contact with women (doubtless women priests were also in corresponding ways restricted from physical contact with men) for a period beginning several days before temple duty commenced. They were not to wear certain clothing, like wool and leather, which are made from materials obtained from animals. The maintenance of Maat demanded an eco-friendly practice. Hence priests wore linen clothes and shoes constructed of plant fibre. The vessels and other utensils used in the rituals were also to be kept ritually clean; therefore they were regularly washed in the ritual lake.⁸⁰ It is quite possible that priests fasted regularly, most likely especially before performing ceremonies.

Ritual purity is not normally possible without physical and moral cleanliness (and purity), for external or physical purity was consdered a representation of internal or spiritual purity. The helpers of the officiating priests were physically clean and ritually pure also, for it is certain that they were made ritually pure during the ritual of washing in the special pool.

The idea of purity was not restricted to the priests and priestesses. It was taken very seriously by the majority of the people of Kemet. Besides regular baths there was a ritual washing of the hands before every feast, and before every meal. This was called the rite of ⌐∩ s3t, that is, "water-pouring."⁸¹ The ritual washing of hands and feet was considered a way of purifying the person, both externally (physically) and internally (i.e. spiritually). There are references to this in the spiritual texts of Kemet. Examples are to be found in the ⟨hieroglyphs⟩ ru prt m hrw: *Chapters of Going Forth By Day (Into Light)*,⁸² popularly known in the west by the erroneous and misleading term, "The Egyptian Book of the Dead." In Chapter 172 we find this reference to offerings, libation and foot washing in very close association with each other:

> May you make offerings in the Upper Houses, may you propitiate the Lords of Heliopolis ⁸³, may you present to Re water in a vase and two large jars of milk. May your offerings be raised up on the altar; may your feet be washed on a stone of . . . on the slab of the God of the Lake . . . ⁸⁴

It is necessary to conclude from this passage that in Kemet there was a ritual washing of the Pharaoh's feet. Foot washing was a fairly widespread ritual in Kemet.⁸⁵ Christian Jacq considers this ritual of Kemet to be the basis for the washing of feet in the Christian bible,⁸⁶ where it is mentioned at Luke 7:38 and John 13: 5–14.

At an even more rigorous level, it was considered important to keep the mouth clean so that one's words (speech) would remain pure and therefore beautiful. In Kemet, 𓌃𓂧𓏏𓆑 Mdw nfr: *Medew Nefer* or Beautiful Speech was speech that was true, morally correct and consistent with action.[87]

Keeping the mouth clean is a well understood ritual preoccupation from the time of the *Pyramid Texts*, the oldest writings of the people of Kemet and in the world. These most probably represent the practice stretching back into the time before the invention of writing or the establishment of the state of Kemet, in the very least before 30,000 BCE, probably even before then. Utterance 210 of the *Pyramid Texts* says: "My mouth is pure, the Two Enneads cense me, and pure indeed is this tongue which is in my mouth."[88]

The importance of keeping the mouth clean is underlined in the *Book of Going Forth by Day*, a much later development and elaboration of themes in the *Pyramid Texts*. The *Book of Going Forth by Day* clearly sustains the idea that purity and beauty are subverted, and the practitioner rendered impure, if he or she speaks but does not do actions that are consistent with his/her speech. For example, in the Address to the Divinities in the Hall of Justice, immediately after the pronouncement of the Declarations of Innocence in Chapter 125, the Ba or Soul of the deceased is made to say: "I live on truth, I gulp down truth, . . . save me, protect me, . . . for I am pure of mouth and pure of hands."[89]

It is clear from this context that dissonance, or worse, divergence, between the mouth (as the representation of the word/speech) and the hands (as the representation of action,) was regarded as a source of impurity. This very idea is rearticulated in Chapter 182 of the "Theban Recension," a version of the *Book of Going Forth by Day* retrieved from papyri found in the vicinity of the Ancient Egyptian city of Thebes, where 𓅝[90] *Djhwty* gives a synopsis of his job description:

I am [Djhwty] the skilled scribe whose hands are pure, a possessor of purity,
who drives away evil, who writes what is true, who detests falsehood.[91]

The ideal was to be morally consistent in thought/word and intention/action. Hence the admonition to "Speak Maat; Do Maat,"[92] which has also been rendered as "Speak Truth, do Truth."[93]

Chapter 172 of the "Theban Recension" begins with these words:

I am purified with natron, I chew natron, incense . . .
I am pure, and pure are the recitations which
come from my mouth.[94]

Thus because the mouth is made pure—by chewing natron, a powerful cleanser widely used in Kemet, and by [burning] incense—the utterances coming forth from that mouth are therefore pure also. The importance of purity is reinforced by the location of this ritual. The heading of this chapter makes it plain that it is to be performed in "God's Domain," that is, in the temple,[95] which is a pure and sacred space.

The state of purity was considered essential for gaining "secret" (i.e. spiritual) and sacred knowledge and power and for gaining access to and being in unity and harmony with the spiritual and divine forces of the universe: the ancestors, the divinities and the Creator. This is very clearly the basis for such Nile Valley practices as the libation, censing with incense, the use of natron and other acts of purification reflected in the earliest writings in the Medew Netjer.[96] Impurity, including the ritually impure, was therefore considered not merely against, but in direct opposition to the state of harmony, i.e. to Maat, and so to life itself. Physical and moral purity constitutes the basis for carrying forward the aspirations of our ancestors and of The Supreme One.

The nature of ritual purity, as well as the many functions performed by the ritually pure person, is clearly indicated in the writings of Kemet. For example, one papyrus reads thus:

> Shall be recited chapter this by a person purified [and] washed, [one who] hath not eaten animal flesh [or] fish. . . .[97]

This is clearly a reference to vegetarians, and by extension the role of vegetarianism in the spiritual system of Kemet.

Chapter 64 of The Theban Recension gives further details:

> It should be recited while one is pure, without going near women, without eating goats, without consuming fish.[98]

This notion of ritual purity as abstinence from sex and abstinence from the consumption of certain named foods, which is present in the earliest writings of Kemet, is reinforced elsewhere in the literature of this country:

> This spell must be read when one is in a state of purity and without blemish, and has not eaten small animals or fish, and has not had carnal relations with a woman.[99]

The last two notions of ritual purity may be taken to imply that only men were considered to be candidates for this state of distinction, but this appears to be a contradiction of the fact that women were quite clearly members of the priesthood in Kemet, as is demonstrated earlier in this chapter. It appears logical to conclude that the taboo against sex in a period beginning sometime before commencement of priestly duty applied to men as well as to women.

We are more certain about the other taboos. (In the Medew Netjer the term for taboo is bwt.) For example, in the mythology of Kemet, the pig was taboo to Heru (Greek Horus,) first because it was his sacrificial and perhaps his representative animal and doubly so because Setekh (Seth,) his rival, disguised himself as a pig in order to inflict a grievous wound on him.[100] Fish and sheep were considered ritually impure, unclean, and so were not eaten by persons who were sanctified, nor were these two items offered to the deceased. However, fish and sheep were eaten by many persons in the population.[101]

The importance of being in a ritually pure state when undertaking spiritual functions is underscored on many other occasions in the *Book of Going Forth by Day* as well as in other writings of the people of Kemet. Ritual purity was a very important aspect of the spiritual practice of the Nile Valley. Ritual purity, along with abstinence and other spiritual practices, were all part of festivals of Kemet, which form the basis of carnival as it is known today. The spiritual aspects of carnival have been de-emphasised among some participants, but these remain a most important part of the festival for most conscious Afrikans.[102] One of the most important bases of the spiritual practice of Kemet was the principle that ritual purity helps to guarantee higher forms of consciousness and ensure contact with the divine.

Today Afrikans have also continued this part of the tradition. Afrikans regularly fast and undertake purification before performing the Ritual of Libation, particularly on special occasions. In the modern Afrikan practice of ritual purity it is not only the person that is purified. Space is also purified, especially homes and any space that will host a ceremony. A good example of an elaborate practice of this concept is the daapa, the day of preparation that falls immediately before an Adae festival of the Asante in Ghana. On this day the Asante clear bushes in the environment, clean their houses, clean paths to their farms, clean wells, rivers, etc., clean court accoutrements, re-tune musical instruments, and generally cleanse and prepare for the Adae. Ritual purification of space is usually accomplished by cleaning with certain substances and/or sprinkling the latter after cleaning. In the Diaspora, Florida Water features regularly among these cleansing substances. It is believed that this condition of purity is maintained and enhanced by burning incense.

The important notion of abstinence is observed today in several ways. Certain foods are taboo at all times or at certain times, to certain groups or to everyone. Women experiencing a certain stage of the menstrual cycle are considered both sacred and profane and so are not expected to enter into sacred places such as shrines, or to touch sacred objects, or to perform certain rites. New yams are not to be eaten until a specific time, for example, at the first sighting of a new moon. The notion of abstinence exists in many manifestations and is common throughout contemporary Afrika.[103] It s not unknown in Afrikan communities abroad either.

The benefits of abstinence are many. These include emotional, mental and spiritual strength including greater focus, increased will power, power of concentration and clarity of vision derived from persistence in the face of self-imposed denial. They also include physical strength and endurance derived from rest and fasting and therefore the recuperation of organs, including the mind. In certain conditions benefits may also include solidarity gained from the knowledge that one is part of a spiritual community, so that one undertakes the same practices in sustained commune with a number of others and with the higher powers.

It should be recalled here too that the libation performed before the morning meal happens before the person has broken the fast they had effectively undertaken from the time of the previous meal, which is usually during the early evening of the day before. Therefore in reality this is most often abstinence from eating that began at the end of the meal consumed on that previous evening. Afrikans understood a long time ago that in certain situations abstinence increases the powers of concentration and perception. Washing of at least the mouth, face and hands is common before this Morning Libation. In the early morning the mind and body are therefore in the best condition for libation and general communion with the higher powers and for focusing upon the tasks of that particular day.

It must not be forgotten that at some point in the ritual the entire space in which the gathering is assembled is transformed into a sacred space by both ancestral and Supreme Presences. These ancestral and Supreme Presences, and therefore connection, cannot properly be achieved without the ritual purity of the physical space in which the ritual is to be performed, the purity of the libator(s), the purity of the moment and its purpose(s), and by extension, the purity of all the participants also.

The deep, unifying and powerful meaning and symbolism in the ritual of libation manifest themselves in these ways and at these levels.

Today, as ever-increasing numbers of Afrikans are returning to themselves by reclaiming their identity, they are also reclaiming, refurbishing and reinvigorating Afrikan rituals, Afrikan ceremonies and Afrikan cultural traditions as a generality. This reclamation, termed 𓎛𓅓𓏌𓏥 wḥm mswt: *Wehemu Mesut* (the repeating of the births) in the *Medew Netjer*, and or or *Sankofa* (a return to the past to reclaim something valuable) in Twi, adds other levels of purity and strength to Afrikan existence.[104] Reclamation contributes towards that process that hopefully will be a constant repeating of our birth in the sense of always re-inventing ourselves as necessary, but without losing our Afrikan identity, because every re-invention is both based upon our authentic cultural principles and values and is also sensitive to the age in which it is undertaken. Cultural authenticity in periodic renewal and psychic and spiritual purity will ensure that Afrikans survive, as Afrikans, throughout eternity.

NOTES

1. Bruce Williams. "The Lost Pharaohs of Nubia," pp. 29–43; Williams (1996). "The Qustul Incense Burner and the Case for a Nubian Origin of Ancient Egyptian Kingship" in T. Celenko (ed.). *Egypt in Africa* (Indianapolis Museum of Art and Indiana University Press), pp. 95–97; Brunson. *Before the Unification: Predynastic Egypt*, pp. 107–111.

2. Wilkinson. *The Complete Temples of Ancient Egypt*, p. 16; Hertaus, "Nabta Playa."
3. Janice W. Yellin (1982). "Abation-style milk libation at Meroe." N. B. Millet and A. L. Kelley (eds.). *Meroitica.* (Akademie-Verlag, Berlin), pp. 151–155.
4. Diana Delia (1992). "The Refreshing Water of Osiris" *JARCE*, Vol. xxix, pp. 181–190.
5. Herodotus (trans. A. de Sélincourt, 1972). *The Histories* Book II (Penguin), pp. 129–201, *passim*; G.G.M. James (1954). *Stolen Legacy* (Philosophical Library, New York); C. A. Diop (1974). *The African Origin of Civilization: Myth or Reality* (Lawrence Hill, Westport, Conn.); Théophile Obenga (1995). "La parenté égyptienne: Considérations sociologiques" ♀☥ *Revue D'Égyptologie et des civilisations africaines* Nos.4/5, pp. 139–183; Obenga (1989). "African Philosophy of the Pharaonic Period (2780-330 B. C.)" in I. Van Sertima (ed.) *Egypt Revisited* (Transaction Publishers, Trenton, New Jersey), pp.286–324; Obenga (1992). *Ancient Egypt and Black Africa.* (Karnak House, London); Martin Bernal (1987, 1991) *Black Athenia: The Afroasiatic Roots of Classical Civilization.* Vols. I & II. (London: Free Association Books).
6. Homer (trans. Robert Fagles, 1990). *The Iliad* (Penguin Classics), pp. 92–93 and Homer (trans. E. V. Rieu, 1964). *The Odyssey* (Penguin Classics), *passim* for the general offering context that included sacrifice, prayer, libation and a communal meal. Identical to the Kemetic practice in both form and function, among the Greeks this ritual was normally referred to in the plural, *loibai* or *spondai*. In Latin it is *libationes*, hence "offerings (to the gods.)" Consult M. C. Howatson (ed., 1990). *The Oxford Companion to Classical Literature* (Oxford University Press), p. 323.
7. Versions of this myth may be found in several texts. Examples include Ayi Kwei Armah, *The Eloquence of the Scribes*, p. 207; J.A. Wilson (trans.1969) "Deliverance of Mankind from Destruction" in J.B.Pritchard (ed.). *Ancient Near Eastern Texts Relating to the Old Testament 3rd Edition.* (University of Princeton Press, Princeton, NJ), pp. 10–11; M. Lichtheim (trans., ed. 1976). *Ancient Egyptian Literature Volume II: The New Kingdom* (University of California Press, Los Angeles), pp.197–199; Joseph Kaster (trans. and ed.,1995). *The Wisdom of Ancient Egypt: Writings from the Time of the Pharaohs* (Michael O'Mara Books Ltd., London), pp.66–70; George Hart (1990). "The myth of cataclysm." *Egyptian Myths* (The British Museum Press, London), pp. 46–49; L. H. Lesko (1991). "Ancient Egyptian Cosmogonies and Cosmology" in B.E. Shafer (ed.). *Religion in Ancient Egypt*, pp. 110–111, A. P. Thomas (2001). *Egyptian Gods and Myths* (Shire Publications Ltd., Princes Risborough); Joyce Tyldesley (ed. 2004). "The Destruction of Mankind" in *Tales from Ancient Egypt*, pp. 9–15 and Théophile Obenga (Trans. A. K. Armah, 2004). *African Philosophy: The Pharaonic Period: 2780–330 BC* (Per Ankh, Popenguine), pp.165–178, with some details that vary slightly from those in other texts.
8. Lesko, "Ancient Egyptian Cosmogonies and Cosmology," p. 111.
9. Ayi Kwei Armah, *The Eloquence of the Scribes*, p. 207.
10. Hart, *Egyptian Myths*, p. 46.
11. Obenga. *African Philosophy*, p. 177.
12. Wole Soyinka (1976). *Myth, Literature and the African World* (Cambridge University Press), p. 27.
13. Modupe Oduyoye. *Words and Meaning in Yoruba Religion*, p. 16.
14. R. O. Faulkner, *Pyramid Texts*, Utterances 23 on p. 4, 32 on p.6, 33 on p.7, etc.
15. Faulkner, *The Coffin Texts*. Vol II, p.193.
16. Maulana Karenga (ed., 1984) *Selections from the Husia: Sacred Wisdom of Ancient Egypt.* (Kawaida Publications, Los Angeles), p. 53. See also M. Lichtheim (1976). *Ancient Egyptian Literature: Volume II: The New Kingdom* (University of California

Press, Berkeley, Los Angeles and London), p. 137. For a different translation see R. M. Janssen and J. J. Jannsen (1996). *Getting Old in Ancient Egypt* (London: The Rubicon Press), p. 50.

17. Gardiner, *Egyptian Grammar*, p.583.
18. Faulkner, *Concise Dictionary*, pp. 179–180.
19. Gardiner, *Egyptian Grammar*, pp. 172 and 583.
20. Ibid., pp. 500 and 608. This term may also mean "torch," "flame" and the like, as in Faulkner. *A Concise Dictionary*, pp. 301–302, which does not give "candle."
21. Faulkner, *A Concise Dictionary*, p. 253.
22. Gardiner, *Egyptian Grammar*, pp. 524, 563; Faulkner, *Concise Dictionary*, pp.73 and 76. Note the variation wdḥw on p. 73.
23. M. Smith (1993). *The Liturgy of Opening the Mouth for Breathing* (Griffith Institute, Oxford), p.16.
24. Smith. Ibid., p.41.
25. Gardiner. *Egyptian Grammar*, p. 529.
26. Leo Depuydt (1999). *Fundamentals of Egyptian Grammar I: Elements* (Frog Publishing, Norton, Mass.), pp.14–16; J. P. Allen, *Middle Egyptian*, pp. 2–3 and 23.
27. From the Latin *amphorae* (singular *amphora*), derived from the Greek *amphoreus, amphiphoreus*.
28. Gardiner. Ibid., pp. 529, 596.
29. Faulkner, *Concise Dictionary*, p. 278.
30. A. Erman and H. Grapow (1926, 1963, 1982). *Wörterbuch der Aegyptischen Sprache*, Vol. 5 (Akademie Verlag, Berlin), p. 22.
31. Gardiner. *Egyptian Grammar*, p. 529; Faulkner. *Middle Egyptian*, p. 176.
32. Gardiner, *Egyptian Grammar*, p. 596; Faulkner, *Concise Dictionary*, p. 277; A. Erman and H. Grapow, *Wörterbuch der Aegyptischen Sprache*, Vol. 5, pp. 22–31.
33. Erman and Grapow, *Wörterbuch*, Vol. V, pp. 22–31.
34. J. Okoro Ijoma (2010). *The Igala and their Neighbours*, p. 15. Emphasis added.
35. For example, John Coltrane's use of the term, in an interview on Swedish radio in September, 1960, to describe the album "Giant Steps," released in 1959. Conversation with Prof. Herbert Ekwe-Ekwe. 4th October, 2006.
36. Erman and Grapow, Vol.V, p. 27.
37. Faulkner, *Concise Dictionary*. p. 277 regarding "pour a libation" and p. 211 for the case of "make libation."
38. Jomo Kenyatta (1965) *Facing Mount Kenya* (Vintage Books, New York), p. 223.
39. Sarpong, *Libation*, p.15.
40. Ibid.
41. Gardiner, p.560; Faulkner, p. 57; Allen, *Middle Egyptian*, p.56.
42. Faulkner, *Concise Dictionary*, p.57.
43. *Wörterbuch*, Vol. I, p. 283.
44. Obenga, "La parenté égyptienne …," pp. 141, 151, etc.
45. Allen, *Middle Egyptian*, p. 56.
46. Note the honorific transposition. The term ⌐Nṯr: *Netjer* is written first although it is pronounced last. This is to show respect for divinity. (For further explication consult "The Spiritual Significance of the Flag" in Chapter Six). Obenga, "La parenté égyptienne …," pp. 145, 146, translates this term as *prophète*, that is, "prophet," probably following Faulkner. *Middle Egyptian*, p.169, and Gardiner. *Egyptian Grammar*, p. 581, who adds that this was "the highest grade of priests." The descriptive title "servant of the divinity," a literal translation from the *Medew Netjer*, will be preferred in this work. For possible

objections to the rendition "prophet," a term first imposed by the Greeks, consult I. Shaw and P. Nicholson (1995). *British Museum Dictionary of Ancient Egypt* (British Museum Press, London), pp.228–229; Adolf Erman (1894, 1971). Trans. H. M. Tirad. *Life in Ancient Egypt* (Dover Publications, Inc., New York), p. 289; and, notably, Alan Gardiner (1961). *Egypt of the Pharaohs* (Oxford University Press), p. 87, note 1.
47. Gardiner, *Egyptian Grammar*, p. 555. See also p. 621 for this term.
48. A.M. Blackman (1916). "Libations to the Dead in Modern Nubia and Ancient Egypt" *Journal of Near Eastern Studies*. Vol. III, p. 32.
49. Herodotus, *The Histories*, p. 143.
50. Consult, for example, Anne K. Capel and Glenn E. Markoe (1996. eds.) *Mistress of the House, Mistress of Heaven: Women in Ancient Egypt*. (Hudson Hill Press Inc., New York), pp. 115–117. The reference to Libation is on p. 116. Note also Miriam Ma'at Monges. (1997) *Kush: The Jewel of Nubia: Reconnecting the Root System of African Civilization*. (Africa World Press, Trenton, New Jersey), pp. 137–140; Rosalie David, *Religion and Magic in Ancient Egypt*, pp. 199, 306–307, 331; S. Pernigotti (1997). "Priests" in S. Donadoni (ed.) *The Egyptians* (The University of Chicago Press, Chicago and London), pp. 140–141; J. G. Wilkinson, *The Ancient Egyptians* Vol. I, pp. 316–319.
51. Karenga. *Maat: The Moral Ideal in Ancient Egypt*, p. 78.
52. Théophile Obenga (1996). "La parenté égyptienne: Considérations sociologiques" ⸻ *Revue D'Égyptologie et des civilisations africaines*. Nos.4/5,p.146.
53. Clinton A. Hutton (2005). *The Logic and Historical Significance of the Haitian Revolution and the Cosmological Roots of Haitian Freedom* (Arawak Publications, Kingston, Jamaica), pp. 80, 85 and 118.
54. Jessie Gaston Mulira (1991), "The Case of Voodoo in New Orleans" in Joseph E. Holloway (ed.) *Africanisms in American Culture* (Indiana University Press, Bloomington and Indianapolis), pp. 49–56.
55. Faulkner, *Concise Dictionary*, p.57.
56. Gardiner, *Egyptian Grammar*, p. 553.
57. Faulkner, *Concise Dictionary*, p.16.
58. Erman and Grapow, *Wörterbuch*, Vol.I, p. 64.
59. Gardiner, *Egyptian Grammar*, p.560.
60. R. M. Janssen and Jac J. Janssen (1996). *Getting Old in Ancient Egypt* (The Rubicon Press, London), pp. 50–51.
61. Christian Jacq (Trans. J. M. Davis, 1985). *Egyptian Magic* (Aris & Phillips, Ltd., Warminster), p.12.
62. "Nefer-rohu: The Prophecy" in Asante and Abarry (eds.). *African Intellectual Heritage*, p.65, from J. A. Wilson (trans.) "The Prophesy of Nefer-rohu" in J. B. Pritchard (ed. 1969). *Ancient Near Eastern Texts Relating to the Old Testament*. 3rd *Edition (Princeton NJ, The University of Princeton Press)*, pp. 444–446.
63. M. Lichtheim (trans. and ed.,1975). *Ancient Egyptian Literature. Volume I: The Old and Middle Kingdoms* (University of Los Angeles Press, Berkeley), p. 144.
64. R. B. Parkinson (trans., 1997). 'The Words of Neferti' in *The Tale of Sinuhe and Other Ancient Egyptian Poems, 1940–1640 BC* (Oxford University Press), p. 139.
65. Smith. *The Liturgy of Opening the Mouth*, pp. 30–31.
66. Ibid., p. 42.
67. Papyrus No. 10188, BM, as quoted in Wallis Budge, *From Fetish To God In Ancient Egypt*, p. 527.
68. R. O. Faulkner. (Translator) *The Ancient Egyptian Pyramid Texts*, p.4.

69. *The Pyramid Texts* as quoted in Blackman,"The Significance of Incense and Libations in Funerary and Temple Ritual" *ZÄS*. Vol. 50, p. 71.
70. Adapted from Ibid.
71. Jacob H. Carruthers (1984). *Essays in Ancient Egyptian Studies* (University of Sankore Press, Los Angeles), pp. 19–23; C. A. Diop (1991) *Civilization or Barbarism: An Authentic Anthropology* (Lawrence Hill and Company, New York), p.108. See also W. E. B. Du Bois (1915) *The Negro* (Henry Holt and Co., New York), pp. 21, 46 and du Bois (1965). *The World and Africa: An inquiry into the part which Africa has played in world history*. (International Publishers, New York), p. 106 for this general conclusion about the origins of the people of Kemet.
72. Blackman, "The Significance ..." p.71; Smith. *The Liturgy of Opening the Mouth*, p. 43.
73. Gardiner, *Egyptian Grammar*, p. 596. Gardiner's orthography omits the final consonant, ⌘:w, which is easily attested from the variations given above from the *Wörterbuch*, the first of which is a full phonetic spelling.
74. Erman and Grapow, *Wörterbuch*, Vol. V, p. 29.
75. Gardiner, Ibid., p. 560.
76. Charles Finch (1994). "Nile Genesis: Continuity of Culture from the Great Lakes to the Delta" in Ivan Van Sertima (ed.). *Egypt Child of Africa* (Transaction Publishers, New Brunswick and London), pp. 38–39.
77. Erman and Grapow, Ibid. Literally "Master of the Cataracts," but more precisely "Owner of the Cataracts;" from ⌣ = "owner of."
78. Chancellor Williams (1976). *The Destruction of Black Civilization: Great Issues of a Race From 4500 B.C. to 2000 A.D.* (Third World Press, Chicago), pp. 36, 110, 136.
79. Christian Jacq. (trans. J. Davis 1988?). *Egyptian Magic*. (Aris & Phillips Ltd., Warminster), p.64.
80. Serge Sauneron (trans. D. Lorton, 2000). *The Priests of Ancient Egypt* (Cornell University Press, Ithaca and London), pp. 36–42; David, *Religion and Magic in Ancient Egypt*, pp. 200–202; Pernigotti, p. 123, quoting Herodotus, and pp, 134, 136 and 142–143; Wilkinson, *The Ancient Egyptians Vol. 1*, pp. 324–325, 333, 335; Herodotus, pp. 143–144.
81. Alan H. Gardiner (1938). "The Mansion of Life and the Master of the King's Largess." *Journal of Egyptian Archaeology*. No. 24, p.87; Erman and Grapow, *Wörterbuch*, Vol. III, pp. 422–424 and 489.
82. There is a significant difference among scholars on the interpretation of this term. E. A. Wallis Budge (Translation and transliteration, 1895, 1967). *The Egyptian Book of the Dead* (Dover Publications, Inc., New York), p. xxx; Maulana Karenga (1990). *The Book of Coming Forth By Day: The Ethics of the Declarations of Innocence* (University of Sankore Press, Los Angeles), and others, render it "Coming Forth" while R. O. Faulkner, O. Goelet (see below) and others render it "Going Forth." Part of the difficulty encountered by some scholars appears to reside in the fact that in the *Medew Netjer* the verb ⌘ prw in this position means "coming forth," "going forth" as well as "going up." (Gardiner. *Egyptian Grammar*, pp. 609 and 614; R.O. Faulkner. *A Concise Dictionary of Middle Egyptian*, p. 90; J. P. Allen, *Middle Egyptian*, p. 458). Goelet's observation, which is that "the work was written from the viewpoint of the deceased, not of the living," seems decisive. Consult Ogden Goelet, Jr. "A Commentary on the Corpus of Literature and Tradition which constitutes The Book of Going Forth by Day" in R.O.

Faulkner (Trans. 1988, 1994). *The Egyptian Book of the Dead: The Book of Going Forth by Day*. (Chronicle Books, San Francisco, 1988), p.158. Consideration of the third meaning of this term, especially when we recall that this verb refers to the motion of the *Ba* or "soul" of the deceased, which we know that the Egyptians believed did "go up" to the heavens among other things, appears even more decisive in favour of the notion of "going forth" or "going up." All of this, when taken in conjunction with the notion of "day"—the final term in the title—suggests that the exact rendition of the title of the text is something of the order of "The Book of Going Forward into Enlightenment," with a less figurative meaning being "The Book of Developing Greater Understanding."

83. The correct name of this town is 'Iwnw, which has been rendered variously as *Iunwu* and *Anu*, and as On in the Bible.

84. Faulkner (trans. 1994, 1998). *The Egyptian Book of the Dead: The Book of Going Forth by Day*. (Chronicle Books, San Francisco), p. 129.

85. J. G. Wilkinson, *The Ancient Egyptians Vol. I*, p. 76.

86. Jacq, pp. 36–37.

87. For a good explanation of this important idea of good and beautiful speech in Kemet consult Jacob Carruthers (1995). *Mdw Ntr. Divine Speech*. (Karnak House, London).

88. Faulkner (trans.). *Pyramid Texts*, p. 39.

89. R. O. Faulkner (trans. 1985, 1996). *The Ancient Egyptian Book of the Dead* (The British Museum Press, London), p. 32

90. Variation, full phonetic writing is : dhwty: Dhwty, a name that was widely written with the appellation : nb mdw ntr , hence : *Djhuty, neb medew netjer*: Djhuty, Lord of Knowledge, often given in the literal meaning 'Lord of the words of God'.

91. Faulkner (trans. 1994, 1998). *The Egyptian Book of the Dead: The Book of Going Forth by Day*. (Chronicle Books, San Francisco), p. 133.

92. Karenga. *Maat: The Moral Ideal in Ancient Egypt*, pp.69–71.

93. Carruthers, *Mdw Ntr. Divine Speech*, p. 45.

94. R. O. Faulkner (trans. 1985, 1996). *The Ancient Egyptian Book of the Dead*, p. 170; See also Faulkner (trans. 1994, 1998). *The Egyptian Book of the Dead: The Book of Going Forth by Day*. (Chronicle Books, San Francisco), p. 129.

95. Faulkner. *The Egyptian Book of the Dead: The Book of Going Forth by Day*. (Chronicle Books, San Francisco), p.129.

96. For example, Faulkner, *The Pyramid Texts*, (Oxford University Press, 1969; Warminister, England: Aris and Phillips, nd), Utterances 32, 33, 34, 35, 36 on pp.6–8, etc. Consult also Obenga, *African Philosophy*, p. 241.

97. E. A. Wallis Budge. Trans. (1895). *The Egyptian Book of the Dead: The Papyrus of Ani* (Dover Publications, Inc. New York), p.15.

98. Faulkner, The Egyptian ... Book of Going Forth by Day, p.107.

99. The Ancient Egyptian *Book of the Heavenly Cow*, as quoted in F. Lexa (1925). *La magie dans l'Egypte antique, de l'ancien Empire jusqu'à l'époque copte*. Vol.II, Paris, pp. 51–52, as quoted in turn in C. Jacq. *Egyptian Magic*, p.37.

100. J. A. Wilson (trans.) "The Mythological Origin of Certain Unclean Animals" in J. B. Pritchard (ed., 1969). *Ancient Near Eastern Texts Relating to the Old Testament* 3rd Edition. (University of Princeton Press, Princeton, NJ), p. 10; Faulkner, *The Egyptian ... Book of Going Forth by Day*, Chapter 112, p. 114.

101. R. H. Wilkinson (1998). *Reading Egyptian Art* (Thames and Hudson, London), p. 61. For similar observations see J. G. Wilkinson, *The Ancient Egyptians, Vol. I*, pp. 322–325; Herodotus, p.148.

102. Kimani Nehusi (2000). "The Origins of Carnival: Notes from a Preliminary Investigation." In Ian Smart and Kimani Nehusi (eds.). *Ah Come Back Home: Perspectives on the Trinidad and Tobago Carnival.* (Original World Press, Washington, DC and Port of Spain), pp.77–103.

103. For examples see Opoku, pp. 76–78.

104. For further explanation of these terms consult Kimani Nehusi. "Language in the Construction of Afrikan Unity …", pp. 223–225.

Chapter Three

The Origins and Evolution of the Offering Complex

The collection of related values, attitudes, ritual behaviours and material aids, which we have chosen to term the offering complex, arose from the way in which humanity conceptualised divinity in Afrika. Much of this is founded upon the powers Afrikans attributed to the divine—or more accurately, the divine status Afrikan humanity gave to nature, its manifestations and its power. The offering complex exerted a profound influence on how humanity, first in Afrika and then in other parts of the world, has sought to propitiate the divine. There is evidence to suggest that at first, the notion of offering was in practice represented in a single ritual. However, for much of the known history of the practice of offering, it has been represented by a number of distinct rituals. These include sacrifice or blood offering in which life was offered; libation or drink offering; censing or the offering of burning incense; voice offerings, including prayers, praises and the libation statement; first fruits or the offering of the first and best of the harvest; and the offering of miscellaneous other material things. Each of these offerings was also considered the best that humanity had to give. The two apparently contradictory trajectories of integration and separation have resided side by side during the known history of this offering complex. This constellation of related rituals, and the beliefs upon which they were founded and which they articulate in dramatic fashion, became a very powerful force in regulating society in Kemet, as well as in other Afrikan societies both before and after Kemet.

4.1: *The Origin and Purpose of Offering Rituals*

There is a latent and often unarticulated threat, though perhaps a not inarticulate one, which is resident in the presence of the ritual complex of offerings in human society. It is the devastating consequences for not obtaining and maintaining the satisfaction of the divinities. This understanding points towards both the origins and the ultimate purpose of this ritual complex. Undoubtedly, the idea of pleasing the divinities, and so pacifying them, is a very ancient one, born when humanity may have scarcely understood the world and often felt threatened, at times even overwhelmed, by some of its uncontrollable elements—those natural forces that still cause havoc among us today, such as earthquakes, volcanoes, fire, floods, droughts, lightning, and thunder. Some of these forces were envisaged as aspects of the Creator and were therefore regarded as divine. They were also invested with human attributes. Some were benevolent, some malevolent; others a combination of the two. In Kemet the divinity Shu was air; Tefnut was moisture, Geb the earth, and Nut the sky. It was the widespread belief that they visited when the divine was displeased. The fear of disorder led to the development of powerful concepts, aimed at bringing order and security to society, such as ˧sema, the basis of ᛗSematawy or the United Two Lands, ⁂dd *Djed*, the representation of stability,[1] and the notion of ⸺ (variation ⸺) M3ꜥt: *Maat*, which has been discussed in Chapter One.

The periodic ravages of nature occasioned great insecurity in human populations, especially those repeatedly touched by these forces. There was a need for permanent psychological, social and material security in the face of these constant threats to existence represented by danger that appeared to originate beyond human comprehension or control. Why would the social order and security be periodically disrupted? What force or forces could offer such profound threat to humanity and its relations to the world? The only force that humanity admitted as greater than humanity itself was the divine. And surely, the catastrophic nature of such visitations dictated that they be born of anger or of some other expression of great displeasure. But none can conquer that which they do not understand or control. It was this particular understanding of these forces which led humanity to the conclusion that even though with time they might have eventually understood such forces, they could not exercise direct control over them. They needed to be pacified instead.

The line of reasoning that led to the conclusion above must have soon arrived at another deduction. This was that it was much better not to await te next eruption of chaos, but to act strategically to stave off some such event before it could reoccur. Such a desirable outcome was to be achieved through ensuring the continuous pacification of these cosmic powers by making them regular gifts or offerings, in kind, of the best humanity had to give, with of course the accompanying appeals in words. Hence, the solution to the fundamental threat posed to humanity would be found in the realm of spirituality. It is here that we once again encounter ideas, material aides and practices that demonstrate how humans relate to the Creator and to other cosmic forces.

So was born one of the most important ideas of humanity, and the practices through which people sought to make it real in daily life: Offerings; gifts to the divinities, the better in quality and the greater in frequency and intensity, the greater the chance of pleasing these most powerful beings in the universe and so of preserving the cosmic order and the human place in it. First in Afrika, then elsewhere, humans made offerings of life and liquid (liquor or not,) and an assortment of other articles that were thought to represent the best that humanity had to give, and to do so even in circumstances that were often materially challenging. It was a burden of giving imposed upon all givers by the regime of offering, a burden accepted fully, even willingly and joyfully, by the most conscientious celebrants. This is an attitude that illustrates the deeper meaning of sacrifice—and demonstrates that this idea may embrace all forms of offerings. For those who believed in this concept, and performed with sufficient regularity and commitment the necessary sacrifices, including libations and other offerings, nature held less terror now, or even none. The idea and practice of giving up the best to the most powerful, in order to receive in return something valuable that one cannot provide for oneself, constitute the basis of a very ancient complex of values, beliefs, attitudes and attendant ritual action that throughout the world came to be associated with divinities. This complex was in some instances also occasioned by attitudes to ancestors and potentates—who were both just as often considered divine.

4.2: ḥtp: *Pleasing the Divinities*

In Kemet the effort to please the cosmic forces came to be represented in the term ḥtp: "peace," "satisfied," etc. Its significance was pointed out in the previous chapter. In order to understand more about the ritual of libation itself, especially its origin, early transformation and development, it is necessary to revisit this term and seek to trace and understand its full ramifications. It is also necessary to examine terms that designated material aides used in the offering complex as well as terms designating ritual ideas and activity in this complex. The results appear to throw much light upon the origins, nature and development of the entire offering complex. Our understanding of libation is enhanced significantly when we consider its historically more recent manifestations against the background of what we have learnt about these ancient origins, organisation and purpose of this and related ritual activity.

It is important to recall that the range of meanings supplied in the previous chapter for the term ḥtp includes "rest, go to rest, be at peace, pleased, be pleased, be happy, be gracious, pardon, be peaceful, become calm, satisfy, make content" and "pacify." All of these meanings are captured and conveyed in the causative verb sḥtp, meaning "propitiate," "pacify;" that is, to make peaceful, to make satisfied, and so on: to bring about the state(s) articulated above in ⟨ḥtp⟩. This is exactly the objective of libation, sacrifice and indeed all other offerings and activities in the offering complex, which were always primarily a collection of ritual behaviours aimed at appeasing the divine powers.

4.3: ⟨⟩ *The Offering Table and the Altar*

The structure of the term ⟨⟩ is significant. It is composed of three parts. The first is ⟨⟩, which is in turn made up of θ, a loaf that is placed on a reed mat. In the Old Kingdom ⟨⟩: the loaf on a reed mat, had the phonetic value of Htp and signified "altar"[2] or offering table, as well as "offering."[3] This is exactly reflective of reality in early Kemet, for this arrangement of a loaf on a reed mat "doubtless reflect[ed] the most basic method of presenting an offering."[4] At that early stage there appeared to be no distinction between an offering table and an altar, for no such separation is reflected in the language at this time.

The consonants ⟨t⟩ and ⟨p⟩ add phonetic reinforcement to ⟨⟩ and ensure that there is no doubt about the orthography and so the term intended. In this position they are known as phonetic complements. Hence the signs in this term read, literally, ḥtp+t+p, but the word intended is ḥtp. The consonant t here is also represented by another kind of loaf: ⟨⟩. But unlike the loaf in ⟨⟩, it is only the sound that is conveyed in this case; the actual object has nothing to do with the meaning of the term.

Both the loaf and the reed mat held great and long-standing practical and symbolic value to the people of Kemet. A reed mat, to sleep upon, was one of the few personal possessions of the rural folk, mainly agricultural workers, who made up the vast majority of the people of Kemet. It was an essential item, known from the earliest times.[5] Bread was an essential item in the diet of all in the land and the only staple of the ordinary people. It was produced in loaves of different shapes, with the round, oval and conical predominating. In New Kingdom times (ca 1550–1070 BCE), there were some forty terms for different types of bread and cakes produced in Kemet.[6] However, both this importance and this complexity had been reflected in the Medew Netjer from the very beginning of the latter, long before the New Kingdom era, and so this item must have been of very great value even before the invention of writing. In the Old Kingdom the sign for the half-loaf of bread: ⟨⟩ was the ideogram or determinative for the concept "food," as is illustrated in words such as wšb: "eat" and ⟨⟩, variation ⟨⟩, wnm: "eat" and even in ⟨⟩ snw: "food-offerings."[7] The great significance of bread to the ancient Egyptians is also reflected by the popularity of signs for this item in Gardiner's sign list at X, which accords "Loaves and Cakes" an entire section, listing some eight different signs.[8] More recent scholarship attests a significantly greater number of signs in this group.[9]

There can be no doubt about the above interpretation of ⟨ḥtp⟩, for the stroke under the sign signifies that the meaning is exactly what is physically represented. Since both the loaf and the reed mat were very old articles used extensively in the daily life of Kemet and since they are also the basis of signs representing certain concepts in the Medew Netjer, a loaf on a reed mat as a sign in the Medew Netjer also suggests a very early date; it must have been one of the earliest kinds of altars known to the people of Kemet. Wilkinson concurs: "From prehistoric times offerings were made to the gods and to deceased persons on small mats of woven reeds."[10]

Later altars, introduced at the beginning of the Old Kingdom, were far more elaborate and durable, being constructed of stone. There was clearly evolution in form, and to some extent function, from offering mat to offering table then to altar. The offering table was essentially a more robust and permanent version of the offering mat of reed. Small, and constructed of more durable material, it was individual rather than private and used extensively in personal and family shrines as well as in temples. The altar was the grand version of its two predecessors. Huge and permanent, it was constructed from the hardiest of materials and designed as the focus of the major activity during rituals. Conceived and constructed as the ritual cornerstone of the temple, it still serves this function to this day.

The terminology of the Medew Netjer appears to reflect this evolution from reed mat to permanent altar. Faulkner translates ḥtp as "altar," while Gardiner gives both "altar" and "table of offerings."[11] However, both also supply ḫ3wt and its variations as "altar,"[12] though Gardiner also lists it as "table of offerings."[13] The loaf on the reed mat is absent from the second term. It is quite possible that this is a new term which is tied to the relatively new concept of a large and permanent offering table, an object that is significantly different from its forerunner. The new concept is distinguished by this perhaps new and certainly different term. In time the new concept would be designated almost exclusively by the new term, altar. Here a change in terminology reflects a change in physical and conceptual reality. Again we behold language as a faithful witness to and record of reality.

But it was the ancient model, consisting of the woven mat with offerings upon it, which proved archetypical. The predominant material offering was bread, and so the loaf became symbolic of offerings in general. This model remained very dominant, even in the new reality of altars. As it dominated the origin and conception of altars, so too did this archetype influence the more minute details of their design. Altars were often made in the form of the offering sign, complete with a frontal projection that represented the bread loaf, or with the hieroglyph for the offering mat carved on top. Sometimes the woven mat and bread loaf were carved on the stone altars, as were other offerings such as jars of water, ducks, meat and so on. Channels as well as cups and grooves were cut into the table top to receive liquids poured in libation out of special ceremonial vessels. It is these ceremonial vessels, (singular $\bigcirc$: hst in the Medew Netjer; amphora in Egyptology), that form the five signs from W14 to W18 in Gardiner's sign list. Carvings of the Htp or offering sign dominate some of the most impressive surviving examples of stone altars, such as the altar in the sun temple of Nyuserra (2445–2421 BCE) at the site now called Abu Gurab on the west bank of the Nile, between Giza and Sakkara, and the pink granite altar in the temple of Amun at Karnak.[14] The pictures at numbers 17 and 18 of the photospread show offering tables, which are personal miniature altars with vessels and channels carved out on their surfaces.

There can be hardly any doubt about the factors that occasioned ⌒ becoming representative of the very idea of offering, as well as an important part of the representation of a number of related concepts in the Medew Netjer. First was the great spiritual significance of the reed mat in the offering complex. The second factor was the overwhelmingly huge economic and social importance of the loaf, which propelled it to very great spiritual significance also. These added up to the tremendous economic, social and spiritual importance of the offering mat. Clearly, the offering mat dominated the ancient Egyptian's idea and practice of offering, and did so for the entire existence of the state of Kemet, perhaps from even before its inception. It is for this reason that the dominant sign of the offering mat with a loaf upon it became the determinative in an entire class of words that signify offering rituals, some of the ritual activity, as well as some of the items used in these rituals.

The further significance of the notion of ⌒ in Kemet is therefore illustrated in the terms for a number of the articles (and practices) by and through which the divinities were propitiated. Such terms are conceptually and structurally rooted in ⌒. They all refer to different types of invocation offerings made to ancestors or to divinities. At first the theory was that the giver of all offerings was the nsw or king, as Heru, son and heir to Wsir (Osirus), ruler of the afterlife. By the Middle Kingdom certain divinities, such as Inpu (Anubis), Wasir and Geb, were also givers. But in practice it was the person and his/her family who gave, for it was they who provided the material offerings. This is the understanding current among practitioners today. Here are some examples of terms rooted in the idea of giving:

⌒ htp(w), htp: "offerings;" "food offerings."

⌒ htpw ntr, "offerings to the divinities" or ⌒: pr(t)-hrw-(htpw)-ntr literally, "sending forth/sending up of voice offerings,"[15] i.e. "voice offerings" to the divinity, hence "divine offerings." This is the oldest recorded reference to what would become, over millennia of evolution, prayers and the Libation Statement. These developments are discussed below.

⌒ shtpy: censer. This term may be analysed grammatically as the following elements: ⌒, a causative particle; ⌒ = "peace," etc. ; ⌒, a noun ending or suffix and ⌒, the graphic representation of a censor, here indicating literally the same. In this context it has the function of a sense sign or determinative. The meaning is thus "the thing that causes to be at peace." That is a statement about the fundamental purpose of censing, which is to help create a calm and otherwise enabling atmosphere for spiritual presences in the process of propitiating ancestors and divinities, a process that itself ensures peace. This instrument was very often made in the form of the "offering" arm, which will be discussed presently. The design consisted of a handle that was normally the length of a forearm, a hand at one end holding a bowl in which the incense was burned, and sometimes a small box near to the other end of the "arm" for keeping the pellets of incense. Many designs were based upon this basic concept. It is very likely that the use of censer arms was instructed by the necessity to avoid holding the hot censer bowl as well as the duty to present the incense to a divinity in a way that avoided touching the divine image while maintaining a respectful distance from it.[16]

The central idea of pleasing the divine, as well as the range of ritual activity calculated to achieve this objective, and too, some of the paraphernalia generated by these rituals, were therefore rooted in the notion of ⚱. This objective of pleasing the divinities, and therefore creating and maintaining peace between these most powerful beings and humanity, was at the centre of all these practices that constitute offerings, including libation or drink offering, sacrifice or blood offering, where blood signifies life, and the offering up of other articles that were neither drink nor the life of an animal, but were also regarded as among the best humanity had to offer. It is this idea of presenting the best to the divine beings, who are the highest class of beings in the cosmos, that in Kemet dictated the formulaic ḫt nb(t) nfr(t) wꜣb(t) ꜥnḫt nṯr, literally: "all things good and pure (upon which) a divinity lives," which has been mentioned before. To the ancient Egyptian, giving the best to the most powerful was the quintessential representation of giving. The articles in this category presented were each distinguished by being of the best quality, which also implied that they were the purest, for example, linen, perfume, oils; or of the greatest significance in some other regard: the first fruits of the harvest, or the best returns from the same, the choicest cuts of meat, or possessing some such mark of distinction. Born of desperate times when humanity felt perpetually threatened by cosmic forces, this very idea of presenting only the best to divinity in return for protection is still fundamental to offering rituals in Afrika and elsewhere.

Offerings, by both derivation and meaning, are special gifts to the divine in return for the promotion of the wellness of the offerer and those on whose behalf the gifts are offered. In Kemet a list of offerings was intended to sustain the ka (i.e. vital force, spirit) of the deceased. However, it is also clear that offerings, praises (often in the form of praise names or epithets) and petitions were also addressed to divinities. These practices, and the values and beliefs that instructed them, are alive in contemporary Afrika.

Offerings have been of such great importance in the Afrikan spiritual tradition from the earliest times that declarations that one did not default in this important regard are required and so included at several points in the Declarations of Innocence,[17] in Chapter 125 of *The Book of Going Forth by Day*:

I have not destroyed the food-offerings
I have not lessened the food-offerings in the temples.
I have not destroyed the loaves of the gods;
I have not taken away the food of the spirits.
I have not neglected the dates for offering choice meats;
I have not withheld cattle from the god's offerings.[18]

Even after the spirit of the deceased person has been found pure and true, through not having transgressed these and other rules, an affirmative declaration on this matter is needed as part of the address to the divinities in the Great Hall of *Maati*, the Great Hall of Justice:

I have given god's-offerings to the gods and incantation offerings to the spirits.[19]

As can be expected, the influence of a concept as powerful as ☥ was felt well beyond its initial location in the offering complex. A large number of names from Kemet also incorporated the concept ☥, where it means 'peace' or 'satisfied' and was often appended to the name of a divinity, though this was not the only combination employed. Examples used in this text include 𓇍𓏏𓊵𓏙 Imhotep, 𓇋𓏠𓈖𓊵𓏙 Amenhotep, son of Hapu and Ptahhotep in Chapter Four. Other examples include Neithhotep *et al.*

The ancient Egyptian word ☥ htp, vocalised as *Hotep* and meaning, literally, "[I/we wish you] peace" or "Greetings," and its plural form, ☥ htpw, *Hotepu*, have been revived by some elements of the Afrikan centered community as an appropriate form of greeting, in a similar way to which the Yoruba term Asé has gained popular currency in the conscious Afrikan community around the world, as is partly shown in Chapter One. This is a restoration of a very ancient and profound notion and wish for peace and therefore balance, harmony and the other aspects of Maat, not only within the self and on earth, but in the entire cosmos.

4.4: *Notions of Giving*

The idea and practice of offering were so important in ancient Egyptian life, and must have been so from very early times, that when the 𓊹𓌃𓂧𓏛 *Medew Netjer* was invented, the signs that represent notions of giving, that is the ideograms or determinatives for words for giving, were predominantly selected from the offering complex. Examples are found in the words for "give:" 𓂞, variation 𓂝, which reads rdi: *redi*, 𓂞 variation 𓂟: di *di*, meaning "(that) (he) may give;" the imperative 𓇋𓅓𓂝: imi ("You) give"—a command—and the infinitive 𓂞 or 𓂟, both read rdit redit: "to give."

Four determinatives or sense signs predominate in these words. The first is 𓂞; the second 𓂟, the third is 𓂝 and the fourth 𓂟. Each of these had its origins in, and was chosen from, the offering complex. Gardiner explains the origin of 𓂞:

The sign 𓂞 characteristic of the verb ['give'] is probably an ideogram representing a loaf brought as a gift; for this, from the early Middle Kingdom onwards, is often substituted as a purely graphical variant 𓂟, 𓂝, or even 𓂟, the latter two being due to confusion of the signs in hieratic.[275]

The sign ⌒ is composed of a forearm: —, which is holding an offering loaf: ∧. In the Middle Kingdom, especially in the Eighteenth Dynasty, the forearm with a hand holding a rounded loaf: ⌒, was employed as the determinative in the command "(You) give" as above. The forearm with hand holding an offering bowl ⌒ provides the central meaning or determinative for both 𓂝𓈖𓎡 ḥnk: *henek*: "present" and 𓂟𓂉 drp *derep*: "offer."[20] Hence the components of the determinatives, and so the determinatives themselves, in words that signify "give," "offering" and "present," are taken from the offering complex. This frequency of choice indicates how very popular and important offerings were, for this origin of these terms must mean that the central idea was likely to be known to most, if not to all, of the people of Kemet, and therefore the ideograms or determinatives—and so terms based upon them—were readily understood by many or most, if not by all in the speech community served and represented by the 𓏏𓏤𓃀𓀔. To the ancient Egyptian, the offering complex contained the most popular and representative notions of giving.

4.5: *The Offering Arm*

The human arm and hand, with forearm extended as in the act of giving, predominate in these graphic significations of give and giving. Of particular importance is the sign ⌒, which is known to Egyptologists as the "offering" arm. It is a composite of a forearm and a hand holding ○: an offering bowl of the kind held by *Nsu* (Pharaoh) Hatshepsut in the picture on the front cover of this text and by *Nsu* Pepi I and *Nsu* Taharka in Figures 7 and 8 respectively in the photospread. This composite sign "was used to signify the presentation of a libation offering to the [divinities]."[21] This "offering" arm became a very popular motif in the art of royalty in Kemet. Wilkinson is instructive on this point:

> The motif of a pious king presenting an offering before one of the gods was a favourite one in royal Egyptian art, and many monarchs were portrayed in this way from Middle Kingdom times on. In the reliefs and statuary showing this gesture, the king holds an identical bowl in each hand—one for each of the two parts of the kingdom—and usually the bowls are said to be filled with wine or milk, or simply cool water. In virtually all representational examples the king does not hold the offering out at arm's length, but the upper arms are kept parallel to the body and only the forearms are extended—in exactly the position of the hieroglyph.[22]

Surely, this was art imitating life, for in reality it was the glyph that was made to mirror humanity's pose when giving to the divine, not the other way around. The popularity of this representation indicates the importance attached to libation by the rulers of Kemet, a significance that obviously held implications for everyone in the country. The earliest known representation of this posture in the art of Kemet is a green slate statue of Nsu Pepi I (2278–2184

BCE), now in the Brooklyn Museum and reproduced at the afore mentioned Figure 7 in the photospread. These dates place Pepi near to the end of the Old Kingdom, yet firmly within it, a fact which appears to contradict Wilkinson's assertion, in the quote above, that this portrayal dates from the Middle Kingdom onwards. In Figure 8 in the photospread, Taharka, *nsw* in the Twenty Fifth Dynasty of Kemet, is shown in exactly this posture. This and the many other similar portrayals that are extant, including the one of Nsu Hatshepsut referred to above, illustrate a significant difference between the dominant practice of libation in the state of Kemet for most of its existence and in the modern Afrikan world. Pepi I, Hatshepsut and Taharka present the drink offering with two hands, one bowl in each, a format that evidently became predominant in Kemet during the Old Kingdom and was thereafter repeated for the remainder of that state's very long history, in fact right down to the Late Period.[23]

However, the foregoing does not mean that libation was always presented with both hands in Kemet. There is evidence to suggest that at least on some occasions, the pouring of libation, and indeed the presentation of any offering, continued to be made either with one hand or with both hands.[24] There are many extant illustrations which show this clearly. The New Kingdom *Nsu*, Seti I (1291–1278 BCE), is depicted in two of these.[25] Further, figures 3 and 4, referred to in Chapter Two, show that in early Kemet offerings were presented with both hands (Figure 4) or with either hand, with the right hand being used in Figure 3. Other extant figures show that offerings could be made with both hands or with one hand.

The passage quoted above from Wilkinson provides the reason for the eventual predominant use of both hands, especially on official occasions. It was a double offering by the leader of the Two Lands (Upper and Lower Kemet), one bowl and so one offering was made for each part of the state.[26] The custom of a double offering was the way in which the powerful concept of the Two Lands came to be institutionalised in the official public performance of the ritual drama of libation in Kemet in order to symbolize the unity of the two aspects of the state and much more.

In the modern Afrikan world libation is made only with the right hand.[27] How and why this happened must be a line of future research. At the moment it is only to be speculated that for those who migrated from the Kemet/Nile Valley area, the powerful notion of the Two Lands ceased to hold sway over them, perhaps gradually. At present it is only to be imagined how the challenging conditions of migration and the increasing physical and emotional distance from the Two Lands loosened the bonds with this principle and lessened the need to give it dramatic effect in the ritual. In time, the new reality of a different environment was represented in a different way. Libation was now presented only with the right hand. Yet, again, this aspect of the ritual drama was a reflection of a social value and the social reality it instructed, for in modern Afrikan custom, the presentation of drink, like the eating of any food, falls into the sphere of those things that are done only with the right hand. This custom may indicate how in practice the presentation of the libation offering was changed so that the continuation of the ritual was assured.

4.6: ⸺𓂀𓂀 nis 3ḫw: *Invoking the Spirits*

The locations of the ritual offering were predominantly in the temple, the tombs and in private dwellings: "before the shrine, statue, or stele of the god or deceased parent."[28] There is significance in these locations. These were dedicated spaces, places specially constructed and consecrated; reserved for sacred ritual activity. They were the principal sites at which offerings were made to the divine and/or to the propitiated—the divinities and the ancestors, some of whom, we must remind ourselves, were divine. Offering tables and ancestral altars still abound in the living tradition of Afrika. Today they are to be found in personal, family and clan shrines as well as divinity centres, called churches or temples in some traditions.

A posture of respect and reverence, even devotion, was adopted by the offerer—devotee or not—in the sacred place. The Medew Netjer term for this posture is ⸺𓂀 *nis*: "calling or invoking,"[29] "call, summon."[30] Here, "[t]he offerer ... stands with arm upraised (𓂀) in the attitude of invocation ..."[31] in front of the statue or other sacred representation of the 3ḫw or spirits to be invoked. Postures and other acts of reverence when in the divine presence are discussed in Chapter Two. There is a famous representation of Pharaoh Seti I and his young son, later Ramesses II the Great, in the Hall of the Ancestors, intoning the names of previous Pharaohs in order to invoke their spirit. Intoning and invoking the names and so the spirit of the ancestors and the divinities, normally to give libations and/or other offerings and to ask for certain often specified favours, is known subsequently in the history of Afrikan spirituality. It is still current practice throughout the Afrikan world, including Afrika, the Americas and the Caribbean, where it is a very important aspect of libation and many other rituals.

In the 𓂋𓏏𓊪 the ritual offering of food was termed 𓂋𓏏𓊪𓏙 irt ḥtp-di-nsw, that is, "performing (the ritual named) Hotep-di-nesu." This last noun phrase may be translated as "a gift that the nsw gives" and, like the other foundational concepts through which the idea of offerings were articulated, is of a very ancient vintage. In the Old Kingdom it was used to indicate various kinds of gifts given by the nsw to his subjects and included "clothing, coffins, a sacrificial ox, ... or even the rank and title of prince."[32] The term also referred to various kinds of funerary gifts and benefits solicited from the nsw (who we must remember was regarded as a living divinity) or from *Inpw*, or *Wsir* or *Geb*. Some of the earliest known examples of the *hotep di nesu* occur in the Pyramid Texts. Utterance 172 runs thus:

> A boon which the [Nsu] and Gēb grant to this [Nsu]; there is given to you every offering and every oblation which you can desire, whereby it will be well with you before the god for ever and ever.[33]

80   *Chapter Three*

The last two paragraphs of Utterance 599 say:

> A boon which the [Nsu] grants and Gēb grants of these choice joints, invocation offerings for all gods who shall bring into being all good things for the [Nsu] and who shall cause to endure this construction and this pyramid of the [Nsu], in accordance with what the [Nsu] wishes in the matter, for ever and ever.
>
> O all you gods who shall cause this pyramid and this construction of the [Nsu] to be fair and endure: You shall be effective, you shall be strong, you shall have your souls, you shall have power, you shall have given to you a boon which the [Nsu] grants of bread and beer, oxen and fowl, clothing and alabaster; you shall receive your god's-offerings, you shall choose for yourselves your choice joints, you shall have your oblations made to you, you shall take possession of the Wrrt-crown in the midst of the Two Enneads.[34]

It may be of some significance that Faulkner terms this part of the utterance "A prayer for pyramid and offering." The people of Kemet called this a ⌑prt-ḥrw: a voice offering, which was a vocal appeal that always accompanied some material offering. Technically this is not a prayer, since the divinities are promised the usual gifts, which were at first all material. The trajectory that led to prayers, which are a vocal appeal without any accompanying material offering or inducement, is described in the discussion below.

The *hotep di nsw* formula was usually recorded on false door stelae,[35] other funerary stelae and the exterior of coffins. Examples are recorded in a variety of sources. Gardiner quotes a Twelfth Dynasty offering inscription:

𓏏𓊵𓂧𓇓𓈖𓇓𓏏 𓊨𓊨𓏏 𓎟𓊖 𓊹𓉻 𓎟𓍋𓃀𓈋𓊖 𓂞𓆑 𓉺𓐍𓂋𓏏𓈖𓉺𓅱 𓏏𓉺𓏥 𓇥𓏏𓅓𓃾𓅆𓏪 𓈙𓋴𓈘𓅓𓐍𓏏𓏪 𓏎𓏏𓎟𓏏𓄤𓏏𓋴𓃀𓏏 [36]

> A gift which the nsu gives to Wsir, Lord of Busiris, the great divinity, lord of Abydos, that he may give invocation-offerings consisting of bread and beer, oxen and fowl, alabaster and clothing, all things good and pure on which a divinity lives, to the spirit of the revered Senwosret, the justified one.

The form and structure of these and other examples of formulae suggest the following:

The divinities invoked and propitiated were, in this era, primarily the Nsu (a living divinity), as well as Gēb, Wsir and Inpu (Greek Anubis).

1. The articles offered were usually those thought to be the best material things of the land.
2. The list soon became formalised into specific named articles: "bread, beer, oxen, birds, alabaster and clothing," which was followed by the general enunciation of "all good and pure things upon which a divinity lives."
3. The things solicited were either very specific, as in the second example above, in which the construction of a pyramid was

the goal of the offering, or the general wellness in the relationship between the offerer and the divinity served, which is the first desire expressed in the same example.

4. Praises or acclamations were given to the divinities, often in the form of epithets or praise names. An example may be taken from Utterance 936 of the *Coffin Texts*, which is further analysed below:

> Anubis, Lord of the coffin, Lord of internment, Lord of invocation-offerings in the w3g-festival, in the Djhuty-festival, in the Sokar-festival, in the festival of the First of the Year, in the festival of the Opening of the Year, in all the goodly festivals of [Wsir].[37]

Praises and praise names were vocal wishes for honours to the divinities, including the nsu, as well as recitations of their roles and accomplishments. Praise names, praise poems, praise songs and praise hymns to the divine became aspects of a distinctive part of the offering practice of Kemet. Akhenaton's Hymn to the Aten, Neferhotep's Hymn to Ra as the owner of Maat and Montemhet's Prayer to Amen, are but three of the many known examples of praise hymns. The embellishment of these forms of praises and praising constitute evidence of the evolution of this vocal form of ritual expression into a distinctive Afrikan tradition of the voice. This is the first known notice of what would become a significant aspect of salutations on the Afrikan continent.

Lichtheim's translation of the Eighteenth Dynasty "Great Hymn to Osiris" contains one hundred and fifty nine lines of praises—and twelve lines of the standard offering formula.[38] The praises are translated in poetic format and the offering formula as narrative, but this spatial distribution provides a good indication of the evolution of what started out as the epithets of the divinities within the archetype offering ritual. By this time (roughly 1570–1293 BCE) the initial salutation, of which the epithets were a part, had grown to become an elaborate format of praises, which is still attached to the offering formula, though this latter is accorded far less space. Over time this trajectory led to a physical separation of one set of the praises and praising from the offering formula. A detailed reconstruction and analysis of the evolution of epithets into various forms of praises and blame is best not undertaken in this text. However, the conceptual and therefore physical separation of the epithet cum praise name/praise poem/praise song/praise hymn from the offering formula marked a decisive stage in that development. It announced the assumption of a separate ritual identity of yet another aspect of the archetype offering formula. The results are alive all over the Afrikan world today. The priesthood in contemporary Afrika continues to offer praises to various divinities, as their ancestors did in the ancient Nile Valley. The Supreme Being is often conceptualised and represented as Grand Ancestor[39] and Her/His attributes and roles articulated as Creator, King, Omnipotent, Transcendent, Immortal, Judge, and so on.[40] Such vocal renditions are offered particularly on formal occasions, including libation rituals.

There were further developments in the spoken and sung forms of expression that originated in the offering complex. Some aspects of praises and blame, such as adulation and ridicule of rulers and heroes, are now mostly independent of the offering context. Rulers, heroes and other successful persons are accorded numerous titles and salutations, and many poems and songs are composed, recited and sung in the honour or ridicule of them and their families. Today praise names, praise poems and praise songs are aspects of a very distinctive tradition of praise and blame that is still very much in use throughout the Afrikan world and in fact mark Afrikan culture as distinctive. Both the good and bad qualities, attributes and achievements of gods, rulers and heroes are articulated and celebrated in a tradition that currently includes the *jali* (griots) among the Mandinka speaking Afrikans in Senegal, Mali, Guinea and the Gambia, the *kwadwumfo* among the Akan in Ghana, the *maroka* in Northern Nigeria, the *imbongi* among the Nguni of southern Afrika (Zulu, Xhosa, Ndebele, etc.), the *umusizi* in Ruanda in Central Afrika, the *nyatiti* among the Luo in Kenya and the *udje* poetry that is sung among the Urhobo people in south western Nigeria.[41] This tradition also includes the *kaiso*, a specific form of this expression which is popular in the Caribbean, extends the subject to scrutiny of anyone and anything in society, and is delivered in song.[42] It also includes such related forms as the Mento, and has also influenced Rap, Hip Hop and similar forms in the Caribbean and the Americas. But ultimately all these forms of the word have at least part of their genesis in the original offering ritual.

4.7: *An Integrated Ritual*

Praise poems, praise songs and praise hymns, and in fact the tradition of praise and blame, do not form an isolated example of a developmental trajectory out of and away from an archetype offering ritual. It may be noticed that the other examples of rituals mentioned above were in most instances also only parts of a much larger ritual that appears to have been the first format for offerings. It integrated various aspects, each of which subsequently became more distinct and in some cases separate offering rituals. The early rudimentary and integrated format is illustrated in one example of an early offering ceremony that is intact in Utterance 936 of R. O. Faulkner's translation of the *Coffin Texts*. Consuming six pages and clearly a funeral ceremony, it is much too large to reprint in full here. But it is apposite to examine its form, content and functions.

The entire ceremony consists mainly of a series of ritual actions, almost every one of which is followed by a corresponding utterance that contains some praises to the divinity, followed in turn, regularly but not in every instance, by an expression of a wish of the offerer(s) or an even more direct solicitation of something specific from the divinity being propitiated. The first part is occupied by a *hotep di nsu* ceremony. This is followed by libation with water, then censing, the expression of wishes, another libation, more censing—here with three different types of incense, presentation of five different types of oil, then presentation of a substantial number of different articles. At this point an invocation offering is presented and the instruction to sit down to eat it follows. This instruction suggests that the first part of the ceremony was undertaken with the participants standing. It demonstrates a dramatic element that reminds the observer of the origin and essence of the offering complex in the ritual dramatisation of a deeply felt need to propitiate cosmic forces.[43] The ceremony proceeds with the presentation of an even more substantial number of other articles to the divinities, followed by the by then typical wish for "a thousand of bread and beer," oxen, fowl, alabaster and clothing. The Reversion of Offerings follows. The ceremony closes with a series of pronouncements for the protection and escorting of the spirit of the deceased by a number of divinities,[44] presumably on its journey through the underworld, perhaps eventually to the heaven of Kemet.

The first part of this ceremony is presented in the greatest detail. In the light of what is now known about the subsequent evolution of the entire offering complex, it is the only fully developed and so the most distinctive segment of the entire proceedings. It is a typical *hotep di nsu* ritual. The divinities who are thought to give the gifts on behalf of the real offerers are the nsu and Inpw (Anubis), the latter here accorded the praise names "Lord of the coffin, Lord of internment, Lord of invocation-offerings in"—a number of named festivals. The articles offered, in real and/or imaginary terms, are the typical "thousand of bread and beer, oxen, fowl, alabaster and clothing" for the deceased, "consisting of everything which Wsir desires and which comes forth to him (at) the voice . . ." The latter is clearly a reference to the as yet nascent voice offering. These offerings are in return for the "opening of the mouth" of the deceased.[45]

Remembering that libation is supremely the presentation of a drink offering. and censing that of incense, and that the giving of these gifts is in return for stated favours, it seems clear that, in this ceremony, neither the libation drink nor the censing incense, is conceptualised as being radically different from the other articles that are also presented. In this instance, the offering complex is a single integrated ritual. Its various aspects are still rudimentary and part of a larger entity. These aspects have not yet been invested with the distinct identities that would develop later as this integrated ritual evolved. (Sacrifice does not appear to be part of this ceremony, for it is not mentioned.)

The fusion of these elements (censing, libation, voice offerings, etc.) into a single ceremony, as well as the underdeveloped state of almost every one of them, may suggest that at first, nearer to the dawn of history, humanity practiced a single offering ritual in which each of these elements was perceived and enacted as an integral part. However, such a conclusion is based substantially upon the evidence of what we shall term the integrated ceremony that is analysed here. But the danger of generalization based upon a single example is considerably relieved by three very significant other pieces of evidence culled from different sources within this ritual context.

First is the term ḥtp, which is central to our understanding of what happened so many millennia ago. The great age of this term, which is mentioned by Gardiner,[46] and attested in the discussion above, appears to recall and represent a very early state of the offering ritual in which offerings in kind, whether liquid or solid, and word offerings, were not yet much differentiated from each other. The relative absence of differentiation may itself indicate that at this early stage the ritual actions were not conceptualised as different. The meaning of ḥtp, which is a general term that encompasses almost all the ritual actions and processes, as well as much of the paraphernalia of this complex, appears to sustain this conclusion. Further, the very fact of the causative verb sḥtp appears to add credence to such a conclusion. sḥtp is rooted in the idea of ḥtp and means "to cause to be at peace, to cause to be satisfied" etc. In reality these meanings represent the attainment of the ultimate objective of the entire offering complex.

There is a certain logic and consistency in certain of these facts surrounding this word ḥtp. First is its great age. There is also its meaning that embraces almost the entire offering complex. A third consideration is its being the basis of the verb that describes the objective of all the ritual activity in the complex. ḥtp represents the earliest known and most rudimentary stage in the conceptualization and practice of the offering complex, as well as its objective and meaning. It is the archetype of all the rituals that were nascent in and subsequently evolved from within itself.

Another consideration concerns the conservative nature of rituals. These are dominated by the desire to and the practice of preserving the ritual drama exactly as it was inherited. In normal conditions change within rituals is therefore an infinitely slow process. Therefore rituals tend to persist relatively unchanged through space and time. This characteristic assures us of much certainty in our understanding of form, content and function of these rituals.

The third aspect of our evidence is constituted by the availability of other examples of these rituals from different sources, including the *Pyramid Texts*, published tombs and stelae, tomb inscriptions such as the Harageh tomb 290[47] and secondary sources that combine many of these, like the work of Assmann.[48] These are important for comparative purposes. The examples indicate that separate performances of many—though not all—of the component parts of this offering ritual may be established from since the time of the *Pyramid Texts* (ca 2323–2150 BCE), in which libation,[49] purification (with natron and cool water, i.e. libation,)[50] purification with natron,[51] censing,[52] a censing prayer,[53] the ritual meal[54] and Reversion of Offerings[55] all appear to be presented as separate performances. The existence of this feature of separate performances of some of its elements, contemporaneously with this integrated ceremony, suggests that the trajectory towards separate and distinct ritual identities for some of its components was already being described in practice at the times we have the first glimpses of the offering complex in action.

The picture that emerges is that what would grow and change to become the entire offering complex was initially conceived and practiced as a single ritual. Further, it seems that both the integrated ceremony, containing all or most of these elements, as well as distinct ceremonies for libation, sacrifice, praising and perhaps censing, were practiced side by side from a very long time ago, certainly at the time of the *Pyramid Texts*, perhaps even before. This is precisely the performance model of the offering complex that exists in the living reality of Afrika today. It also seems clear that in the integrated ritual we find the archetype ritual, the ritual of rituals, the mother of much subsequent development in ritual activity.

The term 𓉔𓂋𓏏: prt-ḫrw: "invocation offerings" is also important for our understanding of Libation. Gardiner is certain that this term evolved from 𓉔𓂋𓏏𓀁 pr ḫrw: 'the voice goes forth' and that they both refer directly to the voiced *hotep-di-nesu* formula, which accompanied material offerings. He provides further clues to the real meaning of this expression, (though the meaning itself appears to have eluded him). First, he observes that "[t]he actual offerings were . . . so closely associated with the expression that this often received the determinative 𓊻 and practically acquired the meaning 'make an offering.'" His next sentence provides another clue: "Throughout the Old Kingdom pr was treated grammatically as a transitive verb with ḫrw as object, whether or not the whole was consciously felt to mean 'send forth the voice' with evocative magical intent."[56] Whether or not the intention was "magical" is a very subjective opinion—and besides the point here. It is clear, from both the determinative 𓊻, which is used for terms in the category of offerings, as well as the fact that from their point of view the voice offering was sent forth, in essence projected by the agency of the offerer, that the people of Kemet meant and understood this phrase as a voice offering that was sent up by the offerer to the beseeched divinities.

The fact that simultaneously with pr-ḫrw, the ancient Egyptians employed the compound noun 𓉔𓂋𓏏prt-ḫrw, which in this ritual context is known to mean "a sending forth of the voice,"[57] leads us to the above conclusion with greater certainty. Once we retain the fact that the purpose of this ritual context was to contact the divinities to offer them goodies so that they may be pleased, another conclusion becomes irresistible. This is that, eventually so much attention was focussed on the actual verbal formula accompanying the physical offerings, that this formula became an offering in itself, a voice offering that was sent forth by the offerer. The very high regard the people of Kemet held for the word, something replicated in the very term Medew Netjer, further supports this conclusion.

Attention to the actual voice offering tells more. It was a formula, a particular form of words that started life as the mere verbal accompaniment of the material offerings, which were at first considered the only offerings. But the vocal accompaniment underwent a distinctive evolution towards standardization, a development which indicates that the practitioners of this ritual were attaching increasing importance to this aspect of the drama. The resulting formulaic uttering was always employed to address the divinities on the particular occasion of making ritual offerings. The content shows that certain divinities, especially the *nsw* or pharaoh (who was regarded as the manifestation of a living divinity), *Wsr* (Greek: Osiris), in the lore of Kemet both a crucified *Nsw* and the *nsw* of the afterworld; *Inpw* (Greek: Anubis), divinity of embalmment, and *Geb*, the Earth Divinity, were each invoked or called out, that they were accorded praises and praise names, were presented with certain choice gifts (actual or imagined) and that they were asked certain specified favours in return, which varied from the general well-being of the offerer to specific requests, and that the ultimate objective was to ensure the satisfaction of the cosmic forces thus propitiated. As can be seen from Chapter One, these are still the major aspects of the libation statement in Afrika today. It is therefore impossible to escape the conclusion that the 𓉐𓂋𓏏𓊤-ḫrw, or sending forth of the voice or voice offering is in fact the earliest known version of a libation statement.

But though its genesis may be in Kemet, there is no text of a fully blown libation statement available from that state. The available evidence suggests that there will never be any, as there was never such a thing in Kemet, certainly not the fully developed and even intricate and detailed libation statement that is the norm in contemporary Afrika. It seems that while libation, praising, censing, first fruits and other aspects of the archetype ritual of rituals assumed distinctive and eventually separate ritual identities long before the collapse of the state of Kemet, the same is not true for the voice offering. In its evolutionary trajectory the voice offering did not attain the form of a current libation statement until some time after the migration from Kemet.

4.8: *Continuity and Change*

The present state of scholarly knowledge does not permit any great certainty about all that occurred in the evolution of the offering complex in general, or about libation in particular. But against the background of the offering complex in Kemet we can compare what is known about libation in ancient times with what is current in the Afrikan world today and arrive at some conclusions about both the changes and the continuities in the ritual, and perhaps why they occurred. The changes and retentions appear to be the following:

1. In the beginning libation was more closely integrated with other rituals in the offering complex, but as the complex evolved libation grew to become more distinctive—a feature it shares with some of the other rituals in this complex: sacrifice, censing, prayers, praising and first fruits. This ritual continued to be performed both separately and as part of an integrated offering ceremony. These features are still found in the practice of libation in the Afrikan world today.

2. In this current era, libation is expected to be poured only with the right hand. This was not always so, for it was poured with either hand or with both hands in ancient Egypt.

3. The tendency to pour libation once, at the beginning of a ceremony, is almost universal in the Afrikan world today. This was not always so. In Kemet it seems that libation was poured at several points in a ceremony.

4. The taking of kola nut appears to be a historically more recent development and is a popular custom in West Afrika[58], though it has been also observed in Papua-New Guinea.[59] It appears unknown in Kemet and except for West Afrika, it is not regularly practised in other parts of Afrika or in the communities overseas, except for some recent migrants from the western region of the continent. However, the communal nature of this practice is a characteristic of Afrika from ancient times, where it is illustrated in the recension of offerings in Kemet, to the present. A thorough examination of this practice in its spiritual context across the region represents another line of investigation in the project to retrieve, refurbish and reinvigorate Afrikan traditions.

5. In Kemet the voice offering was already formulaic, though it was brief and not as distinct an aspect of the complex as in later times. This evolutionary path is already evident. The voice offering grew out of a vocal accompaniment to each physical offering. At first it was something much less distinctive and less elaborate than its final form. It was also regarded as less important than the actual physical offering. But this vocal accompaniment eventually became an offering in itself, the voice offering, then prayers and praising. Each of the latter would henceforth continue an independent existence. The voice offering of Kemet would become prayers, the libation statement and praises of later historical epochs.

6. Praises and praise names, praise poems and praise songs are also forms of vocal offering that are all rooted in the spoken word which accompanied material offerings.

7. In Kemet the liquid used for pouring libation could have been water, which was regarded as the ultimate cleanser (both physically and spiritually, hence the ritual of baptism), or wine, beer, milk or honey. In the contemporary Afrikan world it is predominantly locally brewed white spirits: ogogoro in Nigeria, akpeteshie in Ghana and palm wine throughout West Afrika, where beer is also used. Schnapps and gin are also poured throughout West Afrika, beer in Kenya and white rum in the Americas and the Caribbean: clarin in Haiti, babash in Trinidad, Palm in Suriname, though other liquids are also used for this purpose.

8. Incense is still widely used as an enabling fragrance, just as in Kemet. However, there has been a development in communities abroad. In some parts of the Americas and the Caribbean, the liberal use of Florida Water, a sweet-smelling cleanser for external use only, combines the cleansing function of water with the fragrance of incense. A single new medium has thus been created and employed to achieve two different ancient functions that were previously, and are still in many instances, achieved through the deployment of two different substances.

9. The idea and practice of cursing wrong doers was not unknown to the Afrikans in Kemet[60] and the immediate successor Coptic tradition.[61] In fact, some offering formulae requested visitors to the tombs to recite the formula in the belief that the spoken word would be enabling to the offering process. Threats and curses are written in some instances—aimed at the uncooperative visitor. It is not inconceivable that this was also part of at least some offering rituals. However, the very polite people of Kemet omitted threats and curses from most of the written records on the tomb stelae. In any event, asking the divinities and/or the ancestors to curse wrong doers is certainly an aspect of the ritual in the modern Afrikan world.

It seems logical to conclude that in the beginning there was a fusion of all these elements, all of which were evidently present in one offering ritual: libation, censing, food offerings, other material offerings, voice offerings, purification with water and natron, eating a ritual meal and recension of offerings. Each one of these was a somewhat distinctive aspect of this single integrated ceremony. The processes that would eventually result in the development of increasing distinctiveness, and separation in some enactments, were already evident at the time we have the first sight of the offering complex. It may have been only later that some of these ritual acts were invested with distinctive identities occupying separate parts of a single ceremony and eventually sometimes conceptualised and enacted separately.

Structurally, each kind of offering was expanded and some were eventually separated to assume independent ritual identities and often performed separately even while they continued to be aspects of the offering ritual. Hence drink offering became libation; blood offering became sacrifice; incense offering was transformed into censing; the offerings from the harvest and/or the choicest cuts from the hunt developed into first fruits; the voice offering was transformed into prayers and the libation statement, and the according of epithets or praise names initiated the tradition of praising and blaming or ridicule. Each one of these became a well developed ritual occupying significantly more space than before. All other kinds of offerings fell into a single category of miscellaneous offerings. It must be significant that this group of offerings was not given any distinctive label in the literature, where they are identified by the individual name of each article offered or collectively as just offerings. The absence of a distinctive terminology here suggests that at the time of Kemet, none of the ritual actions of presenting these miscellaneous offerings had developed into a distinctive activity that made it stand out on its own and eventually develop into a distinct ritual identity, as was the case with libation, sensing, sacrifice, etc. However, evidence from Afrika in this current era shows that the offering complex continued to develop and change. Examples of such evidence include the breaking of kola nut, the praise tradition and the embellishment of the vocal offering into the libation statement as well as into both prayers and praises.

In each of these instances requests were made to the divine in return for the offerings made—mostly material things proffered. But there arose one group of ritual practices that dispensed with the requirement of material inducement to the divine. This group of offerings began as one integral aspect of the integrated offering ritual, where it accompanied every material offering. It developed into three different rituals that have been continued as more or less indispensable parts of every offering ritual. It evolved into a distinctive group of offering rituals, one of a kind, different from all the other rituals that have their origins in the very ancient integrated offering ritual. The spoken word that accompanied the material offerings in the ancient archetype of offerings evolved into three distinct rituals now known as prayers, praising and the libation statement. The prayer is a voice offering in which there is an outright and straightforward appeal to divinity, in which nothing material is given and strictly speaking nothing at all is promised, save perhaps the often unspoken understanding of continuing devotion to the divinity or ancestor propitiated. The libation statement is a more recent development in which divinities are identified and addressed, a drink offering is made and something solicited in return. Praises and praising arose from the epithets that announced the offices and outstanding qualities and achievements of gods and rulers. Over time these became formalised into a distinctive tradition that is still alive in Afrika, where rulers are regularly accorded praises and praise names which are often elaborated in praise songs and praise poems. Here, too, the Supreme Being is just as often conceptualised as Grand Ancestor, and accorded other epithets which announce Her/His attributes. Praise poems and praise songs to the Supreme Being, more popularly known as praise hymns or simply hymns, originated in the same ritual space and perform the identical function as does praise songs and praise poems to the earthly rulers.

The basic ancient structure of the original offering ritual was thus retained. Ritual actions were each accompanied by a corresponding utterance: the spoken word that eventually developed into praises, praise names, the voice offering, and prayers. As these rituals evolved, this line of development resulted in the libation statement. As with censing, and often purification with natron, the voice offering continued to accompany any kind of offering. However, the role of the spoken word in these rituals was elaborated. This was another manifestation of the evolution of the original integrated offering ritual, but this development was almost certainly aided by the ancient Egyptian's profound respect for the word, a cultural trait still very much alive in the Afrikan world today.[62]

Censing, or the offering of burning incense, appears to have described a remarkably similar developmental trajectory to the voice offering. It too began life as a mere accompaniment to material offerings, the presentation of which was conceptualised as the major activity in the ritual. It is undoubtedly a distinct segment of every offering ritual in the time of Kemet. However, it does not appear to have developed into a separate ritual performed on its own, one that was the only or major activity of a specific ritual occasion. In this way it is unlike libation, prayers, sacrifice or even the offering of the first fruits or other articles. But like voice offerings and prayers, censing has remained an integral aspect, a possible part in the performance of every ritual in the offering complex.

The common origin of both libation and prayers in the integrated offering complex of ancient Afrika assumes great significance in the context of contemporary Afrika. Here, especially in Ghana and Nigeria, there is much debate about the relevance of libation and prayers to Afrikan life. Some Afrikans, who call themselves "Christians," believe that the rituals described by the two terms are so different that they are opposites, and even term libation "devil worship." Such a view reveals a profound and disturbing ignorance of both their own cultural history as well as the history and practices of Christianity, which largely grew out of the Nile Valley spiritual system, and therefore shares many common roots with modern expressions of Afrikan spirituality. Libation is older than prayers; the two are ritual cousins which evolved in ancient Afrika from a single ritual that expressed the same desire expressed today by both: to propitiate and honour divinity and ancestors and solicit favours from them. It is interesting that Peter, Paul, et al are deified ancestors of Europeans and who are worshipped as "saints" in the Christian tradition. Many Afrikans unquestioningly term such worship the "Communion of the Saints." However, they term the propitiation of their own ancestors "Devil Worship" and so subvert the continuation and strengthening of their own cultural history, communities and nation. This racist elevation of Europeans and their history, cultural values and traditions, and the simultaneous degradation of Afrikans as well as Afrikan culture, values, history and traditions, is one of the major aims of European colonization of Afrikans and one of the major causes of the continuing disablement, exploitation and impoverishment of Afrikans. The fact that this practice is part of "religion" shows that some people have abused religion for evil purposes, and illustrates the importance for Afrikan people to interrogate everything that others have imposed upon them, including all histories, all doctrines and the interpretations of these.

Much is known about the archetypical offering ritual and its components that would evolve into separate identities and even sometimes separate performances. But it is not known how long this archetype was in development. We have only Gardiner's testimony that it was very old at the time of the people of Kemet, about 5000 years ago. Scholarship merely lifts the veil of ignorance and permits us a brief and tantalising glimpse of some of the facts. It is necessary to interrogate these—and even on occasion to indulge in informed speculation—in order to develop a clearer picture. Yet, the results provide little more than a blurred and incomplete version of what transpired. We emerge with our understanding somewhat increased, our appetite for more knowledge titillated, but unfulfilled. It is important to remember that we do not have the full facts concerning the process of evolution and transformation of libation and the related rituals. All we possess at the moment are a few "still frames" recovered from the otherwise lost record of the dynamic processes of evolution of the ritual practices under discussion. Our current possession amounts to little more than specks of knowledge from the vast ocean of information that must have been generated by this ritual activity and the paraphernalia it engendered. Comparison with the living tradition of the contemporary Afrikan world, which is a continuation of these ancient processes, establishes and illuminates changes. But more research is needed to fill the gaps and establish a clearer understanding of what transpired and how it did so.

This information and understandings of the origins of libation gained from examination of its earliest records provide a less dramatic picture than the Myth of Libation presented in the previous chapter. But the two accounts are not necessarily mutually exclusive, or even contradictory. The sacred narrative, or myth, is an ancient way of communicating important and often complex information. The well organised and integrated structure of the Myth of Libation, and its focus upon the divine, are characteristics of this particular example of the genre. They suggest a conscious and deliberate organisation of information in order to illustrate and dramatise, rather than explain in today's terms, a particular understanding of the story of libation. Its ancient methodology is an easy and exciting telling to aid the abiding necessity of remembering and emphasising that particular perspective on the ritual. Its objective is not a tour of all the highways and byways leading to the perceived reality. The establishment, recall, consideration and understanding of those numerous details, which are often bewildering to the uninitiated, are parts of a process that is an objective of much of modern scholarship. The ultimate aim of the myth is to impress the point that libation is a creation of divinity that it is therefore sacred, and that regular performance of this ritual drama is mandatory for the maintenance of cosmic harmony. Those details which do not fit this purpose are superfluous and so expendable. Hence we return to Soyinka's observation, which is that of Oduyoye also, that myth is always careless with details.

This way of "explaining" libation posits a very clear, divine, instantaneous and revealed origin that is organised, official, received and even imposed. There is no notion of a process of development here. Further, this origin is presented as independent of other offering rituals. But the truth may well be at once far less orderly and far more complex and intriguing than the myth alone. Reality is seldom, if at any time, as neatly and as conveniently laid out as in the schema invented by humans to make for easy understanding, as in this and other myths. Yet the Myth of Libation is undoubtedly part of the truth about the beginnings of that ritual. Clearly, the myth was invented after the fact of libation was established in daily life, and it was invented in order to account for a long and complicated process that was of much less importance to its authors in the officialdom of Kemet. What mattered, more, or even most, was the facts of the ritual and its great significance. It was these that were of the greatest importance to the state and the people of Kemet. But for all this the basic aim in both the ancient and modern telling may have been the same, to communicate what seem to be the important points about this important ritual of libation. Each of the two methods involves the selection and organisation of what the author considers to be the most important facts, and the rejection of those considered insignificant. The levels may vary, but every teller and every tale is influenced by both the standpoint and the objectives of its author—as well as the nature of the audience.

While the revealed nature of the Myth of Libation suggests a divine and instantaneous origin of this ritual, close examination of the earliest records of libation, and the ritual context in which it was born and in which it evolved, argues quite the opposite. It is almost certain that there was a slow development of this and other offering rituals, especially given the particularly conservative nature of the people of Kemet, with their profound respect for tradition, and the inherently conservative nature of ritual anyway. This ritual, and indeed the entire offering complex of which it was an integral part, has persisted in easily recognisable form from at least the time of the ancient Egyptians. Today, five thousand and more years later, it is to be found throughout the Afrikan world and beyond. But perhaps the real and enduring genius of those who created libation and other offering rituals lies not merely in the persistence of these beliefs and practices, but more so in the fact that in creating divine and comforting order out of nature's threatening chaos, they also inverted reality and persuaded humanity to worship its own creation. By this achievement alone, they motivated humanity to lift its gaze skywards and achieve much more than was possible in the much more trying time before divinity—and so before offerings to the divine.

NOTES

1. For these see, for example, Wilkinson. *Reading Egyptian Art*, pp. 80–81 and164–165 respectively.
2. Gardiner. *Egyptian Grammar*, p. 501.
3. Shaw and Nicholson. *British Museum Dictionary of Ancient Egypt*, p. 209.
4. Ibid.
5. See, for example, R. A. Caminos (1997). "Peasants" in S. Donaldoni (ed.). *The Egyptians*, pp. 14, 23.
6. Wilkinson. *Reading Egyptian Art*, p. 207.
7. Gardiner. *Egyptian Grammar*, pp. 484, 532.
8. Ibid., pp. 531–533.
9. See for example, Nicolas Grimal, Jochen Hallof and Dirk van der Plas (2000). *Hieroglyphica Sign List*. 2nd Edition, revised and enlarged by Jochen Hallof, Hans van der Berg and Gabriele Hallof. (Interniversitaries de Recherches Égyptologiques Informatisées, Utrecht and Paris), pp. 1X-1 and 2X-1–2X-3.
10. Wilkinson. *Reading Egyptian Art*, p. 163.
11. See Faulkner. *Concise Dictionary*, p. 179 for "altar" and Gardiner. *Egyptian Grammar*, p. 583 for both terms.
12. Faulkner. Ibid., p. 183; Gardiner. *Egyptian Grammar*, p. 605.
13. Gardiner. *Egyptian Grammar*, p. 583
14. Shaw and Nicholson. *British Museum Dictionary of Ancient Egypt*, p. 25.

15. Gardiner. *Egyptian Grammar*, pp. 172 and 583.
16. Wilkinson. *Reading Egyptian Art*, p. 53.
17. The Forty Two Declarations of Innocence, also termed the Affirmations of Innocence in the Afrikan centered movement, are often mislabelled the "Negative Confessions" in Eurocentric scholarship. These are rules for good living—reflecting the moral and ethical standards of the society—that evolved from the practice of the people of Kemet. As far as is known they were first fully stated in the *Book of Going Forth by Day*, and later shortened and presented as the ten commandments in the Bible by Moses at Genesis 20: 3–17 and repeated at Deuteronomy 5: 6–21. For autobiographical texts illustrating part of the early evolution of these Declarations, consult, for example, M. Lichtheim (1975). *Ancient Egyptian Literature Volume 1: The Old and Middle Kingdoms* (University of California Press, Berkeley), pp. 4–5, and *passim*.
18. There are several versions of the *Chapters of Going Forth by Day*, and several translations of each version. The translation consulted here is found in R. O. Faulkner. (Trans. 1994, 1998). *The Egyptian Book of the Dead: The Book of Going Forth by Day*. (Chronicle Books, San Francisco). See Chapter 125 of the Papyrus of Ani, See also "The Theban Recension," p.115 and Maulana Karenga (1990). *The Book of Coming Forth By Day: The Ethics of the Declarations of Innocence*, pp. 56, 57, 58, 59, 72, 73.
19. Faulkner, Ibid., p.116; Karenga, ibid., pp. 26 and 77.
20. Gardiner. Ibid., pp. 217, 533, 614; Wilkinson. *Reading* ..., pp. 163 and 207.
21. Wilkinson. *Reading Egyptian Art*, p. 53.
22. Ibid.
23. Peter Clayton (1994). *Chronicle of the Pharaohs* (London, Thames and Hudson), p.65.
24. E. A. Wallis Budge (1911, 1973). *Osiris and The Egyptian Resurrection* Vol. I. (Dover Publications, Inc., New York). See the illustrations on pp. 251–267, *passim*.
25. Ibid.
26. Kemet was known as the Two Lands, Upper Kemet and Lower Kemet.
27. The preference for the right hand appears to find divine sanction— at least among the Igbo. Here, in the process of creation, Chukwu put his right hand in to the pot to withdraw the first piece of white chalk, which became Otolo, the First Son. See Awolalu and Dopamu, p.58.
28. Gardiner. *Egyptian Grammar*, p. 170. See also Morris Bierbrier (1982) *The Tomb-Builders of the Pharaohs* (The American University in Cairo Press), p. 69; Lanny Bell (1996). "Ancestor Worship and Divine Kingship in the Ancient Nile Valley" in T. Celenko (ed.). *Egypt in Africa*, p. 57.
29. Gardiner. *Egyptian Grammar*, p. 170.
30. Gardiner. Ibid., p. 445; Wilkinson. *Reading*, p. 25.
31. Gardiner. Ibid., p. 170.
32. Ibid., p. 171.
33. Faulkner. *Pyramid Texts*, p.32.
34. Faulkner. Ibid., p. 246.
35. A stele is a "slab of stone or wood bearing inscriptions, reliefs or paintings, usually of a funerary, votive, commemorative or liminal nature, although these four categories often overlap." See Shaw and Nicholson, pp. 278–279. The quote is from p. 278.
36. Gardiner. *Egyptian Grammar*, p. 170.
37. M. Lichtheim. *Ancient Egyptian Literature: Vol. II*, pp. 81–86; Faulkner. *Coffin Texts*, p. 70.
38. M. Lichtheim. *Ancient Egyptian Literature*: Vol. II, pp. 81–86.

39. See, for example, Opoku. *West African Traditional Religion*, pp. 25–26.
40. Opoku, pp. 26–29; Awolalu and Dopamu. *West African Traditional Religion*, pp. 37–53; John Onuche (1998). "Theophoric Igala Names" in Adegbola (ed.). *Traditional Religion in West Africa*, pp.347–348; Modupę Oduyọye (1998). "Names and Attributes of God" in Adegbola (ed.). *Traditional Religion in West Africa*, pp. 349–357; Harry Sawyer (1970). *God: Ancestor or Creator?*, pp.x–xi, 5 and 40–67, *passim*.
41. Isidore Okpewho (1992). *African Oral Literature: Backgrounds, Character, and Continuity* (Bloomington and Indianapolis: Indiana University Press, 1992), pp. 25–41. For praising among the Yoruba, see Idowu. *Olódùmare*, pp.9–10.
42. Gordon Rohlehr (1990). *Calypso and Society in Pre-Independence Trinidad* (The Author, Tunapuna, Trinidad), pp. 2 and 523; Hollis 'Chalkdust' Liverpool (2001). *Rituals of Power and Rebellion: The Carnival Tradition in Trinidad and Tobago, 1763–1962*. (Research Associates School Times Publications/Frontline Distribution Int'l Inc., Chicago), pp. 186–210.
43. For an explanation of the dramatic aspect of many texts from Kemet, and consequently of drama as a mode of enquiry into the literature of Kemet, consult Carruthers. *Essays in Ancient Egyptian Studies*, pp. 50–53. For the role of drama in kingship succession in Kemet see Henri Frankfort (1948, 1978). *Kingship and the Gods*. (Chicago and London: The University of Chicago Press), pp. 123–139.
44. Faulkner. *Coffin Texts*. Vol III, Spell 936, pp.70–77.
45. The Opening of the Mouth was a special ceremony performed on the deceased. See Shaw and Nicholson, pp. 211–212; Smith. *The Liturgy of Opening the Mouth for Breathing*; Assmann. *Death and Salvation in Ancient Egypt*, pp. 310–329.
46. Gardiner. *Egyptian Grammar*, p. 170, asserts that the entire phrase, *hotep di nesu*, "is of very ancient date ..."
47. Harageh tomb 290, religious texts'. www.digitalegypt.ul.ac.uk. [Accessed on 20/01/08].
48. Assmann. *Death and Salvation in Ancient Egypt*, pp. 354–361.
49. Faulkner. *Pyramid Texts*, Utterance 23, p. 4.
50. Ibid., Utterance 33, p.7; Utterance 423, p. 140
51. Ibid., Utterances 33 and 34, p. 7.
52. Ibid., Utterance 36, p. 8; Utterance 200, p. 36; Utterance 741, p. 316.
53. Ibid., the first part of Utterance 269, p. 316.
54. Ibid., Utterances 108, 109 and 110, p. 24.
55. Ibid., Utterance 1999, p. 36.
56. All the quotes in this paragraph are from Gardiner. *Egyptian Grammar*, p. 172.
57. Ibid.
58. For an exposition of the significance of the Kola nut invocation among the Igbo, consult Ogonna Agu. *The Book of Dawn and Invocations*, pp. 11–15.
59. Private communication with Mr. Shurwin Semple. 1st April, 2007. The investigation of Afrikan populations in Australia, Papua-New Guinea, the Solomon Islands, Fiji and other parts of the Oceana, which is not attempted in this text, is a necessary development in methodology for a fully comprehensive presentation on the Afrikan world.
60. See, for example, R. B. Parkinson. *Voices from Ancient Egypt*, pp. 125–126; Scott Morschauser (1991). *Threat-Formulae in Ancient Egypt: A Study of History, Structure, and Use of Threats and Curses in Ancient Egypt* (Oxford, Halgo Inc.) and K. Nordh (1996). *Aspects of Ancient Egyptian Curses and Blessings: Conceptual Background and*

Transmission. Uppsala Studies in Ancient Mediterranean and Near Eastern Civilization, No. 26. (ACTA Universitatis Upsaliensis).

61. M. Green (trans. 1987). *The Coptic Share Pattern and its Ancient Egyptian Ancestors* (Aris and Phillips Ltd., Warminster).

62. Note the force of the word here. For Kemet, consult, for example, Allen, *Genesis in Egypt*, pp. 36–47, passim. For more contemporary Afrika see A. Hampaté Bâ (1981). "The Living Tradition' in J. Ki-Zerbo (ed.). *General History of Africa Vol. I: Methodology and African Prehistory.* (Unesco and Hinemann, Berkeley, California), pp. 166–205; K. Nehusi, "From Medew Netjer to Ebonics", pp. 82–83, Sheila Mayers-Johnson (2004), "The Word as a conduit of African Consciousness: MDW NTR Through Ebonics." *JCTAW.* Vol. I, No.2, Winter/Spring, pp. 145–174 and Maulana Karenga. *Maat. The Moral Ideal in Ancient Egypt*, pp. 187–191.

Chapter Four

On the Sacred Ancestors

The status of ancestors in Afrikan cosmology and cosmogony has been second only to divinity from the most ancient to current times. One version of the Book of Going Up into Enlightenment records these words of a supplicant in Ancient Egypt:

> Ancestors, give me your hands.
>
> It is I, who come into being through you.[1]

In contemporary times the tremendous significance of ancestors has been rearticulated all over the Afrikan world. Here is one version from Southern Afrika:

> I am the servant of my ancestors;
>
> My father is the messenger of my ancestors;
>
> My ancestors are humanity;
>
> All I live for is to be the best that I can be.[2]

5.1: At the Foundations of the Individual and Society

The ancestors, those people who have spent a full span of time on Mother Earth, who have done good work and returned to the Other World, have always had a strategic location in the Afrikan family, which has always been an extended one, comprising mother, father, children, uncles, aunts, cousins, ancestors, close friends and those yet to be born.[3] Ancestors are not merely symbolically present in the family. They may be physically gone, but they are always spiritually present, and they have specific living roles that are valuable, even indispensable to the correct and effective functioning of the Afrikan family, of the Afrikan clan, Afrikan community and entire Afrikan Nation. No Afrikan person, or family or any other Afrikan collective is complete and proper—and recognised to be so—without the ancestors. The recognition and propitiation of ancestors is a defining characteristic of the Afrikan people. This has been so from at least the time of the ancient Egyptians, among whom the term ⌂⌐ſ⌐ℓ kr ḥt meant both an ancestral spirit and a local divinity,[4] a fact which shows that the deification of some outstanding ancestors, and normally the propitiation of all ancestral spirits, was general in Kemet more than 5,000 years ago. It was almost certainly so among Afrikans even before then.

Ancestors are the spiritual, ideological, social, psychological, biological and material foundations of Afrikan society. They are responsible for generating the generations who inhabit any aspect of reality, be it past, present or future. This is so not merely and only by the genetic facts of ancestry and descent and the biological fact of procreation. It is so also in the spiritual aspects of the Afrikan personality, for it is not only the physical self that Afrikans inherit from their sacred ancestors; Ancestors pass on to their inheritors part of their spiritual aspects also—including the spirit and the soul, two vital forces within each individual and in every collective. In addition, ancestors are also the origin of the social, institutional, historical and indeed all other aspects of cultural heritage, and so of identity. It is ancestors who give to the living all that they are born with, including themselves, and all that they must inherit: their material, social and spiritual heritage. Ancestors constitute the birthright of those who come after. These are the things which the living must work with in every generation, and even transform whenever necessary, if they are to take the fullest opportunity offered by their own lives to develop all that they possess and so become the best that they can ever be. Our knowledge and consciousness of our ancestors, and their gifts to us, are indispensable to our own best survival.

It is the ancestors who first discerned the principles and developed the values of the Afrikan people. It is they who devised the rituals and founded the institutions in which these principles and values are embedded in daily life and in which they are transmitted, through place and time, from generation to generation, to mould and mark and preserve Afrikans. It is the ancestors, who, through this patterned organisation and institutionalization of their interaction with nature, including themselves and other humans, founded the culture that gives identity and security and makes meaning of daily life and of life itself. It is the sacred ancestors too who initiated the Afrikan story and thus the human story, for they were the first humans and so gave birth to history, for no one else was present when history was born. Our ancestors invented history and society and all therein, which is their legacy to us and our inheritance from them. We truly come into being through our ancestors. And if we appear tall, in these or any other generations, it is so at least in part because we stand upon their shoulders. And if we can see clearly today and beyond tomorrow, it is only with the light they have generated to enlighten us and lighten our progress into the future.

The opposite is also true: those who do not know their own ancestors have at best only incomplete knowledge and awareness of themselves. They are not fully and properly aligned to themselves, to their own history and cultural heritage, or to the world. Therefore they are not properly aligned to their interests, and so they cannot consistently and fully identify, defend or promote their own interests and so achieve their fullest potential. Such people will never stand as tall as they may stand and see as clearly as they may see, for they have neither the foundations of their ancestors, nor their light. Those who do not know their ancestors do not embrace and possess the platform offered by the experience, knowledge, wisdom and vision of their ancestors. So they remain small and blind. And their disablement is a direct consequence of their condition of disconnection from their ancestors.

5.2: Ancestor Veneration

The fact of ancestorship, like that of the closely related fact of the divine, is central to the Afrikan practice of libation. From the earliest known traditions Afrikans have always understood that kinship ties are not severed when someone makes her/his transition from this world into the spirit world or the afterworld. This is what others call death in the belief that there is a final and finite parting. Afrikans know that ancestors are potentially powerful intermediaries on behalf of those on this side of reality. Ancestors are therefore feared, loved, respected and even, on occasion, venerated. Honouring the ancestors has always been and will always be an important aspect of being Afrikan.

It may not be surprising that many scholars of Afrika, including some Afrikan scholars also, have distorted this feature of Afrikan culture, mislabelling it "ancestor worship." This error has been pointed out by Okot p'Bitek[5] and Raul Canizares,[6] among others. It has been authoritatively dismissed by Mbiti,[7] Fu-Kiau[8] and also by Ogbaa. It is the latter who, referring to one Afrikan group, notes that "... the Igbo know that the ancestors are 'honoured', not 'worshipped' in the strict sense."[9] It is clear that Afrikans held this view from millennia before, for in writing about ancient Egypt (Kemet), the English scholar, John Baines, says that "[t]he [nsw] is said to 'propitiate' the gods rather than to 'worship' them..."[10] Sarpong has explained this situation. "With all their importance," he asserts, "the ancestors are not worshipped. They are venerated—veneration being a higher form of respect and honour. ... They are in no way deified. ... They are revered because they have attained an old age, something Africans in general respect."[11] More recently Ayi Kwei Armah has also undermined the false view of ancestor propitiation put out by scholars who are either ignorant about Afrika or hostile to the truth about Afrikans—or both. Armah notes, incisively, that "[w]hat is involved is not worship, but respect."[12] The inescapable conclusion is that from the earliest recorded times to the present, Afrikans have consistently propitiated their ancestors, not worshipped them as some scholars have deliberately or mistakenly concluded. The according of very great respect to elders, ancestors and divinities may appear to differ only slightly in the degree to which the being is esteemed. Oduyoye has noted that "[f]rom honour to worship is an intensification of adulation."[13] In this continuum of appreciation and adoration that ranges from respect to reverence, elders are respected and honoured, ancestors are respected, honoured and propitiated, and divinities are respected, honoured, propitiated and worshipped.[14]

This relationship among elders, ancestors and divinity has been clearly established and expressed in the classical tradition of the Afrikan people many millennia ago. Listen to Ptahhotep, a wise ancestor whose 𓂋𓂧𓏏𓀁 (variations 𓂋𓂧𓏏; 𓂧𓏏; 𓂧𓏏𓀁) sb3yt: *sebayt* or written teaching, instructions, or even maxims, have been widely quoted and much studied.[15] Ptahhotep is one of the most outstanding sages of Kemet. We shall meet him again later in this chapter. He speaks to us from over four and a half thousand years ago:

𓂋𓂧𓏏𓀁𓏛𓏥
iḫ ḏd=i n=f mdw
Then I will tell him (the) words

𓂋𓂧𓏏𓀁𓏛𓏥
sḏmyw sḫrw[16] imyw-ḥ3t
(of) those who obeyed (the) counsels (of the) ancestors

𓂋𓂧𓏏𓀁𓏛𓏥[17]
p3w sḏm[18] n nṯrw
who obeyed the divinities (gods).

A clear hierarchy of wisdom, power and authority is articulated in this teaching. These attributes, indispensable for any successful society, originate from divinity and are passed down to ancestors, to elders, and thence to the younger generations. The younger people are being instructed by Ptahhotep, who is a wise elder—more—a sage. But Ptahhotep says that his words come from the sḏmyw: literally 'the listeners' or 'those who obeyed,' but also 'judges'[19] and therefore persons who are wise because they listened to and obeyed the ancestors. And the ancestors obeyed the divinities. This is a detailing of the hierarchy of wisdom, power and authority as well as the connections among various beings in the cosmos, which are set out in Chapter Two. It is the same wherever Afrikans have retained their culture. Once again it should be noted that a fundamental principle in Kemet is continued, alive and well, in contemporary Afrika.

5.3: Becoming an Ancestor

The criteria for becoming an ancestor differ only slightly among Afrikans over the tremendous measures of both space and time that have been occupied by the Afrikan experience of life. Among the Akan, someone was excluded from the circle of ancestors if that person's transition was 'caused by unclean diseases such as lunacy, leprosy, small pox, dropsy or epilepsy' or 'an accident, suicide or another form of violent death' or during labour, which was the worst form of disqualification for women.[20] There are similar rules throughout West Afrika.[21]

Despite these variations, Afrikans in all times and places have agreed unanimously that producing children, attaining old age, acquiring wisdom and making one's transition are fundamental to the condition of ancestorship. Throughout the existence of the state of Kemet, a period of over 3,000 years, an ideal age of 110 years was normally attributed to anyone attaining old age, irrespective of the actual age attained. This is an ideal articulated at the end of the *Sebait of Ptahhotep* as well as in many other sources from Kemet.[22] It is an ideal inherited and echoed millennia later in the Eurochristian tradition represented in the Bible at Genesis 50:22 and 50:26; Joshua 24:29 and Judges 2:8. This attitude of respect for old age is attested within all Afrikan experience including the communities abroad.[23] It is indicated in such names of respect and veneration as *Mzee* on the continent (Kiswahili speakers), *Gang Gang* abroad (Guyana, Suriname, most likely from the Kikongo *nganga*) and *los sabios*[24] (literally, "those who know and understand much,") the old ones, those who have much knowledge. (Afrikans in the Spanish dominated Americas).

We may ground our understanding of old age, and its association with experience and wisdom, in some of the facts and the millennia of practical experiences from which it has been distilled. The association of age, and more certainly of great or long experience, with knowledge and wisdom, is very important. Wisdom is the essence. A person of great age, or of many experiences and even of much knowledge, is not automatically held to be wise. From the earliest recorded time to the present Afrikans have, whenever necessary, made associations among great age, much experience, much knowledge and wisdom. But they have made the relevant distinctions also. The *Instructions of Ptahhotep* tells that "No one is born wise,"[25] a basic assertion that is the beginning of the educational wisdom and practice of Kemet.[26] More than three millennia later in the Afrikan experience, Chinua Achebe amplifies this principle: "Experience is necessary for growth and survival. But experience is not simply what happened. A lot may happen to a stone without making it any wiser. Experience is what we are able and prepared to do with what happens to us."[27] It is the memorising and analysis of experience to obtain the knowledge and lessons it offers, and the deployment of the knowledge and implementation of the lessons, that constitutes wisdom and leads to achievement. Ogbaa speaks, and eloquently so, for the Afrikan world view when he observes that "age is respected but achievement is revered."[28]

The attainment of old age has been a basic criterion for ancestorship across Afrika for millennia. From the time of ancient Kemet to now, Afrikans have consistently associated old age with much experience and therefore with knowledge, wisdom and authority, since all humans can and do intellectualise their experiences. No one is therefore expected to live to old age without having an accumulation of experience to be analysed and interpreted, mined for wisdom and deployed as example—as lessons and as guidance to those who come after.

There is no fear of old age here. Old age is widely recognised as a natural condition, a consequence of birth and life that is willingly and fully, even joyfully, embraced and valued highly in Afrikan society. Old age is simultaneously a privilege and a great practical advantage in providing the benefits of accumulated knowledge and wisdom while linking the generations on this side of reality and providing pointers towards the ancestors. The aged are cherished and hold much importance and attention in Afrikan communities. That is why elders and ancestors remain incorporated into the family, the clan and the community. They are great repositories of experience, often of knowledge, insight and wisdom. They therefore serve as fountains of valuable advice and guidance to the younger generations, who are the less experienced and often less knowledgeable members of the family, the clan and the community. In Afrikan communities elders are not shunted off to some "old peoples' home" where their great value is unutilised and their dignity diminished. The scourge of ageism: of a negative view of elders as useless, which is so rampant in western society, is not possible in a real Afrikan society. In fact, all over Afrika before the *Maafa*, from the smallest and most humble to the most complex societies, elders were tutors and advisors to rulers, or rulers themselves. It was their experience and wisdom that made society accord them these important roles, among others. Elders were valued, encouraged, stimulated and even challenged by their roles so that they "had to be informed and alert because of their responsibilities."[29]

We should not allow to go unnoticed more historically recent demonstrations of the value of tradition and the tremendous spiritual and intellectual resources possessed by elders in Afrikan society. Several studies of the Afrikan struggle to repossess their continent illustrate the importance of spiritual tradition in the capacity to win.[30] A spirit medium is a repository of age, experience, knowledge, wisdom and cultural and spiritual power; an important functionary from deep within Afrikan social history who combines the considerable advantages of age and ancestorship. Spirit mediums were deployed very effectively in both the First and Second Chimurenga (or Wars of National Liberation) in the struggle of Afrikans in Zimbabwe against European settler colonialism. Spirit mediums illustrate the role of ancestors and the aged as potent sources of wisdom and an Afrikan vision of a dignified and valuable future. They also demonstrate resistance to disempowerment and its terrible consequence of disablement. The mediums imposed a complex set of abstentions upon the guerrillas of the Second Chimurenga: no sex, no physical contact with menstruating women and no eating of food cooked by women in this condition, no killing of wild animals in the bush, and a number of others.[31] These abstentions are in some instances exactly the same as those observed in Kemet, ancient Egypt, especially by priests but also by the general populace. (See Chapter Three.) It is an ancient and enduring spiritual heritage they brought to the battlefront, though some may have been unaware of just how ancient this heritage is and observers from afar may wonder whether the heat of a physical battle is the best place for such reflections. Nevertheless, Afrikans effectively deployed ancient ancestral knowledge and wisdom in the struggle for Zimbabwe.

The abstentions were designed to achieve discipline and cohesion among the humans who resisted European domination, to assure their harmonious integration with the land, with each other, with the other (i.e. the wild) animals and with the vegetation that inhabited the land. Taken to their logical conclusion, such abstentions recognised the fundamental contradiction of being inculcated with the oppressor's cultural values, and sought to avoid the resulting trap. The fighters for Zimbabwean independence were not a mass of traditionless humanity fighting against inhumanity. The notion of a traditionless group of humanity is false, even when there are humans who believe and act as though they have no traditions, a condition that is almost always the result of oppression. These fighters were Afrikan revolutionaries fighting for their freedom and the dignity of an entire people. The genius of the spirit mediums and the guerrillas was to unite with each other and modernise and re-site the struggle firmly within the historical and cultural traditions of that particular group of Afrikans we know today as the Zimbabweans. Some of the ancient Afrikan principles were re-articulated in ways that were suitable to Zimbabwe and perhaps peculiar to that context. While the spirit mediums represented ancient ways, the guerrillas, with their automatic weapons, represented modernity. The combination of these two elements ensured historical depth and continuity in the struggle from the time of the first Chimurenga, as well as an equally necessary modernization of the techniques of warfare, including ideology. The fighters were therefore empowered to achieve Maat: order and balance within themselves and with all in their environment. This objective was achieved, and so the struggle was won. So today Afrikans pour libation to Mbuya Nehanda, the grandmother of both Chimurengas, whose vision, knowledge and inspiration guided the Afrikan guerrilla forces. She was uncompromising to the end and outstanding in her resistance. For consistently sustaining these qualities in all political weather, Mbuya Nehanda is a revered ancestor.

On the other hand, in Kenya, the Mau Mau rebellion of the Gikuyu against European settler colonialism was not firmly and effectively anchored in the spiritual tradition of the Afrikan people. While there were indeed some Afrikan spiritualists, there was no core of active Afrikan practitioners solidly grounded in the long spiritual tradition of the Afrikan people. It was not that this tradition was unknown to the people of modern Kenya. The simple reason is that the

Afrikan spiritual system had been comprehensively replaced by Eurochristianity. The identity of these Afrikans has been erased and/or distorted:

> There were no venerable traditional spirit mediums to offer focus to peasant radicalism nor were the 'tribal elders' inclined to endorse the revolt. ...the 'tribal elders' were no longer those who had stuck to their traditional customs, but they were the chiefs, evangelists, the educated elite, and other propertied persons. Power, influence, and prestige had shifted towards these groups away from undiluted traditional institutions. These new 'tribal elders' failed to embrace Mau Mau.[32]

The tribal elders were no longer tribal elders. They thought to themselves that they had become "Christians," but they had in fact become Europeanised Afrikans. They had exchanged the traditions of their ancestors for the mental prisons of their oppressors. Miseducated and propertied at the expense of the majority, they were well integrated into the Eurocentric system. They had become the handmaidens of their oppressors. They had fallen prey to cultural genocide that masqueraded under the cloak of Christianity, which was falsely and widely equated with modernity and progress. Basil Davidson's conclusion about the chiefs of West Afrika is equally valid about these chiefs of East Afrika: They "were the agents of foreign domination instead of being, as in the past, the guardians of African tradition and self-respect."[33] True, there were other weaknesses in this fight for *itaka na wiyathi*, for land and freedom. But the key factor in the defeat of the movement lay in the failure to continue their traditions in a modern context. In the face of impending military defeat some of the guerrillas desperately sought to introduce new forms of oaths as a way of spiritually reinforcing themselves and sustaining the fight. But they were not politically astute enough and the British government was able to oversimplify, distort and misrepresent their oaths as backward and evil. The military defeat of Mau Mau was accompanied by numerous British crimes against humanity and other atrocities, including mass arrests, concentration camps and hangings and other forms of genocide.[34] These "measures" were followed by a program of pacification in which a key component was indoctrination with Eurochristianity.[35] British authorities later on tried to "disappear" the evidence of these crimes against humanity in Afrikan skin.[36]

Most of the leaders of the Gikuyu had in fact become westernised, perhaps believing that they had become modernised. Many Afrikans have mistaken westernization for modernisation. It is always necessary to modernise, to continually interrogate, update, re-interpret, extend, enrich and reinforce our traditions. Humanity does this as a matter of course, and does so especially when adapting tradition to new and challenging circumstances. However, no group of people have ever become successful by deserting their history, their culture and their identity and trying to adopt those of another group, especially their oppressors. The Europeans have for over five hundred years incorporated numerous ideas and practices from around the world, but they have remained

Europeans. The Japanese have adopted western technology and become massively successful, but have remained Japanese. The Chinese have adopted socialism, then the rival market system, but have throughout remained Chinese. But most Afrikan leaders have failed to remain Afrikan. This is quite clearly a root, perhaps the root, of Afrikan disablement, exploitation and underdevelopment. Many scholars, including Kotkin,[37] Lee Kuan Yew[38] and Amy Chua,[39] have pointed to the role of culture and identity in the economic success of large cultural groups. Others, most notably Cabral,[40] Kwesi Prah[41] and this writer,[42] have pointed out the role of culture in the liberation and development of Afrika. In fact, Cabral has concluded that in the face of imperialist cultural oppression, "national liberation is necessarily an act of culture."[43] These experiences and observations tell that those who retain their identity and so remain themselves are more likely to be successful at beating off foreign oppression and developing themselves. And, as has been shown, an important aspect of remaining the Afrikan self is maintaining spiritual, cultural, historical and other connections with the ancestors.

Another basic criterion for ancestorship, from the earliest times to the present, has always been living a life of exemplary moral fortitude. Afrikans have always been unanimous on this point also. In Kemet, on arrival at the Hall of Maati after many challenges, a person's soul had to recite the Forty Two Declarations of Innocence without any hesitation while the heart, literally the person's moral conscience, was weighed against a feather, which was a representation of Maat: Truth, Justice, Righteousness, Balance, Harmony, Reciprocity and Order. Failure meant being devoured by a fearsome beast and cast into Amenti (Hell). Success was rewarded with a permanent place in an ideal land and the title 𓂝𓏤𓊹𓋴 mꜣꜥ ḥrw: *maa kherew*: literally, "True of Voice," but Vindicated or Justified or Blessed Departed. Today Afrikans have retained this criterion for ancestorship. Other criteria include parenting, leaving at least one heir who will inherit one's life work and seek to extend it, and, of course, making one's transition in a good way and being accorded full transition rites.[44]

5.4: Relationship with the Ancestors

For Afrikans, ancestors are close to the Creator, with whom they can intercede on behalf of the living. Ancestors have knowledge, inspiration and power to give to succeeding generations. But no one can receive that which they are not prepared to receive.

The relationship with the ancestors is therefore an extremely important aspect of the Afrikan way of life. In Kemet, ancestors were included in the family. Family ties were not severed by death and ancestors continued to play a very important part in the lives of the living, even punishing them for improper behaviour. Ancestors were intermediaries between this world and the world of the spirits and Divinities, and were often asked to intercede on behalf of the living,[45] and letters were written to them asking them to grant certain favours.[46]

Ancestors may visit the living and even intervene in their lives in ways that may be recognised by some. Sometimes the ancestors were angry because of neglect by the living. Such neglect always risks condemning both ancestors and the neglectful living to cosmic death through severance of the connections between the two groups. In the rest of the continent, in the current era, the exact beliefs dictate the same attitudes to ancestors, who are still considered part of the family, and it is still believed that they can intercede with higher powers on our behalf.[47]

These attitudes to ancestors and the related practices have been continued among Afrikans in communities abroad. One example will be enough here. In 1813, during a funeral ceremony in Berbice, Guyana, enslaved Afrikans "sent messages to their uncles, aunts, and other relatives who were dead."[48] This appeared to be part of the custom. It is most certainly an important aspect of Cumfa, a belief system practised by Afrikans in Guyana today. These are identical to beliefs and practices in other Afrikan communities abroad today, where they are easily recognised in Candomblé in Brasil, in Santería in Cuba, Puerto Rico, Mexico, Panama and other places, in Voodoo in Haiti, in Orisha in Trinidad and Tobago, in Kumina in Jamaica and in other forms of Afrikan spiritual continuity in other parts of the Americas. Each of these is increasingly being represented among Afrikans in the USA. The system of communing with Afrikan ancestors is called Lucumí (its Yoruba name) or espiritismo in Santería, which is alive in Cuba, Puerto Rico, the United States of America and other countries. In Haiti we are told that "reduced to its simplest terms, vodun is a cult of ancestor [propitiation]" and that "the chief rites extending these beliefs are propitiatory and seasonal, ancestral and agricultural."[49] The tremendous importance of the proper relations with the ancestors, and by extension of Afrikan traditions, for the well being of the entire Afrikan nation world wide, was well understood since many generations ago by the practitioners of this variety of the Afrikan spiritual system:

> [T]here was great and protective interest in the recognition of 'Guinea'[50] blood ties and great concern for my ancestors, who had not received the proper ritual attention because that group [of enslaved Afrikans] taken further north had been cut off from their [sisters and] brothers in the Caribbean and had forgotten these practices. In some instances ... it seemed that the welfare of the entire [Afrikan] race might be improved if these unfortunates to the north might be acquainted again with the rituals of ancestor [propitiation] and the vodun.[51]

5.5: Ancestor Veneration Today

There is much evidence that Afrikans in North America are aware of the shortcomings mentioned in the quote above and are taking the necessary action to repair the damage. Growing numbers of Afrikans in the USA are indeed beginning to reacquaint themselves with Afrikan culture. Further, it does appear that this is a very pivotal development that could have significant effects upon the fortunes of the entire world community of Afrikans. The cultural and historical bases of Pan-Afrikanism were very clearly understood by at least some Afrikan practitioners of Voodoo in Haiti a long time ago.

Many Afrikans in communities abroad who had been separated from the idea and practice of ancestor veneration and other aspects of the Afrikan cultural heritage are now beginning to recognise the centrality of the proper relations with the ancestors to Afrikan unity and so to Afrikan liberation. This is perhaps the most significant development in the Afrikan world in centuries. One example is Minister Ra Ifagbemi Babalawo, who, like many others, is very clear and forthright on this question:

> There is no such thing as an African based or 'Afro-centric' being without there being Ancestor communion. It is our tradition and sacred way, and the rituals of honouring our beloved Dead rundeep within our blood.[52]

Reconnection with the sacred ancestors is an essential aspect of the restoration of Afrikan culture as the dominant and decisive factor in Afrikan life, which in turn is the most strategic aspect of Reparations. This reconnection will help to end the psychic pain experienced by Afrikans to this day, for it will help to restore balance within their individual selves, within their families, their communities and within the world community of Afrikans. At this moment such a community is more a necessary idea than a reality. But it must be brought into existence, for such a community is at once both a precondition and a necessary objective of Afrikan healing and Afrikan redemption.

Recognising the importance of our ancestors in Afrikan lives is an important basis of Afrikan unity. This is demonstrated at several levels of conceptualisation and practice in the Afrikan communities abroad. For example, in the United Kingdom, every year, on the First of August, the Melchesidek Spiritual Baptist Church, in Boundary Road, Walthamstow in London, under the leadership of Mother Ann and Bishop Godfred Hercules, organise the 'Emancipation Day' activities that inevitably have a focus on the ancestors. On this very first day of August, Afrikans in the United Kingdom are also brought together, this time by the Afrikan Remembrance Day Committee (ARDC), to meet and observe Afrikan Remembrance Day in the common knowledge and understanding of the great suffering of the ancestors and of their role in the lives of Afrikans. The first of August is a day of very special significance for Afrikans from parts of the Caribbean that had been colonised by the British, for it marks the anniversary of the legal termination of physical enslavement. Countless acts of remembrance of ancestors form part of the observations that take place each year in Trinidad and Tobago, where the Emancipation Committee takes the lead, in Guyana, where the Afrikan Cultural Development Association (ACDA) is the leading force and organises the annual Afrikan Holocaust Day on 12th October, in Barbados, Jamaica and indeed all across the region. In London the Marcus Garvey Organising Committee organises occasions honouring this outstanding ancestor on the seventeenth day of August, which is his earth-day.

In the USA, in Galveston, near Houston in Texas, Afrikans are brought together each year by the Houston Chapter of the National Black United Front (NBUF) on the third Saturday in October for the Annual Sankofa Caravan to the Ancestors. Two thousand and six marked the 9th anniversary of this Caravan. Galveston is a very historic space for Afrikans. Many enslaved ancestors were landed there to labour for life without wages and contribute very significantly to the construction of the USA. "The caravan is a venue which is a means to reconnect to our ancestors, effecting internal repair to the damage caused through our loss of language, culture, history and spiritual traditions."[53]

The spread of ancestral observations to other parts of the USA and beyond has been rapid. There are now annual observances in New York, at Ocean Beach, in San Francisco, in Seattle, in Washington, D.C., and in numerous Afrikan communities abroad as well as on the continent of the common ancestors. Afrikan traditional acts of homage abound in the rites and ceremonies that decorate these events: the wearing of white, the wrapping of hair, the Unity Circle, intoning the names of ancestors, and of course libation, the cleansing smell and smoke of incense, the drums.[54] This movement represents another important advance in the continuing rehabilitation of Afrikans through the rehabilitation of the ancestors in their lives. The profound damages and great pain suffered by the ancestors, which are a direct cause of the continuing damage and suffering among subsequent generations of Afrikans, constitute one part of the largest crime against humanity and a just cause for urgent Reparations to Afrikans.

These instances of remembering and honouring the ancestors are comparatively recent manifestations of this ancient Afrikan principle and its practice. Afrikans in many communities abroad have several practices that amount to older manifestations of this tradition of remembering and honouring the ancestors. For example, ancestors were invoked in certain rites performed in burial grounds in order to "mount"[55] the sticks of stick fighters, to ensure victory of a village team in a cricket match, or success in some other venture. In addition to all of these manifestations there are in existence uncountable numbers of personal and family altars and billions of thoughts and acts of recognition and honouring of the ancestors every day in the Afrikan world.

Remembering and honouring the ancestors is an aspect of the Afrikan worldview that reflects itself in the products of the creative imagination of Afrikans throughout the world. Ancestral spirits populate the stories of the Afrikan people. They are present in the work of Toni Morrison, Jacques Roumain, Erna Brodber, Ben Okri and numerous others.

The increasing awareness of the importance of the ancestors is a part of the growing cultural and spiritual awareness of Afrikans which dictate actions that arise from a greater and more profound urge to propitiate, to give thanks to ancestors and to the Divine. Today giving thanks for the First Fruits or harvest is celebrated or observed as *Homowo*, *Afahye* and *Odwira*, all in Ghana, in the yam festivals which abound in West Afrika, and as *Kwanzaa* in communities abroad. Kwanzaa is a seven day festival in which the *Nguzo Saba* or seven principles of

Umoja (Unity), *Kuichagulia* (Self Determination), *Ujima* (Collective Work and Responsibility), *Ujimaa* (Co-operative Economics), *Nia* (Purpose), *Kuumba* (Creativity) and *Imani* (Faith) are also observed and celebrated.

Libation is a central ritual in each one of these festivals.

5.6: Deified Ancestors

When we begin at the beginning of Afrikan history, which is the beginning of all history and is therefore the longest history on this planet, it will be noticed that once we had our own cultural integrity, Afrikans have always held their ancestors in great reverence, second only to the Supreme Spirit and the ꜣꜣꜣ: the Ntrw, the Netjru or Divinities. Some of these divinities were ancestors who have been given the very rare honour of being deified, that is, raised up from ordinary humans through the categories of hero, legend and myth to the permanent status of divinity. (The meaning of ꜣNtr: *netjer* as well its connection with ancestors are explained in Chapter Six.) It is the same in Haiti, where "Gods are created from important persons who manifest themselves after death."[56] This is another detail in which the Afrikans of Kemet are the direct cultural progenitors of present-day groups of Afrikans, who also venerate but rarely deify ancestors. Such present-day groups include the Akan,[57] and others throughout West Afrika.[58]

In Kemet it was normally only the pharaoh who could have been elevated from humanity to divinity. Very few other humans had any chance of that extremely rare distinction. Examples of deified people of Kemet include ⟨hieroglyphs⟩ (variations ⟨hieroglyphs⟩ and ⟨hieroglyphs⟩): Ii-m-Htp, Imhotep, a name which means, literally, 'He who comes in peace.' This great ancestor lived in the time of the Old Kingdom in Kemet, over four thousand years ago. He is the first multi genius known to history, having been a famous medical doctor, an architect (his design initiated pyramid building), Chief Lector Priest, the Grand Vizier or Prime Minister of Kemet, an astronomer, a poet and a sage. So profound has been his influence upon succeeding generations that he was worshipped thousands of years later as a divinity as far away as Greece, where he was known as Asklepios. In Kemet, Imhotep's influence was repeatedly proclaimed equally long after he made his transition to the Spirit World. For example, as late as the New Kingdom (about 1550–1080 BCE), every scribe would pour libation to him with water from the waterbowl that was a regular part of the scribe's equipment. The libation was poured into Mother/Father Earth before the scribe began to write anything.[59] Each scribe's libation to Imhotep constituted recognition of his outstanding example and his consequent elevation to divine status. Moreover, this libation, poured exclusively to Imhotep, distinguishes him from almost every other human who was propitiated in Kemet and establishes beyond any doubt that Imhotep was regarded in a special category of being, the commoner who had become a divinity. Since this is the text found on the books held by his figures in surviving statues, it is likely that the formula of this libation was as follows:

"Water from the waterbowl of every scribe to thy k3, o Imhotep."

Further corroboration of both the fact of this libation to him and of Imhotep's status is provided by a text from a tomb at Thebes, from the time of Amenhotep III, during the XVIIIth Dynasty. It reads thus:

[hieroglyphs]

"May the wᶜb-priests stretch forth for you their hand with water upon the ground, just like what is done for Imhotep from the end of the waterbowl."[60]

Gardiner concludes that this is the most explicit as well as the oldest reference to the divinity of Imhotep. However, it is entirely likely that this is but the oldest known *surviving* reference. The outstanding status of Imhotep had been established while he was alive, and since devotion to him was also centered on his burial place, we may be certain that the trajectory that would eventually take him into divinity was already established by the time of his transition into the afterlife. It is therefore entirely reasonable to conclude that references of this kind would have been made before the XVIIIth Dynasty, the time of the text that occasioned Gardiner's comment, which is more than a thousand years after Imhotep's death.

Of interest here is also the writing of Imhotep's name in the inscription: [hieroglyphs] Ii-m-ḥtp, with the determinative [hieroglyph] signifying a revered person. As is discussed below, this may provide another clue to the fact that by the time of the writing of the inscription reproduced above, the status of Imhotep was already in the realm of the illustrious ancestors.

Other deified ancestors include [hieroglyphs] Amenhotep, son of Hapu, of the XVIIIth Dynasty, worshipped for his wisdom and his medical skill; Hardedef, son of Pharaoh Khufu of the IVth Dynasty, famous for his prodigious knowledge and wise sayings, and Khaemwaset, high priest of Ra at Mennefer (Memphis of the Europeans) and son of Pharaoh Ramesses II. Khaemwaset was one of the first known archaeologists in the world, restorer as well as builder of many monuments in Kemet, knowledgeable about many documents that were ancient even in his time, inspirer of two tales of wonder (or magical occurrences.) Yet others include Ptahhotep and Kagemni of the Old Kingdom. To each of these ancestors was attributed wisdom literature embodying ethical values,[61] a fact that constitutes an eloquent comment upon the humanist preoccupations of Nile Valley civilization.

5.7: Ancestral Festivals Today

Less remote in time from our era, but remote nevertheless, is the earthly era from which springs a number of individual spirits and groups of ancestral spirits who are regularly acknowledged, communed with and propitiated in contemporary Afrikan practice on the continent. One Yoruba myth tells us that Ifa was an outstanding ancestor who was deified after his transition. Shango, the *Orisa*, is another deified ancestor, a historical figure who may be partly recovered from some of the many myths about him. He was the fourth *Alafin* (king) of Oyo. Agẹmọ, Egungun, Eluku and Gẹlẹdẹ are groups of Yoruba ancestral spirits who are regularly communed with at festivals that bear their names. Other festivals in which the ancestors are remembered and propitiated include *Homowo* of the Ga people in Ghana,[62] *Akwaside* among most Asanti, *Odwira* or *Ojira* among the Akwapin and Akwamu groups of the Asanti in south-east Ghana, (this is also a First Fruits or harvest festival), the *Adge* Festival, at which the king is ritually purified, the *Eguadoto* and *Ahobaa* festivals of the Fante, the *Egungun* and *Oro* of the Yoruba, the *Mmo* of the Igbo[63] and a great number of others. Many of these festivals show remarkable continuities from the practice of Kemet. Such continuities suggest a relationship which ought to be the basis of meaningful research about Afrika.

J. O. Lucas is particularly expansive on these Ancestral Festivals. In addition to many of those just mentioned, he also discusses the Adae and its many variations, the Afira-bi Ceremony of the Asanti and the Fon ancestral venerations, which are closely connected to water divinities. Lucas also discusses the Skull, Royal and Isọgbetọ or Zangbetọ of the Egun, the Mmo Society (with its branch, the Ayaka Society) and the Odo society of the Igbos. He examines the royal ancestral veneration centered around the Ogwedian Shrine in Benin and a number of Yoruba ancestral venerations, including the Abiku, Adimu, Agẹmo, Egungun, Eluku, Gẹlẹdẹ and Oro festivals. The ancestral spirits who are the foci of many of these festivals are also the centres of highly organised and elaborate year-round devotion with priests and adherents of their own.[64]

Quite logically, just as the culture of the Nile Valley, the heartland of Afrikan culture, has been taken with them and continued, with variations, by Afrikans who migrated to other parts of the continent and/or were children of a common cultural parent, so too has Afrika continued itself in the Afrikan communities abroad. In Haiti the practitioners of Voodoo hold *services ancêtres*: services in honour of the ancestors. In the Yoruba sub group of Afrika the *sàaráà* is common. This term is contracted from *sàrákà*, an older term once employed in Trinidad to refer to the same annual ceremony of ancestor propitiation. Sàrákà is in turn descended from the Hausa term *sadaka*: a ceremony in which gifts are made to those in need. "The saraka is an act of ancestor reverence, and often, neglected ancestors—those whose descendants failed to offer *saraka*—will visit a series of misfortunes upon the living offenders, or will appear in a dream to chide the descendants. *Saraka* are also given as thanksgiving ceremonies after recovery from illness or after job promotion."[65]

In the saraka, the echoes from Kemet are as unmistakable as the similarities to ceremonies throughout the rest of the Caribbean and the Americas. Similar honours are awarded to ancestors in Cuba and Guadeloupe.[66] In Guyana the name for this ceremony has been rendered *s'iku*, a term obtained in 1917 from a group of Yoruba Afrikans who resided at Canal No. 1 Polder on the West Bank of the Demerara River.[67] This is a variant orthography, and quite possibly a variant vocalization also, of the preceding terms. In Sierra Leone, in West Afrika, the same ceremony, with some variations, is termed a *sara*. In this writer's home village of Queenstown, on the Essequibo Coast in Guyana in South America, the same ceremony was known in the local language as *jumbie dinner*,[68] i.e. a feast in honour of the spirits, which is quite clearly an exact translation, in word and practice, of this concept of the Afrikan ancestral feast.

Year over year, throughout Afrikan communities outside of Afrika, observations of Kwanzaa continue to be on the increase. Libation is a central aspect of each of these festivals to the ancestors. Libation was and still is a major part in maintaining the proper relationship with the ancestors. It is therefore an important ritual in the maintenance of Maat: the proper order and balance, both within each and among all categories of beings and things in the cosmos.

Examples of ancestors from the more recent history of the Afrikan experience who have been made divinities or who appear to be approaching that status include Sojourner Truth, Mbuya Nehanda, General Dedan Kimathi, Emperor Haile Selassie, especially for the Rastas, Marcus Garvey, Bob Marley, Walter Rodney, Kwame Nkrumah, Omowale Malcolm X, Nanny of the Maroons, Paul Bogle, Martin Luther King, John Henrik Clarke and many others. In the conscious community of Afrikans in the United Kingdom, Baba Kwame Ani and Nana Bonsu, whose lives of proud humility and dedication to the cause of Afrika amount to glowing examples and a significant challenge to all Afrikans, appear set to join this list of distinguished ancestors. In Atlanta, Georgia, in the US, the NSAA Family, a group of Afrikan volunteers, has organised the Abakosem Sunsum every year since 2004. This group "is dedicated to making Abakosem Sunsum a yearly celebration and veneration of Baba [John Henrik] Clarke and a time of communing with our never-ending procession of warrior ancestors." The purpose of this "powerful African ceremony" is "to raise up Nana John Henrik Clarke and other African warrior ancestors."[69]

These are Afrikan icons. Most have used their lives to illuminate the way forward out of our long, long night of misery and psychic pain. Each has her or his own story, which is a part of the Afrikan story and a fundamental aspect of the human story. All of them are held in such high esteem because of their outstanding works here on Mother Earth on behalf of the Afrikan people. It is of the greatest significance that their names are normally intoned at Libation Rituals. Indeed, it is becoming increasingly customary within the Afrikan communities abroad to intone these names, as well as the names of remembered lineage and the obligatory reference to those whose names are not and perhaps cannot be known, in a unique communal call and response aspect of the Libation Ritual that is developing in this part of the Afrikan world. These names form a very illustrious, sacred and powerful company of ancestors and therefore constitute a strong tool for the invocation of the revered, the sacred and the divine and of understanding of and focus upon the most urgent and necessary task facing current Afrikan generations, the task of liberating themselves from the Maafa and its effects.

We must pause to remind ourselves here, as is said on the preceding pages, that scribes in Kemet poured libation to Imhotep with water into Mother Earth before they would write anything. This was their way of remembering and keeping alive the powerful example of this outstanding ancestor, a foremost representative of their profession and their race.

Times have changed. Afrikans all over the world today inhabit the midnight of the Maafa, and nowhere is Afrikan people free to fulfil their fullest potential, individually or collectively, as Imhotep and other Afrikans who lived before the Maafa could do in their chosen professions, or in professions that chose them. Self-Liberation has therefore been a sacred duty from the inception of the Maafa, and liberation shall be the foremost duty until Afrikans, by their own efforts, put an end to this downpressing Maafa. It is not surprising, therefore, that the most outstanding Afrikans of these times of continuing terror tend to be those who are foremost in undertaking this most important and sacred duty. So libation is poured to them, the foremost warriors in these times of the greatest terror, of the continuing war against Afrikan culture, Afrikan identity and Afrikan people. And libation is also poured to those ancestors who distinguished themselves in times before these Maafa times, when oppression did not bar the way to the fullest human growth and flowering. Those ancestors represent, simultaneously, both the humanity and the ultimate objective of the Pan Afrikan struggle.

It does not matter in which era these glorious ancestors lived and what circumstances challenged them in their duty and their desire to achieve the best for themselves and their communities. These Afrikan icons rose above all or most obstacles to success in whatsoever field they chose—or were chosen—in which to make their contribution. These distinguished ancestors come to the world from time and across times, from historical eras far and near in the long, long march of the Afrikan generations. Each of them represents the best in all of us. That is why, always by popular and very often by universal acclaim in Afrikan communities, they are revered ancestors.

5.8: Elders and Ancestors

Afrikans have always been very clear about the important place of ancestors in their view of things and of their equally important role in the lives of the living. Maulana Karenga explains the wider social and historical context of Kemet in which the idea of ancestorship was first known to have been conceptualised and practised as part of an ethical system and a way of life, which "is marked by its strong and profound reverence for tradition and the past. This was expressed in terms of both ancestor [veneration] and elder veneration and a profound respect for ancient knowledge and achievement. In Maatian sacred literature, there are abundant models of virtue from the past used to instruct."[70]

Respect for the aged and veneration of ancestors became central principles of the ethical system throughout Afrika. These principles are articulated in the social life of Afrika through the rules governing age grades, forms of address and greetings, performance of genuflection, prostration and other formal and semi formal behaviours. Walter Rodney mentioned respect for all humanity, especially respect to elders, as one of the principles of Afrikan culture. It is therefore not surprising that he also mentioned "the role and treatment of the aged" as a notable aspect of Afrikan social behaviour,[71] for the one was a consequence of the other. Herbert Ekwe-Ekwe and Femi Nzegwu list "Respect for Elders and the Old" among the eight essential elements or traits which make up the Afrikan. "Respect for the elders and the old is a crucial feature of African spirituality which sees the old as part of the revered circle of the forebears of society, linking them inevitably to ancestors and the gods that make up the pantheons of the order of the cosmogony. The old act as 'meaning,' a continuing thread from the past to the present, and those soon to play the role of 'continuity' with the future as the respected and adorable subject of reincarnation."[72] Today the continuing decay of Afrikan communities around the world is often described by the disconnection from elders and ancestors, the consequent distortion and/or cessation of the conversation among the generations and other principles and practices that together constitute the core of the Afrikan and a true measure of Afrikan spiritual, cultural and psychological health. It is therefore not at all surprising that the restoration of the role of the elders and the ancestors is increasingly recognised as central to the rebuilding of the Afrikan nation around the world.

5.9: Ancient Wisdom

In our attempts to understand the full significance of our ancestors, the Medew Netjer, the language of Kemet, one of the oldest known languages, offers considerable help. It is mentioned above that in Kemet, ancestors, as revered persons, are included in the family. This is conveyed in the term ꜣbt: abet, which was used to designate "family,"[73] at least up to the early part of the second millennium. Here again the sign : seated man, indicates "revered person(s)." This is the most common determinative for words for ancestors in the Medew Netjer. It shows that the term ꜣbt: contains the literal meaning of "revered persons" as ancestors. This is an important fact for the understanding of a number of other words that contain this sign—and therefore carry this meaning, irrespective of whether it is primary and so active and dominant, or secondary and passive. In Kemet, as in all Afrika, no one exists without her/his ancestors. More details are provided in the following etymologies of various terms for ancestors in this primary language of Afrika.

The conception of the individual was based upon the very sound idea that every individual inherits at least a part of the self from his or her ancestors. This is conveyed in the term ꜣḫ: akh, meaning spirit or ancestral spirit (variations include ⌇⌇, ⌇, ⌇ and ⌇), which was an aspect of every person.[74] This is a meaning of ancestors that is additional to the widely understood fact that at death each of us "goes to join our ancestors." The meaning of the term akh therefore embraces notions of both coming from and going to the ancestors. The signs, ⌇ and ⌇, are of special interest to us here. Gardiner tells us that they both mean "revered persons."[75] Faulkner adds notions of "splendid," "valuable" and such like,[76] which are sustained by Allen.[77] These are quite likely later derivatives of the fundamental meaning put forth by Gardiner. These nuances do not contradict that basic meaning. They embrace and extend it. And they all claim our attention here.

It is to be noted that the sign ⌇: the seated man without the flail, is an alternative to the signs of the figure with the flail; the absence or presence of the flail does not confer any significant difference on the meaning of the terms written. Nevertheless, it is necessary to give some attention to the meaning of the flail itself. Closer examination of the term ⌇: 3ḫ: akh or spirit reveals that one sign is composed of a seated figure holding a ⋀ nḫḫ3: a *nekhakha* or flail or fly whisk that became part of the royal regalia in Kemet, signified protection, here the duty of the ruler to protect his people. It is carried by potentates in Afrika today, where it signifies the very same thing. This figure and one of a squatting man, also with a ⋀, function as determinatives in writings of terms for ancestors, giving the class or general meaning to be ascribed to the word.

It is necessary to conclude that the notion of "revered person" was integral to the conception of this aspect of the person—and therefore of the entire person. In the known social history of Afrika, from earliest times to contemporary times, the only persons revered have been elders, royalty and, especially, ancestors. We shall shortly see, from an examination of the etymology and structure of terms for ancestors, that in Kemet it was not possible to divorce the notion of reverence from the idea of ancestors, or either of the two from the meaning of family. Another conclusion is therefore necessary: both the concept of the individual person and that of the family related them intimately to their ancestors, who were revered persons. Here again we notice that language provides a faithful record of genetic and social fact, for it preserves both the people of Kemet's understanding of genetic descent and inheritance from ancestors and their attitude of reverence to ancestors. The very conclusion is necessary for modern Afrika, where no one exists without family and community, and the ancestors are a living and integral aspect of all.

There are a number of words for "ancestors" in this language. One of these is ⌇ b3hi. This term originates in ⌇ m-b3ḫ (usual variations ⌇ and ⌇). Structurally, this term is clearly a composite of ⌇ b3 and ⌇ hi: husband (in the sense of the procreative function and duty.) Its most literal meaning is therefore "the soul issuing from a man's husbandly duty to reproduce." However, the normal usage of this term shows that the notion of husband here is representative of the procreative function of humanity in general; that is, of both male and female.

116   *Chapter Four*

The structure of this term, 𓂝 𓂋𓏤 m-bʒḥ, also tells us that the people of Kemet believed that the 𓅿 bʒ, the Ba or soul of a person, was passed on and inherited from their genetic ancestors. The etymology of this term therefore reinforces a conclusion that appears irresistible from our examination of 𓅱𓐍: ʒḫ: akh above: we receive our spirit as well as our souls from our sacred ancestors. Consideration of the determinative 𓀀 leads to the notion of reverence attached to the term 𓂝 𓂋𓏤 m-bʒḥ. Thus rooted in the notion of (male) progenitor, but with the exact meaning of "the revered one who sired," the term was mainly employed to mean "in the presence of," but usually of respected persons, with the extended form of 𓂝𓂋𓂝 m-bʒḥ-ʿ.[78] Again, we see that the fact of respect is closely associated with a word for ancestor. This social attitude is communicated both by the determinative 𓀀 and by the normal usage of the term. Further, deployment of the determinative 𓂝 in contradistinction to 𓂝 seems instructive. The former sign is of restrictive meaning and implies, literally, "what issues from [the phallus] or is performed by it." The meaning of the latter term, 𓂝, is more figurative. It expands the notion of phallus to a much wider concept, meaning "of the organ and all that is characterised by it."[79] Clearly then, the etymology of the term in question is rooted in the fact of male progenitor, but is used to represent genetic progenitor or ancestor, its meaning thus embracing both male and female roots.

One group of words for ancestors is founded upon the root 𓄂 ḥʒt, hat, which means "front" and "beginning" and is the basis of terms that mean "in front of," "before" and "formerly." When combined with the prepositional term 𓅓𓏤: imy, meaning "who/which is in," the resulting term, 𓅓𓏤𓄂 imy-ḥʒt: *imyhat*, literally "who/which is in front," therefore "prototype," "earliest example," is a composite in both structure and meaning. It is instructive that one word for ancestors arises directly from this term. It is simply 𓅓𓏤𓄂𓀀: imyw-ḥʒt,[80] imyuhat, the plural form of the foregoing term with the seated-man determinative 𓀀, which we have met above. (We have also encountered this entire word for ancestor in the words of Ptahhotep, the wise ancestor, who is quoted above.) The literal translation of this word is therefore "revered ones who are in front," that is, revered prototypes or earliest examples; "those revered ones of former times" or "those revered ones who are at the beginning." The tremendous significance of the idea of anteriority, of being before, in the meaning of this word may be gauged from its origin in 𓄂 ḥʒt. One resonance of the morpheme 𓄂 ḥʒt that is worthwhile noting here lies in the notion of being foremost. This idea is resident in the name 𓄂𓊃𓊪𓏏: Hatshepsut. (From = ḥʒt: "head," "foremost," and 𓊃𓊪𓏏 = špst: "noble woman;" hence "Foremost of noble women," a real leader.) We have encountered this name above, at the beginning of the Introduction and also in Chapter Three. Ancestors are valuable and revered because they are our prototypes, the ones who stand at our very beginnings and provide the first examples and models we constantly try to emulate, reinterpret and surpass in every generation. They are the very platform upon which we exist. Once again, morphology and etymology reveal a fact that is simultaneously both historical and sociological.

The combination of ⟨imy⟩ and ⟨leads⟩ to ⟨imy-bȝḥ⟩, yet another term for ancestor, but also with the meanings 'who is in the Presence', (usually of a Divinity and therefore an extremely revered presence) and 'who existed aforetime.'[81] This term is a composite in both structure and meaning. Yet again we see that great value is attached to the idea of ancestry.

Another word for ancestors is tpyw-ʿ, a word that means, literally, "those revered ones who are at the head or at the beginning," "those who are first," "those of previous times." This term is rooted in the word tp: "head" or "chief," and so also conveys the secondary notions of being in front, "example," "the best of" and so on.[82]

There is yet another term for ancestors in this language. It is founded upon the term ḏr: end, limit and includes the idea of revered persons, a fundamental one in the meaning of ancestors. ḏrtyw: ancestors[83] means that ancestors are revered ones who represent a finite and profound limit; it is not possible to go beyond them, for beyond the ancestors there is nothingness. No one existed before them in any real sense. We therefore return to the meaning of our ancestors as our revered spiritual, social, moral and material beginnings and foundations.

Some important observations emerge from these facts. The first is that we inherit important aspects of ourselves, spiritually, genetically and socially, from our ancestors. The second is that there does not appear to be any word for ancestor in the Medew Netjer which does not incorporate this meaning of "revered one from before times." Thirdly, it cannot be coincidental that in this language the words for ancestors stress their revered presence at, and therefore their representation of, the beginning—our beginning. This is one of the most important reasons why we are compelled to begin our idea and account of ourselves, of our history: our deeds and our thoughts about ourselves and the world, at our beginning and therefore with our ancestors. We commit the sacrilege of forgetting and negating our earliest ancestors when we do not begin at our beginning. When we behave in this illogical way we negate the largest part of our history, which is also the first and fundamental part, without which nothing else is possible or fully intelligible or intelligible at all. If we do not begin at our beginning we assassinate the memory of our ancestors; we weaken our psychic, psychological and social foundations. If we forget our ancestors we condemn our ancestors and so ourselves to cosmic death, which is the worst fate that can befall any section of humanity. Those who come after stand upon the foundations laid down by their ancestors and must be in constant communion with their ancestors, otherwise, their story is distorted and misunderstood, and their lives and their communities are dysfunctional—and most probably disabled. Maintaining and generally nurturing the links with the ancestors are therefore of critical importance. It is the recognition of this great importance of ancestors which led the people of Kemet to always honour, revere and, sometimes, to venerate ancestors.⁸⁴ Libation and other offerings are fundamental to this constant communication with the ancestors.

The authority of previous example is central to the concept of ancestor in Afrikan culture. This is a basic meaning of the term, as is illustrated in the language and therefore in the social history of Kemet, where the concept for "old person" had strong association with "greatness" and "authority," as can be seen from the word ⌇wr, which means both "great one" and "ruler." (Only the determinatives or sense signs are different.) It is very much the same all over the Afrikan world today wherever Afrikans have kept their cultural values intact. Understanding this will place Afrikans at a very distinct advantage in the ordering of their own affairs.

Again, in the Medew Netjer, Ȝw: iaw, the word for "old" or "the old ones," is the same as Ȝw, the word for praise or adoration (only the determinatives or sense signs are different) as well as Ȝw = "old man" and Ȝyt = "old woman." Clearly, in this language the words for elders (that is, "old man," "old woman," "the old ones") and for "praise," share a common root and are of very close affinity. Here, as in many other instances, language articulates a social reality. We are permitted to understand how Afrikans in this ancient society regarded their elders. Respect, adoration and veneration of the aged, is an unmistakable social fact conveyed in these linguistic relationships. As is shown above and below, respect, adoration and veneration of the aged and of ancestors, as well as occasional deification of ancestors, constitute one of the distinctive features of a culture that runs from Kemet to contemporary Afrika.

The structural and semantic similarities between the Medew Netjer word iȜyt: *iayt* ("old woman") and the Yoruba word *iya* (literally "mother" but also "grandmother,") should therefore not surprise us. The genetic relations between the Medew Netjer and contemporary Afrikan languages have already been illustrated⁸⁵ and the more general context of many cultural similarities and continuities between the Nile Valley and contemporary Afrika has been pointed out in this and other works. However, the specific relationship between these two terms merits further investigation and consideration.

Other terms used for ancestors are ⌇(variation ⌇) it = "father" (including forefather,) which gives rise to ity (variation ⌇), Ity = sovereign.⁸⁶ The feminization of this term provides ityt = "queen regent."⁸⁷ This etymology appears to indicate the sociological fact that ancestor veneration was a considerable basis, if not the only basis, of the kingship system in Kemet, which in turn was a tremendous force in the regulation of the society. The transmission of these related concepts of fatherhood and kingship from Kemet to contemporary Afrika may well be indicated in the continuing and exact replication of the relationship between words for "father" and those for "king." It is of the utmost importance to refrain from generalisations based upon a single instance. Nevertheless, in the context of other linguistic relationships indicated, it ought not to be surprising that oba, the Yoruba term for "king," is derived from the same root as iba, the word for "father."⁸⁸ All we are permitted to conclude from this evidence is that Yoruba notions of fatherhood and kingship appear to parallel those of the earlier people of Kemet. It is clear, however, that once again we encounter the need for a comprehensive investigation of this matter as well as its indication of a necessary perspective in the study of Afrika.

In the Medew Netjer the terms such as *itw* = "fathers," and those that mean "mother," or "mothers," collectively "fathers and mothers," all carry the meaning of progenitors, i.e. "ancestors," who, as we have seen above, are revered persons. The *Pyramid Texts* contains this usage of "fathers" and "mothers" (i.e. meaning grandfathers or grandmothers.)[89] This illustrates how ancient this usage is among Afrikans. An unusual but not unknown writing of "fathers" is of some significance here. It is ⸗ ⸗ ⸗ 𓀢, itw, with variations of 𓏺𓏺𓏺 and ⸗ ⸗ ⸗ 𓀢𓀢𓀢.[90] It was extant during the Old Kingdom, when some of the conventions of the Medew Netjer were being established. Of special interest here is the fact that in the first example, the word was written with the ideographic determinative 𓀢, which has been shown to mean "revered person." This is instructive, for it shows clearly that at the formative stage in the development of their writing, to the Ancient Egyptians, fathers were revered progenitors. We can therefore be certain that, for all Kemet, the root of the concept 𓇋𓏏 : *it*: "father" lies in a notion of progenitor or ancestry that is revered, even sacred. Again, the same must be true for the concept of 𓅐𓏏 mwt: *mut*: mother. Our understanding of all this may be reinforced by another term in the Medew Netjer that articulated another but related social fact. Here it is necessary to repeat something that has been said above, in the opening paragraph of this chapter: the term 𓉐𓂋𓏏𓏤 ḳr ḥt means both an ancestral spirit and a local divinity, which again shows that ancestors were revered.

This fact of sacred ancestry meant that the concept was not necessarily restricted to the immediate progenitor. Therefore "father" could also mean "grandfather" or father many times removed, in fact any male progenitor, a meaning that is alive in contemporary Afrikan usage of words for father. The same must be true for mothers. The people of Kemet, in the Old Kingdom, must have inherited this notion of father, and also mother, from preceding generations and passed it on to succeeding ones, for the evidence presented above compels us to conclude that this very understanding of fathers and mothers was transmitted to the succeeding generations of Kemet and later still to contemporary Afrika.

These are the identical meanings employed in many Afrikan languages to this day. Examples include Yoruba: *Baba* = father, forefather; *Iya* = mother, foremother. In Afrika, all progenitors are revered.

In fact, it may be demonstrated that the very lexical item, 𓇋𓏏 it, with the identical meanings, have been passed on from Kemet to modern Afrika. Théophile Obenga is very instructive on this point. He shows us the morphological and phonetic replication of this lexical item, as well as other terms in the Medew Netjer that relate to kinship, in the languages of modern Afrika.[91] 𓇋𓏏 it, with some meaning of "father" (i.e. either male parent of male grandparent) reproduces itself in many current Afrikan languages. Hence, in

Coptic, the last known dialect of the Medew Netjer and the language of the Coptic church, *iotĕ* = fathers, and there are also *iatĕ* and *iati*. In Kikongo, *tá* = father, with the duplication *táata*. In Mbochi there is *táa* = father; so too do *táyi* and *téyi*. (In both Kikongo and Mbochi, which are Bantu languages, this item demonstrates the phenomenon linguists call metathesis, where the order in which syllables are pronounced and so written, is reversed.) In Tagbu (Bar-el-Ghazal,) *ate* = "grandparent;" in Mondu (Bar-el-Ghazal), *àtá* = "grandparents." In Efik (Nigeria) *èté* = "father;" in Fali (Cameroon), *to* = "father," Ngbandi (Zaire) *to* = "father;" Sénoufo (Minianka) *to* = "father."[92] Similar morphological and semantic correspondences exist in the case of the words for mother,[93] and indeed for many others.[94] This frequency of correspondences cannot be accidental. They can mean only a genetic relationship among the Medew Netjer and the other Afrikan languages. Obenga's conclusion is important:

> On constate sans difficulté que tous les mots de base de la parenté égyptienne se retrouvent tels quels dans bien d'autres langues négro-africaines modernes.[95]
> [It is noticed without difficulty that all the words at the base of Egyptian kinship are the same as those of many other modern black African languages.]

Again, in the Medew Netjer there are terms reserved for royal ancestors and which reflect social conditions. *Nsyw, bityw* or *nsyw-bityw* and *isyw* = 'royal ancestors'. In Kemet royal ancestors had basically the same attributes as every other ancestor. The major difference was that royalty, particularly the Pharaohs, were able to represent this understanding of the relationship with ancestors in a far more elaborate and impressive way because of their access to far greater material resources—and perhaps, by virtue of their leadership position, a greater compulsion to respect, represent and perpetuate the rituals of heritage, since as leaders they were expected to set the example. Like all others in Kemet, they acknowledged their ancestors in various ways. A well known example is the famous scene in the Hall of Ancestors in the temple of Nesu (Pharaoh) Seti I at Abydos, which shows Seti standing with his son, Rameses, later Rameses the Great, in front of the *shenw* (cartouches) enclosing the ⌧, rnw, the *renu* or names of those they thought were the seventy-six most important royal ancestors. The young Prince Rameses and his father are performing a ritual of offering and praises to these ancestral kings, with Rameses intoning their names from a papyrus while his father burns incense in a censor. In Kemet, as in modern Afrika, a name is a very potent possession. One by one the names of ancestors who served as nsw are intoned and their spirits invoked. The spirit of *Aha* (literally the "Fighter" and therefore one who must have been a great warrior) was called forth. So too were Ahmose ("Child of the Moon") and a host of others stretching right down to Sety I. These names describe a vast tradition. They form a long, long chain that stretches back through the generations to the very dawn of the state of Kemet. This chain links every Nesu with every other Nesu, consciencising and ordering ancestors and descendants, including those as yet unborn; linking Past, Present and Future in an unbroken continuum that, at every performance of this ritual,[96] energised and renewed the current Nesu and united him with all his ancestor pharaohs and with all those pharaohs who were yet to come into being.

There is a lesson about ancestorship and descent that is to be reclaimed from this example from Kemet. It is that ancestorship and descent are not simply or only matters of biological or blood relationship, for in the long history of Kemet the kings arose from different families. (Each family is termed a dynasty in modern scholarship.) Therefore relationship among the pharaohs was also, perhaps even primarily, the ideological and related programmatic matters of maintaining the identity and stability of the world of Kemet. All who managed this project, and by extension all who were involved in it, were ideologically related. All the Pharaohs, past, present and future, therefore formed a recognisable community of like-minded souls who bore relationships of ideological progenitors and descendants among themselves. Common interests and the joint actions that arise from them are occasions for solidarity. Here is perhaps an unparalleled example of solidarity of such great and enduring history that it is therefore historic.

Keeping the names of the ancestors alive was a most sacred duty that was achieved both by calling out their names and by carving them enduringly in stone. Such knowledge of genealogy provides a firm basis for the location of an individual or group in place and time as well as for invocations. Several lists of royal ancestors are known to modern scholarship. They are termed "King Lists" by Eurocentric scholars and include those known as the Turin Canon and the Table of Saqqara. These are all survivors from numerous examples, formerly extant in Kemet, that attest to the importance of genealogy and the rituals based upon it.[97] These are not merely lists of kings, as is shown in the preceding paragraphs. Today when Afrikans recite the names of their sacred ancestors during libation, they follow a very ancient practice that keeps alive the names and memory of those ancestors and so helps to unite and order their generations and supply the profoundest meaning to the humanist endeavours resident in Afrikan tradition.

Ritual reunions and communion with ancestors were celebrated at festivals such as the Opet Festival, at which the Pharaoh's divine ancestry was confirmed, the festival to the fertility divinity Amun-Min-Kamutef, at which statues of deceased Pharaohs were paraded, and the Festival of the Valley, at which royal as well as non-royal ancestors were celebrated.[98]

We are compelled by the evidence to conclude that in the Medew Netjer the terms for ancestors and the elderly, and those for male ancestor and sovereign, share common roots; that in this language each of these two groups of terms contains words that are structurally and semantically of very close affinity. These relationships reveal genetic and sociological facts that were acknowledged in cosmogony and cosmology, where humans ultimately descended from the Creator. It should not be surprising that Afrikans have kept these traditions alive in the practice of their culture. Harry Sawyerr, Kofi Opoku and Modupẹ Oduyọye show how many West Afrikan groups have titles for the Creator that translate as Father, Mother, Grandfather, Grandparent and Paramount Chief or king. Further, the Creator is conceived as Grand Ancestor who gives each individual a part of her/his spiritual inheritance, which is therefore inherited from Him.[99] In the Diaspora this idea of the Creator is alive in the notion of Papa God, a common nomenclature in the Caribbean. Therefore, in both the ancient and current manifestations of this principle, Afrikans are linked to the Creator through their elders and ancestors, for their Creator is their first ancestor. This is the meaning of the Creator making Afrikans in his/her own image and likeness, an idea that is re-articulated in the Eurochristian tradition in the Bible at Genesis 1: 26. This shows that in order to be genuine the Creator one worships must of necessity look like that person and/or their ancestors; anything else is very likely to be a sign of disconnection from ancestors, and therefore from the self and one's mission in life. Any God who does not look like those who worship it is almost certainly false, demeaning, oppressive and disabling. Afrikans indulge in the greatest and most self destructive folly when they worship gods that do not look like them and were not passed down to them by their ancestors. Such behaviour is even more ridiculous when it is remembered that the gods of foreign creeds were violently imposed upon Afrikans by their oppressors as part of the very process of oppression, which is the biggest crime against humanity.

In Kemet as well as elsewhere in later Afrika where our culture has not been eroded or supplanted by alien cultures, the ancestors were always numbered among the family, remembered and propitiated, sometimes even venerated. The normal arrangement for each family to have an ancestral shrine is still maintained in many parts of the continent. This arrangement has been transferred to the Afrikan communities abroad, where its incidence is now noticeably on the increase. It seems that the pattern has been, from time immemorial, for heads of households, and lineage heads in particular, to ensure the correct relationship is maintained with the ancestors. A profusion of artefacts, including the shrines, but also masks, sacred groves, incense, and other materials that are in use all over the Afrikan world, illustrate this as a living expression of this ancient attitude to Afrikan ancestors. In Afrika today, and increasingly among Afrikans abroad, those who observe tradition in this matter may put the first morsel of food on the ground and pour the first drop of any drink, including water, onto Mother Earth. Sometimes a plate of food and some drink are formally set aside during a communal meal or during a particular ceremony. These are for the ancestors. The food and drink may later be disposed of in special ways, usually by putting them in the sea or in the ocean or a river, or by just leaving them out for at least a day. In many parts of Guyana and the Caribbean children are taught that it is good manners to leave aside a small portion of their food. Some refer to this left aside portion as 'manners piece'. It is almost certain that this custom is a remnant of the propitiation of divinity and ancestors by the offering up of food. In some circumstances, particularly if the food was formally offered to the ancestors and/or to any divinity, or if the drink was offered in libation, they became the basis of a communal meal or a community cup. This is the joint and equal participation in the sharing, sometimes symbolically, of food and/or drink that has been sanctified by the divinities and/or by the ancestors.

NOTES

1. T. G. Allen (trans. 1974). *The Book of the Dead or Going Forth by Day.* Studies in Ancient Oriental Civilization No. 37 (The University of Chicago Press), p. 28.
2. Jordan K. Ngubane (1979). *Conflict of Minds: Changing Power Dispositions in South Africa* (Books in Focus, Inc., New York), p. 100.
3. For example of this conception of the Afrikan family, see Théophile Obenga (1995). "*La parenté égyptienne: Considérations sociologiques*" † • *Ankh: Revue D'Égyptologie et des civilisations africaines.* Nos. 4/5. pp. 139–183.
4. Gardiner, *Egyptian Grammar*, p. 596.
5. Okot p'Bitek (1985, 1998). "The Sociality of Self" in E. C. Eze (ed.). *African Philosophy*, p. 73.
6. Raul Canizares, *Walking with the Night*, p. 78.
7. Mbiti, *African Religions and Philosophy*, pp. 8–9
8. Kimbwandende Kia Bunseki Fu-Kiau (2003). *Self-Healing Power and Therapy: Old Teachings from Africa* (Inprint Editions, Baltimore, MD, USA), pp.8–9.
9. Ogbaa, *Gods, Oracles and Divination*, p. 19.
10. Baines, "Society, Morality, and Religious Practice", p. 128.
11. Sarpong, *Libation*, p.4.
12. Armah, "Who were the Ancient Egyptians?" *New African*, April, 2006, p. 13; *The Eloquence of the Scribes*, p. 198.
13. Modupe Oduyoye. *Words and Meaning in Yoruba Religion*, p. 30.
14. For a different ground of objection see Awolalu and Dopamu. *West African Traditional Religion*, pp. 25–26. They object not to the term itself, but to the fact that some western scholars misrepresent the West African spiritual system as being only about ancestor veneration.
15. Ptahhotep's instructions form the subject of texts such as William Preston (ed. 1990; trans., introduction and appendix by B. Gunn, 1906). *The Instructions of Ptah-hotep and Ke'gemni* (Phyllis Preston Collection, Waddington, New York) and Asa G. Hilliard III, L. Williams and Nia Damali (eds., 1987). *The Teachings of Ptahhotep: The Oldest Book in the World* (Blackwood Press and Co., Inc., Atlanta, GA) and have been discussed in numerous texts on Kemet in general and its literature in particular.
16. ⟨hieroglyphs⟩: sḫrw = 'counsels', in the sense of advice. This term may also be translated as 'custom' or even 'tradition', terms which indicate greater authority and power than

mere advice. This translation is not strange to the Afrikan understanding and practice. In fact, it is completely in harmony with it.

17. The *Medew Netjer* signs are taken from the papyrus known in Egyptology as P. Prisse. See K. Sethe (1924). *Ägyptische Lesestücke*. (Leipzig), p. 36.

18. ⊿🕊sḏm. Literally, 'to hear', but also 'to listen', 'to understand' and 'to obey'. The verb 'to hear' still has these very same meanings in most Afrikan languages, including Ebonics. 'Obeyed' is preferred here because of the greater force of tradition, in the form of ancestors and divinity, which are very significant aspects of this context.

19. M. Lichtheim. *Ancient Egyptian Literature*. Volume I, p. 76.

20. Rt. Rev. Dr. Peter Kwasi Sarpong (1996). *Libation*. (Anansesem Publications: Accra), pp. 3–4.

21. Kofi A. Opoku. *West African Traditional Religion*, p. 36; Awolalu and Dopamu, pp. 254–255, 274.

22. See, as examples, the rubric of Utterance 228 in R. O. Faulkner (Trans. 1973). *The Ancient Egyptian Coffin Texts*. Vol. I (Aris & Phillips Ltd.: Warminster, UK), p. 181 and a number of instances ranging from the Old Kingdom to the Late Period quoted in Rosalind M. and Jac. J. Janssen (1996). *Getting Old in Ancient Egypt*. (The Rubicon Press, London), pp. 67–68; the papyrus known as Papyrus Pushkin 127, as translated in Ricardo A. Caminos (1977). *A Tale of Woe: Papyrus Pushkin127* (Griffith Institute, Ashmolean Museum, Oxford), pp. 11 and 15.

23. For example, Bryan Edwards (1801–7). *The History of the British Colonies in the West Indies*. Book 4, pp. 98–99, as referenced in Orlando Patterson (1967, 1973). *The Sociology of Slavery* (Sangster's Book Stores Ltd., Kingston, Jamaica), p.158; Vega (2000). *The Altar of My Soul, passim*.

24. Vega. *The Altar of My Soul*, p. 150.

25. Instructions of Putahhotep as quoted in Miriam Lichtheim. *Ancient Egyptian Literature* Vol. I, p.63.

26. Jacob H. Carruthers (1995). *Mdw Ntr : Divine Speech* (Karnak House, London), p.45.

27. Chinua Achebe (1975). *Morning Yet On Creation Day* (Heinemann, London),p. xiii.

28. Ogbaa. Gods, Oracles and Divination, p. 68.

29. Rodney. *The Groundings*, p. 54. For details among the Gikuyu consult Jomo Kenyatta (1965). *Facing Mount Kenya: The Tribal Life of the Gikuyu* (Vintage Books, New York), pp. 253–258.

30. Among others see W. O. Maloba (1998). *Mau Mau and Kenya: An Analysis of a Peasant Revolt*. (Indiana University Press and James Currey, Bloomington, Indianapolis and London); T. Ranger (1985). *Peasant Consciousness and Guerrilla War in Zimbabwe: A Comparative Study* (James Currey, London); Lan. *Guns and Rain* and D. Martin and P. Johnson (1981). *The Struggle for Zimbabwe: The Chimurenga War* (Monthly Review Press, New York and London).

31. Lan. *Guns and Rain*, pp. 158–159; D. Martin and P. Johnson (1981). *The Struggle for Zimbabwe*, pp. 75–76.

32. Maloba. *Mau Mau and Kenya*, p. 126.

33. Basil Davidson (1993). *The Black Man's Burden: Africa and the Curse of the Nation-State* (Spectrum Books Limited, Ibadan), p. 48.

34. The most recent texts include David Anderson (2005). *Histories of the Hanged: Britain's Dirty War in Kenya and the end of Empire*. (Weidenfeld and Nicolson, London) and Caroline Elkins (2005). *Britain's Gulag. The Brutal End of Empire in Kenya* (Jonathan Cape, London).

35. Maloba. Ibid., pp. 137–150.

36. There have been a number of recent revelations in the British and international press. Examples include the Tom Rhodes, "The Files Nobody wants—Britain's secret colonial files on Kenya." *Africa Review.* 9th May, 2013. www.africareview.com/Analysis [Accessed 12th May, 2013]; The Communist Party of Great Britain (Marxist-Leninist). "The Kenya Files: Another veil lifted from the murderous face of British imperialism's colonial past." *Proletarian.* Issue 48. June, 2012, and Ian Cobain and Richard Norton-Taylor, "Files that may shed light on colonial crimes still kept secret by UK." *The Guardian.* 25th April, 2013.
37. J. Kotkin (1992). *Tribes: How Race, Religion and Identity determine success in the new global economy* (Random House, New York).
38. Lee Kuan Yew (2000). *From the Third World to the First World* (Harper Collins, New York).
39. Amy Chua (2004). *World on Fire* (Anchor Books, New York).
40. Amilcar Cabral (1980). *Unity and Struggle.* (Heinemann Educational Books Ltd.), especially pp. 138–154.
41. Kwesi Prah (1998). *Beyond the Color Line.* (Africa World Press, Inc., Trenton, NJ and Asmara, Eritrea).
42. Kimani Nehusi (2003). "Language in the Construction of Afrikan Unity: Past, Present and Policy" in Mammo Muchie (ed.). *The Making of the Africa-Nation: Pan-Africanism and the African Renaissance* (London, Adonis&Abbey Publishers, Ltd.), pp. 208–233.
43. Cabral. Ibid., p. 143. Emphasis in the original.
44. Chapurukha M. Kusimba (1996). "Ancestor Worship and Divine Kingship in Sub-Saharan Africa" in T. Celenko (ed.) *Egypt in Africa* (Indianapolis Museum of Art and Indiana University Press, Indianapolis), p. 59; Awolalu and Dopamu. *West African Traditional Religion,* p. 274.
45. Lanny Bell (1996). "Ancestor Worship and Divine Kingship in the Ancient Nile Valley" in T. Celenko (ed.). *Egypt in Africa,* pp. 56–58; Janssen and Janssen, *Getting Old in Ancient Egypt,* p. 55.
46. R.B. Parkinson (1991). *Voices from Ancient Egypt: An Anthology of Middle Kingdom Writings* (British Museum Press, London), pp. 142–145; Ian Shaw and Paul Nicholson (1995). *The British Museum Dictionary of Ancient Egypt* (The British Museum Press, London), pp. 160–161; Janssen and Janssen, *Getting Old in Ancient Egypt,* pp. 55–59; J. P. Allen, 'Introduction' in Faulkner (trans.). *Ancient Egyptian Book of the Dead,* p.16; Armah, *The Eloquence of the Scribes,* pp. 203–204.
47. Mbiti. *African Religions and Philisophy,* pp. 8–9, 59, 160–165, etc.; Sarpong, p.4; Chapurukha M. Kusimba (1996). "Ancestor Worship and divine kingship in Sub-Saharan Africa" in T. Celenko. Ibid., pp. 58–61; David Lan. *Guns and Rain,* p. 32; Armah. *The Eloquence of the Scribes,* pp.23–24, Awalalu and Dopamu, pp. 275–278; Oduyoye. *Words & Meaning in Yoruba Religion,* pp. 108 and 112–113, etc.
48. Emilla Viotti da Costa (1994). *Crowns of Glory, Tears of Blood: The Demerara Slave Rebellion of 1823* (Oxford University Press, New York and Oxford), p. 339, note 61.
49. K. Dunham (1983). *Dances of Haiti* (Center of Afro-American Studies, UCLA, Los Angeles), p.5.
50. Guinea, or *Guiné* or *Ginen* (in Haiti) is another name for Afrika among Afrikans in the Americas. It was in popular use particularly during and just after the time of physical enslavement. An increasingly semi mythical and abstract construct as ties with the cultural wellspring of the homeland became progressively weakened, *Guiné* is paralleled by a similar though geographically restricted view of Ile Ife among practitioners of Santeriá, for whom the city has become, in the estimation of Canizares, p.3: "an abstract,

almost subliminal memory." It retains its status of cultural centre for many Yorubas, as is evidenced by Idowu. *Olódùmare*, pp. 11–17. Among the Igbo, the cities of Nri, in upper Anambra, and Amaigbo, in Orlu, are centers of dispersal of people and culture, and the spiritual and ideological centers and headquarters. See M. A. Onwuejeogwu (1980). *An Outline of an Igbo Civilization: Nri Kingdom and Hegemony, A. D. 994 to present.* Tabansi Press Ltd. for the Odinani Museum, Nri. Ibadan, Nigeria.
51. Dunham, p. xxiv.
52. Babalawo, pp. iii and 7–8.
53. National Black United Front, Houston Chapter. "Fifth Annual Sankofa Caravan to The Ancestors." Press Release of Wednesday, October 2, 2002. See also Press Releases for subsequent years.
54. For example, see Sayyaddina Thomas (2003). "Maafa is Kiswahili for Great Calamity." Email of 23 October, 2003. See also Reshma Ragoonath (2003). "Rain Fails to Dampen Kwanzaa Festival." *The Guardian* (Port of Spain, Trinidad and Tobago). Tuesday, 22 July, 2003.
55. That is, to invest them with the spiritual strength and dexterity of the Ancestors as well as with the inspiration derived from knowing them.
56. Katherine Dunham (1983). *Dances of Haiti*. (Los Angeles, Center for Afro-American Studies, UCLA), p. xi.
57. Sarpong. *Libation*, p.4.
58. K. S. Opoku. *West African Traditional Religion*, p. 53.
59. C. Jacq. *Egyptian Magic*, p. 12. For a substantial attempt to account for the life of Imhotep consult J. B. Hurry (1926, 1987). *Imhotep: The Egyptian God of Medicine* (Ares Publishers, Chicago). For the most up to date treatment see Charles S. Finch (1988). "Imhotep the Physician: Archetype of the Great Man" in I. Van Sertima (ed.). *Great Black Leaders: Ancient and Modern* (Journal of African Civilizations Ltd., Inc.), pp. 213–231 and D. Wildung (1977). *Egyptian Saints: Deification in Pharaonic Egypt* (New York University Press). Note also George Hart, "From history into legend" *Egyptian Myths*, pp.62–65; Budge. *Herb Doctors*, p. 11; Shaw and Nicholson. *The British Museum Dictionary of Ancient Egypt*, pp. 29–30, 139–140; Heinrich Schäfer (1898). *"Eine altägyptische Schreibersitte" ZÄS* 36, pp. 147–148 and Alan H. Gardiner (1902–03). "Imhotep and the Scribe's Libation" *ZÄS* 40, p.146.
60. The inscription is taken from Alan H. Gardiner, "Imhotep and the Scribe's Libation." p. 146. The translation is based on Gardiner, Ibid. For translation see also Wildung, p. 34 and Schäfer, *"Eine altägyptische Schreibersitte,"* p.148.
61. David. *Religion and Magic in Ancient Egypt*, p.278
62. See for example A. S. Abarry, "The Ga Homowo (Hunger-Hooting) Cultural Festival" in Asante and Abarry, *African Intellectual Heritage*, p. 254.
63. Opoku. *West African Traditional Religions*, pp. 35–53; Peter Sarpong, "The Akan Blackened Stool and the Odwira Festival" in Asante and Abarry, pp.251–253.
64. J. O. Lucas. *The Religion of the Yorubas*, pp. 119–149; Lucas. *Religions in West Africa and Ancient Egypt*, pp. 149–183. Unfortunately, Lucas adopts Eurocentric terminology in referring to these Ancestral Festivals as 'cults', thereby, perhaps unintentionally, ascribing negative value to them.
65. Maureen Warner-Lewis (1991). *Guinee's Other Suns: The African Dynamic in Trinidad Culture* (The Majority Press, Dover, Mass.), p.115, emphasis in the original. See also pp.5, 50, 55, 116, 122 and 191 and Warner-Lewis (2003). *Central Africa in the Caribbean: Transcending Time, Transforming Cultures* (The University of the West

Indies Press, Mona, Jamaica), pp. 148–153. For Carriacou and Grenada, with variant orthography, see R. Allsopp. *Dictionary of Caribbean English Usage*, p. 488.
66. Warner-Lewis. *Central Africa in the Caribbean*, pp. 152–153.
67. J. G. Cruikshank (1917, 1999). "Among the Aku (Yoruba) in Canal No.1, West Bank, Demerara River" in David Granger (ed.). *Scenes from the History of the Africans in Guyana*. (free press, Georgetown), p. 49. Note also B. L. Moore (1995). *Cultural Power, Resistance and Pluralism: Colonial Guiana, 1838–1900* (The Press University of the West Indies and Mc Gill-Queens University Press), p. 118 and Barbara Josiah (1997). "After Emancipation: Aspects of village life in Guyana, 1869–1911" *The Journal of Negro History*. Vol. LXXXII, No. 1. Winter. p. 115, where the term is rendered *seku* or *s'iku*.
68. Interviews with several Villagers of Queenstown, mostly from the Primo family, provided corroborated information: Ms. Patsy Russell, 54 years, Toronto, Canada, 6th May, 2006; Mrs. Vera Venture, 82 years, New York, 7th October, 2006. Telephone; Interview with Ms. Lorine Grace Simon, 44 years. New York, 19th November, 2006. Telephone; Mrs. Voi James, 68 years, Queenstown Village, Essequibo Coast, Guyana, 20th November, 2006. Telephone; Ms. Evelyn James, 40 years, New York. 20th November, 2006. Telephone; Mrs. Eunice Walcott, 72 years. Queenstown Village, Essequibo Coast, Guyana. 22nd November, 2006. Telephone.
69. The NSAA Family, "Special African Ceremony to honor Dr. John Henrik Clark and other African Warrior Ancestors." Email of 27 April, 2006.
70. Maulana Karenga (1989). "Towards a Sociology of Maatian Ethics: Literature and Context" in Ivan Van Sertima. *Egypt Revisited*. p. 367.
71. Rodney. *The Groundings*, p.53.
72. Herbert Ekwe-Ekwe and Femi Nzegwu (1994). *Operationalising Afrocentricism* (International Institute for African Research, Reading), p. 11.
73. R.O. Faulkner (Trans.1973). *The Ancient Egyptian Coffin Texts*. Vol. I (Aris & Phillips Ltd., Warminster), p.118, note 1. Later writings of *abet*: 'family' included 𓊪𓂋𓉐 and its variations 𓊪𓂋𓉐 and 𓊪𓂋𓉐.
74. The other aspects of the person were the ⊔:k3 (ka) or soul, ♔: b3 (ba), ♡:ib (literally 'heart', but really the seat of consciousness, intelligence and morality; the mind in modern translation), ⊂:rn *ren*: name, 𓄡:ḫ3t, *khat*: body, and 𓇳𓇳:šwt: shadow.
75. Gardiner. *Egyptian Grammar*, p. 447.
76. Faulkner. *Concise Dictionary*, pp. 264 and 265.
77. Allen. *Middle Egyptian*, p. 468.
78. Gardiner. Ibid., pp. 132 and 456.
79. Ibid., p.456.
80. Gardiner. *Egyptian Grammar*, pp. 447, 539, 553, 580; Faulkner. *Concise Dictionary*, pp. 18 and 19; Allen. *Middle Egyptian*, pp. 459, 463, Erman and Grapow. *Wörterbuch* I, pp.72–77.
81. Faulkner. *Concise Dictionary*, p. 18.
82. Gardiner. *Egyptian Grammar*, pp.599–600, 605; Faulkner. *Concise Dictionary*, pp. 296 and 297.
83. Gardiner. *Egyptian Grammar*, p. 604.
84. The *Medew Netjer* term for venerated state is 𓇋𓐛𓐙𓐍:imȝḫ, which is almost certainly the same or very similar to the word for spinal cord, which supplies the root of a number of cognates like honour, venerated one, etc. See Gardiner. *Egyptian Grammar*, p. 553; Faulkner. *A Concise Dictionary*, p.20.

85. See, for example, C. A. Diop (1977). *Parenté Génétique De L'Egyptien Pharaonique Et des Langues Négro-Africaines* (Institut Fondamental D'Afrique Noire, Dakar); T. Obenga. *Ancient Egypt and Black Africa*; Obenga. "La Parenté égyptienne: Considérations sociologiques;" Nehusi, "From Medew Netjer to Ebonics." This is far from an exhaustive listing.
86. Lanny Bell (1996). "Ancestor Worship and Divine Kingship in the Ancient Nile Valley" in Theodore Celenko (ed.). *Egypt in Africa* (Indianapolis Museum of Art and Indiana University Press, Indianapolis), p.56; J. P. Allen. *Middle Egyptian*, p. 30.
87. Faulkner. *A Concise Dictionary*, p. 33; Erman and Grapow, Vol. I, p. 143.
88. Modupe Oduyoye. *Words & Meaning*, p.36.
89. R. O. Faulkner (trans.). *The Pyramid Texts*. Note 2, p. 294.
90. Faulkner (1929). *The Plural and the Dual in Old Egyptian* (Édition de la Fondation Égyptologique Reine Élisabeth, Bruxelles), pp. 18, 20 and 24.
91. Obenga, "*La parenté égyptienne*" pp. 157–163. This is not necessarily an undisputed view among scholars.
92. Ibid., pp. 157–158.
93. Ibid., pp. 158–162, *passim*.
94. Obenga. "*La parenté égyptienne*", *passim*; Obenga (1992). *Ancient Egypt and Black Africa* (Karnak House, London), pp. 105–141; reprinted in Obenga (1996). "Genetic Linguistic Connections of Ancient Egypt and the Rest of Africa," in M. K. Asante and A.S.Abarry (eds.). *African Intellectual Heritage: A Book of Sources*, pp. 262–281.
95. Obenga, "*La parenté égyptienne*", p. 162.
96. For possible details of this Ancestor Ritual consult Alison Roberts (2000). *My Heart My Mother: Death and Rebirth in Ancient Egypt* (NorthGate Publishers, Rottingdean, East Sussex, UK), pp. 72–92.
97. Donald B. Redford (1986). *Pharaonic King-Lists, Annals and Day-Books*. (Benben Publications, Mississauga); T. C. H. James (1984). *Pharaoh's People*. (The Bodley Head, London), pp.132–133; Alan Gardiner (1961). *Egypt of the Pharaohs* (Oxford University Press), pp. 47–51.
98. Bell, Ibid., p.57.
99. Harry Sawyerr (1970). *God. Ancestor or Creator?* (Longmans, London), p. xi; Opoku, *West African Traditional Religion*, pp. 25—26; 91—100. See also Modupẹ Oduyọyẹ (1983). "Names and Attributes of God". E. A. Ade Adegbola (ed.). *Traditional Religion in West Africa*, p. 349.

Figure 1. Pouring libation onto the body of Asuru, the Corn Divinity. Source: Charles Finch III, MD (1992). *Echoes of the Old Darkland*, p.182

Figure 2. A woman making offerings in early Kemet (UC 14417). Source: Petrie Museum of Egyptology, University College London.

Figure 3. Another illustration of a woman making offerings in early Kemet (UC 14417). Source: Petrie Museum of Egyptology, University College London.

Figure 4. Libation today in Afrikan communities abroad. The naming ceremony of the author's niece, Nia Nyasha Abenni Drakes, Ifetayo Cultural Arts Center, New York, USA. July, 1995. From left to right: Bashir Mchawi, Nana Baakan, Dr. T. Olufemi Drakes, and Ms. Helen Drakes. Photograph courtesy of Kamau Drakes.

Figure 5. An offering table from Kemet, the 12th Dynasty. Note the grooves for running water and the loaves and libation vessels carved into the surface. A Des Robinson photograph.

Figure 6. Another offering table from the 12th Dynasty Kemet. A channel for running water links both registers while libation vessels and birds, loaves, and other articles offered are carved into the upper register. Photograph supplied by Des Robinson

Figure 7. Pepi I making a two-handed offering of libation (BM 39.121). Notice the use of both hands and his kneeling posture of humility. Source: Brooklyn Museum.

Figure 8. NSU Taharka offering libation to Hemen the Falcoln Divinity. Notice the use of both hands, the angle of his arms, and his kneeling posture of humility. The Louvre, Paris. A Des Robinson photo.

Figure 9. A message from the Ancestors. A message asking urgent questions of every generation. Do you remember? Do you know from whence you came or were brought, and how, and why? Do you know who you are? Do you really know? A Denese Ellis photograph.

Figure 10. Sylvia Thomas, informant of Colihaut, Dominica. Photograph by Villeneuve George.

Figure 11. Albert Severen, informant of Colihaut, Dominica. Photograph by Villeneuve George.

Figure 12. Vera Venture-Hinds informant of Queenstown Village, Essequibo Coast, Guyana.

Figure 13. Water of Life in Kemet. The Divinities Heru and Djhwty pouring Libation with Divine (holy) water over an nsw to purify (baptise) him in a ritual that every nsw underwent as part of his coronation. The divine water is represented by ⚱ ankh and ⚱ was sceptres, which respectively confer long life and power to rule. Temple of Sobek, Kom Ombo. Late Period. A Des Robinson photograph.

Chapter Five

Transmission Across Space and Time

We can tell that libation was transmitted across Afrika, most probably with the periodic out-migration of the Afrikan people from the Nile Valley to possess the land, though it is necessary to recognise the possibility of pre-existing groups of Afrikans in other parts of the continent, for example the San speech community of Southern Afrika. This writer has previously shown that:

> When a people migrate, especially en masse, or, as in the case of most Afrikans in Arab lands and in the West, were made to migrate, they do not leave their culture behind. They take their culture with them, for culture cannot be peeled off and separated from a people like a discarded shirt and left behind like another forgotten or unwanted garment or a house or a farm or like any other material possession. Modifications, the consequences of challenges of space, place and time, which often translate into the compulsion to work with new or differing materials in new and differing environments, account for variations, transformations and discontinuities.[1]

This is the major reason for the presence of words for libation in the entire linguistic map of Afrika and the presence of the libation ritual and the libation complex among Afrikans. These facts point to the existence of a common core of cultural values and institutions among all Afrikans and the common origin of the Afrikan nation. Clinton A. Hutton has enunciated the fundamental consequence of the natural drive for continuity among Afrikans in the Americas:

> When enslaved West African peoples began the recreation of their lives in the Americas, their ancestral conception of community became an important guide in the construction of African diasporic community.[2]

The Afrikan blueprint was not the only source of ideas and practices in community formation among Afrikan people in the Americas. We shall see in the discussion below that Native American and European forms were also available and were often incorporated in the Afrikan project of re-creating their lives, though we must note that there was a sustained attempt by Europeans to distort or erase Afrikan culture and enforce their own formats.

6.1: Camouflage

Afrikan strategies for survival in the hostile world of the plantations were critical to the survival of libation and other aspects of Afrikan culture in the Caribbean and the Americas. On the plantations of the Americas and the Caribbean a major preoccupation of the enslavers was the assassination of Afrikan identity because of the realisation that Afrikans who know themselves may be forced into captive labour but can never be enslaved in the most profound ways, that is, spiritually and mentally. So the plantation owners and managers would constantly face a war of extermination by Afrikans who were conscious of their history and their culture, in one word, who retained their identity. The history of resistance and revolt against enslavement illustrates this generalization very clearly. It shows a high positive correlation between the possession of Afrikan culture and therefore of Afrikan identity, and the capacity to resist, and even to make revolution. Hence Afrikans in Haiti, where they retained Voodoo and those in Berbice in Guyana, where Afrikan culture was also retained, militarily defeated European forces (in 1791–1804 and 1763, respectively) and placed revolutionary governments in power. Communities of Resistance, rooted in Afrikan culture, were permanent fixtures in this history of resistance. Palanque do Palmares existed in Brazil from 1595 to 1695. The resistance of the Maroons of Jamaica and Suriname also illustrates this truth very eloquently, though it cannot be claimed that the vacillation, and worse, of some Maroons in Jamaica at some important historical moments contributed to this tendency. The plantation system and the maintenance of the Afrikan cultural heritage and Afrikan dignity were mutually exclusive. Afrika and things Afrikan: values, spiritual system, language, indeed every aspect of Afrikan culture, was therefore relentlessly attacked by being outlawed, given negative value and subjected to a range of other oppressive measures. Cultural genocide was an aim of the plantation system. Cultural genocide became institutionalised and has been reproduced and perpetuated as a basic and often unvoiced objective of the institutions and systems that oppress Afrikans all over the world today.

AFRIKAN DIVINITY	EUROPEAN CAMOUFLAGE(S)	DISTINGUISHING FEATURES	COUNTRY
Yemanyá	La Virgen de Regla	Female divinity of the oceans. Mother of all orisas.	Cuba, Puerto Rico, USA
Yemanjá	Nossa Sra. Da Concieçcão Da Pria		Bahia, Brasil Trinidad, USA
Shango (The Warrior)	Santa Bárbara	Epitome of manly beauty. Lord of thunder and lightening, drumming and dancing.	Cuba Puerto Rico Trinidad USA
Obotalá	La Mercedes	Male divinity of creativity	Cuba
Ochun (Goddess of sweet water, Love giving and Community)	La Caridad del Cobre	Queen of rivers. Epitome of feminine beauty and sensuality. Protector of pregnant women. Protector against intestinal disorders.	Cuba Puerto Rico Trinidad USA
Ochosi (The Hunter)		Male divinity of hunting	Cuba, Haiti, Trinidad
Ellegisa	El Niño de Atocha		
Agwé, Divinity of water	St. Ulrique		Haiti
Babalz Ayi Baba Ayé	St. Lazarus	Lord of leprosy, small pox and other skin ailments.	Haiti Cuba
Elegbara, Esu, Elegba Legba	St. Anthony St. Lazarus	Opener of the Way. Lord of crossroads and cemeteries.	Cuba Haiti, Puerto Rico Trinidad, USA
Ogun	St. Peter	Lord of iron and war.	Cuba, Brasil, Trinidad, USA.
Damballah	St. Patrick		Haiti
Oyá		Ruler of storms. Resident at gates of cemeteries.	Cuba Trinidad

TABLE 6.1: AFRIKAN DIVINITIES CAMOUFLAGED IN EUROPEAN SAINTS SOURCES: Z. N. Hurston. *Tell My Horse*; M. Vega Moreno. *The Altar of My Soul*; Nascimento. *Orixás*; Deren. *Divine Horsemen*; Thompson. *Flash of the Spirit*; Lucas. *Religion of the Yorubas*; Canizares. *Walking with the Night*.

Being Afrikan conscious was a very dangerous occupation in "New World" plantation society, for in a world dominated by institutions and processes of cultural genocide against Afrikans, it was, still is, and will be always, the most revolutionary condition of Afrikans. Those Afrikans who escaped from the plantations and set up their own independent Afrikan-centered communities were assiduously hunted down by Europeans, who aimed to destroy them. Such communities, called Kilombos, Mocambos, Palenques and so on, are generally termed Maroon Communities in some literatures. They are really Afrikan Communities of Resistance. In such communities Afrikan life was organised along Afrikan cultural principles as much as was possible: spiritually, socially, politically, militarily, economically, etc. It was necessary for Europeans to try to destroy these communities totally because each one represented the living practice of an Afrikan-centered alternative to the barbarities of European domination and enslavement in plantation society. The existence of Afrikan Communities of Resistance was therefore diametrically opposed to plantation culture and the interests of European enslavers.[3]

There was far more Afrikan unity in the Americas than Eurocentric sources commonly acknowledge. Violently thrown together in the common plight of enslavement in particular, and the Maafa in general, Afrikans from various parts of the continent united to forge common and distinctive cultural institutions and expressions out of often differing manifestations of the same cultural principles brought from Afrika. This unity was achieved not only because of their common predicament of enslavement and therefore their common objective of liberation, but also because of the bedrock of Afrikan cultural unity that is also not commonly credited in Eurocentric sources.[4] They built communities. In this creative response to a harsh new environment, there unfolded the processes of reinforcement of similarities and the merging and (re)blending of communities which always had much in common. The common possession of libation is one expression of this cultural unity and continuity.

Those sacred Afrikan ancestors who remained on the plantations and so could not openly practice Afrikan culture, realised that in their situation, an open, permanent and direct confrontation with their enslavers was almost certainly suicidal. So they thought out a series of tactics, each of which contributed to the grand strategy to make it appear that they were surrendering their cultural autonomy, while in fact they were trying to preserve it. It was a trickster's twist, one of the best 'Nancy stories ever, all the more so because it was real and alive with myriad dangers in a world made very dangerous by enslavement and the oppressors' objective of cultural genocide against Afrikans.

The Afrikan strategy has worked very well in the case of spirituality, where Afrikans on the plantations gave European names and European clothes to Afrikan divinities while maintaining their Afrikan substance. This is deemed "syncretism" in Eurocentric terminology because Eurocentric scholars believe that the predominant motive for Afrikan appropriation of aspects of the form of European culture was admiration for the European culture. Nothing could be further from the truth. The facts are that Afrikans appropriated European saints that suited the Afrikan purpose and were therefore selected and used by the ancestors.

Throughout the years some of the most astute and discerning observers have reported on this matter. In 1915 W. E. B. Du Bois, the great Afrikan American Pan Afrikanist scholar, who, despite his impeccable intentions, was not free of some of the terminology that reflected the widespread prejudices of the time, wrote this:

> At first sight it would seem that slavery completely destroyed every vestige of spontaneous movement among the Negroes. This is not strictly true. The vast power of the priest in the African state is well known; his realm alone—the province of religion and medicine—remained largely unaffected by the plantation system. The Negro priest, therefore, early became an important figure on the plantation and found his function as the interpreter of the supernatural, the comforter of the sorrowing, and as the one who expressed, rudely but picturesquely, the longing and disappointment and resentment of a stolen people. From such beginnings arose and spread with marvelous rapidity the Negro church, the first distinctively Negro American social institution. It was not at first by any means a Christian church, but a mere adaptation of those rites of fetish which in America is termed obe worship, or "voodooism." Association and missionary effort soon gave these rites a veneer of Christianity and gradually, after two centuries, the church became Christian, with a simple Calvinistic creed, but with many of the old customs still clinging to the services. It is this historic fact, that the Negro church of to-day bases itself upon the sole surviving social institution of the African fatherland, that accounts for its extraordinary growth and vitality.[5]

The very same conclusion, based upon first hand observations of expert eyewitnesses, has been consistently returned over the last six decades. Listen to Zora Neale Hurston in 1938: ". . . right here, let it be said that the Haitian gods, mysteres, or loa are not the Catholic calendar of saints done over in black as has been stated by casual observers . . . over and over in print."[6]

In 1953 Maya Deren arrived at the same conclusion, even though, not understanding that Afrika is the immediate source of many of the similarities between Afrikan spiritual systems and Christianity, she incorrectly attributed the similarities she observed to Afrikan borrowings from the Europeans:

> Where, at first glance, it might seem that Christianity has triumphed over Voudoun, it becomes clear, on closer study, that Voudoun has merely been receptive to compatible elements from a sister faith and has integrated these into its basic structure, subtly transfiguring and adjusting their meaning, where necessary, to the African tradition.[7]

More recent testimony has upheld this observation. In 1983 Kathleen Dunham found that:

> [t]he Catholicism with which the African vodu merged is still superficial, being principally adapted as an expedient to satisfy the [Eurocentric] moral demands of visiting priests and government officials, and as a source of saintly effigies to replace those representations of deities lost in the process of transculturation.[8]

We must note here, *en passant*, that the Afrikan representations of Afrikan gods were not merely "lost." They were consistently repressed, often violently, by European enslavers. Still, in 1983, Robert F. Thompson added this observation to the corpus of more objective conclusions about Voodoo:

> In the course of supposed Westernization, Haitians actually transformed the meaning of the Catholic icons by observing their similarities to African spirits. Haitians restructured the identity of the saints of the Catholic Church in terms of their own religious language.[9]

In 2000, Martha Moreno Vega, in the quote reproduced below, stated very clearly that the Orishas are not the same as the Catholic saints that are employed for the purpose of camouflaging them.[10]

It is therefore clear that Afrikans in Haiti, Brazil, Cuba, Trinidad and elsewhere in the Americas and the Caribbean have adapted a veneer of Catholicism for the purpose of better preserving the Orishas, and that this has been so from near to the inception of their captivity in these places.

This strategic incorporation of European form and labels to disguise Afrikan spiritual substance, as well as its persistent misrepresentation by Eurocentric scholarship, amount to two conflicting interpretations of the same situation. This has enabled Ishmael Reed to echo a certain popular conclusion about Haiti that in turn echoes both interpretations, but with a clear recognition of the great predominance of Voodoo: "the people are ninety-five per cent Catholic and one hundred per cent Voodoo."[11] Reed's observation describes not only Haiti. Trinidad is a 'Catholic country' where the people stage one of the biggest carnivals in the world and a growing number are adherents of Shango. Varying degrees of formal adherence to Christianity alongside the simultaneous practice of Afrikan spiritual systems may also be found in Brazil, Cuba, Jamaica, Puerto Rico, Santo Domingo, many families and communities in the United States and other parts of the Caribbean and the Americas, where, in the teeth of oppression,

> . . . Africans culturally re-created their belief systems, grounding them in the traditions of their tribal heritages. In this way, ancestor [propitiation] and the age-old tales of the African divinities were preserved in the memories of their descendants, secretly passed down through more than four hundred years of enslavement.[12]

6.2: Revolution

A much truer representation of the faith of the Haitian people than that provided by Eurocentric scholarship is clearly shown in how Haitians behaved in times of the gravest danger which, not co-incidentally, was when they launched their greatest undertaking to date. The occasion was the Haitian

Revolution. The military stage of this Revolution, which was launched on the night of August 22, 1791, was preceded, on the night of August 14, by a Voodoo ceremony in which Boukman Dutty, a Houngan[13] or Voodoo Priest, led the revolutionaries in a celebration of Ogun, the Yoruba, Fon and Voodoo personification or Orisha (Divinity) of Warfare and Iron. Carruthers' observation on this point is not merely accurate; it is unerring:

> Boukman . . . planned the launching of the revolution with Ogun's celebration in keeping with the time tested tradition among African people that human events must be coordinated with cosmological forces and ancestral spirits. The revolution, thus, had its roots in the African Worldview.[14]

Clinton A. Hutton travels further along the road to a secure understanding of the great revolutionary process in Haiti. His brilliant work begins the location, exploration and explanation of 'the centrality of Africa and the African diaspora in the making of the Haitian revolution', mainly through uncovering some of the cosmological roots of Haitian revolutionary thought and practice.[15] Hutton, like Carruthers before him, has raised the fundamental question of the centrality of Afrikan thought and practice to this Afrikan revolutionary undertaking in the Americas. Other scholars, either through prejudice or ignorance, or a combination of both, have sought to locate the origin and basis of the Haitian Revolution in the ideals of the French Revolution, and therefore in Europe. Hutton's work is an important intervention that demonstrates Afrikan agency and Afrikan cosmology as the root of the Haitian revolution.

Boukman Dutty's names are significant, as are all Afrikan names. His family name, Dutty, is from the term dɔte in the Twi language.[16] It means soil, earth. His first name, Boukman, is from Kwéyòl (Creole,) a language invented by Afrikans in parts of the Caribbean dominated by the French. The word Boukman is, literally, book + man = Book-man: "the man who could read," a most dangerous crime of the inventors of reading and writing under the civilizing mission of Europeans in the time of enslavement. Here is a literate son of the soil who placed his skills at the service of Afrikan revolution, a conscious and determined defender of Mother Earth and of the Afrikan worldview in general. Here, too, is one whose very Afrikan ceneterd existence was on many levels in direct contradiction to the Eurocentric plantation system. First was his existence as an Afrikan who was conscious of his spiritual heritage. Second was the fact that Boukman was a literate Afrikan in the barbarous season of enforced Afrikan illiteracy and the profound and damaging ignorance of self that was imposed across generations through cultural genocide and the attempted ethnic cleansing of history of all Afrikan achievement. Boukman's Afrikan centered socialization aligned him with the interests of his people and prepared him for leadership.

It is therefore not surprising that Boukman's actions illustrate the centrality of Afrikan Spirituality in the Haitian Revolution. Here, the spiritual actor is just as important as the political actor and the military actor. In fact, in the holistic practice encouraged by the Afrikan worldview, the three were fused in the person of Boukman Dutty. We have seen that this worldview and understandings that are derived from it, such as the need for cosmic harmony and therefore the necessity to synchronise human activity with cosmic forces, have been in the possession of Afrikans from at least 5000 years ago in the Nile Valley. It was this Afrikan worldview that enabled Afrikans in Haiti to recognise their interest with such clarity and to act in its name so decisively. Boukman's address to the revolutionaries on the eve of the physical attack on the plantation system is, very significantly, completely Afrikan centered; that is, in form, in content and in context. His address was delivered in the Afrikan Caribbean language of Kwéyòl (Creole) and illustrates this recognition of reality and the resultant clarity of vision:

> The god of the white man calls forth crime but our god wills good works. . . . Throw away the likeness of the white man's god who has so often brought us to tears and listen to liberty which speaks in all our hearts.[17]

Boukman's observation is still accurate today. Unfortunately, his advice is yet to be heeded by some sections of the Afrikan people who still worship the gods of their oppressors, gods that were not given to them by their Ancestors and which do not look like their own people. The Haitians went on to defeat two armies of France, then the world superpower, an army of the British, who would soon successfully challenge French dominance of the world, a Spanish army and an army of local whites and mulattoes. These triumphs of Afrikan arms amount to an achievement of the most gigantic proportions, made possible by the retention of Afrikan identity and so the Afrikan worldview and an unshakeable confidence in their own abilities to recognise their own interests and pursue them to their logical conclusions.

6.3: More Resistance

There is another piece of evidence which invalidates the erroneous idea that Afrikans chose European saints because they were enamoured with European culture. As in the instance illustrated by the Indian chief who hid Ochosi, the Hunter, it was not only European Christian sources that Afrikans raided to acquire materials they found to be appropriate to their needs. Afrikans also chose Native American camouflage for the divinities. They also incorporated the charada from China and aspects of spiritualism from non Christian Europe.[18] Further, the parallels noted and camouflage adopted varied from area to area and even from one shrine to the other.[19]

Afrikan genius in effectively disguising cultural resistance to the European objective of cultural genocide in the Americas was not at all limited to the practice of spirituality, narrowly defined. This very feature of Afrikan resistance may be noted in the art form known as capoeira. Capoeira is a dance form in which Afrikans in Brasil hid their unarmed martial arts during the time of enslavement. The objective was clearly to preserve this martial arts tradition while making it appear to their oppressors that they were just dancing.

Cultural resistane in language was widespread. Prevented from speaking their own languages on the plantations, Afrikans invented Ebonics, a new language. Since most of the lexicon of most varieties of Ebonics was appropriated from the language of whichsoever European nation oppressed its Afrikan makers, it was easy for many Eurocentric scholars to conclude that Ebonics was really a 'broken' variety of some European language. Later classifications as English-based, French-based, Dutch-based 'pidgins and creoles' further subscribe to that mistaken belief, which was rendered even easier by the prejudice of much Eurocentric scholarship. In fact, such classification inverts the rule for classifying languages, which is that the lexicon is the superstructure and the grammar is the base of a language. It is profitable to argue that in inventing Ebonics, Afrikans retained Afrika at the base or deep levels: grammar, wisdom sayings and world view, and dressed them up in European lexical clothing at the surface level.[20]

There is yet another example of this Afrikan genius for effective cultural camouflage that should be brought to our attention. In this writer's village of Queenstown, on the Essequibo Coast of Guyana, Afrikans erected a church in the shape of an upturned 'slave' ship that brought some of the ancestors to that place in chains. (See Figure 10 in the photospread.) It is an unusual act of remembrance and therefore of resistance, a concrete and permanent statement of the horrors inflicted upon Afrikans by some of those who still call themselves Christians. It is also an example of Afrikans inscribing their own narrative, in symbolic architecture, in the very place that is a bastion of their degradation.[21]

Here is a church in the shape of a ship, a message inscribed in concrete, wood and zinc; permanent and enduring, asking urgent questions of every generation. Do you remember? Do you know from whence you came or were brought, and how, and why? Do you know who you are? Do you really know?

The parallels among the divinities in Orisha, Candomblé, Santería, Kumina, Voodoo, etc., capoeira, language and the church in Queenstown Village are very powerful and striking indeed. In each one of these instances Afrikans have continued their culture by camouflaging it in European external wrapping. The reality is that Afrikans resisted European barbarism from the very inception and did so continuously and in all forms. Every opportunity was exploited to wage resistance, and sometimes revolution, against oppression. The practice of employing European forms to hide and continue Afrikan cultural traditions was not confined to European saints, or to a particular dance form, a church in one village, or to language in general. Every cultural garment the European attempted to force upon the Afrikan was examined for its suitability for this purpose of liberation. It is true that there were cases of Afrikan accommodation with and even outright capitulation to European domination. But all of these examples show how many European attempts at cultural domination were exploited as occasions for resistance.

These facts show clearly that Afrikans chose whatever they believed would work best for them; that it was not some sick infatuation with European culture that instructed all of their actions. That sickness arose and maintains itself among some Afrikans precisely because they forget their own story, and so they forget the reason why their embattled ancestors made the Anancy choices that they did.

We must conclude where the evidence leads us. Afrikans chose the European saints as convenient and partially accommodating receptacles in which to hide and so preserve the Afrikan divinities. That is why, in the Orisha tradition in the western hemisphere, "practitioners understand that there is a sharp line demarcating the differences between Orishas and the Catholic images that are used to camouflage them."[22]

The evidence therefore does not support the belief in Afrikan admiration of European cultural elements, except possibly among those Afrikans who were ignorant and/or confused about their own culture and filled with prejudice against it. The ignorance, prejudice and confusion are very direct results of mis-education and deeply flawed socialization of Afrikans under European oppression, which led to distortion and even erasure of identity. In circumstances in which Afrikans retained their identity they behaved differently. They acquired aspects of European culture because they elected to appear to do so under force of circumstances, in order to better preserve the very thing they appeared to give up. The alternative was often physical demise but certainly cultural genocide leading ultimately to cosmic death.

The dichotomy between an official European religion and an unofficial majority Afrikan spiritual system represents the current reality of most Afrikan populations (and even some non-Afrikan ones.) It is the same with language, where most Afrikan populations, on the continent of the sacred ancestors as well as abroad, have their own Afrikan languages but are subjected to an official foreign language, mostly a European language or Arabic. These truths point towards a greater truth, which is that the state as it exists today over most Afrikan people was not organised by Afrikans in the traditions and interests of Afrikans. A state that does not service the traditions and interests of its citizens is by these very facts oppressive to those citizens. The state in which Afrikans live is therefore oppressive to the vast majority of Afrikans, both on the continent of Afrika and in the Afrikan communities abroad.

The camouflage is more than merely Afrikans dressing up their divinities in the garb of European saints. It is a metaphor for the current condition of most Afrikans, who continue to try to fulfil their spiritual needs through the Arab religion of Islam or through the European religion of Christianity. But each of these two religions was introduced to Afrikans as an intimate part of the *Maafa*, the greatest crime in history. Their common function was to achieve the passification, social control and exploitation of Afrikans through the assassination of Afrikan identity and the imposition of Arab and European values and world views upon Afrikans. Both Islam and Christianity continue to fulfil that role today, despite the sincerity of some of their adherents, because these religions articulate mainly Arab and European male middle class cultural values, institutions, behaviours and worldviews. The pursuit of Islam and Christianity by Afrikans therefore raises deep and demeaning contradictions. From an Afrikan perspective it is not logical or possible for Afrikan spiritual needs to be fulfilled by these deeply flawed cultural vessels of the oppressors of Afrikans.

Part of the problem may well rest with the tremendous need of Afrikans to practice their spirituality, for Afrikans have always been a deeply spiritual people. However, much of the Afrikan spiritual system has been destroyed or distorted by the purveyors of the Maafa. These bringers of the great evil have also erased and distorted knowledge of the Afrikan spiritual system, and taught Afrikans to look down upon their own traditions, the longest traditions in history. Amidst this evil destruction, the destroyers offered their own religions, complete with fanciful claims of revelation, inspiration and much more, when in fact much of the doctrines and practices of their religions were appropriated from Afrikans in the Nile Valley without any acknowledgement of this Afrikan source, and the major purposes of their doctrines were the disablement and control of Afrikans in the interests of these despoilers. The current condition of Afrikans all over the globe attests to the fact that these creeds have failed Afrikans. The only way out of the disablement of Afrika is to become the Afrikan self again. A big part of this repair job is a return to practising Afrikan spirituality in traditional ways, adjusted for changes in the modern world. That is one reason why libation is a path to Afrikan liberation and redemption.

6.4: New Strategy

Today it is no longer necessary to preserve Afrikan rites and rituals within European packaging for camouflage, which is exactly how many of Afrikan cultural practises were eventually handed down in plantation exile. The need now is to recognise that those conditions which compelled the camouflage have changed, particularly through the sustained action of enslaved Afrikans, who played the most decisive role in the processes leading up to the legal termination of physical enslavement, an event often mistaken for and so mislabelled emancipation. But among many practitioners of the Orisha and other aspects of Afrikan tradition there is a deep and often desperate reflex to preserve inheritance exactly as it was handed down.

That mindset is understandable. This is especially because that way of thinking arose in those desperate circumstances inhabited by that company of ancestors who dwelt within the fiercest part of the open warfare on Afrikan culture and identity. It was a context of enforced ignorance and desperation that dictated just such intense dedication and fierce determination as the best means, and often the only means, of cultural continuity and therefore of survival with some dignity. This mindset is just as often combined with an absence of knowledge of the original and perhaps authentic forms and functions of Afrikan institutions, rituals and ceremonies; those ancient archetypes and models that are the truest sources of authenticity and understanding. As the Maafa intensified, the destruction and distortion of Afrikan culture increased. Pockets of knowledge and practice survived. But these were unconnected to each other and often distorted in other ways. The constellation of institutions functioning together to educate and socialise every Afrikan generation was compromised and penetrated by Arab and European values and institutions. It became easier for pretenders to abuse the tradition; charlatans, evil doers and even well meaning ignoramuses often worked in the guise of a profound knowledge of Afrikan culture.

Much of the dominant tendencies in the current cultural practice of Afrikans in the diaspora were therefore dictated by the barbarism of enslavement. Such tendencies account for an often inflexible practice in which there is adherence to form above understanding of substance, simply because form is more remembered and known, an easy inheritance from a traumatic past, something precious to be guarded and bequeathed in times of continuing trouble. The converse is more often true about certain things of greater substance, such as the Afrikan origins of our spiritual practices, and the correct explanation and understanding of these sacred possessions. These are most often unknown, either completely or partially. The reason is that time, patience and continuity, prerequisites for the nurturing, from one generation to the other, of such immensely important intangibles of worthwhile individuals and communities, prove easy victims in times of massive and prolonged psychological, social and psychic upheaval and trauma. The bald fact is that it is this trauma that is inherited and passed down through the generations, not so much the examples, knowledge and explanation of origins. Therefore, instead of self-knowledge and the security that springs from it, the Maafa delivers instability and deep pain. Afrikans will continue to suffer massively unless they intervene on their own behalf with reparation and restoration: the repair of self through the restoration of awareness of their own history and knowledge and practice of their own cultural institutions. There is no other guarantee of Afrikan individual and community health—psychological, social, economic, political or otherwise.

The deficit mental condition has persisted and expresses itself in rituals that are still petrified in European packaging, antique as well as antiquated and perhaps worse; still hostage to bygone times and to circumstances that have long been changed by the action of Afrikans themselves. Those who exhibit this condition have failed to keep abreast with the leading edge of the Afrikan people's struggle and have been left defending frontiers that no longer exist. The struggle has moved on; new battle lines have been established. Re-deployment at or near to the frontlines, specifically in this instance throwing out the European packaging and undertaking a full re-engagement with Afrikan traditions, will constitute a decisive victory in the continuing war for a secure future for Afrikans.

In some instances this mindset has provided fertile ground for the mystification of knowledge and rituals. In other instances the result has been even worse, for it has engendered mysticism instead of spirituality. The consequences of mysticism have been at best severely limiting to spiritual growth and overall development. In such a context the descent into the exclusivity and narrowness of the esoteric often limits crucial knowledge to a privileged and more often self-serving few, who are generally uncritical of the knowledge they possess and uncreative in the use of this precious resource. This state of mind prevents Afrikans from engaging in the healthy process of periodic interrogation and re-interrogation and updating of existing knowledge and understanding, leading to more and more self-knowledge, self-awareness and progress. The predominant narrowness therefore severely limits a person's capacity for self-transformation and so for further and continuing liberation.

The history of the Afrikan people, and indeed of any people, shows that those who do not possess all the relevant information about themselves and their environment are, as a consequence, not equipped to make the best decisions about the issues that confront them on their journey through life. Knowledge, particularly self-knowledge, is a strategic asset which must be carefully cultivated, vigilantly guarded, passed down and enhanced from generation to generation and fully deployed among any people if their general well being and progress are to be permanently guaranteed.

The possession of libation by Afrikans in the Diaspora is only partly explained by the growing movement for self repair. There is evidence of the continuation of this ritual among enslaved Afrikans as well as after the legal termination of that system. In 1790 John Stedman recorded the contemporary observation that an Afrikan in Suriname never "eat or drink without offering a libation."[23] Esteban Montejo, an Afrikan enslaved in Cuba, attested morning libation and prayers among the Yoruba in that country during his lifetime.[24] But as time passed, Afrikan culture in the communities abroad in the time of physical enslavement became cut off from the well-springs of culture in the Motherland. Most Afrikans in "New World" plantation society were estranged from the Source in the time of naked cultural terrorism that made the Source most needed. One factor that explains the resulting forgetfulness, ossification and stasis, is separation from the cultural dynamics of the Afrikan heartland, a separation that made it much more likely for the new trajectories to develop and take root in a different environment. Another factor is loss of sustained cultural and intellectual contact with the homeland, a consequence of the separation that endured until recent decades. The cultural defensiveness of many Afrikans abroad, under the sustained cultural genocide practised by Europeans, merely added to this condition. The more historically recent breakdown of inter-generational links among Afrikans abroad further contributed to this process of disablement.

6.5: A New Era

Today Afrikans are launching a new era. In increasing numbers and in greater and greater depth, they are rediscovering their ancient heritage and repossessing it fully while rejecting European culture and values that were forced upon them. This European culture has proven bankrupt and confusing to Afrikans. It has led us nowhere. The lesson from this 500 year long experience of European domination, as with the 1500 year long experience of Arab domination, is clearly that those who do not live their own culture and identity are doomed to failure. One part of this new movement is a growing assertiveness among the initiates, practitioners, followers and supporters of the Orisha tradition, which has spread from its initial bases in West Afrika and certain parts of the Americas and the Caribbean to many other countries, including Argentina, Columbia, Mexico, Venezuela and parts of Europe.

There must be some significance in the fact that the Yoruba people in Western Nigeria and their Fon cousins in Benin provide the backbone of the dominant Afrikan spiritual expressions in the Americas and the Caribbean: Candomblé, Voodoo, Santería, Orisha, Kumina and so on, though we must be careful to note the similarities and continuities that run throughout Afrikan culture. Devotees from Afrika and Afrikan communities abroad are reaching out for each other and building a togetherness where before, for too long, there was only a lack of communication, ignorance and suspicion of each other, a disabling unawareness of roots and the past, disunity and other manifestations of weakness. A World Congress of Orisa has been organised. It has met in Ile Ife, the spiritual center of Orisa, in Nigeria, in 1981. Conferences have also been held in Brazil, USA, Trinidad and Tobago (1999), Cuba and elsewhere. Afrikans from Nigeria and representatives of the continuation of their spiritual tradition in the Americas: Voodoo in Haiti, Candomblé, Shangó, Kumina and indeed from all over the world, have attended. Brilliant public ceremonies have been organised and executed as part of these gatherings of Afrikan spiritual practitioners.

There is no longer any reticence, among many, about observing this branch of Afrikan spirituality. Benin has thrown out the European religion of Catholicism and reclaimed Voodoo as its national spiritual system. Haiti, under President Aristide, has recognised Voodoo as a national religion, thereby officially acknowledging the right of Voodoo leaders to legally perform naming ceremonies, marriage ceremonies, and other rituals that are consistent with their spiritual system.[25] The state of Trinidad and Tobago has officially recognised Orisha as one of its national religions.[26] Perhaps the time has at last arrived to throw off the Catholic images, as some Afrikans have already done,[27] in the full recognition that the circumstances which compelled that accommodation have passed and so it is no longer necessary to hide their Orishas in the clothing of their oppressors' religion. In the same way that some Afrikans have thrown out Catholic images, it is necessary for all Afrikans afflicted by Eurochristianity to abandon their oppressors' religion and return to their own spiritual traditions. Afrikans cannot continue the fundamental contradiction of trying to express and develop Afrikan spirituality in and through the European church, with European scriptures and European values. Those are deeply flawed European vessels imposed upon Afrikans during the time of the Great Terror, and their fundamental purpose was to aid that terrorism by demeaning Afrikan spirituality, and indeed everything Afrikan and replacing it with Eurochristianity. The Afrikan experience of the Arab religion of Islam offers an almost exact parallel to their experience of European Christianity. Afrikans face the task of retrieving and developing further their own existing Afrikan alternatives to such institutions. The continued Afrikan dependence in spiritual matters upon those who committed the worst crimes against Afrikans continues the most illogical and self-defeating behaviour. Self-knowledge and self-reliance in spiritual matters is as fundamental a necessity for liberation and redemption as self-knowledge and self-reliance in all other matters. Libation has survived the evil and destructive processes of Arabs using Islam and Europeans employing Christianity. Libation remains lodged in the culture and therefore refracted in the creative imagination of Afrikans on the ancestral continent and among Afrikans abroad. But it did not survive unchanged. Often, when Afrikans in the Americas open a new bottle of liquor, some is poured out onto the floor or on the earth. Sometimes this is done in silence. This may be a sacred silence as the appropriate words are silently intoned. Sometimes this silence signifies little more than adherence to form, as the person pouring does not know that something must be said, or what is to be said. Silence in this matter is a practice that was first instituted in the hostile plantation environment, where anything more than a brief and silent gesture in the practice of Afrikan culture could have meant death. Sometimes the one who pours or anyone else present says: "To absent friends," or "For those who are not here, Past, Present and Future," or "Salutations to absent friends, to the East, to the West, to the North and to the South'. Sometimes someone says "Throw (or pour) one [i.e. a drink, a libation] for . . . ," at which point is intoned the name of a loved one who has made her or his transition, or who is not physically present for some other reason, but who is present spiritually because they would have understood and agreed with the ritual and its meaning. This formula has been artfully extended to "Play one for . . . ," as in kaisoes by The Mighty Stalin (Leroy Caliste, later Black Stalin,) "Play One" a tribute to Winston Spree Simon[28] and the Mighty Sparrow's "Tribute to Melody."[29] Others who are around often join in these greetings to the Divinities, to the ancestors and to living relatives and friends who are absent, and to the symbolic orientation of the liquid. Sometimes, less often, the liquor is just poured out and consumed.

There is a famous Afrikan Caribbean declaration, "One for de road" that has an exact replication in the Brazilian Portuguese in "*Un por saideira.*" Such a statement is only fully understandable from within the Afrikan philosophical system. Once placed in this context the meaning is revealed to be: ["Let us pour] one [i.e. a drink, a libation] for [the challenges of] the road [and the spirits of the road]." We find out that such a statement almost certainly has its origin in the practice of libation. Here, "de road" [the road] represents the journey ahead: contemplation of the various challenges upcoming, ranging from the physical to the spiritual, the ancestral and divine spirits which guard the road and the last chance for a communal drink on a particular occasion. "One for de road" is simultaneously a declaration of a sometimes purely mundane determination to have that last drink as well as an adherence to the Afrikan spiritual system, in which instance the Road is the Way. The existence of another popular declaration in the Brazilian Portuguese language helps to clarify this understanding. "*Isi é por santo*" ("This [drink] is one for the saint/spirit.") The spiritual nature of the understanding that instructs this practice certainly lies in the Afrikan conception of being and reality that has already been explained in Chapter Two of this work.

In this writer's experience among Afrikan people in the villages and towns of Guyana, there will sometimes be threats to knock a drink of liquor out of the hand of anyone who dares to pour from a bottle that has not in this way been first offered to the Creator, the ancestors and others not physically present. Additionally, a spilt drink will invariably occasion enquiries about whether some of the liquor from that particular bottle had been poured (in libation) for "unseen guests." Sometimes the spilt liquor will occasion observations along the lines of "Dem come foh dem own" ["The unseen guests (i.e. the Spirits) have come to demand their drink (i.e. a libation.)"]

Other evidence from contemporary times shows that libation has also survived among Afrikans in North America. Unsurprisingly, the context and representation of this ritual in the living tradition of Afrikan Americans present striking similarities with its survival among Afrikans in the Caribbean. These are not two mutually exclusive cultural categories of humanity, and the art forms of Rap and Hip Hop, though born in Afrikan communities in the USA, are known by Afrikans from the Caribbean and the world over, and in fact have been added to by them. Rap, Hip Hop, Reggae, Kaiso, Blues, R&B, Jazz and many other art forms of the western hemisphere are the products of Afrika in exile. They are rooted in the Afrikan experience and are related to each other. It is therefore not at all surprising that artistes from one aspect of this diaspora, or from the Afrikan continent, easily identify with and contribute to forms that arose in another part of the Afrikan experience.

Few knowledgeable persons would resist the conclusion that 2Pac Shakur and Nas are two of the leading exponents of Hip Hop. Both have contributed to the continuation of the ritual of libation in the west. 2Pac's "Pour Out a Little Liquor"[30] and "Just a Moment" by Nas[31] are but two of the lyrics that reflect the presence of libation in the folkways of Afrikans in the USA. Content analysis of the lyrics of these two songs establishes, without any doubt, that libation is an important part of the folk memory and popular culture of inner city USA. The following analysis is based upon the main elements identified in the definition of libation given above, that is, in the categories of thought, word and action.

The thought that instructed the audible word and visible action is very clear. 2Pac mentions his best pal in jail, his cousin who died the year before, a death he still couldn't get over, and the "so called G's," that is, successful gangsters, who are heroes in the community. His purpose is to reminisce about his buddies who have died.

Nas introduces this ritual in rap with a request for a moment of silence. This request is in fact a demand for respect for the ritual and those whom he memorialises. He in effect creates a silent, peaceful space within the background of continuous violence against which the lyrics are set. This is a moment not merely of silence, but of power. Nas then goes on to invoke the spirit of beloved ones to whom the moment and the portions of liquor are dedicated, memorializing in rhyme his buddies in jail and those who have died. He repeats his demand for a moment of silence in which to consider that though those absent through death or confinement are not physically there the love that binds them to those present is still there. 2Pac terms it reminiscing; Nas says that it is symbolizing. In both lyrics the desire to remember and appreciate beloved ones who were not physically there, both dead and alive, but not physically present, give birth to the thoughts which instruct the word and the action. It is necessary to recall here that remembering and honouring those not there, both the dead and the absent living, is one of the expressed purposes of what we may call classical libation.

The word which announces these libations can hardly be separated from the ritual action. On the surface Nas' reference may be read as a respectful request, but in this context it has the power of a command. Hence, in both instances this word is a descriptive instruction. That instruction to pour out some liquor is repeatedly given throughout both lyrics, for in each case it is the emotional centre of the song and so a part of the refrain. Hence Nas asks "Can we please pour out some liquor?" and 2Pac instructs us to "Pour out a little liquor!" 2Pac repeatedly contrasts the consumption of large amounts of liquor, of which he plainly disapproves, with this act of pouring out a little of the liquid in honour of those beloved not present, of which he certainly approves and promotes by repeatedly instructing us to do so.

This is the classic description of a libation in liquor, even though neither 2Pac nor Nas employs that term in a single instance. "Pour out a little liquor" or "pour out some liquor." Not just any amount, but a little; no not just anything, but liquor. These commands are strikingly similar to the ancient descriptive commands of "pour libation" and "pour water." The fact that Afrikans in West Afrika and the west pour libation mostly with liquor should make it clearer that this is the ritual of libation. The video which accompanies the song banishes any doubt; 2Pac and company go to the grave of their dearly departed and offer libation of liquor.

The physical and psychological context in which these lyrics are put forth is clearly a gathering of like minds, that is, of those who would agree with the sentiments expressed and the action undertaken, in essence, with the ritual. Hence, both lyrics address themselves directly to an unnamed group physically present as well as to the listener/participant who is not necessarily physically present, but is nonetheless a witness, a sympathiser or even a participant on the emotional level who is effectively included in the ritual by the communications media of this digital age.

The available evidence leads us to the conclusion that as the distance from the Afrikan wellspring grew, our connections with the ritual and our understanding of it were lessened. We have seen that 2Pac and Nas do not have a name for the ritual. It is the same with Stalin and Sparrow and also informants in Dominica and Guyana. Yet, in form and function they recall the ancient Afrikan practice of libation, of recognising and honouring the dead and others not physically present. This ritual is powerfully present in the folk memory and living tradition of the Diaspora. But it survives as a ritual which does not speak its name, or proclaim its origins too loudly. Yet even that is not the full picture, for the movement towards reclamation of self-knowledge among Afrikans is a trend that embodies the very opposite to distance and loss of full understanding.

Libation has been truncated by time and circumstances, especially in those Afrikan communities abroad that were not communities of resistance. These are the direct inheritors and continuations of plantation enslavement and its myriad forms of cultural genocide and other processes of dehumanization. But libation has survived even in places like these. Every one of these pronouncements and questions, brief as each may be, is uttered on the often unspoken but not unarticulated understanding and acceptance, at some level, of the practice of libation. They all attest to the knowledge that those who are not physically present in a particular space may be there spiritually. We have seen that this understanding is a part of the philosophical and spiritual foundations that render libation necessary and therefore possible. The close association of the act of pouring a small portion of a new bottle of liquor, significantly termed *sagua* in Antigua (See Chapter Three), with these utterances, shows beyond any doubt that the ritual performed is libation, even though it is severely truncated and other aspects of the ritual context have been lost or are no longer associated with the act of pouring. We have also seen that this ritual is a continuation of the practice of Afrikan ancestors and has been attested over 5000 years ago in the Nile Valley of Afrika.

Libating with liquor predominated among Afrikans who were forced to migrate to the West. This tradition, brought mainly from West Afrika, was accentuated by the easy availability of liquor on the "New World" plantations, where it was and still is a major by-product of sugar production. That is most probably how it came to be the tradition in this part of the Afrikan world also. Whatever the reason for libating almost exclusively with liquor in the Americas, it is noticeable that the entire ritual has not survived in the popular consciousness of all the Afrikan communities in this part of the world. This is exactly parallel to the ritual offering of food, which often forms part of the context of libation. It has been mentioned in Chapter Three that children in some homes are taught that it is good manners to leave uneaten a small portion of their food. Like libation, the ritual context has not been retained. In fact the ritual of libation has survived intact only in those Afrikan communities where cultural resistance to European genocide was a cornerstone of existence. It is therefore not surprising that before the current era of cultural revival in the Americas, wherever libation survives as a full and fully understood ritual, the tendency is that it survives as part of a greater Afrikan cultural context that has been preserved by Communities of Resistance in the Diaspora.

It may also be argued that the full significance of libation has until now escaped the majority of Afrikans who exist away from the Homeland. They know only that it is important to pour out the first portion of liquor; less often do they know that they must put by the first portion of food, or why it is necessary to perform these tasks. They almost always do not understand that pouring the first portion is a part of libation, and that libation is an inescapable aspect of being Afrikan. They just follow a fractured and disjointed tradition inherited and passed down, unaltered from those dangerous times of enslavement on the plantations when open retention, or indeed any form of retention, of Afrikan culture and therefore of Afrikan identity, was a dangerous business, precisely because it is the most sacred, fortifying and important business of all Afrikans.

It still is. In these times of the continuing *Maafa*, being Afrikan is a difficult and revolutionary business. But it is the only genuine identity Afrikans everywhere may have, and the most rewarding way to be. Being Afrikan will forever be the most important business of all Afrikans, for without their identity Afrikans shall continue to be the disabled cultural orphans of their oppressors.

NOTES

1. Kimani Nehusi (2001). *"From ꮥ Medew Netjer to Ebonics"* in Clinton Crawford(ed.). *Ebonics and Language Education of African Ancestry Students.* (Sankofa World Publishers, New York and London), p. 61.
2. Clinton A. Hutton (2005). *The Logic and Historical Significance of the Haitian Revolution and the Cosmological Roots of Haitian Freedom* (Arawak Publications, Kingston, Ja), p.60.
3. There is an extensive literature on these Afrikan Communities of Resistance, which are often labelled "maroon." A selected list ought to include Richard Price (ed. 1973, 1979, 1996). *Maroon Societies: Rebel Slave Communities in the Americas* (The Johns Hopkins University Press, Baltimore); John G Steadman (1790, 1992). *Narrative of a Five Years Expedition against the Revolted Negroes of Surinam* (The Johns Hopkins

University Press, Baltimore); Jacob Carruthers (1985). *The Irritated Genie: An Essay on the Haitian Revolution* (The Kemetic Institute, Chicago), C. L. R. James (1938,1963,1994). *The Black Jacobins: Toussaint L'Ouverture and the San Domingo Revolution* (Allison and Busby, London) and Mavis C. Campbell (1990). *The Maroons of Jamaica 1655–1796: A History of Resistance, Collaboration and Betrayal* (Africa World Press, Inc., Trenton, New Jersey).

4. Apart from the works of Diop *et al* already cited on this matter, several observers of Afrikans in the Americas and the world over have noted this predominant commonality in Afrikan culture and an increasing number of scholars write from the recognition of this basic truth, which does not deny many variations and even differences among Afrikans. Examples of those who made this observation include Octavio Da Costa Eduardo (1948, 1981). *The Negro in Northern Brazil: A Study in Acculturation* (The African Publication Society, London), p. 10; Walter Rodney (1975). "Africa in Europe and the Americas" in Richard Gray (ed.) *The Cambridge History of Africa* Vol. 4 (Cambridge University Press), pp. 619–20; Maureen Warner Lewis (2003). *Central Africa in the Caribbean: Transcending Time, Transforming Cultures* (University of the West Indies Press), pp. 143–144, 331–333; Maya Deren (1953, 1970). *Divine Horsemen: The Living Gods of Haiti* (McPherson and Co., New York), pp. 58–59; Campbell. *The Maroons of Jamaica*, pp. 3–4; Hutton. *The Logic and Historical Significance* ..., pp. 115–117 and Basil Davidson. *The Black Man's Burden*, pp. 62–63. The Afrikan-centered school presents the foremost examples of those who begin with this truth. See, for example, Asa G. Hilliard III (2002). *African Power: Affirming African Indigenous Socialization in the Face of the Culture Wars* (Makare Publishing Company, Gainesville, Florida); Marimba Ani. *Let the Circle be Unbroken*, Oba T'Shaka (1995).*Return to the African Mother Principle of Male and Female Equality* and numerous others.

5. W. E. B. Du Bois. *The Negro*, pp. 113–114

6. Zora Neale Hurston. (1938, 1990.) *Tell My Horse*, p. 114.

7. Maya Deren. Divine Horsemen: The Living Gods of Haiti, p.56.

8. K. Dunham. *Dances of Haiti*, p.5.

9. R. F. Thompson. *Flash of the Spirit*, pp. 169–172. Emphasis added.

10. Vega. *The Altar of My Soul*, p. 33.

11. Ishmael Reed (1990.) 'Foreword' in Zora Neale Hurston. *Tell My Horse*, p. xii.

12. M. Moreno Vega. *The Altar of My Soul*, p.2. See also pp. 32–33, 82, etc.

13. A fully initiated Voodoo Priest. The etymology of this title appears to lie in the Kongo/Bantu term *Nganga* = "chief priest" and the Fon (West Afrika) word *Houn* = "spirit," with which it is prefixed. His female counterpart is designated by the Kongo/Bantu term *Mambo*. See M. Denning, O. Phillips and G. Rudolph (1979). *Voudoun Fire: The Living Reality of Mystical Religion* (Llewellyn Publications, St. Paul, MN), pp.148 and 149. Both the etymology of the term *houngan* and the easy incorporation of elements from various aspects of Afrika to achieve Voodoo in Haiti and other forms of Afrikan spiritual continuity in the Americas and the Caribbean demonstrate the underlying cultural unity of Afrika.

14. Jacob Carruthers, *The Irritated Genie*, p.21.

15. Hutton. *The Logic and Historical Significance of the Haitian Revolution*. The quote is from p. 121.

16. Richard Allsopp (ed., 2003.) *Dictionary of Caribbean English Usage* (University of the West Indies Press, Kingston, Jamaica), p. 208; Frederic G. Cassidy (1982.) *Jamaica Talk* (Macmillan Caribbean and Sangsters Book Stores Ltd.), pp. 119, 396.

17. Boukman Dutty, as quoted in Pauleus Sannon (1920.) *Historie de Toussaint L'Ouverture* (Port-au-Prince,) p. 89, as quoted in Carruthers. *The Irritated Genie*, p. 22. See also C.L.R. James. *The Black Jacobins*, p. 87, where the quote appears unsourced. Compare Boukman's words with Paul Bogle's exhortation to his brothers and sisters on the occasion of the 1865 Afrikan Rebellion in Jamaica: "Join your colour and cleave to the Blacks." See Richard Small's Introduction in Rodney. *The Groundings*, p. 9.
18. Canizares. *Walking With the Night*, pp. 74–84, 106–110.
19. Thompson. *Flash of the Spirit*, p. 273, note 30.
20. Kimani Nehusi, "From Medew Netjer to Ebonics." pp. 74–79; Sheila Mayers Johnson, "The Word as a Conduit for African Consciousness." *JCTAW*, Winter/Spring, 2004, pp. 146–174.
21. Kimani Nehusi (2003). "St. Bartholomew's Church: The Story of a National Monument" *Emancipation*, Vol. 2, No. 11. 2003–2004, pp. 6–9; Nehusi (2004). "Fragment of Memory? The Building that houses St. Barts Anglican Church" *Queenstown Anniversary Publication 2004*. (The Queenstown New York Association, New York), pp. 30–43.
22. Vega, *The Altar of My Soul*, p.33.
23. Price and Price. *Stedman's Surinam*, p. 263. See also pp. 31 and 276.
24. Montejo. *The Autobiography of a Runaway Slave*, p. 55.
25. Nowa Omoiyui (2003). "Haiti Officially Sanctions Voodoo." Email of 10 April.
26. Frances Henry (2003.) Reclaiming African Religions in Trinidad: The Socio Political Legitimation of the Orisha and Spiritual Baptist Faiths (The University of the West Indies Press.)
27. M. Moreno Vega. *The Altar of My Soul*, pp. 199–200.
28. The Mighty Stalin (1979). "Play One." *To the Caribbean Man*. LP. (Wizards MCR-147, Makossa M2342), Side A, Track 1; See also Stalin (1979). "Play One" *Play One/Caribbean Unity* 7-inch vanyl. (Wizards MC-147), Song 1 and Black Stalin (1991). *Roots, Rock, Soca*. CD. (Rounder C-5038), Track 5, all at www.calypsoarchives.co.uk. Accessed on 16 March, 2007.
29. Mighty Sparrow [Slinger Francisco] (2000, re-issue). "Play One for Melo" *Down Memory Lane*. CD. Millennium Series, Track 6.
30. 2Pac. "Pour Out A Little Liquor." Lyrics and accompanying video available at youtube.com [Accessed 10.05.08.]
31. Nas. "Just a Moment" from the album *Street's Disciple*. Lyrics available at anysonglyrics@hotmail.com [Accessed on 01.05.08].

Chapter Six

Ritual Significances

In the Afrikan spiritual system and in Afrikan culture in general, certain articles and practices have assumed very great importance, sometimes even greater importance, than their practical utility may at first suggest. The reason for this is often to be found in the fact that the article in question does indeed have significant practical value to Afrikans in the spiritual, psychological, social and physical aspects of the environment in which they exist. Additionally, however, over and above its immediate practical value, is the fact that a thing of vital ritual significance often symbolizes ideas and understandings of very great importance in the Afrikan spiritual system. A particular article or practice may thus be invested with great symbolic value. We must remind ourselves that Afrikan spirituality may be said to be primarily concerned with ways of maintaining harmony and balance at all levels in the entire cosmos; that is, within the person, the family, the clan, the community, the nation and the environment in which all must exist. Libation, the very subject of this text, is a fine example. Other examples chosen here include water, spitting, the number three, the flag and other items and ideas that are associated with the ritual of libation. Understanding what these articles and practices represent, and how they have come to represent what they do represent, will enable a clearer and deeper understanding of both the ritual of libation and the cultural context to which it belongs.

7.1: The Significance of Water

In one of his most known poems Langston Hughes proclaims the Afrikan engagement with rivers and their deep knowledge and development around these waterways from the earliest times.[1] The ancient Afrikan fluvial environment had a profound impact upon the Afrikan spiritual system, which in turn impacted back upon Afrikan humanity by giving order and significance, as well as deeper meaning and higher purpose to daily life. Nowhere is this more dramatic and obvious than in Kemet. It is here that the River Nile, which is referenced by Hughes, and an imaginary underground river, of which the Nile was undoubtedly the prototype, respectively ordered and regulated the life of the living and that of the dead, and in fact influenced all existence and conceptions of existence. Over time the Nile has become the archetype of many rivers that populate the human imagination and thus the spiritual systems and religions of Afrika as well as of other cultures. In the mythology of humanity, rivers often represent boundaries and zones of transition from one state to another, as well as challenges to be overcome along the road of life and death.

The Nile is the longest and most dominant river in the world. It runs for over four thousand miles from south to north through East Central and North East Afrika to its estuary in North Afrika on the Mediterranean Sea. This course takes the river from its two sources, first the White Nile in the region of the snow capped, five thousand meter high Ruwenzori ("Rain Makers") Mountains near the Great Lakes of Afrika on the Kongo-Uganda border and secondly the Blue Nile in Lake Tana in Ethiopia. It is a journey from the place of the beginnings of humans in inner Afrika through to the places of the beginnings of human civilization, in Kush, Ta-Seti and Kemet, which are still in Afrika. From close to the dawn of humanity, people as well as progress have also flowed northwards, following this ancient waterway from the heart of Afrika where humanity was born. The Nile Valley was the world's first trans-continental cultural highway. But it was not only water, people and their culture that this river has carried as it arose in the highlands of Afrika and journeyed across varied terrain to empty itself into the Mediterranean. Fertile silt has always been transported in its yearly flood and deposited in places that would have been part of the largest desert in the world but for this annual nourishment from this, the longest river in the world.

But how does the Nile perform its miraculous transforming feat and accomplish it with such unfailing regularity? From whence come the millions of tons of silt, bearing its rejuvenating nutrients? Not from the Sudd in southern Sudan, through which journeys the White Nile; the world's largest swamp is not the source of the world's most fertile flood. It is from Ethiopia, which possesses eighty percent of Afrika's volcanic mountains. Clouds from the Kongo basin hug the peaks, the highest four and a half thousand meters up, and shower these highlands with rain every year from June to August. In this part of Afrika, where offerings are made to Gion, the River Spirit, rivulets soon turn to streams, which beget rivers, most of which flow into Lake Tana. Where over sixty rivers flow into this lake there is but one exit. That is the Blue Nile, which soon swells to fifty times its dry season size, taking an annual bounty of one hundred and forty million tons of silt from these highlands and eighty five percent of the water reaching Egypt on its way to join the White Nile beyond Khartoum, then to flow as part of one through the Sudan to rejuvenate and transform the parched and grateful land of Kemet.

The Nile has run through Afrika and the lives of Afrikans for millennia. In Kemet, the land which possesses the termini of this long journey, the Nile at first brought devastating and fearful floods to vulnerable settlements which clung precariously to thin margins of land along both banks, rich with the silt deposited as the pace of the water slowed on nearing its juncture with the sea, and so rich also with agricultural, economic and other possibilities of human advancement. Then, as human knowledge and technology developed, and predictability and flood control evolved, threat became promise, and the Nile flood a welcome deluge to provide for an increasingly more productive and secure future. Here, besides its annual rejuvenating silt, the river also "provided irrigation, transportation, communication, drinking water, water for washing, a disposal system, and plentiful fish, fowl, and game."[2] Soon this part of the Nile Valley had become a magnet which attracted more and more settlers from all directions. It became the heart of Kemet. So was born the foremost country in the ancient world, owing much of its life to water in the form of the Nile, always one of the foremost rivers in the world. More than any other single factor, save humanity itself, the Nile was the cause of Kemet. Yet, if Kemet was indeed the gift of the Nile,[3] it is Afrika that was the giver of that gift,[4] and through this river her gifts are many, and wonderful.

The people of Kemet, not coincidentally the most bountiful recipients of this annual act of nature, certainly recognised the importance of this river in their life. They made the river in flood into the divinity they called ℩╦‵⸗[Middle Kingdom variation ℩ ▱]: ḥʿpy, *Hapi*. The Nile was sacred, and, as we shall see in details below, running water was a sacred thing: to dam up Nile water and so detain or prevent it from flowing over the land was an offence under the Declarations of Innocence. So too was wrongfully diverting water in the season of inundation[5] when the flow was strongest and the water was most needed for irrigation. Social ideals arising from the best daily practice derived from the communal use of the Nile were invested with the highest sanction and restated as religious and spiritual norms, or as dogma. Thus was a population encouraged to aspire to the highest standards of humanity—or to behaviours that tended to keep an elite in power.

Human habitation dominated the east bank of the river; the west bank was *Amenta*: "the hidden land," "the region where the soul of the departed journeys after it quits the body,"[6] the preserve of cemeteries, mortuary temples and other things to do with the deceased. People crossed the river to bury their dead. These material conditions strongly influenced images of life and death in Ancient Egypt. The east bank of the Nile became synonymous with this world, with the rising sun and transformation, rejuvenation and resurrection; the west bank with the setting sun, death and the underworld. Crossing the river became symbolic of making the transition into the underworld, which was envisaged as "a sphere of security and divine presence" to be achieved only by the righteous.[7] The dead were called the westerners. A dead body was transferred from the place of death, usually on the east bank, to the embalming hall on the west bank in a neshmet boat, a fully ceremonial boat that was towed by a normal craft in a "ritual riverine procession."[8] Later, the mummified body was pulled along on a boat-shaped sledge on the final physical journey, from the embalming hall to the tomb. Apart from the boat and the mythical river itself, the entire notion of the transition came to be dominated by images of ferrying and of the ferryman, that now ubiquitous conductor of souls across the Great Divide.[9] The journey from this world into the next is still, for most peoples, conveyed mainly by images based upon these ancient archetypes founded by Afrikan people and first attested in the Nile Valley those multiple millennia ago. This symbolic significance of "crossing the river" has also been retained by many Afrikan people in an unbroken tradition down into contemporary times. Examples include the Akan in Ghana[10] and the Igbo in Nigeria.[11]

The image and significance of the river, its running water and of crossing it are among the influences from Kemet that are retained in the scriptures, songs and sermons of Christianity, Judaism and other faiths. Here, the significance of the Nile has been transferred to the Jordan, belief in the purifying effects of running water is illustrated in baptism and the image of crossing the river may also retain their ancient meanings of death and rebirth, sometimes spiritually, as in Kemet.

The notion of a river as a very significant boundary therefore may have first arisen in the living reality of Kemet. The image of crossing the river became a metaphor for crossing a very significant frontier, for taking a decisive or an irrevocable step. It was from Kemet that this metaphor was cast into the popular consciousness of humanity. Its ripples may well still be present in many well known metaphoric images of the river, from Caesar crossing the Rubicon[12] to the Afrikan American spiritual, 'Roll Jordan Roll,' with its coded message of transformation as resistance to enslavement, to Afrikan Jamaican Jimmy Cliff's powerful and profound word-picture of "Many Rivers to Cross"[13] emphasising the maintenance of focus and endurance in the face of tribulations and trials.

Every people have their story of the beginning. In the first known Afrikan account of the beginning, which is also the first known account in the world, water is fundamental.[14] In Chapter One it is shown that in the creation story of Kemet, the oldest in the world, the ∞∞≡ *Nun*, or primordial waters, is the oldest and most fundamental substance in the cosmos, containing all the possibilities of existence. So profound was the impact of water upon the psyche of the people of Kemet that, for them, a river separated this world of the living from the Duat, the underworld, the place of the departed, which is not only a different world, but a different kind of world also. Every manifestation of water in the Duat was in fact an aspect of the ○○○═ *Nun*. Notions of water as primary to the cosmology and cosmogony of the people of Kemet are sustained in a 𓊝𓂻 wiȝ: *wia*, a boat (or barque), or a fleet of boats, which sail along this underworld river and dominate their conception of the Duat and the associated explanations of the nightly disappearance and daily reappearance of the sun, and of death, decay, transformation, rejuvenation and creation. Water also greatly influenced the ancient Egyptian conception of the daily movement of the sun across the sky, though in an indirect way: the sun is the sacred boat in which the Divinity Ra rides across the sky during the day.

In reflecting upon the ways of the Duat, Erik Hornung makes these observations:

> These Underworld ways are mostly reflections of earthly ones. Just as the River Nile is the thoroughfare in this world, in the underworld the normal route of the barque is a wide river . . . This river is part of Nun, the primeval water, which stretches back into the world before its creation, surrounds the created world on all sides, and also forms the route of the sun in the sky.[15]

The people of Kemet certainly did not imagine any world in which water did not exercise a predominant and determining presence. Perhaps they could not imagine a world without water at the centre precisely because of the profound impact of water upon their lives and so upon their worldview.

It is very likely that this fundamental role of water in the cosmology and cosmogony of Kemet was in the very least a contributory factor to that country's understanding of pure water as a sacred substance. This view was enhanced by the "aura of fertility and power" attributed to water because of the annual rejuvenatory role of the Nile in the agricultural cycle[16] and, indeed, in the entire society.

This predominant presence of water in the physical environment and in the mind of Kemet is reflected at the level of language. Water is present in the very conception of libation, both mythically and etymologically, as is shown in Chapter Two, where it is also shown how water from a certain part of the Nile was regarded pure and so the best for libation. It is therefore scarce wonder that the inhabitants of Kemet called water the 𓏞𓏞𓏛 : It Nṯrw, meaning "Father of the Divinities," and referred to the Nile River as "the water of life"![17] It was also believed that objects could be purified with water, and that water which had been poured over statues and other sacred objects (while the appropriate incantations were uttered) was considered to have thus been imbued with magical and healing properties. This idea of sanctification through running water is enacted by pouring in every performance of the ritual of libation and is central to this ritual. In fact, so important is this act of pouring that, from at least the era of Kemet, words for both pouring and for libation have been employed by Afrikans interchangeably to refer to the ritual. (Examples are provided in Chapters One and Two.)

In the last illustration in the photospread (No. 14,) water of life, in the form of a stream of *ankh* (life) signs, is poured over Nsu Ramesses at his coronation by the two divinities, Heru and Djhwti, who thus give him eternal life. This is the origin of the ritual now known in non-Afrikan faiths as baptism or christening. It was a part of the coronation rituals of every nsu (pharaoh) in Kemet millennia before it became known in other parts of the world. Today the ritual complex to which libation belongs is present in the European Christian church, disguised as rituals which, some claim, began with Europeans. Hence many rituals invented by Afrikans, such as baptism, communion (from the communal meal and the communal drink), harvest (First Fruits, still present all over Afrika), sacrifice, prayers and hymn singing are passed off as of Eurochristian origin. This is not a complete list. In normal circumstances such cross cultural borrowings are healthy and should not matter once the truth of their origin is told. However, the silence on the origins of much of Christianity is but one aspect of the ethnic cleansing of history of Afrikan achievements by European institutions. The church is not alone in this ungodly practice, the aim of which has been to present Afrika as 'uncivilized, backward, primitive' and so on, and therefore justify enslavement and other crimes against humanity committed by some Europeans against Afrikans.

In Kemet, water was universally recognised as the supreme agent of both spiritual and physical purification. This latter is a practical necessity for proper human hygiene and therefore of tremendous daily importance. All humans, by the very act of living, accumulate impurities: sweat, dirt and other pollutants obtained through work, play and the basic biological fact of constant respiration. Therefore everyone needs periodic physical purification. It is a necessary part of the forever alternating cycle of pollution and purification that is an intimate aspect of the human reality. Water is therefore fundamental for respiration and for getting rid of the pollutants.

These understandings and beliefs, widespread in Kemet, may well be the foundation of the profound importance of water in contemporary Afrikan society. The waters of the Niger, Kongo-Ubangi, Senegal, Senqu (Orange) and Zambezi river systems serve the same cosmic, social, economic and other functions today as those of the Nile did yesterday.[18] Water figures prominently in the creation stories of most contemporary African people. Examples include the Yoruba, Igbo, Dogon, Bambara, Bassa, Akan and the Edo in West Africa and the Bapedi, Venda and other Bantu Africans who predominate in Central, Eastern and Southern Africa. There is great reverence for designated portions of naturally occurring *running* water, in rivers, creeks, falls, lakes, seas and other waterways. This attitude is widespread throughout the Afrikan world today. Water appears to have been the base of the majority of medical remedies employed in Kemet, certainly of most of those known today.[19] The Afrikan ancestors in Kemet knew this tremendous importance of water and other liquids. They recognised that to drink is a sacred act. We will do well to be guided by their wisdom.

Afrikan people the world over have retained this huge significance of water as well as other aspects of the Nile Valley blueprint. These retentions and continuities remain even though many Afrikans have migrated away from the Nile Valley, which is the heartland of Afrikan culture and the cradle of Afrikan and world civilization, and divergences and differences have developed in their cosmology and cosmogony.[20]

Afrikans in Haiti articulated a cosmological model of the world in which *Kalunga* is a body of water that separates the living from the dead.[21] This is remarkably similar to the conception and explanation of the world developed in Kemet and described above. The Haitians inherited this model from their Kongo ancestors,[22] who in turn must have inherited it from the Nile Valley or from some parent common to both Kemet and Kongo. But the Haitians did not pass on this cosmic understanding exactly as they inherited it. They adapted the doctrine to their own purpose in their specific circumstances of the *Maafa*. Hence Hutton tells us that:

> The transatlantic voyages into [enslavement] in the Americaswere interpreted in the diaspora (the Haitian model of interpretation) as passages through Kalunga, that body of water in Kongo cosmology separating the living from the dead into a realm of kindoki, hitherto unknown to Africans in the extremity of its expression of evil. Transmigration (repatriation) through kalunga (the voyage of the dead to Ginen through the bottom of the Atlantic Ocean in Haitian Vodou thought) was thus a cosmological expression of freedom . . .[23]

Once again we encounter the association of *Ginen*, here a variant orthography of *Guiné* and *Giné*, with freedom in the struggle of Afrikan communities in the Americas and the Caribbean against the effects of the largest crime in history.[24] *Ginen/Guiné/Giné* is always a synonym for Afrika in a state of freedom. The Afrikan resistance against the *Maafa* has always understood the critical importance of cultural identity in the achievement and maintenance of human freedom and progress.

Water divinities populate the spiritual system of people all over Afrika and naturally, in Afrikan communities abroad. Such divinities abound in West Afrika. Among the Akan in Ghana, *Bosomtwe* is the name of both a sacred lake and the divinity that inhabits that lake. *Tano* or *Ta Kora* is a major river divinity in the Ivory Coast and Ghana. *Ta Gbu* is the sea divinity of the Ga people in Ghana. *Ta Tale* is the Ga female lagoon divinity. *To Nu* or *Ta Nu* is an Egun river divinity. *Otaomi* is a Yoruba river divinity. *Yewa* and *Oshun* are Yoruba female river divinities. *Yemoja* is the Yoruba female sea divinity while *Olokun* (literally, "owner of the sea") is the male and is very important in Ilè Ifè and among the Edo. *Ọta Miri* is an important male water divinity in Igboland. *Bin'abu* ("water people" or "water spirits") are divinities of ocean and waters among the Ijo of the Niger delta. *Ngalwe* and *Kaene* are river divinities of the Mende and Kono in Sierra Leone.[25] In view of the peopling of West Afrika, to a significant degree by migration from the Nile—Great lakes region of the continent, it may be of some significance that *Tana* is the ancient name of a lake in Ethiopia. Lake Tana is significant as the beginning of the Blue Nile and the annual fertilizing flood. The name *Tana* and its variations feature prominently in the names of water divinities in West Afrika. Such correspondences may not be co-incidental. This is another aspect of pan-continental Afrikan experience and culture which needs to be pursued by research.

In Brazil, Candomblé initiates worship two female water divinities: Yemanjá and Oshun. The latter's special day is Saturday. Yemanjá (from Yoruba: *ye* = mother; *maja* = "water": Mami Wata, Water Mother, etc) is Orisha of the Sea and patroness of fishermen. Oshun was originally a divinity of a river of the same name in Nigeria. Today Oshun is the Orisha of all sweet waters. She symbolises love and fertility. In Guyana and other places, *Mingi Mama* or *Water Mamma* or Water Mumma, the Female Divinity of Water, is an important and respected divinity.

In 1808 an Englishman, John Wray, was a Christian missionary in Demerara, Guyana. The Brazilian scholar Emilia Viotti da Costa has concluded that Wray was "profoundly distorted by his ignorance and biases"[26] against Afrikan cultural retentions. In fact, his diaries show that he was deeply prejudiced against Afrikan culture and identity,[27] a conclusion that is also inescapable from the very fact of the conflict between Afrikan culture and his Christian missionary activity. Yet, as is so often the case, even the ignorant and the prejudiced may provide history with hard evidence about the objects of their scorn, ever so often through eyewitness accounts. So it was with Wray. He is an historical witness to the continuity of Afrika in Guyana in spite of himself. The diary of this hostile witness yields much irrefutable evidence of "the pervasiveness among [enslaved Afrikans] of African beliefs and rituals, which were indeed found throughout the Caribbean."[28] As a result of his observations of Afrikans in Guyana, Wray believed that Afrikans there "worshipped water and would walk eighteen or twenty miles to do so." They also ". . . poured into the grave the water they had used to wash [a dead] body."[29] Wray does not say so directly, but it is very clear that the water Afrikans walked so far to reach was considered by them to be very special, perhaps even sacred. Wray functioned on the coast of Guyana, which was the locus of the European colonial project in the country. The very word Guyana is derived from a Native American language and means "land of many waters." It is a fluvial environment; water is of predominant influence, especially in the region where Wray was located. It was therefore very easy for the Afrikans to reach water; it was all around them. They were not compelled to walk so far to reach it. It is therefore highly likely that the water Wray observed them congregating around must have been running water, perhaps black water from a particular creek or river that was in any event considered sacred by those who walked so far to reach the spot. Black water[30] has a particular spiritual significance for Afrikans in Guyana.

This importance of water has been transmitted to succeeding generations of Afrikans gi Mama,in Guyana. In this writer's recollection, the 'calling out' or invocation of the Water Spirit was a very important rite conducted at the very beginning of *Comfa* dances held by the Jordanites[31] in Queenstown Village on the Essequibo Coast in Guyana. This ritual was always performed at the side of a black water canal. But the Afrikans in Guyana were never distinguished in this way: water has always been and continues to be an important part of Afrikan spiritual practice everywhere. What John Mbiti has said in this regard for the Afrikan continent is accurate for Afrikans all over the world and has been so from time immemorial:

> We should take note of the very common use of water in many rituals all over Africa. It symbolises purification and cleansing, not only of body but also of mystical impurities contracted through broken taboos, the commitment of crime, and contamination by evil magic or curse. When so used, water becomes a religious object. Often such water is drawn from sacred lakes, rivers or springs.[32]

Mbiti's observation has been independently corroborated by many others.[33] Here we must remember the Ancient Egyptian attitude to running water mentioned above. Comparison of Kemet with contemporary Afrika is once again very instructive.

Water is indeed the supreme agent of purification in Afrikan practice, whether it is in libation, offerings, outdoorings or naming ceremonies, the dedication of a building, ritual baths, baptism or the laying out of an altar or a shrine. An example of the ritual use of water in Afrikan practice occurs in the elaborate ritual of initiation of a Babalawo or Yoruba priest, which includes a "ceremony of purification by water."[34] Among Afrikans in Guyana and elsewhere in the Americas, water is the basis of ritual baths that provide a quick cure for some fevers, to drive out some spirits (jumbie in Guyana), to combat some mental illnesses and to cure some illnesses not curable by western medicine. Such baths are rendered special by certain additives placed in the water.

Seventy five percent of the earth's crust is covered with water. Similarly, seventy five percent of the human body is composed of water. Humans need water for respiration and without this function humans will die. Water is the ultimate cleansing agent, for conscious Afrikans, both internally and externally. If humans cannot live by the proverbial bread alone it is even more certain that all life, human or not, will perish, swiftly, if there is no water. Water is therefore the quintessential expression of a "pure" drink offering. Further, Afrikans have held it to be so from the earliest known times. That is why almost every Afrikan altar, even the simplest, invariably contains a glass of water for the divinities and our sacred ancestors to drink. That is why, too, from time immemorial, water is often sprinkled on shrines (while incense is burnt and appropriate chants made) as part of ritual cleansing and renewal rites.

Before life there was water. The first life forms were resident in water and all life forms, for the first stage(s) of their lives or for all of their lives, are resident in water. All life is conceived in water, develops in water and is then born out of water, and often inside water. Without water any form of life is impossible. Water is essential for life. Before life there was water; after life there will be water. Water is the beginning and end of life. The water (liquid) of libation is symbolic of the beginning of life and of life itself. The pouring of libation signifies, among other things such as offering to the Creator, the lesser Divinities and the Ancestors, a re-enactment of 𓊃𓊪𓏏𓊪𓇳 sp tpy *Sep Tepy*, literally "The First Occasion" or Creation, the first time, that profound moment at which time began and, as our ancestors in Kemet so cleverly put it, "existence began to exist."[35] *Sep Tepy*, the First Occasion, is also a representation of the first moment: the birth of each living thing, form a single cell to an entire organism, as each birth in itself is a minor replication of Creation, the First Occasion.

Water is a quintessential representation of Nature and therefore of the Creator's work. Fermented water, or alcohol, signifies both Nature and industry; both the work of the Creator and the work of humans, who, like nature, are also the creations of the Creator. But even the ingenuity of humanity is possible and can flourish only upon the basis of Nature, the Creator's creations of which we are also a part. It is human ingenuity and industry, working with water as a basis, which produces alcohol. Alcohol represents both good and bad—all the possibilities of human production and of the human condition.

When we libate with water we symbolize, remember and give thanks for Creation and creations, for water is indispensable to both Creation and creations. When we libate with liquor, which is normally clear liquor, we symbolize, remember and give thanks for both Creation and the transformative possibilities of human labour. That is why the liquor that is mostly employed in libation is clear liquor which is also associated with spiritual work: white rum, gin, *akpeteshie, ogogoro, clarin,* bush rum, moonshine, babash and so on.

7.2: The Ritual Significance of Spit

Spit, or saliva, is almost pure water. It contains only about one per cent of solid material. For our purpose it is also necessary to note that spit emanates from within a person. The ritual significance of spit in Afrikan tradition has in the beginning been that of a creative agent, but it has always been visualized as a transformative and healing agent. It has been shown in Chapter One that in some renditions of the Libation Ritual drama, the libationer spits out the liquid of libation three times. Ritual spitting (as well as the number three) has been important to Afrikans from as long ago as Afrikan social history can be reconstructed by scholars.

The great importance of spit to the ancient Egyptians may well be indicated by its location in the realms of myth, divinity, medicine and social practice. In the language of the ancient Egyptians a correspondingly large vocabulary pertaining to "spit," "spittle" and their cognates amount to more than twenty words and expressions.[36] This constitutes linguistic evidence of considerable weight in favour of the conclusion that the people of Kemet attributed very great importance to this act as well as the substance it produced.

The very first reference to spit in the history of humanity occurs in the earliest Creation Story of the Afrikan people, the creation myth of Kemet. Here, ⚱ ℐ Itm, Atum, the Creator Divinity, creates Shu, the Divinity of Air, and Tefnut, the Divinity of Heat, with and from His ◌ 🝖 ⌇psg, his spit.[37] In this archetypal instance spit is a creative agent in the realm of divinity. Numerous examples of the creative force of spit, as well as other applications of this very popular medical remedy, follow in the *Pyramid Texts*, the *Coffin Texts* and other parts of the spiritual literature of ancient Egypt, so that "[g]ods, kings, demons, animals, plants, materials, and even the earth itself may be viewed as the product of spitting."[38] A considerable range of ideas, including "creation, blessing, healing, . . . washing, . . . venom, cursing, decay, and death" are covered by the notion of ritual spitting in Kemet.[39]

The story of Auset (Amharic Isata, Greek Isis) and Ra further illustrates the ritual significance of spit to the people of Kemet. Auset, in order to obtain power over Ra, who has become a drooling old man in his earthly manifestation, picks up some of his saliva from the ground, mixes it with some earth and fashions it into a snake. The snake bites Ra and his consequent suffering forces him to reveal his secret name, and so he surrenders his power to Auset in return for an antidote.[40] In at least one interpretation of this story, the spit of Ra that is employed by Auset represents "one widely used technique in sorcery, which is that of obtaining something emanating from the body of the victim or intimately associated with him by contact, thus embodying his essence."[41] In this instance the ritual significance of the spit lies in the fact that it comes from inside of the person or being. This represents the essence or vital aspect(s) of the person or being, and so his/her power. Further, it may be noted that here Ra was doubly in Isis' power, for since he had not made the snake and did not name it, he did not know its name and so did not have power over it. Isis did.

This notion of spit as a healing and thus a transforming agent is based securely upon a bio-chemical fact. Spit contains, among other very useful enzymes, a potent chemical called *histatin*, a protein with anti fungal properties that is found only in human saliva. *Histatin* functions as a healing agent. It inhibits the growth of yeast and bacteria and so hastens the healing of wounds.[42]

Faulkner says, cryptically, that "spitting is a means of healing in folk-medicine."[43] As shown above, there is some medical basis for this practice of the ancestors.

However, it is possible to arrive at a much more detailed understanding of the significance of ritual spitting. We have already seen that in the spiritual practice of the Ancient Egyptians the mouth must be made ritually clean for true words to come forth from it. The ritual significance of both the mouth and spit is also important in the entire corpus of rituals surrounding libation.

Goelet recognises that spitting upon things, along with licking them, has magical (or ritual) application in the *Book of Going Forth by Day*. For Goelet, "[t]he underlying notion is not as primitive as it may sound at first, for the curative power of saliva has long been recognised."[44] Spitting and licking are employed as healing actions in Chapters 17, 72 and 102 among several others in the *Book of Going Forth*. In Chapter 146 an epithet for a protective female divinity is "She who licks," an epithet that recalls the protective gesture of a cow that licks her young. It is the same with many other animals. The importance of spit is further emphasised in a number of creation stories of Kemet, "where a generative force akin to that of semen is ascribed to it."[45] It is certain that spitting was already a very old practice at the time of the composition of the *Book of Going Forth*, for there is a reference to it in the *Book of Vindication* or *Coffin Texts*, which predate the *Book of Going Forth* by many centuries. Here, Utterance 113 contains the words ". . . for I am one who spits on wounds which [will make them] heal. . ."[46] Spitting as part of healing almost certainly predates the era in which the *Book of Vindication* was produced.

The creative and transforming power of spit is retained rather consistently in the ritual practice of Afrikan people. Spitting is common today in Afrikan communities on the continent. Spitting on cuts, bruises and sores is a fairly common practice among children. This practice is also known among adults. Many traditional healers spit preparations directly onto affected parts of the human body. Spitting is also part of the ritual of libation. As can be seen in Chapter One, the libationer may spit the liquid of libation three times.

Afrikans in the communities abroad have also retained this tradition, but in a truncated form. Many Afrikans in these parts of the world will spit on to Mother Earth, or into their own hands, as a way of showing that what they are saying is a sacred oath, which must therefore be taken very seriously, as Afrikans do not make this oath unless on the most serious of occasions. It is not at all difficult to establish the origins of this behaviour. In West Afrika, among the Kru people in Sierra Leone, spitting on the ground is a way of showing agreement or of emphasising a point.[47] In Suriname a Winti mother licks her child's forehead three times then spits three times in different directions during an after-birth ritual.[48] This demonstrates the ritual significance of spitting, which is the focus of our discussion here, as well as the ritual significance of the number three, which is discussed later.

The ritual significance of spit is, unsurprisingly, recorded in the Bible. In the New Testament, at John 9: 6–7 and again at 9:11, where the incident is recounted by the beneficiary, the Messiah spits upon the earth, mixes it with some earth, then places the resulting concoction on the eyes of a blind man and sends him to bath in the pool of Siloam. He is cured. Similar deployment of spit is demonstrated at Mark 7:33 and 8:23. The similarities between the afore-mentioned action of Auset and those of the Messiah millennia after, should not escape our attention here.

7.3: The significance of the Number Three

The number three is significant in the language and iconography of Kemet because it conveys the notions of plurality and unity held by the people of Kemet.[49] In the mental universe of Kemet, there was singular (1), dual (2) and plural (3 or more.) Additionally, often, very many or an indeterminate number was expressed as 9, that is, "the plural of plurals," which was also, but less often, represented as other multiples of 3.

In keeping with this status the number nine also represented everything in the ancient Egyptian mental universe. This much is conveyed in such terms as ๐|๒||| and ๆๆๆ ๆๆๆ ๆๆๆ: psḏt: "Ennead," literally, "group of nine."[50] This representation of indeterminate plurality was given rather concrete expression in the concept of the Nine Bows, the summation of Kemet's traditional enemies. Again, in the story known in Egyptology as the "Tale of the Eloquent Peasant," it may be significant that the peasant made nine speeches. For at least one observer, this number represents "a cycle, a complete literary work."[51] The idea that the number nine, the "plural of plurals," may signify an indeterminate but very large quantity, is quite possibly conveyed in some other observations about this story. This appears to be true especially when the notion is combined with substantial length, as it was in this context. Jacob Carruthers quotes John Wilson, Miriam Lichtheim and Alan Gardiner, all of whom suggest that the farmer may have made a large number of speeches of indeterminate length. Wilson concludes that "'His eloquence was so admired that he was kept talking on and on, for the enjoyment of the court.'" Carruthers reports Lichtheim as observing that the farmer was "goaded to continue speaking." Gardiner says that the farmer "'poured out his complaints.'"[52] Thus although the texts are quite specific that the farmer made nine petitions, the great length of the latter may have contributed to the notion of a considerable quantity.

The number three also represented a closed system of units that are simultaneously complete and interactive and represents the cyclical nature of some aspects of reality.[53] The ancient Egyptian divinity Ptah—Sokar—Wsir may be of relevance here. This is a trinity, a three-in-one divinity that represents "Creation or Birth," "Death or Decay" and "Rebirth or Resurrection;" an entire cycle.[54] It is quite likely that the use of the number three in the contemporary Afrikan world, like so much of the founding principles of Afrikan culture, has its ultimate origin in the Nile Valley, if not more precisely in the most well known representation of Nile Valley culture in Kemet.

It is therefore not surprising that the number three continues to be of great importance in Afrikan rituals in communities abroad. In 1808 Afrikans on the East Coast of Demerara in Guyana, were observed to walk three times around a grave in procession with the coffin before interring the body.[55] In Trinidad part of the saraka rites was to walk in procession three times around the house.

This number arises in a ritual context on a number of other occasions. One of the clearest expressions of this continuity from the ancient past is the libations poured at the Libation and Orison (orientation of important persons and paraphernalia) during the opening ritual of a Voodoo service. In fact, the significance of water as well as of the number three may be observed here. First, the water is oriented (that is, presented to East, West, North and South) as their ancestors oriented themselves throughout the history of Kemet, in the Old,[56] the Middle[57] and the New Kingdom.[58] (Among the Spiritual Baptists this orientation is today called surveying.) Next, the Divinities are invoked, especially Legba: the Opener of the Way and Guardian of Crossroads and cemeteries. This is an exact continuation of the ancient Afrikan tradition known to us first at Kemet, where 𓂀𓏏𓃣𓀀 Inpu, called Anubis in Greek and by Egyptologists, was also the Divinity of Crossroads, bore the epithet (descriptive name) of "Opener of the Ways" and was the intermediary between this world and the Afterworld and the Guardian of cemeteries and the Underworld.[59] This tradition was inherited by the Voodoo practitioners through the Yoruba Orisa called Legba or Elegba in Nigeria and the Fon divinity called Legba or Alegba in Benin. We must note that Nigeria and Benin are contiguous countries in West Afrika. Geographically speaking, they are far away from both the "New World" countries where Voodoo is practiced, and the Nile Valley, where Legba/Alegba was first attested, as Inpu, millennia before its presence in this western region of the continent, and even longer before the birth of those specific reformulations and expressions of Afrikan spirituality called Voodoo, Orisha, Santería, Candomblé and so on, in those terrifying circumstances inhabited by the Afrikan people not so long ago in the Caribbean and the Americas. The ancient Nile Valley, West Afrika for most of its long history and the Americas and the Caribbean of modern times may be separated by huge measures of geography and time, but they are all united by the presence of Afrikan people and the continuation of Afrikan culture. Each is an aspect of the Afrikan world.

The water is then poured three times before the centre post or *Poteau-Mitan*, then three times at one entrance, sometimes at each of three entrances to the peristyle (the building or part thereof in which the service is held). Next, lines are traced to the peristyle, which is then kissed three times. Water is then poured three times before each of the three drums, which together form the *batière*. These libations are then repeated by important visiting initiates, then by the members of the hounfor or temple.[60] At a certain point in the rites marking the initiation or 'baptism' of someone into the followers of the divinity Erulie Freida, the *houngan* "recites three Ave Marias, three Credos and the Confiteor three times."[61] (As discussed previously, this content is a comment on how Afrikans have hidden Afrikan symbolism in European clothes.) There are a number of other actions which are repeated three times during other ceremonies.[62]

The number three also resounds in the drums, which constitute a most important part of Afrikan sacred rituals and indeed in general Afrikan cultural expression. Esteban Montejo, an Afrikan Cuban who refused to be enslaved and ran away from the plantation, recalls that for a particular dance called the *yuka*, three drums were played: 'the *caja*, the *mula*, and the *cachimbo*, which was the smallest one.'[63] This is important eyewitness testimony to a specific example of a trinity of drums among Afrikans in Cuba sometime around the 1850s. The following examples show that the trinity was indeed a cultural pattern in drumming among Afrikans in the Caribbean. They also prove that a gradation in pitch that was somewhat related to the size of the drums was and still is in fact part of this cultural reality.

Three drums are played in most Afrikan spiritual ceremonies. In Voodoo the three *Rada* drums are called *bula* or *petit*, the smallest; *seconde*, the second or middle drum, and maman, which is the largest.[64] The pitch of each is related to the others, so that the smallest emits sounds in the highest range, the *seconde* sounds in the middle range and the *maman*, sounds in the lower or bass range. It is the drums that are always sacred, not the drummers,[65] who may be inducted to become "sacred" drummers.

The trinity of drums also lives among the Rastafari. Ras Kwende's description and explanation repeats the fundamentals of the Voodoo expression of this tradition and helps to lead us to a greater understanding of this aspect of Afrikan culture. "Rasta drums, called the *akete*, come in a trinity. The repeater, also called the *kete*, and the *funde* are similar in size and are types of bongo drums except that they are longer and more mellow sounding. The repeater gives the high-sounding melody while the lower-sounding, mid-range funde keeps the time, or syncopates. The double-ended base drum is much larger and it also keeps the time and produces the rhythm and depth."[66]

In Santería too, the batá drums are also three in number and are sacred and ceremonial. Each is double-headed and shaped like an hour glass. They vary in size and sound. The largest is the *iya* (*iya* in Yoruba means mother), the *itotele* is the middle one, and the *okonkolo* (also *okonkilo* or *orele*) is the smallest. Both drums and drummers are consecrated by *Añya* (or *Aña*), the Orisha of the drum, in a special ceremony and the drums are considered the material representation of *Añya*. In Yorubaland these drums are called *Iyá Ilú*, *Omele* and *Kudi*.[67]

In Candomblé there are also three drums. These are collectively called *atabaques* and are believed to have been war drums in Afrika. Each also has its own identity and its own name. Hence *rum*, the largest and deepest-toned, *rumpi*, the middle drum in size as well as tone and *lé*, the smallest drum and the one with the highest tone.[68] These sacred drums "are intermediaries, for they take believers' petitions to the gods through special rhythms peculiar to each Orisha. The drums are mythical entities, and they consume sacred produce: palm oil, honey, sacramental water, and hen's blood."[69] In reality the drums do not literally consume these articles. The priest makes an offering in a sacred ceremony or ritual.

In the French dominated aspects of the Caribbean, especially Martinique, Guadeloupe and Cayenne, "[t]here must be three drums, the one to 'damme' (to announce), the other to 'refoule' (to send the rhythm back), the third to 'coupe' (or cut) . . ."⁷⁰

Afrikan informants in Guyana, the direct descendants of Kongo people, have also preserved this significance of the number three in drums. Junga, a man from Kongo, "owned three drums: the rondel, the tampalin, and the sassi [*nzazi*?] suzina, a small drum with a high, rapid staccato sound."⁷¹ Another drummer from Central Africa was reported to give the names of his drums, again three in number, as "the tuta, the ja and the base."⁷²

Afrikans in Tobago follow this very pattern. Here, the drums are also three in number. Further, the bum or base is the biggest drum and provides the deepest sounds. The cutter is the middle drum in both size and range of sound. The roller provides the highest pitch in sound. We must note a variation here. The roller is not necessarily the smallest drum in size. It attains the highest pitch because the goat skin covering, which is beaten to produce the sound, is pulled the tightest.⁷³

7.4: The Ritual Significance of Wearing White

The spiritual significance of the colour white originated in our earliest ancestors' conceptualization of beings in the spirit world as translucent, luminous and radiant, but also physically intangible, elusive and impermanent. This very idea of spirits has been passed down to us. The colour white is the nearest representation of this appearance in the colour spectrum. Therefore this colour was, naturally, the one which was employed to give visual representation to beings and things from the spirit world. Sometimes off-white or yellow was also used. In ancient Egypt, this was especially so for the ҉●҉҉, the *akhu* or ancestral spirits who made a successful transition into paradise. We must remind ourselves that, as discussed above, the determinatives or sense signs in both variations of the word *akh* also indicate revered status. Reverence for ancestors certainly reinforced this idea and provided concrete occasions to practice the representation of spirits as luminous and translucent. The colours which best capture these qualities are white or yellow. So it is these colours that the ancient Egyptians employed in their physical representation of spirits.

In the *Medew Netjer* there is a group of words that refer to beings in the spirit world and to associated things, qualities and states:

҉●҉[variation ҉!҉] 3ḫ = "blessed spirit," spirit.

҉!3ḫ = "the spirit-state."

҉●3ḫ = "be, become a spirit" (verb); "glorious, splendid, beneficial, profitable," "effective." (adjectives).

҉●҉[variations ҉҉, ҉●҉, ҉●] 3ḫw = "power of god."

҉●҉[variation ҉҉] 3ḫw = "sunlight, sunshine."

⛤ [variation 🝆●⌒] 3ḫt = "horizon."⁷⁴

These words often convey something of the condition of being in the spirit world, certainly the quality and the appearance. Forman and Quirke tell us that the meaning of *akhu* is bound up with the notion of light, that these spirits exist in a paradise that is conceptualised in terms of light, and that to the people of Kemet, the term ⛤ *akht*, translated into English as "horizon," meant the home of light.⁷⁵ It may not be misplaced here to recall that in the Afrikan spiritual system, light may be symbolic of knowledge, understanding and sometimes revelation. A good illustration of this symbolism resides in the name ⸻ ru prt m hrw: *Chapters of Going Forth By Day (Into Light)*, the title of a very important book that was introduced in Chapter Two. One term in this title, ⸻ hrw, is normally read as "day." However, in this position it carries the added significance of "enlightenment." This notion is arrived at through the idea of "light." This idea clearly resides in the very bright Egyptian day, especially when contrasted to the darkness of the grave or sealed tomb from which the liberated spirit of the deceased would "go forth" into the light of day. Here darkness is symbolic of ignorance, the lack of knowledge or light, and light symbolises the possession of knowledge and enlightenment. The idea communicated by the title of this text is that a person in possession of the knowledge contained in the text will attain eternal enlightenment in the Ancient Egyptian heaven.

The link between light and enlightenment may not be purely semantic or symbolic. It may also refer to actual physical stages of human evolution, for the act of standing up, of walking on two legs rather than on four, was simultaneously both a decisive stage in the transformation into humanity and physically reaching towards the sun, towards both sunlight and a higher order of consciousness we term enlightenment. This great evolutionary leap forward happened in Afrika. The process was fired by melanin, a historical and genetic chemical marker which absorbs light and propels itself towards it.⁷⁶

These conclusions are sustained in the physical representation of the akhu or blessed dead in Kemet. In the illustrations of the *Book of Going Forth By Day*, the colour white dominates the clothing of both the akhu or Ancestral Spirits and those who attend to them, such as priests. Further, the rubric to the profound Chapter 125, the Address to the Divinity in the Hall of Justice in which the deceased spirit pronounces the Declarations of Innocence, makes it clear that wearing white is part of the correct procedure:

> The correct procedure in this Hall of Justice. One shall utter this spell
>
> pure and clean and clad in white garments.⁷⁷

Of some relevance here is the fact that the people of Kemet regarded ivory and alabaster as extremely valuable because they were thought to be pure substances. Scarce, durable, widely desired and so precious, they were very important articles in most rituals in Kemet. Both are white and, in certain conditions, even translucent in appearance. These are reasons that added to their importance.

These facts suggest that the wearing of white was a conscious convention on occasions connected to the Ancestors and to divinity. The colour white symbolized purity, cleanliness, the spirit state and spirituality. This symbolism has been continued by Afrikans as they moved away from the Nile Valley to inhabit other parts of the continent and also when they were forced to migrate to the Americas and the Caribbean during the *Maafa*. For example, in the classical cosmology of Shonghai the colour represents the quality of the elusive, the impermanence and the disappearing. People put white clay on their bodies during funeral ceremonies to symbolize the physical disappearance from among them of the person who has made his/her transition.[78] The same or similar ideas and practices abound in many parts of Afrika. For example, in describing ritual drama of the kind in honour of a local divinity or held in a family shrine, Isidore Okpewho observes that "[t]he celebrant is often dressed in white handwoven cloth and has white chalk smeared around her eyes . . ."[79]

Wearing white clay on the face or the entire body on ritual occasions is practised in many parts of Afrika. This tradition was taken to the Caribbean and the Americas during the Great Holocaust. It still survives, sometimes in mutated or truncated forms, wherever Afrikans live today. A brilliant and radiant white or yellow-white is the dominant colour of both the apparel and the bodies of ancestors and divinity who appeared in the visions of Marta Moreno Vega, an initiate of Santería.[80] Altars are regularly draped in white. Priests and those performing libation, particularly on formal occasions, often wear white. White is the dominant colour in the apparel of initiates and practitioners of Afrikan spirituality. It is this fact which led one western scholar to describe the Jordanites, an Afrikan centered spiritual movement in Guyana, as the "White Robed Army."[81] Today, on occasions where the Ancestors are to be specially honoured, such as the Annual Caravan to the Ancestors in Gainesville, Texas, the annual Emancipation Day observations in the Caribbean and the UK, Kwanzaa, and so on, wearing white is very often specifically requested by organisers.

7.5: The Spiritual Significance of Flags, Flag Planting and related ideas

Over their dwellings they hoisted a white cloth on a pole the ideogram for divinity in Egyptian hieroglyphics. That white cloth is the babaláwo's symbolic way of announcing: 'Here you may ask of God.' . . . wherever in Yorubaland, in Igboland or in Dahomey one sees that white cloth fluttering atop a pole, one knows wordlessly that there dwells a wise man, a medicine man, perhaps also a magician, invariably a man of God.[82]

Flags are regularly planted in special rituals and ceremonies held within the Afrikan spiritual community today: in Voodoo, in the Orisha tradition, and indeed all over the Afrikan world. Flags are considered symbolic, especially to particular social and religious groups, and may even be held as sacred by some. Where do these attitudes come from? How did these rites begin? What are their significances?

Flag planting belongs to the same complex of ideas and practices that produced libation. The fundamental understandings that instruct flag planting are the connection of all beings and things in the cosmos and the critical importance of humans maintaining connections with the Creator, with other gods, with our Ancestors, among the living and the unborn and with the environment in which we live.

The flag is especially significant because one of its functions is to connect human beings and symbolise the connections among human beings. It is a marker of love and remembrance. It connects and unites into one community all humans of the group: those "past" (the ancestors), those living (we who are in this dimension of time) and those who are yet to come (the unborn.) The flag also connects the members of this community to divinity, for, as the divine symbol of a particular community (a family, a clan, a nation), it may also recall and represent a founding ancestor. However, a flag may also represent an animal or an object that equally may also embody the principles, vital forces or soul of the community in question. A flag may also represent an army, a part of an army, any other military force, a civilian group, or a civilian organisation, such as a particular spiritual community.

In Kemet flags, standards, ensigns, pennants and streamers, which were notalways one and the same thing, were flown just outside of buildings that housed representative institutions of the group. Such buildings were the family home, the tomb of a leading ancestor, the shrine of the family, the clan, the district and the state, and the residence of an nsw or pharaoh, who was the spiritual and political leader of the nation. On ceremonial occasions, for example at the heb sed or rejuvenation and jubilee ceremony of an nsw, the standards or pennants, as well as the shrines, of each of the divisions or sections of the greater entity represented by their coming together, were taken to the location of the ceremony. Thus flown together in one place, the flags symbolized a great demonstration of unity and strength.

Many Afrikan families and clans, sometimes occupying entire communities and even districts, take their family names from the ancestral person or the sacred animal or object represented and recalled in their emblem and displayed on their flag. The members of a particular group do not eat their representative animal or a particular part of it, or interact with it in certain other specified ways. For example, if the representative thing is an object, then it must be avoided. Each of these representative animals and things is taboo to those it represents. The penalty for not respecting this rule may be illness or some other form of punishment to someone, not necessarily the one who made the infraction, but one related to him or her. The tremendous implications of this aspect of the Afrikan world-view, as well as the practices that are instructed by it, for species protection and environmentalism in general have already been noted above in Chapter One.

Some surviving palettes suggest that at first, the actual object or body of the animal thus sacred to and representative of the group was placed atop a long pole and carried aloft to represent the group, either permanently at institutions and/or on ceremonial occasions. Examples may be seen on the Narmer Palette, which is reproduced in the photospread. However, there must have been problems with such a practice. For example, it would not have been practical, or even possible, to carry the body of a large animal atop a pole or a standard. It is here that artistic representation further aided the development of symbolism. Whatever the details may be, it is certain that over time the visual image of the person, animal or object came to be artistically represented, often stylized, on a piece of cloth, which was then placed at one end of a long pole and flown as a flag or standard to represent the group. The evolutionary trajectories that resulted in this development may not have even been begun in Kemet.[83] However, by 4000 to 3050 BCE a system had evolved in Kemet whereby each town, district, nome (state) and often a family, identified itself by the representation of its collective symbol mounted atop a flagpole or a standard. Some of these symbols were inscribed on pottery.

It is these meanings of the flag that instructed the inventors of the Medew Netjer to choose the flag, ⸸:ntr: *netjer* (singular); ⸸⸸ ntrw: *netjru* (plural), as the symbol that in the written language would also represent ideas of divinity and the divine.

Every written language attempts to give graphic representation to a spoken language. Language, in both its spoken and written forms, is ultimately an expression of the culture, including its values, attitudes, patterned behaviours and world-view, of the particular speech community in which the language originated. It is also an inventory of that community's social history. Hence, once its social history is known, the meaning of the flag in the *Medew Netjer* should not surprise us. Nor should anyone be taken unawares by the significance accorded the flag by the inventors of the *Medew Netjer*. The *Medew Netjer* demonstrates the very special significance the community attached to this sign of the flag by writing it first in words containing the sounds it represented, irrespective of whether or not these sounds were pronounced first. Examples employed in this text include ⸗ ḥtpw nṯr, "invocation offerings" or ⸗ pr(t)-hrw-htp(w)-nṯr "voice offerings" and ⸗ snṯr; [variation ⸗ : snṯr] *sen-netjer* "incense" and ⸗ (variation ⸗) ḥm nṯr: "servant of the divinity" on previous pages, and, of course, the term ⸗ Medew Netjer, which is used throughout this work. This change in the written order of the netjers, in general called transposition, indicates that the idea, things or beings represented by the flag are of the greatest importance, even sacred, and must therefore be shown to be so. The device by which this is effected in the writing, that is, the inversion of the order of the netjers and sometimes the word order of an entire sentence, is called Honorific Transposition in Egyptology. This must be distinguished from Graphic Transposition, which is an inversion of the signs to suit the aesthetics of physical space.

It is noted above that flags, standards, ensigns, pennants and streamers are not always one and the same thing. Strictly speaking, a flag is a piece of cloth that is flown attached to a pole. Its colour(s) and/or the representation upon it of an animal, a place or an idea, or any combination of these, may signify that it represents a particular group of people.

Sometimes one or more long, thin pieces of cloth are attached to the flagpole, mostly below the flag. These are called streamers. If flown on their own (without a flag,) they may be referred to as pennants and may carry an emblem.

The standard evolved as a wooden framework attached to a long pole and supported an emblematic animal or thing, often a religious object. When it was decided to write the language of Kemet, the inventors of the Medew Netjer deployed ⸗, the picture of a standard, especially those used for carrying religious symbols, to represent the idea of 'religious standard' and related ideas such as the names of particular divinities.

The word for standard in the Medew Netjer is ⸗ i3t: iat. The fact that there is the term ⸗ [84] i3t sryt, which translates as 'military standard', shows that different military forces and/or parts of the army and navy were identified by standards peculiar to them.

NOTES

1. Langston Hughes (1997). "The Negro Speaks of Rivers" in H. L. Gates, Jnr. and N. Y. McKay (eds.). *The Norton Anthology of African American Literature* (W. W. Norton and Co., New York and London), p. 1254; Hughes (1994). 'The Negro Speaks of Rivers.' *The Collected Poems of Langston Hughes* (Alfred A. Knopf Inc.) Available at www.poets.org/viewmedia.php/prmMID/15722. [Accessed on 15 July, 2008].
2. L. H. Lesko. "Ancient Egyptian Cosmogonies and Cosmology," pp. 116–117.
3. Herodotus. *The Histories*, p. 131.
4. Yosef A. A. ben-Jochannan (1986). *Abu Simbel-Gizeh: Guide Book/Manual* (The Author, New York), p. 47.
5. Faulkner (trans.). *The Book of Going Forth by Day*, p. 115.
6. Charles Finch. "Nile Genesis: Continuity in Culture from the Great Lakes to the Delta" in Van Sertima (ed.). *Egypt: Child of Africa*, p.39.
7. Jan Assmann (trans. D. Lorton, 2005). *Death and Salvation in Ancient Egypt* (Cornell University Press, Ithaca and London), pp. 304–305.
8. Assmann, Ibid.
9. See, for example, the series of "ferryman" and "ferrying" texts in R.O. Faulkner (trans.). *Pyramid Texts*, Utterances 516–520, 522, 528, 531, etc. on pp. 190–199; Faulkner (trans.). *Coffin Texts*, Vol. II, Spells 395, 396, 397, 398, on pp. 22–41; 775 on pp. 303–304, etc.; Assmann. *Death and Salvation*, p. 304.
10. For example, most recently by Armah, *The Eloquence of the Scribes*, pp.212–214.
11. Sabine Jell-Bahlsen. "The Lake Goddess, Uhammiri/Ogbuide: The Female Side of the Universe in Igbo Cosmology," p. 44. For a reflection of this notion in the creative imagination of the Igbo, See also Nwapa, *Idu*, p. 210.
12. The Rubicon is the ancient name of a small stream that formed part of the boundary between southern Gaul (France) and northern Italy. Julius Caesar crossed it into Italy to begin a civil war with Pompey.
13. Jimmy Cliff "Many Rivers to Cross" Island Music Ltd., 1969.
14. Théophile Obenga (1989). "African Philosophy of the Pharaonic Period (2780 330 B. C.)" in I. Van Sertima (ed.). *Egypt Revisited*, pp. 293–309; Obenga, *Afrikan Philosophy*, pp. 46–50; E. A. Wallis Budge (1927, 1978). *Herb-Doctors and Physicians of the Ancient World: The Divine Origin of the Craft of the Herbalist*, pp. 20–23; J. P .Allen (1988). *Genesis in Egypt: The Philosophy of Ancient Egyptian Creation Accounts*.
15. Erik Hornung (Translated Irmela Stevens, 2005). *The Ancient Egyptian Books of the Underworld* (The Intef Institute, Karnak House, London), p. 16.
16. Ian Shaw and Paul Nicholson. *British Museum Dictionary of Ancient Egypt*, p. 304.
17. Budge. *Herb Doctors*, p. 20.
18. Aboubacry Moussa Lam (1997). "Égypte ancienne et Afrique Noire: autour de l'eau" ⸸ Ankh: Revue d'égyptologie et des civilisations Africaines Nos. 6/7, pp. 55 73. See also Molefe Asante. The History of Africa, pp. 81–89.
19. Budge. Ibid., p.21.
20. See, for example, Chukwunyere Kamalu (1990). *Foundations of African Thought* (Karnak House, London), pp. 1–28; 111–126, etc.; Asante and Abarry. *African Intellectual Heritage*, pp. 6, 11–13, etc.; Jacques Habbib Sy (1989). "Theophile Obenga: At the Forefront of Egypto-Nubian and Black African Renaissance in

Philosophy" in Ivan Van Sertima (ed.). *Egypt Revisited,* pp. 277–285; Théophile Obenga. "African Philosophy of the Pharaonic Period (2780–330B.C.)" in Van Sertima, *Egypt Revisited,* pp. 286–324.
21. Hutton. *The Logic and Historical Significance of the Haitian Revolution,* p. 109.
22. Ibid.
23. Hutton. Ibid.
24. See also Chapter V, note 49.
25. J. O. Lucas. *Religions in West Africa and Ancient Egypt,* pp. 113–130; Awolalu and Dopamu. *West African Traditional Religion,* pp. 87–114, *passim*; Oduyoye. "The Spirits that rule the World," pp. 84–85.
26. Emilia Viotti da Costa (1994). *Crowns of Glory, Tears of Blood: The Demerara Slave Rebellion of 1823* (Oxford University Press, New York and London), p. 105.
27. Da Costa, Ibid. 12. The Rubicon is the ancient name of a small stream that formed part of the boundary between southern Gaul (France) and northern Italy. Julius Caesar crossed it into Italy to begin a civil war with Pompey.
13. Jimmy Cliff "Many Rivers to Cross" Island Music Ltd., 1969.
14. Théophile Obenga (1989). "African Philosophy of the Pharaonic Period (2780 330 B. C.)" in I. Van Sertima (ed.). *Egypt Revisited,* pp. 293–309; Obenga, *Afrikan Philosophy,* pp. 46–50; E. A. Wallis Budge (1927, 1978). *Herb-Doctors and Physicians of the Ancient World: The Divine Origin of the Craft of the Herbalist,* pp. 20–23; J. P .Allen (1988). *Genesis in Egypt: The Philosophy of Ancient Egyptian Creation Accounts.*
15. Erik Hornung (Translated Irmela Stevens, 2005). *The Ancient Egyptian Books of the Underworld* (The Intef Institute, Karnak House, London), p. 16.
16. Ian Shaw and Paul Nicholson. *British Museum Dictionary of Ancient Egypt,* p. 304.
17. Budge. *Herb Doctors,* p. 20.
18. Aboubacry Moussa Lam (1997). "Égypte ancienne et Afrique Noire: autour de l'eau" ☥ Ankh: Revue d'égyptologie et des civilisations Africaines Nos. 6/7, pp. 55 73. See also Molefe Asante. The History of Africa, pp. 81–89.
19. Budge. Ibid., p.21.
20. See, for example, Chukwunyere Kamalu (1990). *Foundations of African Thought* (Karnak House, London), pp. 1–28; 111–126, etc.; Asante and Abarry. *African Intellectual Heritage,* pp. 6, 11–13, etc.; Jacques Habbib Sy (1989). "Theophile Obenga: At the Forefront of Egypto-Nubian and Black African Renaissance in Philosophy" in Ivan Van Sertima (ed.). *Egypt Revisited,* pp. 277–285; Théophile Obenga. "African Philosophy of the Pharaonic Period (2780–330B.C.)" in Van Sertima, *Egypt Revisited,* pp. 286–324.
28. Da Costa. Ibid.
29. Ibid. See pp. 108–109 for the importance of water to Afrikans in Guyana at this time.
30. The water is really dark brown in appearance from fairly close up, black from further away. The colour is due to the release of chlorophyll from rotting leaves.
31. An Afrikan centered group of spiritual practitioners in Guyana. See Judith Roback (1973). *The White Robed Army: Cultural Nationalism and a Religious Movement in Guyana.* (PhD Thesis. Dept. of Anthropology, Mc Gill University, Montreal); Francis Drakes [Kimani Nehusi] (1982). *The Jordanites: The Study of a Black Cultist Movement* (Curriculum Development Centre, Ministry of Education, Social Development and Culture, Georgetown).
32. Mbiti. *Introduction to African Religion,* p. 48.

33. For example, in the case of Ghana see Casely Hayford (1903). *Gold Coast Native Institutions* (Sweet and Maxwell, Limited, London), p. 88; for the Yoruba in Nigeria consult E. B. Idowu (1960, 1994). *Olódùmarè: God in Yoruba Belief*, p.73; for Afrikans in Zimbabwe see David Lan. *Guns and Rain*, p. 144.
34. Lucas. *The Religion of the Yorubas*, p. 72. See also p. 204 for the example of the *Iwenumo* or Outdooring.
35. Obenga. "African Philosophy of the Pharaonic Period ..." in Van Sertima (ed.). *Egypt Revisited*, p.304, quoting an ancient Afrikan text from Kemet known, misleadingly, as the Bremmer Rhind Papyrus. See also J. P. Allen. *Genesis in Egypt*, pp.27–31.
36. R. Ritner (1993). *The Mechanics of Ancient Egyptian Magic*. (The Oriental Institute, University of Chicago), p. 74.
37. For this act of Creation see R. O. Faulkner (trans.). *The Pyramid Texts*. Utterances 600, p. 246 and 660, p. 271. (See also Utterance 527, p. 198, regarding the creation of the twins by Atum through masturbation); Faulkner (trans.). *The Coffin Texts*, p. 80; J. P. Allen (1988). *Genesis in Egypt*, p. 14, etc.
38. Ritner. The Mechanics of Ancient Egyptian Magic, p. 75.
39. Ibid., p. 92.
40. W. Budge. *The Egyptian Book of the Dead*, p. xc for the reference to spit, pp. lxxxix–xci for the entire story. See also George Hart (1990). *Egyptian Myths* (The British Museum Press, London), pp. 45–46, and Aude Gros de Beler (1999, 2002). *Egyptian Mythology* (Todtri Book Publishers, New York), pp. 48 and 50.
41. Joseph Kaster (1968). *The Wisdom of Ancient Egypt: Writings from the Time of the Pharaohs* (Michael O'Mara Books, Ltd., London), p.61. Emphasis added.
42. Rosie Mestel (2002). "The Wonders of Saliva." *Los Angeles Times*. 21 January.
43. R. O. Faulkner. Trans. (1969). *The Ancient Egyptian Pyramid Texts*. (Oxford University Press. Aris & Phillips), p. 104, Note 6 to Spell 324..
44. Goelet. 'Commentary...', p. 147.
45. Goelet. Ibid.
46. Faulkner. *Ancient Egyptian Coffin Texts* Vol. III, Spell 1113, p. 162.
47. James Graham Cruikshank (1919, 1999). "African Immigrants after Freedom" *Timehri* VI, 3rd Ser. Reprinted in David Granger (ed.) *Scenes from the History of the Africans in Guyana* (free press, Georgetown), p. 36, Note 2.
48. H. J. Stephen. (1998). *Winti Culture*, (The Author? Amsterdam?), p.73.
49. R. H. Wilkinson. *Symbol and Magic in Egyptian Art*, pp. 142–143.
50. J. P. Allen. *Genesis in Egypt*, p.8.
51. Oleg Berlev (1997). "Bureaucrats" in Sergio Donadoni (ed.). *The Egyptians*. p. 99.
52. J. Carruthers (1995). *MDw NTr: Divine Speech*, p. 143. Emphasis added.
53. R. H. Wilkinson (1994). *Symbol and Magic In Egyptian Art*, pp.131–133, 142 143.
54. The anteriority of this notion of Trinity to Christianity ought to be noted.
55. Da Costa. *Crowns of Glory*, p. 106.
56. See examples in Faulkner. *Pyramid Texts*, Utterance 217, pp. 44–45; Lichtheim. *Ancient Egyptian Literature*, Vol. I, pp. 30–34.
57. For an example consult Faulkner. *Coffin Texts*, Vol. III, Spell 1018, p. 120.
58. Budge. *Book of the Dead*, p. 2.
59. See, for example, Aude Gros de Beler. *Egyptian Mythology*, pp. 14–15; M. Denning, O. Phillips and G. Rudolph (1979). *Voudoun Fire: The Living Reality of*

Mystical Religion, pp. 148,149, etc.
60. M. Denning *et al. Vodun Fire*, p.55.
61. Hurston. *Tell My Horse*, p.124.
62. Ibid., pp. 142, 147, 153, 160, 171, 175, 225, *passim*.
63. Esteban Montejo. *The Autobiography* ... , p.50.
64. K. Dunham. *Dances of Haiti*, p. 73 renders these as *mama, seconde* and *kata*.
65. Deren. *Divine Horsemen*, pp. 184, 185, 235, 245, 326, 332, 336, *passim*.
66. Kwende Anbessa-Ebanks (1983, 2004). *Rastafari Livity: A Basic Information Text* (Kwemara Publications, London), p. 68.
67. Vega. *Alter of My Soul*, pp. 171–172, 281; R. Canizares. *Walking With the Night*, pp. 69–72; Judith Bettelheim (2000, ed.). *Cuban Festivals: A Century of Afro-Cuban Culture* (Ian Randle Publishers, Kingston, Jamaica and Markus Wiener Publishers, Princetown, NJ), pp. 179, 192 and 195, where the orthography varies into *Iya, Iyá* or *Chaworo, Itotels, Okónkilo, Kónkolo* or *Orele* or *Omelé* .
68. Abdias Do Nascimento. *Orixás: Os Deuses Vivos da África*, pp. 149, 155, 159, *passim*.
69. Ibid., p. 57.
70. Madiana (1934, 2002). "The Biguine of the French Antilles" in Nancy Cunard (ed.). *Negro*, p. 247.
71. Monica Schuler (2000). "Liberated Central Africans in Nineteenth-Century Guyana" Harriet Tubman Seminar, York University, Canada. January 24, 2000.
72. Schuler. Ibid., note xxiii.
73. Interview with Mr. O. Bacchus (Tobago Krusoe). London. 19th November, 2007.
74. Faulkner. *A Concise Dictionary*, pp. 4–5; Gardner. *Egyptian Grammar*, p. 550; Allen. *Middle Egyptian*, p. 453.
75. Werner Forman and Stephen Quirke (1996). *Hieroglyphs and the Afterlife in Ancient Egypt*. (British Museum Press, London), pp. 7, 24 and 182.
76. Edward B. Bynum (1999). *The African Unconscious: Roots of Ancient Mysticism and Modern Psychology*. (Teachers College Press, Columbia University, New York and London), pp. 5 and 13, *passim*.
77. R. O. Faulkner (Trans., ed. Carol Andrews). *The Ancient Egyptian Book of the Dead*. (British Museum Press, London), p. 33. For a fuller version of this rubric see Faulkner (trans.). *The Egyptian Book of the Dead: The Book of Going Forth by Day*, p. 32.
78. Telephone interview with Dr. Hassimi Maiga, Askia Mohammed Centre. Atlanta, Georgia, USA. 1 May, 2006.
79. Isidore Okpewho (1992). *African Oral Literature: Backgrounds, Character, and Continuity* (Indiana University Press, Bloomington and Indianapolis), p. 262.
80. Vega. *The Altar of My Soul*, pp. 90, 138, 192, 236 and 242–243.
81. Judith Roback (1973). *The White Robed Army*. (Montreal).
82. Modupẹ Oduyọye (1998). "The Medicine-man, the Magician and the Wise man" in Adegbola (ed.). *Traditional Religion in West Africa*, p. 66.
83. Finch. "Nile Genesis: Continuity in Culture from the Great Lakes to the Delta", pp. 35–54.
84. Gardiner. *Egyptian Grammar*, pp. 502, 550 and 625; Erman and Grapow. *Wörterbuch* I, p.26; Faulkner. *Middle Egyptian*, p.7.

Chapter Seven

Some Conclusions

Libation is a drink offering, made nowadays with the right hand, though it has not always been so in the very long history of this ritual. But it is more than a mere drink offering. The little seen symbolises the great unseen. Libation is poured in order to ensure good and proper relations among the forces of the cosmos: the Divine, (composed of the Creator and lesser divinities), the sacred Ancestors and those who are not yet born (i.e. those who exist in the spirit world), those who inhabit the present, and Mother Earth (the mountains, rivers and other aspects of the environment). Libation and other offerings are made to these forces. Libation is a ritual drama that ensures maintenance of the proper personal, social, ecological and spiritual relations within the cosmos. In this way, libation maintains *Maat*: cosmic unity and harmony, truth and order, reciprocity and balance, righteousness and justice; the fully integrated and proper functioning of the universe on all levels, from the smallest and simple organism to the largest and most complex systems. Libation ensures cosmic order by maintaining the optimum relations among the various beings and things in the cosmos, by preventing any of these relations from being impaired, by repairing or restoring good relations when they are impaired, or by nullifying any threat of such impairment.

Libation belongs to a collection of related beliefs, values, attitudes, ritual behaviours and special articles that includes sacrifice, incense, prayers, food, flowers and indeed, as is said in the offering formula of Kemet, "all things good and pure upon which a divinity lives." It is through this offering complex that humanity has, from perhaps before the dawn of history, made manifest in the daily life of society the belief that powerful cosmic forces must be continuously propitiated in order to ensure psychological, social, material and spiritual security and general wellness.

In looking towards the heavens in this way, the practice of libation, and indeed the entire offering complex to which it belongs, raised the bar of human progress. It did so by identifying the highest standards in human relations among themselves and with every other aspect of the cosmos and by incorporating those standards into daily life. In this way, libation and the offering complex also provide evidence that Afrikans possessed an intelligently organized world for uncounted generations before the disruptive arrival of foreigners.

Libation was first recorded and handed down to posterity for certain by Afrikans in Kemet, but its origins clearly predate the foundation of that state. So important is this ritual drama that its archetype is to be found in the domains of the heroic, the legendary, the mythical and the divine. Eventually, it is in this latter category, elevated to a level beyond and above humanity, that the people of Kemet chose to locate the origins of libation. So it was, according to the myth, that the first libation was poured at the behest of *Djhuti* and *Maat* in order to restore and ensure proper cosmic relations and so save humanity from divine wrath that was occasioned by human frailty and the Creator's disappointment and anger, which had been aroused by this human weakness. Hence libation is of such importance that it did not merely receive divine sanction; the very first libation was the work of divinity itself. And, not content with this invention or demonstration of divine approval, and quite possibly perhaps to emphasise this divine agreement also, Afrikan ancestors in the Nile Valley made mandatory the regular performance of this ritual drama, for the pouring of libation is inscribed as a command in the sacred literature of the earliest known tradition of the Afrikan people.

But there is another explanation for the origin of libation and the entire offering complex to which it belongs. More mundane, more gradual, less orderly and less spectacular than the afore-mentioned Myth of Libation, this explanation is based upon careful interrogation of the earliest available records of the Nile Valley. These show that the offering concept and its attendant practices were extant before the time of the society of Kemet. The strongly felt need to propitiate divinity, ancestors and other cosmic forces occasioned the birth and development of a single offering ritual that contained various elements that would later become recognisable as distinctive aspects, some even later as distinct rituals, which evolved from this original rudimentary and integrated form. Thus libation, sacrifice, censing, prayers and first fruits developed as distinct forms of offering. In time, some were enacted separately. Hence two parallel traditions were established and practiced contemporaneously in the state of Kemet. The integrated offering ritual continued to be performed alongside separate renditions of some of its constituent parts, each of which became more and more elaborate and distinctive. Libation, censing, prayers, sacrifice and First Fruits are examples from early Kemet.

The voice offering started life as a vocal accompaniment of each material offering. It grew to become a specific offering in itself. But it was different from all the other offerings, for no material goods were offered in return for the things sought, through this Word, from the divine and/or from the ancestors. This voice offering evolved, through different historical eras, into the prayers and the libation statement that are so common in Afrikan communities today. In addition, praises, praise names, praise poems, praise hymns and praise songs now form a distinctive tradition of the voice in Afrika. These forms of the voice together almost comprise a 'voice complex' in its own right. Like libation, sacrifice and other forms of offering, each of these forms of the voice is rooted in and evolved from the early form of the integrated offering ritual.

The function of libation in ensuing cosmic harmony is of the greatest importance. The cosmic order gives rise to the Afrikan world-view, to a system of morality, of values, principles and ethics. This system orders both the individual and society and proposes to regulate how humans should conduct themselves in every conceivable kind of relationship: with the Creator and with lesser divinities, with the Ancestors, with the unborn, within each individual and with each other, and with the environment in which Afrikans live. It is this world-view that provides context, purpose, relevance, order, meaning, significance and peace to the various elements in the cosmos, including Mother Earth and all her occupants, both human and non-human. It is a world-view that is fundamental to the construction of the person and personality as well as family, community and nation in Afrikan culture. Through myths, legends, folk tales, proverbs, riddles and history—sacred and secular narratives—this world-view provides explanations of the fundamental questions of the cosmos and the human condition. It supplies archetypes, models and examples of Afrikan ethics and morality. Through these it tells what is good and just, what is right and what is wrong; what is acceptable and what is not acceptable.

Libation also functions to give thanks to the Supreme Being, to the Divinities and to the Ancestors for all life and for the things which sustain life, for example for a meal, or a successful hunt, or a catch of fish, or anything else reaped from Mother Nature and/or derived through the processes of human production. Through libation, the petitioner or petitioners may also seek general blessings of the Divine Spirit, the lesser Divinities and the Ancestors; solicit the help and guidance of these forces in work to be undertaken; give thanks to these higher powers for guidance, sustenance or help in achieving some milestone, including the completion of a project; request that evil doers be damned, and/or appeal to the Supreme Being and or other divinities or Ancestors to intervene to restore the cosmic balance or Maat if any of the spiritual relationships that constitute it is ruptured or endangered or is understood to be threatened in any way through some forthcoming action or actions.

It is obvious that today these cosmic relations have been undermined; that the integrity and effectiveness of the institutions that expressed and maintained

Afrikan beliefs, values and principles and ensured these relations in good order, for many millennia before foreign intervention, have been impaired or destroyed. As a direct consequence, either individually or collectively, Afrikans are not fully, securely and properly aligned to their ancestors, to themselves, to their history, their heritage or in their world. Afrikans no longer know and understand who they are. Afrikans have no stable and secure relationship to the cosmos. So they have become disabled, dysfunctional, confused and ineffective in identifying, defending and advancing their own interests. The uncomfortable truth is that Afrikans are mostly disabled and ineffective in whatsoever circumstances they inhabit across the earth today.

Where are the Afrikan national shrines to the Ancestors? Who pours libation at these and other Afrikan sacred sites? Where is the system of explaining and passing on these Rituals of Heritage to the upcoming generations? Who are the guardians of these traditions? There is hardly a place in the Afrikan world where a definite affirmative may be supplied to these important questions about the fundamentals of Afrikan identity.

It is equally obvious that a return to the Afrikan self in this most fundamental way, to this world-view and the morality it instructs, is both necessary and urgent if Afrikans are to survive and contribute their full and fair share to humanity's progress in today's world. To contribute meaningfully to this world, Afrikans face a clear choice: heal themselves through becoming Afrikan again and therefore be the best they can be, or continue on the road to the worst of all possibilities, that of cosmic death.

Libation may therefore provide the opportunity to establish renewal as the context for healing the many grievous wounds of Afrika, particularly but not only through the employment of the languages of the vast majority of the Afrikan people wherever they are, sipping together from a common cup, participating in a common meal, doing libation together. Joint participation in community rituals builds and maintains community unity. Preparation for libation may also encourage purification of body, mind and spirit through ritual cleansing, fasting or other kinds of abstinence which also develop will power, clarity of vision and other kinds of strength.

The purification of physical space is also encouraged by libation. The surroundings in which the libationer prepares, as well as the site of the performance if these are not the same, are cleansed of all negative and discordant energies. An appropriate atmosphere is created. This is an atmosphere that is encouraging and receptive to the spiritual presences to be invoked and stimulating to the tasks at hand. Incense and sweet smelling oils, as well as candles and other appropriate forms of lighting, may be employed to help achieve this goal.

The transmission of libation from the Nile Valley to the rest of Afrika and to Afrikan families and communities overseas, especially in the Americas, the Caribbean and Europe, illustrates the connections among the Afrikan people and demonstrates the oneness of their story. The time/space dimensions of this distribution define the Afrikan world and help us to imagine the parameters, and often the content, of the Afrikan Studies curriculum, its history, sociology, literature, science, philosophy and other areas of organisation of learning experiences of the relevant values, knowledge and skills that together ensure the best education and socialization of every Afrikan wherever s/he may be. In illustrating these connections among Afrikan people, the ritual of libation, and the cultural complex to which it belongs, provides answers to some fundamental questions and issues about the history, the culture and the identity of Afrika and Afrikans: how this ritual and this complex come to be distributed all over the Afrikan world, so that they virtually define that world, and the meaning and significance of this common possession by Afrikans. The story of libation shows that it is no longer possible to present the history, the culture or the identity of Afrikans anywhere as though they are separate from the history, culture and identity of Afrikans everywhere.

The history of the ritual of libation is in many ways an exact parallel of and a metaphor for the greater Afrikan story of which it is but one part. Libation has been in the possession of Afrikan people from the earliest times to this time. It too has been distorted, has suffered dismemberment, and lies half-buried and unremembered by some and not practised by others who know. It demonstrates, demands and ensures awareness of the most important forces in the cosmos and the most important forms of unity. It emphasises love, respect, appreciation and a connectedness across space and time among ancestors, elders and the living generations, as well as those yet to come. Libation announces a covenant of the generations that Ayi Kwei Armah calls a vast community of affection which is the birthright of all Afrikans. It is this truly Pan-Afrikan community, at once all-inclusive of all Afrikans and therefore everlasting, which is a basic objective of the Afrikan struggle. Libation is an occasion for the most important aspect of Afrikan Reparations, that of repairing themselves through the recovery, restoration, and modernization wherever necessary, of their own traditions. This is the securest road to Pan-Afrikan unity.

Today and forevermore, wherever libation is poured, in gatherings all across the Afrikan world, Afrikan people are beginning to reclaim historic space and their own rituals, to link previously isolated and not fully understood facts and bridge chasms long gouged out of their collective story. Afrikans are beginning to make the fullest sense of their disconnected wanderings among the scattered, half-buried, half remembered and unremembered treasures of their common cultural and historical inheritance, to reclaim their collective mind; to remember their own story and therefore to know and repossess their own selves. The work of restoration and renewal links the generations of Afrika across times and time, and place and places, so that today Imhotep is summoned from five millennia ago in the Nile Valley, Nehanda from the First Chimurenga in Zimbabwe and again from the same space one hundred years later in the Second Chimurenga. Boukman, Dessalines, Cecile Fatima, Harriet Tubman, Malcolm X and Martin King, Kwame Nkrumah and Cheikh Anta Diop, Walter Rodney, Maurice Bishop, the roll call of Afrikan heroes and sheroes from across the Afrikan world ensure that the Afrikan struggles and the Afrikan story become the common possession of Afrikans around the world. The spirit, the vision, the energy and the inspiration of all Afrikan ancestors become their spirit, their vision, their energy and their inspiration also.

The significance of libation transcends the ritual itself. The distribution of this ritual throughout the Afrikan world illustrates that journey of journeys, the great migrations of Afrikan people from the birthplace of themselves and so of humanity in Afrika. Some first went mainly northwards down the Valley of the Nile to invent civilization in Nubia, Kush and Kemet and so transform themselves and humanity. Humanity spread out from the Nile Valley and doubtless other parts of Afrika in periodic migrations to rejoin, commingle, revitalize and be revitalized by previous streams of migrants to eventually populate and possess the entire continent, later the world, and propagate the ideas and always the practice of civilization. It is they who thus gave to humanity its humanity.

But it was not people alone who migrated north along the Nile Valley and over desert lands those uncounted millennia ago, or who migrated out of the valley and other places to populate Afrika much later. Nor was it culture alone that arrived, bereft of its human agents, in all those places that were and have since become the Afrikan world. The truth is that both people and culture have made this immensely long journey, for when a people migrate, or are made to migrate, they do not leave their culture behind. That is not possible, for culture is inseparable from its human inventors and agents. A culture is a defining characteristic of a people.

Undoubtedly ancient, even in those ancient times about which we are now beginning to know more, the ritual of libation has never been antiquated, nor even antique, for it has constantly been updated and modernized; modified and renewed by the challenges of space and time. Libation may therefore be varied in form according to time, place and occasion. But its basic format remains easily and clearly identifiable and its purpose has remained the same throughout the ages over which this ritual has evolved and the vast number of spaces in which it lives in the lives of the Afrikan people today. The different ways of pouring libation illustrate the fact that there are different ways of being Afrikan, that there is no one way of living that ancient heritage and that no one way may be either less authentic, or more so, than the others. This ritual has remained a constant and fully functional aspect of Afrikan life. It is a marker of Afrikan identity.

Both libation and the world-view that instructs it are to be found all over the Afrikan world. Libation may therefore point towards the possibility of real and lasting unity based upon awareness and understanding of cultural continuities and similarities, with all their diversity, as a secure basis of Pan Afrikanism, Afrikan repair and Afrikan redemption.

Chapter Eight

Some Questions and Answers

9.1: Who Can Pour Libation?

Anyone who is willing to do so. On formal occasions, this person may be expected to have the necessary spiritual and social status among the gathering at the ritual, to be ritually clean and to have the knowledge and understanding of the Ritual of Libation and its purpose. However, the Libationer may be anyone appointed by a gathering and may be helped by special assistants or by anyone in the gathering, whether or not they are specially trained to do so.

This practice of anyone pouring libation is alive throughout the modern Afrikan world. Many Afrikans pour their own private libations at the beginning of each day in order to give acknowledgement and thanks to the Supreme One or to particular lesser divinities, and to one's ancestors. Other important objectives of these private libations are to identify the challenges of a particular day or period, to meditate upon them, and to imagine their solutions. This planning and psychological preparation puts the pourer into the best frame of mind and therefore sets the correct tone for a successful day. Libation may also be poured, and is indeed often poured, on several other occasions during the day: at the beginning of each meal, at the opening of a bottle of spirits/alcohol, at the end of each day and indeed at any moment one feels the urge to do so.

In addition to the above there are very grand occasions when a special functionary, normally a person in charge of the spiritual welfare of the community, but in any event a spiritual leader, is expected to either perform the Libation Ritual or take the lead in its performance. In the latter instance the leading functionary in the ritual may be assisted by others. On family occasions this person may well be the eldest male in the family or someone else designated to play this role, by tradition and/or by popular consent of a particular gathering.

9.2: When should Libation be poured?

At meal times, at the formal opening of any occasion or ceremony, and generally at any time someone feels the urge to do so.

Any time is the best time for pouring libation. However, it is usual to pour libation on certain occasions: at the beginning and end of the day, at the beginning of each meal, at the beginning of any ceremony or event to mark a special personal or community occasion, at the beginning of a ceremony to mark some important venture or achievement, like the construction of a building, at the completion of that or any other task, at the beginning of festivals of sowing and at the end of reaping, at a saraka or other ceremony to honour the ancestors, and so on.

Libation should be poured anytime someone feels the need to do so and/or at the beginning of any formal occasion in the family, the clan, the community or the nation.

9.3: Where is the best location to pour Libation?

Anywhere. But especially at any central place within a formal gathering, in the entrances to cities, towns, villages, dwelling places, yards, farms, or at any other strategic points in our environment. By doing the correct incantation, anywhere may be transformed into a sacred space.

In order to liberate ourselves from the worst kind of enslavement and the worst kind of sickness, Afrikans must insist on doing our own rituals and living our own culture every minute of our existence, for this is the only authentic way of being, and therefore of maintaining spiritual, cultural, economic, social and psychological health. For those Afrikans who exist daily in the harsh realities of Babylon, the spiritual transformation of social spaces in the belly of the beast is even more critical to dignified and fruitful existence. In any space such transformation releases much positive energy within ourselves, our families, our clans and within our communities. This kind of transformation makes a valid contribution to any space Afrikans inhabit. Such transformations may be induced by a variety of visual and audio media, for example murals and Kwanzaa decorations. Decorating our built environment with our own aesthetics is one of the best ways of promoting the social, psychological and spiritual health of the community and liberating ourselves from the clutches of foreign spiritual domination. This latter is undoubtedly the worst affliction that can befall anyone, for a spiritually enslaved soul is condemned to a life of servility, a severely limited existence and certain cosmic death.

9.4: Why is Libation poured?

To maintain *Maat*: the spiritual, psychological, social and ecological order inherent in the Afrikan world view. In practice this means to give acknowledgement and thanks to the Supreme Spirit, to the lesser divinities and to our sacred ancestors. Hence we must connect with these forces and with kindred souls who may not be physically present in our midst. The proper practice of libation also compels us to respect and care for our physical environment.

We acknowledge these existences, for it is by the divine will of the Supreme One and the other divinities that we exist. And it is upon the platform established by the creativity, suffering and struggle of our ancestors that we stand today, as it is upon whatsoever we inherit, construct and pass on that our children and their children after them will stand in turn during their own moment in the glare of history, which is bound to continue unfolding in the environment we inhabit and pass on to them.

In pouring libation, Afrikans acknowledge and maintain connections across generations and form a vast community of affection among all Afrikans for all time: Afrikans past, Afrikans present and Afrikans who are still to be born. Libation is a transgenerational instrument through which these cosmic relations are maintained in an optimum state. Every libation poured is a step closer to the full restoration and continuation of our culture and therefore of ourselves, and a contribution to our own eternity.

9.5: Which liquids can be used in Libation?

Water, any liquor, including rum, gin, beer and wine; or with milk, honey, tea or coffee. Indeed, with any drinkable liquid. Long ago, in Kemet, the liquid was presented with both hands. In more recent historical times it has become customary to pour the liquid with the right hand. Some Afrikans in the west insist on a calabash as the container into which the liquid is poured.

9.6: In which language must Libation be conducted?

Any Afrikan language, including the languages of the communities abroad, like Kwéyòl (Creole), Ebonics, Srantongo, Papiamento, and so on. This is a certain way of ensuring that our Ancestors hear us, and that we value and respect ourselves and our traditions in all their diversity. The use of the 𓏞𓏛𓊪, the *Medew Netjer*, the first writing in the world that was invented by some of our ancestors in Ancient Egypt, throughout this text is one way of encouraging, even challenging Afrikans to reconnect with their roots. Ras Kwende tells us the truth at the heart of this matter: "It is psychologically better for one's language to be compatible with one's ideology and world-view."[1] Any discordance between a people's language and their ideology or world-view is a sign of contradictions and confusion within themselves. Invariably this points to some form of oppression which is normally the source of a widespread affliction of this nature.

However, it is quite all right for the libationer who does not know an Afrikan language to conduct the ritual in any language which is understood by the gathering.

9.7: What preparation is needed for Libation?

Normally not much, for when the occasion is small and private, there is no need for much preparation. But on very grand and public occasions adequate preparation of both the person(s) pouring and the articles needed for the ritual become more important, even essential.

Preparation of the libationer may mean ensuring that the person is of the correct spiritual disposition, is ritually clean, and is in the correct state of mind, including being focused upon the task(s) at hand. Such preparation may take days to complete. But they are based upon millennia of tradition and often, in addition, upon a lifetime of conviction.

One demonstration of spiritual purity is the "Cleansing of the Auras" of the libationer(s) practised by Sister AnkhAmunet in London. In this rite, the auras of the person(s) about to lead a libation ritual are ritually cleansed immediately before beginning the actual ritual.

The libationer has the spiritual direction of the entire gathering and indeed the entire community in her/his hands. This is so not only because libation sets the appropriate tone to the occasion in which the ritual is enacted, but also because libation connects all those who are there with those who are not there, Past, Present and Future. Those who are not there may include both our departed ancestors and living generations who may not be physically present and may be even unaware of the particular enactment of the ritual. Those who are unborn, the Future, may also be recognised and saluted. In the Afrikan worldview, Time is a seamless Unity of Past, Present and Future in which the Present is the future of the Past, just as it is the past of the Future. Our communities are composed of the divinities and those who have gone before (the Past; the ancestors), those who are here now, (the Present), and those who are yet to come (the Future). Afrikans who follow our sacred traditions recognise them all. There is no rigid compartmentalisation of reality and the consequent separation and exclusion of the differing aspects of our existence.

Spiritual and physical preparations are most important and necessary. Fasting, ritual purification and concentrating upon the task at hand are essential aspects of the preparation of the libationer.

Besides the spiritual preparation, it is necessary to have certain material objects. It is also important to possess an understanding of the ancestral traditions (the Classical Afrikan Traditions). A commitment to being and remaining Afrikan is also essential. So too, is a specific occasion such as a feast or a community meeting. But this specific occasion may be just the desire to recognise and thank the Supreme Spirit, or any particular divinity and our ancestors who brought us here. It may also be the desire to recognise ourselves as human beings who are knowledgeable and secure in our culture and identity.

The material objects necessary include water or clear liquor, potted plants or a large receptacle and a small receptacle, preferably a calabash, which is a cultural item of preference used in rituals all across the Afrikan world.

Sometimes water or any liquor will serve the purpose, but on important occasions water or clear liquor is used. The liquid of libation is poured directly into Mother Earth whenever possible. Sometimes this takes the form of pouring into a sacred stream, river, lake, the ocean, or over a shrine, into a sacred recess or some such place. However, if the ceremony is conducted inside a building or in any place out of direct contact with Mother Earth, the liquid may be poured into potted plants or into a container made available especially for this purpose. The pouring may be done with any smaller container, but a calabash is widely preferred.

9.8: Why is it necessary to invoke the Supreme Being, other Divinities, the Ancestors, the Unborn, others not physically present and aspects of the physical environment?

For our own spiritual awareness, our psychological well being, our understanding of our place in the universal order of things and our consequent compulsion—and hopefully desire—to maintain the correct relations among the beings and things in the universe, as well as for the success in our mundane daily lives that we guarantee by keeping these rules always. Cosmic order and social order, personal and group stability and harmony and our ability to always get the best out of ourselves, both as individuals and as groups, all depend upon our orderly, balanced and secure connection to and peace with these most important forces in our lives. It is not possible to live successfully, however we define success, without the example and authority of tradition. All of us usually have the urge to contact our Creator, the other divinities, our ancestors and people who may not be sharing our physical space at a given time. If we know how to do so we can also help to unite our communities, both their seen and unseen aspects, and so unite our people, protect our physical environment and assure ourselves both cosmic life and continuity and the secure environment to guarantee this survival of the Afrikan world. Our future depends upon our will and our capacity to do so. The best guarantee of success in this cosmic venture is our practice of this and other traditions of our people.

NOTE

1. Ras Kwende Ambessa-Ebanks. *Rastafari Livity*, p. 5.

BIBLIOGRAPHY

INTERVIEWS
Interviews conducted by Dr. Kimani Nehusi
Interview with Dr. Hassimi Maiga. Askia Mohammed Centre, Atlanta, Georgia. 1 May, 2006. Telephone.
Interview with Ms. Patsy Russell. 54 years. Toronto, Canada. 6 May, 2006. Telephone.
Interview with Mrs. Vera Venture. 82 years. New York, USA. 7th October, 2006. Telephone.
Interview with Ms. Lorine James. 44 years. New York. 19 November, 2006. Telephone.
Interview with Ms. Voi James, 68 years. Queenstown Village, Essequibo Coast, Guyana. 20 November, 2006. Telephone.
Interview with Ms. Evelyn James, 40 years. New York. 20 November, 2006. Telephone.
Interview with Ms. Eunice Walcott. 72 years. Queenstown Village, Essequibo Coast, Guyana. 22 November, 2006. Telephone.
Interview with Mr. Othneil Bacchus (Tobago Krusoe). London. 19 November, 2007.
Interviews conducted by Ezra Blondel
Interview with Ms. Sylvia Thomas. 76 years. Colihaut, Dominica. 10th October, 2006.
Interview with Mr. Sion Adams. 100 years. Colihaut, Dominica. 9th October, 2006.
Interview with Mr. Albert Severin. 87 years. Colihaut, Dominica. 9th October, 2006.
Interview with Mr. Radcliffe St. Louis. 91 years. Colihaut, Dominica. 9th October, 2006.

Private Communication
Private communication with Dr. Amon Saba Saakana. London. 29th June, 2006.
Private communication with Prof. Herbert Ekwe-Ekwe. Reading. 4th October, 2006.
Private communication with Mr. Shurwin Semple, 1st April, 2007.

Compact Disks, DVDs, Videos, etc.

Caliste, Leroy (The Mighty Stalin, later Black Stalin) (1979) "Play One" *To The Caribbean Man*. LP. Wizards MCR-147, Makossa M2342.
—— (1979) "Play One" *Play One/Caribbean Unity*. Wizards MCR-147.
—— (1991). "Play One". *Roots, Rock, Soca*. Rounder C-5038.
Francisco, Slinger (The Mighty Sparrow). (2000, re-issue). 'Play One for Melo' Track 6 in *Down Memory Lane*. Millennium Series.
Nas. "Just a Moment" *Street's Disciple*. anysonglyrics@hotmail.com [Accessed 01.05.08].
Shakur, 2Pac. "Pour Out A Little Liquor". youtube.com [Accessed 10.05.08].
Sweet Honey in the Rock. (1997). "Breaths". *Selections 1976–1988* Cambridge, Mass.: Flying Fish/Rounder Records Corp.

Articles, Emails, Etc.

Achebe, Chinua (1975, 1998). " 'Chi' in Igbo Cosmology" in E. C. Eze (ed.) *African Philosophy: An Anthology* Blackwell Publishers.
Adams, Frank Kwesi (July, 2002). "Odwira and the Gospel: An Exploratory Study of Asante Odwira Festival and Its Significance to Christianity in Ghana." Thesis submitted for Doctor of Philosophy, University of Wales.
Adams III, Hunter A (1994). "Ma'at: Returning to Virtue—Returning to Self" The Author.
Allen, James P. (2005). "Introduction" Raymond O. Faulkner (trans.) *Ancient Egyptian Book of the Dead* New York, Barnes and Noble.
Armah, Ayi Kwei (April, 2006). "Who were the Ancient Egyptians?" *New African*, No. 450.
—— (2006). "The Identity of the Creators of Ancient Egypt". Ibid.
Bâ, Amadou Hampaté (1972, Trans. Susan B. Hunt). "Remarks on Culture: Wisdom and the linguistic question in Black Africa" in Aspects of African Civilization (Person, Culture, Religion). First published (1972) as *Aspects de la civilisation Africaine: personne, culture, religion* (Présence africaine, Paris). www.ese.upenn.edu [Accessed 12 June, 2008].
Bell, Lanny (1996). "Ancestor worship and Divine kingship in the Ancient Nile Valley" in Theodore Celenko (ed.) *Egypt in Africa* Indianapolis: Indianapolis Museum of Art and Indiana University Press.
Berlev, O. (1997). "Bureaucrats" in S. Donadoni (ed.). *The Egyptians* Chicago and London: The University of Chicago Press.
Blackman, Alward M. (1912). "The Significance of Incense and Libations in Funerary and Temple Ritual" *Zeitschrift Für Agyptische Sprache und Altertmuskunde (ZÄS)* Leipzig, Berlin. Vol. 50.
—— (1916). "Libations to the Dead in Modern Nubia and Ancient Egypt" *Journal of Near Eastern Studies*. Vol. III.
Brathwaite, Edward Kamau (1967, 1968, 1969, 1973). "Libation" in *The Arrivants* Oxford University Press.
Buuba, Boubacar Diop (2006). "Les migrations Sereer: jalons de la saga arficaine et sénégalaise" Ankh: Revue D'Égyptologie et des Civilisations Africaines. Nos. 14/15, 2005–2006.
Caminos, Ricardo A. (1997). "Peasants" in S. Donadoni (ed.) *The Egyptians* Chicago and London: The University of Chicago Press Cruickshank, James Graham (1917, 1999). "Among the Aku (Yoruba) in Canal No.1., West Bank, Demerara River." David Granger (ed.) *Scenes From the History of the Africans in Guyana* Georgetown: free press.
—— (1917, 1999). "African Immigrants after Freedom" Ibid.
Delia, Diana (1992). "The Refreshing Water of Osiris" *JARCE* Vol. xxix
Fairservis Jr., W. A. (1991). "A Revised View of the Narmr Palette" *JARCE* Vol. xxviii

Finch, Charles (1988). "Imhotep the Physician: Archetype of the Great Man" in Ivan Van Sertima (ed.) *Great Black Leaders: Ancient and Modern* New Brunswick, USA: Journal of African Civilizations Ltd.
—— (1994). "Nile Genesis: Continuity of Culture From the Great Lakes to the Delta" In Ivan Van Sertima (ed.) *Egypt Child of Africa* New Brunswick and London: Transaction Publishers
French, Howard (1996). "Voodoo Devotes Mark Tragic Diaspora" *The Guardian* U (K). Tuesday, 19 March.
Freud, Sigmund (1964, 1985). Trans. A. Richards. "Moses and Monotheism" in *The Origins of Religion* London: Penguin
Gardiner, Alan (1902–03). "Imhotep and the scribe's libation" *ZÄS* No. 40.
—— (1938). "The Mansion of Life and the Master of the King's Largess" *Egyptian Archaeology* No. 24.
Guarnori, Sandra and Jean-Luc Chappaz (1983). "Deux tables d'offrandes et un basin à libations du Musée d'Art et d'Historie à Genève. " Chronique d'Égypte LVIII, Nos. 115–115.
'Haraeh tomb 290, religious texts'. www.diitalegypt.ucl.ac.uk [Accessed on 20/01/08].
Hertaus, Jeff. "Nabta Playa." http://www.mnsu.edu/emuseum/archaeology/sites/africa/nabtaplaya.html. [Accessed on 6th April, 2007].
Hughes, Langston (1997). "The Negro Speaks of Rivers" in H. L. Gates Jr. and N. Y. Mc Kay (eds.) *The Norton Anthology of African American Literature* New York and London: W. W. Norton and Co. Hutton, Clinton (2007). "The Creative Ethos of the African Diaspora: Performance Aesthetics and the Fight or Freedom and Identity" *Caribbean Quarterly*. Vol. 53, Nos. 1&2, March–June, 2007.
Jossiah, Barbara P. (1997). "After Emancipation: Aspects of Village Life in Guyana, 1869–1911" *The Journal of Negro History* Vol. LXXXII, No. 1. Winter. Karenga, Maulana (1991). "Towards a Sociology of Maatian Ethics: Literature and Context" in Ivan Van Sertima (ed.) *Egypt Revisited* Trenton, NJ: Transaction Publishers.
Kusimba, Chapurukha M (1996). "Ancestor Worship and Divine Kingship in Sub-Saharan Africa" in T. Celenko (ed.) *Egypt in Africa*: Indianapolis Museum of Art and Indiana University Press.
Lam, Aboubacry Moussa (1997). "Égypte ancienne et Afrique Noire: autour de l'eau" ☥ *Ankh: Revue d'égyptologie et des civilisations Africaines* Nos. 6/7
—— (2004). "L'origine des Peul: les principales thèses confrontées aux traditions africaines et à l'égyptologie" *Ankh: Revue D'Égyptologie et des Civilisations Africaines*. Nos. 14/15, nos. 12/13, 2003–2004.
—— (2006a). "Égypte ancienne et Afrique noire: quelques nouveaux faits qui éclairent leurs relations" *Ankh: Revue D'Égyptologie et des Civilisations Africaines*. Nos. 14/15, 2005–2006.
—— (2006b). La Vallée du Nil: berceau de l'unité culturelle de l'Afrique noir. Kephera, Paris and Presses Universitaries de Dakar
Madiana (1934, 2002). ''The Beguine of the French Antilles '' in Nancy Cunard ed.) *Negro*. New York : Continuum
Mayers-Johnson, Sheila (2004). "The Word as a Conduit for African Consciousness" *JCTAW* Vol. I, No. 2. Winter/Spring.
Mestel, Rosie (2002). "The Wonders of Saliva" *Los Angeles Times*, 21 January.
Mostafa, Maha F. (1993). "Eine Darstellung des Thot als Wasserspender" *SAK*. 20.
Mulira, Jessie G. (1990). "The Case of Voodoo in New Orleans" in Joseph E. Holloway (ed.) *Africanisms in American Culture* Bloomington and Indianapolis: Indiana University Press.

National Black United Front (NBUF). Houston Chapter. (2002). "Fifth Annual Sankofa Caravan to the Ancestors" Press Release of Wedneaday, 2 October.

Nehusi, Kimani (2000). "The Origins of Carnival: Notes from a Preliminary Investigation." In Ian Smart and Kimani Nehusi (eds.) *Ah Come Back Home: Perspectives on the Trinidad and Tobago Carnival.* Washington DC and Port of Spain: Original World Press.

—— (2001). "From 𓏞𓂋 *Medew Netjer* to Ebonics" in Clinton Crawford. (ed.) *Ebonics and Language Education of African Ancestry Students* New York and London: Sankofa World Publishers.

—— (2002)."Mental Enslavement" in David Granger (ed.), *Emancipation* Vol. 2. No. 10. Georgetown, Guyana.

—— (2003). "St. Bartholomew's Church: The Story of a national monument" in David Granger (ed.). *Emancipation.* Vol. 2, No. 11. Georgetown, Guyana.

—— (2003) "Language in the Construction of Afrikan Unity: Past, Present and Policy" in Mammo Muchie (ed.). *The Making of the Africa-Nation: Pan-Africanism and the African Renaissance* London: Adonis & Abbey Publishers, Ltd.

—— (2011) "Introduction: The Strategic Intellectual Importance of Kemet" in Karen Exell (ed.) Egypt in its African Context: Proceedings of the conference held at The Manchester Museum, University of Manchester, 2–4 October 2009. Oxford: Archaeopress.

The NSAA Family (27 April, 2006). "Special African Ceremony to honor Dr. John Henrik Clarke and other African Warrior Ancestors." Email.

Obenga, Théophile (1995). "La parenté égyptienne: considerations sociologiques" ⚨ *Ankh: Reveu D'Égyptologie et des civilisations* Nos. 4/5

—— (1996). "Genetic Linguistic Connections of Ancient Egypt and Rest of Africa" in M. K. Asante and Abu S. Abarry (eds.) *African Intellectual Heritage: A Book of Sources* Philadelphia: Temple University Press.

—— (1989). "African Philosophy of the Pharaonic Period (2780–330 B. C.)" in I. Van Sertima (ed.) *Egypt Revisited* New Brunswick and London: Transaction Publishers.

Obenga, Théophile (2004a). "Comparaisons morphologiques entre l'Égyptien ancient et le Dagara" *Ankh: Revue D'Égyptologie et des Civilisations Africaines.* Nos. 14/15, 2003–2004.

Oduyoye, Modupe (1988). "The Spirits that Rule the World: African Religions & Judaism" in Amon Saba Saakana (ed.). *Afrikan Origins of the Major World Religions* London: Karnak House.

Omidire, Félix Ayoh (2008). "The Yoruba aṣẹ as a social capital among Afro-diasporic peoples in Latin America" in Tunde Babawale and Akin Alao (eds.) *Global African Spirituality, Social Capital and Self-reliance in Africa* Lagos, Benin, etc.: Malthouse Press Ltd.

Omoigui, Nowa (10th April, 2003). "Haiti Officially Sanctions Voodoo." Email.

Pemigotti, Sergio (1997). "Priests" in S. Danodini (ed.). *The Egyptians.* Chicago and London: The University of Chicago Press.

Ragoonath, Reshma (22nd July, 2003). "Rain Fails to Dampen Kwanzaa Festival" *The Guardian.* Port of Spain, Trinidad and Tobago

Richards, Cynthia B. (2003). "Reflections on African Spiritualist Traditions in Jamaica" *JCTAW* Vol.1 No.1. Spring, 2003.

Rodney, Walter (1967) "West Africa and the Atlantic slave trade" *Historical Association of Tanzania. Occasional Paper No. 2.* Dar-Es-Salaam: East African Publishing House.

—— (1975) "Africa in Europe and the Americas " in Richard Gray (ed.) *The Cambridge History of Africa* Vol. 4. London, New York and Melbourne: Cambridge University Press.

—— (1968) "African History in the Service of the Black Liberation" Lecture presented at the Congress of Black Writers, Montreal, Canada.

Sarr, Mouhamadou Nissire (2006). "Cours d'eau et croyances en Égypte Pharaonique et en Afrique noire modern" *Ankh: Revue D'Égyptologie et des Civilisations Africaines.* Nos. 14/15, 2005—2006.
Seattle, Chief. Native American Leader (1786–1866). See Duane Bristow. "Chief Seattle's Thoughts". http://www.kyphilom.com/www/seattle.html.[Accessed on 23rd April, 2007].
Schäfer, Heinrich (1898). ''Eine altägyptische Schreibersitte" ZÄS 36.
Schuler, Monica (January 24th, 2000). ''Liberated Africans in Nineteenth-Century
Guyana" Paper presented at the Harriet Tubman Seminar, York University.
T'Shaka, Oba (1995). *Return to the African Mother Principle of Male and Female Equality.* Vol. I. Oakland, California: Pan Afrikan Publishers and Distributors.
Tempels, Placide (1959, 1998). "Bantu Ontology" in E. C. Eze (ed.) *African Philosophy: An Anthology* Malden, MA: Blackwell Publishing Ltd.
Thomas, Sayyadina (23rd October, 2003). "Maafa is Kiswahili for Great Calamity" Email.
Williams, Bruce (1985). "The Lost Pharaohs of Nubia" I. Van Sertima (ed.) *Nile Valley Civilizations.* New Brunswick, USA: Journal of African Civilizations, Ltd.
—— (1996). "The Qustul Incense Burner and the Case for a Nubian Origin of Ancient Egyptian Kingship" in T. Celenko (ed.) *Egypt in Africa* Indianapolis Museum of Art and Indiana University Press.
Yellin, Janice W. (1988). "Abaton-style milk libation at Meroe". N. B. Millet and A. L. Kelly (eds.) *Meroitica Meroitic Studies. Proceedings of the Third International Meroetic Conference,* Toronto, 1977. Akademie-Verlag, Berlin.
Achebe, Chinua (1958, 1987). *Things Fall Apart* Heinemann
—— (1975). *Morning Yet on Creation Day* Heinemann
Afua, Queen (2000). Sacred Woman: A Guide to Healing the Feminine Body, Mind and Spirit_ New York: One World/Ballantyne
Agyei, Kwame and Akoto, Akua Nson (1999). *The Sankofa Movement: ReAfrikanization and the Reality of War* Washington, D.C.: Ɔyoko InfoCom Inc.
Akoto, Kwame Agyei (1992). *Nationbuilding: Theory & Practice in Afrikan Centered Education* Washington, D.C.: Pan Afrikan World Institute.
Allen, James P. (2000). Middle Egyptian: An Introduction to the Language and of Hieroglyphs London and New York: Cambridge University Press. (1988). Genesis in Egypt: The Philosophy of Ancient Egyptian Creation Accounts. New Haven, Connecticut: Yale Egyptological Studies 2. Yale University.
Allen, T. G. (ed. & trans. 1974). The Book of the Dead or Going Forth by Day: Ideas of the Ancient Egyptians Concerning the Hereafter as Expressed in their own terms. Studies in Ancient Oriental Civilization 37. Chicago: The University of Chicago Press.
Allsopp, Richard (ed., 2003). *Dictionary of Caribbean English Usage* Kingston, Jamaica: The University of the West Indies Press
Amadi, Elechi (1975). *The Great Ponds* London: Heinemann.
Anbessa-Ebanks, Kwende (2004). *Rastafari Livity: A Basic Information Text* London: Kwemara Publications.
Anderson, David (2005). Histories of the Hanged: Britain's Dirty War in Kenya and End of Empire. London: Weidenfeld and Nicolson.
Ani, Marimba (1980, 1997). Let The Circle be Unbroken: The Implications of African Spirituality in the Diaspora New York: Publications.
Armah, Ayi Kwei (1974). *Fragments* London: Heinemann.

—— (1979). *The Healers* London: Heinemann.
—— (2006). The Eloquence of the Scribes: A Memoir on the Sources and Resources of African Literature Popenguine, Senegal: Per Ankh.
Asante, Molefe K and Abu S. Abarry (1996, eds.). *African Intellectual Heritage: A Book of Sources*. Philadelphia: Temple University Press.
Asante, Molefe K and Mazama, A. (2009, eds.). *Encyclopedia of African Religion* Los Angeles, London, etc. : SAGE Publications, Inc.
Assmann, Jan (1997). *Moses the Egyptian: The Memory of Egypt in Western Monotheism*. Cambridge, Mass. and London: Harvard University Press.
—— (2001, trans. D. Lorton 2005). *Death and Salvation in Ancient Egypt* and London: Cornell University Press.
Awolalu, J. Omosade and Dopamu, P. Adelumo (1979). *West African Traditional Religion* Ibadan: Onibonoje Press and Book Industries (Nig.) Limited.
Ayisi, Eric O. (1972, 1992). *An Introduction to the Study of African Culture* Nairobi: East African Educational Publishers Ltd.
Babalawo, Minister Ra Ifagbemi (1999). *Ancestors: Hidden Hands, Healing Spirits. For your Use and Empowerment* Brooklyn, New York: Athelia Henrietta Press, Inc.
Bierbrier, Morris (1982). *The Tomb-Builders of the Pharaohs*. American University in Cairo Press.
Bynum, Edward Bruce (1999). *The African Unconscious: Roots of Ancient Mysticism and Modern Psychology*. New York and London: Teachers College Press, Columbia University.
De Beler, Aude Gros (1999, 2002). *Egyptian Mythology*. New York: Todtri Book Publishers.
Bettelheim, Judith (2001, ed.). *Cuban Festivals: A Century of Afro-Cuban Culture*. Kingston, Jamaica and Princetown, NJ: Ian Randle Publishers and Markus Wiener Publishers.
Du Bois, W. E. B. (1915). *The Negro*. New York: Henry Holt and Co.
—— (1965). The World and Africa: An enquiry into the part which Africa has played in world history. New York: International Publishers.
Brunson, James E. (1991). Before the Unification: Predynastic Egypt. An African- centric View. DeKalb, Illinois. The Author.
Budge, E. A. Wallis. (Translation and transliteration. 1895, 1967). *The Egyptian Book of the Dead.* (The Papyrus of Ani). New York: Dover Publications, Inc.
—— (1911, 1973). *Osiris and The Egyptian Resurrection* Vol. I. New York: Dover Publications, Inc.
—— (1927,1978). *Herb-Doctors and Physicians in the Ancient World: The Divine Origin of the Craft of the Herbalist* Chicago: Ares Publishers, Inc.
—— (1934, 1988). *From Fetish to God in Ancient Egypt* New York: Dover Publications, Inc.
Bynum, Edward B. (1999). *The African Unconscious: Roots of Ancient Mysticism Modern Psychology* . New York: Teachers College Press, Columbia University
Cabral, Amilcar. (1980). *Unity and Struggle: Speeches and Writings*. London: Educational Books Ltd.
Caminos, R. A. (Trans., 1977). *A Tale of Woe: Papyrus Pushkin 127* Oxford: Griffith Institute, Ashmolean Museum.
Campbell, Mavis C (1980). The Maroons of Jamaica 1655—1796: A History of Resistance, Collaboration and Betrayal Trenton, NJ: World Press.
Canizares, Raul (1993). *Walking With the Night: The Afro-Cuban World of Santeria* Rochester, Vermont: Destiny Books
Capel, Anne K and Markoe, Glenn E. (eds., 1996). *Mistress of the House, Mistress of Heaven: Women in Ancient Egypt* New York: Hudson Hill Press, Inc.
Carew, Jan (1958, 2009). *Black Midas* Leeds: Peepal Tree Press.
Carruthers, Jacob. (1995). *Mdw NTr: Divine Speech*. London: Karnak House.

—— (1985).*The Irritated Genie: An Essay on the Haitian Revolution* Chicago: The Kemetic Institute.
—— (1984). *Essays in Ancient Egyptian Studies*. Los Angeles: University of Sankore Press
Carter, Martin (1977). *Poems of Succession* London: New Beacon Books
Cassidy, Frederic G. (1982) Jamaica Talk: Three Hundred Years of the English *Language in Jamaica*. Macmillan Caribbean and Sangsters Bookstores Ltd.
Chinweizu (1975, 1978, 1987). The West and the Rest of Us: White Predators, Black slavers and the African elite. Lagos: Pero Press
Chua, Amy (2004). *World on Fire*. New York: Anchor Books.
Clarke, Austin. (2003). *The Polished Hoe*. Kingston, Jamaica: Ian Randle Publishers.
Clarke, John Henrick. (1994). *My Life in Search of Africa*. Ithaca, New York: Cornel University. Africana Studies and Research Center. Monograph Series No. 8.
Da Costa, Emilia Viotti (1994). *Crowns of Glory, Tears of Blood: The Demerara Slave Rebellion of 1823*. New York and London: Oxford University Press.
Crooks, Paul (2002). *Ancestors*. London: BlackAmber Books Limited.
Cunard, Nancy (ed., 1934, 2002). *Negro: An Anthology*. Edited and abridged by H. Ford. New York: Continuum
David, Rosalie (2002). *Religion and Magic in Ancient Egypt*. London: Penguin
Davidson, Basil (1993). *The Black Man's Burden: Africa and the Curse of the Nation-State*. Ibadan: Spectrum Books Limited.
Davis, Theodore M. (1912, 2001). *The Tombs of Harmhabi and Touatánkhamanou* London: Gerald Duckworth & Co. Ltd.
Davies, Vivian and Friedman, Renée (1998). *Egypt*. London: The British Museum Press.
Denning, M., Phillips, O and Rudolph, G (1979). *Voudoun Fire: The Living Reality of Mystical Religion* St. Paul, MN: Llewellyn Publications.
Deren, Maya (1953, 1970). *Divine Horsemen: The Living Gods of Haiti*. New York: Mc Pherson and Co., Ltd.
Depuydt, Leo (1999). *Fundamentals of Egyptian Grammar I: Elements*. Norton, Mass: Frog Publishing.
Diop, Cheikh Anta. (1963, 1989). The Cultural Unity of Black Africa: The of Matriarchy and of Patriarchy in Classical Antiquity. London: Karnak House.
—— (1987). *Precolonial Black Africa*. Trans. H. Salemson. Lawrence Hill and Co. Westport, Connecticut.
Drakes, F. M. [Kimani Nehusi] (1982). *The Jordanites: The Study of a Black Cultist Movement* Georgetown, Guyana: Ministry of Education.
Dunham, Katherine. (1983). *Dances of Haiti*. Los Angeles: Center for Afro-American Studies, UCLA.
Eduardo, Octavio Da Costa (1948, 1981). *The Negro in Northern Brazil: A Study in Acculturation*. London: The African Publication Society.
Ekwe-Ekwe, Herbert and Nzegwu, Femi (1994). *Operationalising Afrocentricism* Reading: International Institute for African Research.
Elkins, Caroline (2005). *Britain's Gulag. The Brutal End of Empire in Kenya* London: Jonathan Cape.
Erman, Adolf (1894, 1971). Trans. H.M. Tirard. *Life in Ancient Egypt* New York: Dover Publications, Inc.
Erman, Adolf and Grapow, Hermann. (1926, 1963, 1982). *Wörterbuch der Aegyptischen Sprache*.(5 Vols.) Berlin: Akademie Verlag.
Faulkner, R. O. (1929). *The Plural and Dual in Old Egyptian* Bruxelles: Édition de la Fondation Égyptologique Reine Élisabeth.
—— (1962). *A Concise Dictionary Of Middle Egyptian* Oxford: Griffith Institute.

—— Trans. (1969). *The Ancient Egyptian Pyramid Texts* Warminster: Aris & Phillips Ltd.
—— Trans. (1994). *The Ancient Egyptian Coffin Texts.* 3 Vols. Warminster: Aris and Phillips Ltd.
—— Trans. (1985, 1996, 2005). *The Ancient Egyptian Book of the Dead.* London, The British Museum Press; New York, Barnes and Noble.
—— Trans. (1994, 1998). The Egyptian Book of the Dead: The Book Going Forth by Day. San Francisco: Chronicle Books.
Flanagan, Brenda (2005). *You alone are Dancing.* Ann Arbor, Michigan: The University of Michigan Press.
Forman, Werner and Quirke, Stephen (1996). *Hieroglyphs and the Afterlife in Ancient Egypt.* London: The British Museum Press.
Fu-Kiau, Kimbwandende Kia Bunseki (2003) *Self-Healing Power and Therapy: Old Teachings from Africa.* Baltimore, MD, USA: Inprint Editions
Fu-Kiau, Kimbwandende Kia Bunseki and A. M. Lukondo-Wamba (2000). *Kindezi: The Kôngo Art of Babysitting.* Baltimore, MD, USA: Inprint Editions
Gardiner, Alan. (1927,1988). *Egyptian Grammar: Being An Introduction To The Study Of Hieroglyphs* 3rd Edition, revised Oxford: Griffith Institute, Ashmoleum Museum.
—— (1961). *Egypt of the Pharaohs* Oxford University Press.
Goldwasser, Orly (1995). *From Icon to Metaphor: Studies in the Semiotics of the Hieroglyphs.* Orbis Biblicus et Orientalis No. 142. University Press Fribourg, Switzerland and Vandenhoeck and Ruprecht, Göttingen.
Green, Michael (trans. 1987). *The Coptic Share Pattern and its Ancient Egyptian Ancestors.* Warminster: Aris and Phillips, Ltd.
Grimal, Nicolas, Jochen Hallof and Dirk van der Plas (2000). *Hieroglyphica Sign List.* 2nd Edition, revised and enlarged by Jochen Hallof, Hans van der Berg and Gabriele Hallof. Utrecht and Paris: Interniversitaries de Recherches Égyptologiques Informatisées.
Haley, Alex (1976) *Roots.* New York: Doubleday.
Hanson, Ben (1999) *Takadini.* Lagos: Lantern Books, Literamed Publications Ltd.
Hart, George (1990). *Egyptian Myths.* London: The British Museum Press.
Hayford, Casley (1903). Gold Coast Native Institutions: With Thoughts Upon a Healthy Imperial Policy for the Gold Coast and Ashanti. London: Sweet and Maxwell, Ltd.
Heath, Roy A. K. (1978). *The Murderer.* London: Allison and Busby Ltd.
Henry, Frances (2003). *Reclaiming African Religions in Trinidad: The Socio-Political Legitimation of the Orisha and Spiritual Baptist Faiths.* Barbados, Jamaica and Trinidad and Tobago: The University of the West Indies Press.
Hill, Lawrence (2007). *The Book of Negroes.* Toronto: HarperCollins Publishers Ltd.
Hilliard III, Asa G. (Nana Baffour Amankwatia II). (2002) *African Power: Affirming African Indigenous Socialization in the Face of the Culture Wars.* Gainesville, Florida: Makare Publishing Company.
Hillard III, Asa G, L. Williams and Nia Damali (eds., 1987) *The Teachings of Ptahhotep: The Oldest Book in the World.* Atlanta, GA: Blackwood Press and Co., Inc.,
Homer (trans. R. Fagles, 1990). *The Iliad* Penguin Books.
Hornung, Erik (Translated Irmela Stevens, 2005). *The Ancient Egyptian Books of the Underworld* London: Intef Institute, Karnak House.
Howatson, M. C. (ed. 1990). *The Oxford Companion to Classical Literature* Oxford University Press
Hurry, Jamieson B. (1926, 1987). *Imhotep: The Egyptian God of Medicine* Chicago: Ares Publishers.

Hurston, Zora Neale. (1938, 1990). *Tell My Horse: Voodoo and Life in Haiti and Jamaica* New York: Harper and Row.
Hutton, Clinton A (2005). The Logic and Historical Significance of the Haitian Revolution and the Cosmological Roots of Haitian Freedom Kingston: Arawak Publications.
Idowu, E. Bolayi (1960, 1994). *Olódùmarè: God in Yoruba Belief* New York: A&B Publishers.
Ijoma, J. Okoro (2010). *Igbo Origins and Migrations.* Nsukka: Great AP Express Publishers Ltd.
—— (2010). *The Igala and their Neighbours: Historical Glimpses.* Nsukka: Great AP Express Publishers Ltd.
Jacq, Christian. (Trans. J.M. Davis, 1985). *Egyptian Magic* Warminster: Aris & Phillips Ltd.
James, C. L. R. (1938, 1963, 1980, 1994). The Black Jacobins: Toussaint L'Ouverture and the San Domingo Revolution London: Allison and Busby.
James, T.C.H. (1984). *Pharaoh's People: Scenes From life In Imperial Egypt* London: The Bodley Head.
Janssen, Rosalind M and Jac J. (1996). *Getting Old In Ancient Egypt* London: The Rubicon Press.
ben-Jochannan, Yosef A.A. (1986). Abu Simbel-Gizeh: Guide Book/Manual New York: The Author.Kamalu, Chukwunyere (1990). Foundations of African Thought: A Worldview Grounded in the African Heritage of Religion, Philosophy, Science and Art. London: Karnak House
Karenga, Maulana. (ed., 1984). *Selections from the Husia: Sacred Wisdom of Ancient Egypt.* Los Angeles: Kawaida Publications.
—— (1990). *The Book of Coming Forth By Day: The Ethics of the Declarations of Innocence* Los Angeles: University of Sankore Press
—— (ed., 1999). *Odù Ifá: The Ethical Teachings.* Los Angeles: University of Sankore Press.
—— (2004). Maat: The Moral Ideal in Ancient Egypt: A Study in Classical African Ethics. New York and London: Routledge.
Kaster, Joseph (1968, 1995). *The Wisdom of Ancient Egypt: Writings from the Time of the Pharaohs* London: Michael O'Mara Books, Ltd.
Kenyatta, Jomo (1965). *Facing Mount Kenya: The Tribal Life of the Gikuyu.* New York: Vintage Books.
Kotkin, Joel (1992). Tribes: How Race, Religion, and Identity determine success in the new global economy New York: Random House.
Kwayana, Eusi and Kwayana, Tchaiko (1972, 2002). Scars of Bondage: A First Study of the Slave Colonial Experience of Africans in Guyana Georgetown: free press.
Lam, Aboubacry Moussa (2006) La Vallée Du Nil: berceau de l'unité culturelle de l'Afrique noire. Paris: Khepera and Dakar: Presses Universitares de Dakar.
Lan, David (1985). *Guns and Rain: Guerrillas and Spirit Mediums in Zimbabwe* London: James Currey and Berkeley and Los Angeles: University of California Press.
Lichtheim, Mariam. (1975). *Ancient Egyptian Literature. Volume I: The Old and Middle Kingdoms.* Berkeley, Los Angeles and London: University of Los Angeles Press.
—— (1976). *Ancient Egyptian Literature. Volume II: The New Kingdom.* Berkeley, Los Angeles and London: University of Los Angeles Press.
Liverpool, Hollis 'Chalkdust' (2001). *Rituals of Power and Rebellion: The Carnival Tradition in Trinidad and Tobago, 1763—1962.* Chicago: Research Associates School Times Publications/Frontline Distribution Int'l Inc.
Lucas, J. Olumide (1948). *The Religion of the Yorubas.* Lagos: CMS Bookshop

——(1970). *Religions in West Africa and Ancient Egypt.* Apapa: Nigerian National Press

Maloba, Wunyabari O. (1998). *Mau Mau and Kenya: An Analysis of a Peasant Revolt.* Bloomington and Indianapolis and Oxford: Indiana University Press and James Currey Publishers.

Martin, D and Johnson, P. (1981). *The Struggle for Zimbabwe: The Chimurenga War.* New York and London: Monthly Review Press.

Matthews, Donald H. (1998). Honoring the Ancestors: An African Cultural Interpretation of Black Religion and Literature Oxford University Press.

Mazuri, Ali A. (1986). *The Africans: A Triple Heritage.* London: BBC Publications.

Mbiti, John. (1969, 1988). *African Religions and Philosophy.* London: Heinemann.

—— (1975, 1986). Introduction to African Religion. Heinemann

Monges, Mariam Ma'at-Ka-Re. (1997). *Kush. The Jewel of Nubia: Reconnecting The Root System of African Civilization* Trenton, NJ: Africa World Press.

Montejo, Esteban (1968, 1993. Translated by Jocasta Innes). *The Autobiography of a Runaway Slave* London: The Macmillan Press Ltd.

Moore, Brian. (1995). Cultural Power, Resistance and Pluralism: Colonial Guyana, Barbados, Jamaica and Trinidad and Tobago:

The Press University of the West Indies and Montreal and Kingston: McGill-Queens University Press.

Morschauser, Scott (1991). Threat-Formulae in Ancient Egypt: A Study of the History, Structure and Use of Threats and Curses in Ancient Egypt Oxford: Halgo, Inc.

do Nascimento, Abdias (1995). *Orixás: Os Deuses Vivos da África* Rio de Janeiro: IPEAFRO

Ngubane, Jordan K. (1979). *Conflict of Minds: Changing Power Dispositions in South Africa.* New York: Books in Focus, Inc.

Nordh, Katarina (1996). *Aspects of Ancient Egyptian Curses and Blessings: Conceptual Background and Transmission.* Uppsala Studies in Ancient Mediterranean and Near Eastern Civilization, No. 26. ACTA Universitatis Upsaliensis.

Nwapa, Flora (1966, 1978). *Efuru.* London: Heinemann Educational Publishers

—— (1970) *Idu.* London: Heinemann Educational Books Limited.

—— (1975, 1992) *Never Again* Trenton, NJ: Africa World Press.

Nzegwu, Femi (2001) Love, Motherhood and the African Heritage: The Legacy of Flora Nwapa Dakar, Senegal: African Renaissance.

Obenga, Théophile (Trans. A. Sheik, 1992). Ancient Egypt and Black Africa: A Student's Handbook for the Study of Ancient Egypt in Philosophy, Linguistics and Gender Relations London: Karnak House.

—— (Trans. Ayi Kwei Armah, 2004). *African Philosophy: The Pharaonic Period: 2780–330 BC.* Popenguine: Per Ankh.

Oduyoye, Modupe (1996). *Words and Meaning in Yoruba Religion* London: Karnak House.

Ogbaa, Kalu (1992). *Gods, Oracles and Divination: Folkways in Chinua Achebe's Novels* Trenton, NJ: Africa World Press.

Okpewho, Isidore (1992). *African Oral Literature: Backgrounds, Character, and Continuity* Bloomington and Indianapolis: Indiana University Press.

Olmos, M. F. and Paravisini-Gerbert, L (2003). *Creole Religions of the Caribbean: An Introduction from Vodou and Santeria to Obeah andEspiritismo* New York and London: New York University Press

Opoku, Kofi Asare (1978). *West African Traditional Religion* Accra: FEP International Private Ltd.

Parkinson, R. B. (1991). Voices from Ancient Egypt : An Anthology of Middle Kingdom Writings London: The British Museum Press.

—— (1997, trans., ed.). *The Tale of Sinuhe and Other Ancient Egyptian Poems, 940—1640 BC*. Oxford University Press

Patterson, Orlando. (1967, 1973). *The Sociology of Slavery*. Kingston, Jamaica: Sangster's Book Stores Ltd.

Prah, Kwesi (1998). *Beyond the Color Line: Pan-Africanist Disputations, Selected Sketches, Letters, Papers and Reviews*. Trenton, NJ and Asmara, Eritrea.

Preston, William (ed. 1990; trans., introduction and appendix by B. Gunn, 1906) *The Instructions of Ptah-hotep and Ke'gemni* (Waddington, New York: Phyllis Preston Collection

Price, Richard and Price, Sally (eds.) *Stedman's Surinam: Life in an Eighteenth-Century Slave Society*. Baltimore and London: The Johns Hopkins University Press.

Pritchard, James B. (ed., 1969). *Ancient Near Eastern Texts Relating to the Old Testament* 3rd Edition. Princeton, NJ: The University of Princeton Press.

Ranger, Terence (1985). *Peasant Consciousness and Guerrilla War in Zimbabwe: A Comparative Study* London: James Currey.

Redford, Donald B. (1986). *Pharaonic King-Lists, Annals and Day-Books: A Contribution to the Study of the Egyptian Sense of History* Mississauga: Benben Publications.

Ritner, Robert. (1993). *The Mechanics of Ancient Egyptian Magical Practice* Studies in Ancient Oriental Civilization No. 54. The Oriental Institute of the University of Chicago.

Roberts, Alison (2000). *My Heart My Mother: Death and Rebirth in Ancient Egypt* Rottingdean, East Sussex: NorthGate Publishers.

Rodney, Walter (1969, 1970, 1971, etc.). *The Groundings With My Brothers* London: Bogle L'Ouverture Publications.

—— (1972, 1988). *How Europe Underdeveloped Africa* London: Bogle L'Ouverture Publications Ltd.

Sarpong, Rt. Rev. Dr. Peter Kwasi (1996). *Libation*. Accra: Anansesem Publications.

Satell, Stephen C. (2013). *No Gang War in '74 : Past, Present and Future*. Xlibris Corporation.

Sauneron, Serges (trans. D. Lorton, 2000). *The Priests of Ancient Egypt*. Ithaca and London: Cornell University Press.

Sawyerr, Harry (1970). *God, Ancestor or Creator? Aspects of traditional belief in Ghana, Nigeria and Sierra Leone*. London: Longmans.

Seligman, C. G. (1934). *Egypt and Negro Africa: A Study in Divine Kingship*. The Frazer Lecture of 1933, University of Liverpool, 30th November, 1933. London: George Routlege and Sons, Ltd.

Semple, Wosley (Compiler. 1989 & 1990, with updates every 2 years). *The Semple Family Tree*. Washington, D. C.: The Author.

Sethe, K. (1924). *Ägyptische Lesestücke*. Leipzig.

Shafer, Byron E. (ed., 1991). *Religion in Ancient Egypt: Gods, Myths and Personal Practice* Ithaca and London: University of Cornell Press.

T'Shaka, Oba (1995). *Return to the African Mother Principle of Male and Female Equality. Volume I*. Oakland, California: Pan Afrikan Publishers and Distributers.

Shaw, Ian and Nicholson, Paul. (1995). *British Museum Dictionary of Ancient Egypt*. London: British Museum Press.

Smith, Mark. (1993). *The Liturgy of Opening the Mouth for Breathing*. Oxford: Griffith Institute.

Soyinka, Wole (1976, 1990). *Myth, Literature and the African World*. Cambridge University Press.

Stephen, Henri J. M. (1998). *Winti Culture: mysteries, Voodoo and Realities of an Afro-Caribbean Religion in Suriname and the Netherlands* Amsterdam: The Author?

Stephens, Rev. Patricia (1999). *The Spiritual Baptist Faith: African New World Religious Identity, History and Testimony* London: Karnak House

wa Thiong'o, Ngugi (1965). *The River Between.* London: Heinemann.

Thomas, Angela P (2001). *Egyptian Gods and Myths* Princes Risborough: Shire Publications Ltd.

Thompson, Robert Farris (1983, 1984). *Flash of The Spirit: African and Afro-American Art and Philosophy* New York: Vintage Books

Trigger, B.G., Kemp, B.J., O'Connor, D and Lloyd, A.B. (1983). *Ancient Egypt: A Social History* Cambridge University Press.

Tyldesley, Joyce (2004). *Tales from Ancient Egypt* Bolton, UK: Rutherford Press Ltd.

Umeh, John Anenechukwu (1997, 1999). *After God Is Dibia: Igbo Cosmology, Divination and Sacred Science in Nigeria.* Vols. I & II. London: Karnak House.

Umeh, Marie (ed.). *Emerging Perspectives on Flora Nwapa: Critical and Theoretical Essays.* Trenton, NJ: Africa World Press, Inc.

Vega, Marta Moreno. (2000). *The Altar of My Soul: The Living Traditions of Santeria* New York: One World, The Ballantine Publishing Group.

Warner-Lewis, Maureen (1991). *Guinea's Other Suns: The African Dynamic in Trinidad Culture.* Dover, Mass.: The Majority Press.

—— (2003). *Central Africa in the Caribbean: Transcending Time, Transforming Cultures* Mona, Jamaica: The University of the West Indies Press.

Wildung, Dietrich (1977). *Egyptian Saints: Deification in Pharaonic Egypt.* New York: New York University Press.

Wilkinson, J. Gardner (1853, 1994). *The Ancient Egyptians: Their Life and Customs* Vol.I London: Senate.

Wilkinson, Richard H. (1994, 1999). *Symbol and Magic in Egyptian Art.* London: Thames and Hudson Ltd.

—— (2000). *The Complete Temples of Ancient Egypt* London: Thames and Hudson.

Williams, Chancellor (1976). The Destruction of Black Civilization: Great Issues of a Race from 4500 B.C. to 2000 A.D. Chicago: Third World Press.

Williams, Eric (1944, 1964, 1975). *Capitalism and Slavery_* London: Andre Deutsch

Yew, Lee Kuan (2000). *From the Third World to the First World* New York: Harper Collins.

INDEX

2Pac Shakur, 2Pac, xxvii, 45, 144-146

Abarry, Abu S., xxx, 5, 19
Abstinence, 60-62, 180. See also fasting, ritual purity.
Achebe, Chinua, xxviii, 101
Adae festival, 61, 111, See also festivals; ancestral festivals
Adegbola, E. A. Ade, xxvi, xxvii
African divinities (gods) 18, 33, 131, 132, 134, 138. See also Earth Divinities, Water Divinities.
    Ala, 9, 26
    Aker, 9
    Ani 9, 26
    Shu, 69, 161
    Shango, 18, 46, 110, 131, 134
Afrikan (African),
    Circle of Life, 1, 4
    ceremonies, 1, 14, 18, 19, 23, 34, 58, 62, 85, 108, 111, 139, 142, 159, 164, 165, 168, 169
    Communities of Resistance, 3, 4, 130, 131, 146. See also Afrikan centered Communities; *Kilombos; Mocambos; Palenques;* Maroon Communities; *Palanque do Palmares*
    Gods, African, 43–47. See also Divinities
    Holocaust, Great Holocaust or *Maafa*, xxiii, 4, 23, 24, 27, 30, 102, 107, 113, 132, 138–141, 147, 157, 168.
    identity, xxiii, xxiv, xxx, xxxii, 3, 10, 24, 27, 29, 30, 49, 62, 81, 88, 98, 104, 105, 113, 121, 130, 133, 136, 138, 139, 141, 147, 157, 158, 165, 180, 181, 182, 186
    languages, xxvii, 10, 11, 23–24, 28, 30, 45, 47, 49, 52, 55, 56, 57, 72, 73, 108, 112, 114, 115, 117, 118, 119, 120, 121, 130, 133, 135, 136, 137, 138, 143, 155, 158, 161, 163, 170, 171, 180, 185. See also Ga, Twi, Igbo, Yoruba, Mdw Ntr, *Medew Netjer*, hieroglyphs, Gikuyu (Kikuyu)
    nation, xxvi, 12, 16, 19, 23, 25, 29, 33, 90, 98, 106, 114, 130, 151, 169, 179, 184.
    people, xxiii, xxix, xxxi, 2, 6, 23, 24, 28, 30, 33, 45, 49, 51, 90, 98, 100, 103, 108, 112, 113, 129, 136, 138, 140, 144, 154, 157, 161, 162, 164, 178, 180, 181, 182
    perspectives, xxvi, xxx, 46, 91, 119, 138
    points of view, xxix, 85
    popular culture, xxviii, 144
    Movement, Afrikan-centered, xx, 28, 43, 76, 135, 168
    Ritual of Heritage, 1, 14

scholarship. See scholarship and scholars
unity, 3, 107, 132, 181
world/world-view, xxiii, xxviii, xix, xxxii, 1, 2, 5, 7, 10, 23, 25, 26, 30, 34, 44, 54, 78, 79, 81, 82, 86, 87, 88,89, 90, 92, 97, 102, 107, 108, 112, 118, 122, 135, 136, 146, 156, 163, 164, 169, 170, 179, 180, 181, 182, 183, 184, 185, 186, 187
African Cultural Development Association (ACDA, Guyana), 107
Afrikan Remembrance Day, 107
Afrikan Remembrance Day Committee, 107
Afrikan development, xxiii, xxvii, 5, 9, 24, 42, 47, 70, 104–105, 106, 107, 119, 140, 152
chronology of Afrika, xxvii
akh/ akh/ akhs, 4, 114–115, 116, 166–168
Akan, xxvi, 6, 82, 101, 109, 154, 156, 157
alcohol, 3, 17, 18, 34, 43, 52, 160, 183. See also rum, babash, Clarin, Palm, *akpeteshie, ogogoro, babash, Zai-id*
Allen, James P, xxvii, 4, 53, 115
altar, 14, 28, 48, 58, 72–76, 79, 108, 159, 168. See also offering table
Amenta, 153. See West Bank, underworld, death, Duat
Americas, xxviii, 21, 30, 51, 79, 82, 87, 101, 106, 111, 129, 130, 132, 134, 135, 136, 141, 142, 143, 146, 157, 159, 164, 168, 180
Ancestors, 1, 2, 3, 5, 6, 7, 9, 11, 13, 14, 15, 17, 18, 19, 20, 21, 23, 24, 25, 26–31, 32, 33, 42, 43, 47, 48, 49, 51, 52, 56, 57, 60, 71, 74, 79, 81, 88, 89, 90, 97–128, 132, 134, 136, 137, 138, 139, 143, 146, 156, 157, 159, 160, 161, 164, 166, 168, 169, 177, 178, 179, 180, 181, 183, 184, 185, 186, 187
  Becoming an Ancestor, 101–105
  Deified Ancestors, 109–110
  Elders and, 113–114
  Invoking the Ancestors, 26–31
  Great Hall of the Ancestors, 28
  names of, 27-28, 110, 112
  relationship with, 105–106
  roles and significance of, 98–99
  terms for in the Nedew Netjer, 114–123
  veneration of, 99–101, 106–109
Ancestral Festivals, 110–113. See also *saraka, services ancêtres, sàrákà, s'iku, jumbie* dinner. See also festivals
Ancestral spirit, 159
Ani, Elder Kwame, 112
Ani, (Igbo divinity), 9, 26. Also Ala, Ale, Ama
Ani, Sebayat of, 47
ankh, 156
Arabs, xxx, 3, 20, 30, 143
Assmann, Jan, xxv, 84
Asaase Yaa (Adaase Afua in Fanti), 9, 26
Ast/ Auset/ Isis/Isata, 46, 53, 161, 163. See also African Goddess; African Divinity;
Awolalu, J. Omosade, xxvi
Ayi Kwei Armah, xxviii, 7, 12, 26, 43, 100, 181

Ba, 59, 115, 116. See also soul; ka
balkanization, xxxi, 30
barefooted, 21–22. See also ritual; footware
Bible, xxvii, 15, 22, 58, 101, 122, 162
Blondel, Ezra, xxxii

blood offering, 69, 75, 88
Book of Going Forth by Day, 58, 59, 60, 66–67ff, 75, 162, 167. See also *Book of Going Up Into Enlightenment*, 97; *Egyptian Book of the Dead*, xxiv, 58; *Chapters of Going Forth by Day,* xiv, 58; *Sebayat of Ani*, 47
Book of Vindication, xxiv, 47, 162. See also *Coffin Texts*
Brazil/Brasil, 6, 8, 18, 106, 130, 132, 134, 136, 142, 144, 158.

Cabral, Amilcar, 105
Camouflage, 130–134, 136, 137, 138, 139
Candomblé, 6, 12, 18, 106, 137, 142, 158, 164.
Canizares, Raul, xxviii, xxxi, 6, 99, 131
Caribbean, xxviii, 21, 30, 51, 52, 79, 82, 87, 106, 107, 111, 122, 130, 134, 135, 141, 142, 143, 144, 157, 158, 164, 165, 168, 180
Carruthers, Jacob, xxix, xxx, 134, 135, 163
ceremonial complex, 3, 41. See also Nabta Playa
Chimurenga (War of National Liberation), 102–103, 104, 181. See also Zimbabwe; Mbuya Nehanda; abstinence; spirit mediums
Christian/Christianity/Eurochristian/Eurochristianity, xxv, xxvii, 11, 15, 16, 20, 58, 90, 101, 104, 122, 133, 134, 136, 137, 138, 142, 143, 154, 156, 158
Coffin Texts, xxiv, 13, 47, 81, 82, 161, 162. See also *Book of Vindication*.
Colihaut, Dominica, xxxi
colonizers, colonization, xxx, 91
communal cup, 34
conversation among the generations, 114
Cosmic Model, 4-13
Cosmic Order, 2, 7, 8, 10, 11, 12, 13, 15, 19, 44, 45, 71, 177, 179, 187.
Cosmogony, cosmology, xxix, xxxii, 2, 97, 114, 121, 155, 157, 168
Creator, xxvi, 2, 3, 5, 7, 8, 9, 11, 13, 23, 25–26, 45, 57, 60, 70, 71, 81, 105, 121, 122, 144, 160, 161, 169, 177, 178, 179, 187. See also Supreme Being, God, divinities, First Ancestor, Grand Ancestor, Father, Mother, Papa God
creation, creation story, 5, 10–11, 91, 92, 154, 155, 156, 160, 161, 162, 163. See also *Sep Tepy*, the First Occasion
Cuba, Cuban, 6, 8, 18, 106, 111, 131, 134, 141, 142, 165.
culture, xxi, xxii, xxiii, xxv, xxvi, xxviii, xxix, xxx, 2, 3, 5, 11, 18, 24, 26, 29, 33, 41, 42, 49, 52, 82, 90, 98, 99, 100, 104, 105, 106, 107, 108, 111, 113, 114, 118, 121, 122, 129, 130, 131, 132, 136, 137, 138, 139, 141, 142, 143, 144, 147, 152, 157, 158, 163, 164, 165, 170, 179, 181, 182, 184, 185, 186. See also cultural heritage; cultural genocide; cultural highway
cultural genocide, 24, 30, 104, 130, 132, 135, 136, 138, 141, 146
cultural heritage, xxiii, 98, 99, 107, 130
cultural highway, 152

Deren, Maya, xxviii, 131, 133
Declarations of Innocence, 11, 27, 59, 75, 105, 153, 167. See also Ten Commandments
Diaspora, 3, 23, 30, 51, 61, 122, 135, 139, 141, 144, 145, 146, 157
Dinkinesh, 29
discrimination, xxiv
Divine Presence, 21–23, 31, 33, 48, 79, 154. See also sacred presence, divinity; *Netjeru*
Divinity, xxvii, 1, 6, 7, 9, 10, 11, 13, 15, 17, 20, 21, 23, 24, 28, 43, 44, 45, 46, 48, 50, 52, 55, 57, 58, 64, 69, 70, 74, 75, 76, 79, 80, 81, 82, 86, 89, 90, 91, 92, 97, 98, 100,

109, 110, 117, 119, 121, 122, 131, 134, 153, 155, 157, 158, 161, 162, 163, 164, 167, 168, 169, 170, 171, 178, 186. See also Afrikan Gods.
Djhwti/Djhwty/Djhuti, 59, 81, 156. See also African Divinities (Afrikan Gods)
Dopamu, P. Adelumo, xxvi
drink offering, See libation, libation ritual, libationer
drum, drummer, 33, 34, 108, 131, 164–166
Duat, 154–155
Durban Declaration, xxii
Dutty, Boukman, 24, 135, 135, 136. See also African languages, Haitian Revolution

Earth/Mother Earth, 4, 9, 11, 14, 17, 21, 23, 26, 27, 31, 34, 43, 44, 51, 57, 70, 76, 86, 98, 109, 112, 113, 122, 135, 143, 159, 161, 162, 177, 179, 180, 187
earth divinities, 9
Egypt, ancient
 language (Mdw Ntr, *Medew Netjer*, Hieroglyphs), xxvii, 6, 15, 45, 47–55, 60, 62, 72, 73, 74, 76, 79, 85, 114, 117, 118, 119, 120, 121, 166, 170, 171, 185. See also Afrikan languages
 people, ancient Egyptians, *rmt m Kmt*, xxiv, xxix, 2, 4, 5, 6, 12, 16, 22, 27, 43, 45, 47, 49, 53, 55, 57, 58, 59, 61, 72, 73, 74, 75, 76, 77, 80, 85, 86, 88, 89, 90, 91, 92, 109, 115, 116, 117, 119, 153, 154, 155, 161, 163, 166, 167, 168, 178,
 society, xxv
Egyptology, 43, 44, 49, 73, 163, 171
elders, xxix, 19, 29, 100, 102, 104, 114–115, 118, 122, 181
eldership, 1
Emancipation Committee (Trinidad), 107
enslavement, xxix, 20, 24, 30–31, 107, 130, 131, 132, 134, 135, 136, 139, 141, 146, 147, 154, 156, 157, 184. See also Maafa or Afrikan Holocaust
 mental enslavement, 20
 physical enslavement, xxix, 107, 139, 141
 time of terror, xxix, 24, 113
environmentalism, 9, 10, 170
Erman, Adolf (and Grapow, Hermann), xxviii, 35, 90–93, 177, 241, 264
Europe, European, Europeans, xxv, xxvii, xxix, xxx, 3, 4, 9, 18, 20, 26, 29, 30, 90, 102, 103, 105, 110, 146, 156, 158, 164, 180
European cultural genocide, Afrikan reaction to, 129–143
 Language(s), 30, 136, 138
Eurocentricism/Eurocentric, xxv, 42, 53, 104, 121, 132, 133, 134, 135, 136
Ewe, 9, 25

fasting, 61–62, 180, 186. See also abstenance, ritual purity.
father/grandfather, 11, 28, 47, 53, 54, 97, 98, 118, 119, 120, 121, 122, 155. See also ancestor; male progenitor; revered person
Faulkner, Raymond O., xxvii, 47, 49, 51, 73, 80, 82, 115, 161
festivals, 19, 43, 51, 61, 81, 83, 108, 109, 110, 111, 112, 121, 184 See also Ancestral Festivals; *saraka*; *services ancêtres*; *sàrákà*; *s'iku*; *jumbie* dinner
First Fruits, 3, 13, 69, 75, 86, 88, 89, 108, 111, 156, 178, 179. See also harvest, offerings,
flag, flag planting, 151, 169–171. See also Ritual Significances
Florida Water, 61
food/food offerings, 13, 18, 34, 48, 49, 58, 60, 61, 72, 74, 78, 79, 88, 103, 122, 123, 146, 177

Gardiner, Alan, xxx, xxvii, 47, 49, 53, 72, 73, 76, 80, 84, 85, 90, 110, 115, 163

Geb, 9, 70, 74, 79, 86. See also African Divinities
Gikuyu (Kikuyu), xxvi, 29, 52, 103–104
Ginen; Giné; Haiti, 125, 157, 158
gods. see African Divinities
grandfather, 119, 122
grandmother, 103, 118, 119
grandparent, 119–120, 122. See also ancestor
Great Terror, time of terror, xxix, 24, 27, 113, 142. See also cultural terrorism, enslavement
Greece, 42, 109. See also ancient Europe
God's Domain, 59. See also temple; sacred space; pure space;
Guyana, xxxi, 17, 21, 101, 106, 107, 111, 112, 130, 137, 144, 145, 158, 159, 163, 166, 168

Haiti, 6, 17, 18, 24, 54, 87, 106, 107, 109, 111, 130, 131, 133, 134–136, 142, 157
Haitian Revolution, 24, 54, 134–136. See also Boukman Dutty
harvest, 3, 13, 69, 75, 88, 108, 111, 156
Hathor, 43–46. See also African gods, African divinities
Hatshepsut, 77, 78, 116
Hemen, 108. See also African Gods
Herodotus, xxv, 42, 53
Heru, 57, 60, 74, 156. See also African Gods; Wsir; Ausir (Osiris); Ast; Auset
hip-hop, xxviii, 82, 144–145
hotep, 47, 48, 71–72, 73, 74, 76, 84, 85, 109. See also Charlie Parker; chill; chill out; cool; cool runnings; greetings; John Coltrane; Kool and the Gang; pacify; propitiate; purify
Hurston, Zora Neale, xxxi, 131, 133
Hutton, Clinton, xxx, 6, 129, 134, 135, 157

Idowu, E. Bolayi, xxvi
Igbo, Igbo language, xxvi, 6, 8, 10, 19, 26, 28, 99, 111, 154, 156, 157, 169
Imhotep, 55, 56, 76, 109–110, 113, 181. See also Ancestors; Deified Ancestors; Khaemwaset; Amenhotep, son of Hapu; Hardedef; Kagemni; Ptahhotep; Shango.
incense, incense burner, censer, xxiv, 3, 13, 41, 42, 48, 49, 56, 60, 61, 69, 74, 75, 83, 87, 88, 89, 108, 120, 122, 160, 171, 177, 180. See also offerings.
initiation, 1, 19, 159, 164
Inpu (Greek: Anubis), 74, 80, 164. See also African Gods; Heru; Ast; Auset; Isis; Wsir
interview, interviewees, xxxi. See also living witnesses
invocation, invocations, 19, 25–31, 48, 51, 74, 79, 80, 81, 83, 85, 112, 121, 159, 171. See also Divine Presences, Ancestral Presences
Isfet, 12

Jamaica/Jamaican, 6, 17, 51, 106, 107, 130, 134, 154
jumbie dinner, 112

ka, 75, 110
kaiso (calypso), xxviii, 82, 143, 144
Kalunga, 157, See also transmigration; repatriation.
Karenga, Maulana, xxx, 113
Kash, 41. See also Kush, Nubia
Kemet:
    The Book of Ani, x

The Book of Going Forth by Day, xxx, 33, 50, 83, 84, 86,
  The Book of Vindication, xxx, 66, 224
  Chapters of Going Forth By Day (Into Light), 82, 231
  The Coffin Texts, xxv, xxxiv, 18, 53, 55–56, 66, 90, 113, 115, 132, 172, 176, 222, 224, 238, 239, 240, 265
  The Egyptian Book of the Dead, xxv, 33, 50, 82, 93, 94, 95, 131, 174, 239, 241, 259, 265
  Pyramid Texts, xxii, xxxiv, 50, 66, 79, 80, 83, 90, 92–95, 111, 118–119, 131–132, 165, 177, 222, 238–240, 265
    sacred literature of, 65–66
Kenya, 34, 91, 115, 123, 143, 173, 262, 264, 266, 267
Kenyatta, Jomo, xxvi
Kilombos, 130
Kush, 41, 42, 152, 182. See also Kash, Nubia
Kwanzaa, 108, 112, 168, 184

Language, xxvii, 6, 11, 23, 25, 28, 30, 45, 47–55, 56, 57, 72, 73, 108, 112, 114–122, 130, 133, 135, 136–137, 138, 143, 155, 158, 161, 170, 171, 180, 185. See also African languages, hieroglyphs, Mdw Nṯr, *Medew Netjer*.

libation,
See also drink; drink offering
    Ga Libation oratory, 19
    Libation Statement, 14, 15, 19, 25, 48, 69, 74, 86–89, 179. See also petition, request, prayers.
    Myth of Libation, 7, 43–47, 91, 92, 178
libationer, 14–17, 23, 24, 31, 32–33, 53, 54, 57, 160, 162, 180, 183, 185, 186
Lucas, J. Olumide, xxvi, 111, 131

Maafa or Afrikan Holocaust or Great Holocaust. See Afrikan Holocaust
maa kherew, 28, 105
Maat, the Law, 2, 6, 11–13, 14, 17, 45, 51, 58, 59, 60, 70, 76, 81, 103, 112, 113, 177, 179, 184. See also *Maat*, the Divinity; African Gods; African Divinities
Maat, the Afrikan Divinity (Goddess), 44–45, 178
Maati, Great Hall of; Great Hall of Justice, 28, 76, 105
Maroons, 112, 130. See also Communities of Resistance
Mau Mau (Land and Freedom Army), 103–104. See also Kenya; European settler colonialism; Gikuyu
Mazama, Ama, xxv, xxvii
Mbiti, John, xxv–xxvi, xxvii, 5–6, 28, 99, 159
Melchesidek Spiritual Baptist Church, 107
Mende, xxv, 9, 157
Mesopotamia, 42, 43
Middle Kingdom, 43, 53, 54, 74, 76, 77, 78, 153
migration, 3, 78, 86, 129, 158, 182

Mocambos, 130
modernity, xxvii, 9, 103, 104,
modernization, 103, 181. See also westernization; Christianity
Monomotapa/ Mutapa, 22.
Montejo, Esteban, xxix, 18, 141, 165
Moses, 16, 22

Mother, 11, 47, 85, 98, 118, 119, 122, 131, 158, 162, 165. See also *mut*; grandmother, grandparent, ancestor, Mother Earth, Mother Nature, revered person; knowledge; wisdom; respect
Mother Earth, 9, 14, 21, 26, 27, 34, 51, 98, 109, 112, 113, 122, 135, 162, 177, 179, 187
Mother Nature, 17, 179
Mut, 119
myth, mythical, mythology, xxvi, xxix, 2, 28, 43–47, 60, 91, 92, 109, 110, 111, 152, 154, 155, 161, 165, 178, 179
    'Deliverance of Mankind', 44
    'Destruction of Mankind', 44
    The First Libation, 43–47
    Myth of Afrika, xxix
    Myth of Libation, 7, 43–47, 91–92
    Myth of Cataclysm, 44

Nabta Playa, xxiv, 3, 41–42, 49
Nani, Explo Kofi, 25
Narmer, Narmer Palette, 21–22, 170
Nas, xxviii, 45, 144–146. See also 2Pac Shakur; hip-hop
do Nascimento, Abdias, xxviii, 3
Nehanda, Mibuya, 103, 112, 181. See also spirit medium; Chimurenga; Zimbabwe
New Era, 141–147
New Kingdom, 43, 47, 48, 53, 54, 72, 78, 109, 164
Nigeria/ Nigerians, xxvi, 9, 17, 18, 25, 29, 51, 82, 87, 90, 120, 142, 154, 158, 164
Nile River/Nile Valley,xxiv, xxv, xxvi, xxvii, xxxii, 4, 5, 6, 10, 41, 42, 51, 52, 56, 57, 60, 61, 73, 78, 81, 90, 110, 111, 118, 129, 135, 139, 146, 152–157, 158, 163, 164, 168, 178, 180, 181, 182. See also Great Lakes region of Africa; 'Father of the Divinities'; Hapy
nsaguo, 45, 52. See also sagua
Nsu, 43, 77, 78, 79, 80, 81, 83, 156. See also pharaoh
Nsu Pepsi I, 77–78
Nsu Taharka, 77, 78
Nsu Tutankhamon, 22, 43
Nubia, 41, 42, 182
Nun, 5, 154–155

Obenga, Théophile, xxx, 42, 44, 53, 54, 119–120
Oduyoye, Modupẹ, xxvi, xxvii, 91, 100, 122
offerings, xxiv, 2, 3, 12, 13, 15, 16, 18, 42, 43, 47, 48, 54, 56, 57, 58, 69–92, 118, 152, 159, 171, 177, 179
    blood offerings, 45, 69, 75, 88
    ceremonial complex, 3, 41
    First Fruits, 3, 13, 69, 75, 86, 88, 89, 108, 111, 156, 178, 179
    Food offerings, 48, 74, 88
    offering table, 71, 73, 74–75, 79
    voice offering, 15, 48, 69, 74, 80, 83, 85–86, 87, 88, 89, 171, 179
offering arm, 77–79
Old Kingdom, 9, 43, 48, 50, 72, 73, 78, 79, 85, 109, 110, 119
Opoku, Kofi, xxvi, 121
Orishas, 6, 19, 106, 133, 134, 137, 139, 141, 142, 158, 164, 165, 169

Palanque, 130

Pan-Afrikan, Pan-Afrikanism (Pan-Africanism), 107, 181
petition/petitioner, 14–15, 24, 25, 32, 52, 75, 163, 165, 179. See also Libation Statement; requests
Pharaoh, 21, 22, 28, 51, 58, 77, 79, 86, 109, 110, 120, 121, 156, 169. See also *nsu*
'pour water', 45, 56, 145
'pour out a libation', 56
praise, 28, 49, 69, 75, 81–82, 86, 87, 88, 89, 118, 120,179. See also kaiso
praise name, 75, 81–82, 83, 86, 87, 88, 89, 179
praise poems, 81, 82, 87, 89, 179
praise songs, 81, 82, 87, 89, 179
priesthood in ancient Egypt, 53–54, 60. See also wab; priestess; ritually pure; ritual purity
Ptahhotep, 76, 100, 101, 110, 116. See also ancestors; *Sebait of Ptahhotep*; *Instructions of Ptahhotep*
Pyramid Texts, xxiv, 47, 56, 59, 79, 84, 85, 119, 161

Queenstown, Essequibo Coast, Guyana, xxxi, 112, 137, 159
Qustul, Qustul incense burner, xxiv, 3, 41–42, 49

Ra, 5, 6, 43–44, 81. See also African gods; African divinities
'receive water', 56
'receive a libation', 56
Reclamation, xxx, 31, 62, 146. See also Sankofa; *Wehemu Mesut*
reincarnation, 114
religion, xxv, xxvi, xxvii, xxviii, 9, 15, 16, 90, 131, 132, 138, 139, 142, 152, See also spiritual system,
resistance, cultural resistance, physical resistance, spiritual resistance, etc, xxx, 27, 102, 103, 130, 136–139, 146, 154, 157. See also Communities of Resistance
'Reversion of Offerings', 83, 84. See also offerings, sacrifice, First Fruits, libation, voice offering, prayer, etc.
Revolution, 24, 54, 104, 130, 134–136, 137, 147. See also Haitian Revolution; Boukman Dutty; Afrikan Worldview; *Kwéyòl* (Creole)
ritual,
    Libation Ritual, xx, 22, 29, 35, 43, 45, 47, 79, 114, 156, 179, 221, 252, 255
    Opening of the Mouth Ritual, 116
    The Daily Temple Offering Ritual, xxvii
    Ritual reunion with the ancestors, 169
ritual complex, xxiv, 70, 156
ritual purity, 53, 54, 55, 58, 60-62, 186. See also priest; priestess; wab; wabt; 'servant of the divinity'; First Servant of the Divinity; Second Servant of the Divinity; etc.; 'father of the divinity'
Rodney, Walter, 28, 112, 114, 181, 182
rum, 14, 17, 18, 52, 87, 160, 185. See also alcohol; *clarin*; white rum; Palm; *akpeteshie*; *ogogoro*; *babash*; *Zai-id*; Mountain Dew

sacred literature of Kemet, xxiv, 47, 113, 178
sacred presences, 24, 31, 33. See also Divine presence
sacred space, 21–23,31, 33, 59, 62, 184. See also temple; pure space; God's Domain

sacrifice, xxiv, 3, 12, 13, 30, 34, 47, 49, 50, 69, 71, 72, 75, 83, 85, 86, 88, 89, 156, 177, 178, 179. See alsp blood offering
Santeria, 6, 12, 21, 106, 137, 142, 164, 165, 168
Sarpong, Right Reverend Dr. Peter Kwasi, xxxi, 6, 99

Sawyerr, Harry, xxvi, 121
scholarship, scholars, xxiii–xxxii, 41, 42, 72, 90, 91, 99, 100, 105, 121, 132, 134, 135, 136, 160,
Sep Tepy, 160, See also The First Occasion; Creation
Seti I, pharaoh, 28, 43, 78, 79, 120
Shango, 18, 46, 110, 131, 134
shoes, footwear, 21, 22–23, 58
Soyinka, Wole, 46, 91
speech, 50, 58–59, 60. See also *Medew Nefer*; beautiful speech
speech community, 49, 52, 77, 129, 170,
social history (of Afrika), xxvi, xxviii, xxix, xxx, xxxii, 26, 45, 55–62, 102, 115, 118, 160, 170
spirit world, 1, 2, 5, 7, 15, 55, 99, 109, 166, 177
spit, spitting, ritual spitting, 32, 151, 160–163. See also
Ritual Significances
spiritual purity, 58, 62, 186. See also ritual purity
spiritual system, xxiv, xxvi, xxvii, xxviii, 6, 7, 45, 60, 90, 104, 106, 130, 133, 134, 138, 142, 143, 151, 152, 157, 167
syncretism, 132

Taharka, Nsu, 77–78
Ta-Kenset, 57. See also *Ta-Iakhu*, Ta-*Khenti*,
temple, xxiv, 18, 23, 28, 53, 54, 57, 58, 59, 73–74, 75, 79, 120, 153, 164 See also God's Domain
Ten Commandments, 11. See also Declarations of Innocence
Thompson, Robert F, 6, 131, 133
three (number), ritual significance of, 32, 160, 162, 163–166. See also Ritual Significances
Twi, 9, 26, 45, 52, 55, 62, 135. See also African languages
Two Lands, 70, 78

Umeh, John Anenechukwu, xxvi,
Utterance, 13, 47, 56, 59, 79, 80, 81, 82, 146, 163. See also *Pyramid Texts*, etc.

Vega, Marta Moreno, xxviii, xxxi, 131, 133, 168
voodoo, 6, 12, 18, 19, 54, 106, 107 111, 130, 133–134, 137, 142, 164, 165, 169. See also Santeria

wab, 48, 52–53, 54, 75, 110. See also Egyptian priest
Warner-Lewis, Maureen, xxvii
Wasir (Osiris), 74, 86
water, 3, 5, 14, 16, 17, 18, 42, 45, 48, 49–50, 54, 55, 56, 57, 58, 73, 77, 82, 84, 87, 88, 109, 110, 111, 113, 122, 131, 151, 152–160, 164, 165, 185, 186, 187. See also libation; offerings; purification; water divinities; Florida
Water of Life, 155, 156
water pouring, 50, 56
water divinities, 111, 157–158. See also Bosomtwe; Tano; Ta Kora; Ta Tale; Ta Gbu; To Nu; Ta Nu; Otaomi; Yewa; Oshun; Yemoja; Yemanjá; Olókun; Ota Miri; Bin'abu; Ngalwe; Kaene; Water Mamma; Water Mumma

West Africa, xxvi–xxvii, 17, 18, 28, 51, 87, 101, 104, 108, 109, 112, 122, 141, 145, 146, 157, 158, 162, 164
West Bank (of the Nile River), 73, 153, 154
white, 14, 17, 18, 87, 108, 160, 166–168, 169. See also Ritual Significances; *akhu*
Wilkinson, J. Gardner, xxiii, 20
Wilkinson, Richard H., 73, 77, 78
wia (boat), 155.See also *Amenta; Duat;* nun
women, 6, 16, 46, 53–54, 58, 60, 61, 101, 102, 103, 116, 131
Wörterbuch der Aegyptischen Sprache, 50, 54, 57. See also *Wörterbuch*
Wray, John, 158

Yemoja/Yemanjá, 131, 157, 158
Yoruba, Yorubas, xxvi, 9, 11, 28, 29, 78, 106, 110–111, 118, 119, 131, 134, 141, 142, 156, 157, 158, 159, 164, 165
Yorubaland, 6, 169

Zimbabwe, 22, 102–103, 181

www.ingramcontent.com/pod-product-compliance
Lightning Source LLC
Chambersburg PA
CBHW030319020526
44117CB00029B/129